Growing Up in an Urbanising World

This book is dedicated to the children and youth of the international Growing Up in Cities Project.

Growing Up
in an Urbanising World

LOUISE CHAWLA, Editor

Earthscan Publications Ltd
London and Sterling, VA

 UNESCO PUBLISHING

Management of
Social Transformations

First published in the United Kingdom in 2002 by the
United Nations Educational, Scientific and Cultural Organization
and Earthscan Publications Ltd

Copyright © UNESCO, 2002

United Nations Educational, Scientific and Cultural Organization
7, place de Fontenoy, 75007 Paris, France

A catalogue record for this book is available from the British Library

ISBN: 92-3-103817-6 (UNESCO paperback)
      1 85383 828 4 (Earthscan paperback)
      1 85383 827 6 (Earthscan hardback)

The authors are responsible for the choice and the presentation of the facts
contained in this book and for the opinions expressed therein, which are not
necessarily those of UNESCO and do not commit the Organization.

The designations employed and the presentation of material throughout this
publication do not imply the expression of any opinion whatsoever on the
part of UNESCO concerning the legal status of any country, territory, city or
area or of its authorities, or the delimitation of its frontiers or boundaries.

Cover design, book design and layout by Dean Driskell
Printed and bound in the United Kingdom by Bell & Bain Ltd., Glasgow
Cover photographs © Louise Chawla (front) and S. R. Prakash (back)

For a full list of UNESCO publications please contact:
UNESCO Publishing
7, place de Fontenoy, 75352 Paris 07 SP France
Tel: +33 (0)1 45 68 49 30
Fax: +33 (0)1 45 68 57 41
Email: publishing.promotion@unesco.org
www.unesco.org/publishing

For a full list of Earthscan publications please contact:
Earthscan Publications Ltd
120 Pentonville Road, London, N1 9JN, UK
Tel: +44 (0)20 7278 0433
Fax: +44 (0)20 7278 1142
Email: earthinfo@earthscan.co.uk
www.earthscan.co.uk

22883 Quicksilver Drive, Sterling, VA 20166-2012, USA

Earthscan is an editorially independent subsidiary of Kogan Page Ltd and
publishes in association with WWF-UK and the International Institute for
Environment and Development

This book is printed on elemental chlorine-free paper

Acknowledgments

GENERAL COORDINATION: Growing Up in Cities was first conceived and initiated by Kevin Lynch of MIT, an urban designer with vision and heart. He is the inspiration behind the present version of the project. Encouragement to revive Growing Up in Cities was first given by Gary Moore and Sandy Gaster at the Children and the City Colloquium at Monte Verita, Ascona. Initial funding was provided by the Norwegian Centre for Child Research under the direction of Per Egil Mjaavatn, in collaboration with Childwatch International under the direction of Per Miljeteig. UNESCO funded Kevin Lynch's work in the 1970s, and was quick to re-adopt the project under the umbrella of the Management of Social Transformations (MOST) Programme in 1996. Nadia Auriat, Programme Specialist, has been our unfailing link to MOST. From the beginning, her steadfast encouragement and support have made project achievements possible. Gillian Whitcomb, Chief of the Publications Unit of UNESCO's Social and Human Sciences Sector, has been our skilled and dedicated co-worker in bringing this book to realisation. Dean Driskell, book designer, has presented the results of our work to the best possible advantage. Appreciation also goes to experts on the subject of children in cities, who have always been ready to read drafts and answer questions: Roger Hart of the City University of New York, David Satterthwaite and Sheridan Bartlett of the International Institute of Environment and Development in London, and Cristina Blanc of Columbia University. Nora Rubinstein and Mary Rivkin, environmental researchers and authors, have also given helpful suggestions. Our appreciation also to Siebert Kruger, the project's web designer. (You can see his work at *www.unesco.org/most/growing.htm*)

Work at individual project locations has been made possible by an extended network of support.

ARGENTINA: Funding for the Boca-Barracas research was provided by IDRC (International Development Research Centre of Canada), North Carolina State University and the October Foundation of Apartment Building Workers. Victor Santa María, Foundation president, demonstrated enormous commitment to the project.

Many other groups provided in-kind support: La Red Solidaria (the Boca-Barracas Solidarity Network); the Zone 3 Office of the Secretary of Social Promotion of the City of Buenos Aires; the Office of Projects and Management of the Secretary of Urban Planning and Environment for Buenos Aires; El Móvil Verde (the Green Van environmental education program); Mutual Esperanza; San Martin de Tours Girls School; IPA-Argentina (International Association for the Child's Right to Play); School of Social Communication, Buenos Aires University; the Latinamerican Urban Workshop; the Barracas Popular Library; and La Boca Popular Library. Dr. Antonio Battro and Eduardo Ellis, leaders of GUIC research in Argentina in the 1970s, served as mentors for this project revival. The field work was ably conducted by Virginia Guardía, Antollín Magallanes, Cristina Marchesoni, and Maria Suarez, municipal social workers. Heather Manchester compiled the economic and social history of Boca-Barracas and Andres Solomonoff helped prepare the children's photo exhibition. The Children's Hour Helping Fund of the Norwegian Broadcasting Corporation made it possible to create a toy library in the La Boca YMCA as a bequest from the project.

AUSTRALIA: Braybrook research was made possible by support from the Australian Research Council and the Postdoctoral Research Fellowship Programme of Deakin University. The project website and a project-based CD-Rom were funded by the university through its Committee on University Teaching and Staff Development. The Arts Council of Australia funded the Streetspace project through its Environmental Designer in Schools Programme. In-kind support was given by the Australian Institute for Family Studies. Beau Beza ably took charge of photographing and mapping the project site. Rob Walker, Peter Downton, Maggie Fooke, staff and students at Braybrook Secondary College, staff and Council of the City of Maribyrnong, and young people of Braybrook gave advice, encouragement, expertise and support.

UNITED KINGDOM: Research in Northampton was made possible by a doctoral Research Fellowship from Nene University College, now University College Northampton. Hugh Matthews and Melanie Limb at UCN, with Roger Hart from the City University of New York, served as advisors. Staff from the Northamptonshire Youth and Residential Service kindly accommodated the research within their youth projects. Northampton Borough and County Councils helped provide maps, plans, aerial photos, secondary data and reports. Many staff from UCN and the County Youth Service provided assistance with fieldwork and data processing. Thanks also go to all the young people and residents in Semilong and Hunsbury who made the research possible. Special thanks to Clare for keeping things together, and to Chloe, who, more than anyone, helped reflect on what it is to be a child and showed how wise children are, and the extent to which they are able to play a full and active part in everyday life.

INDIA: Research in Sathyanagar was funded by NORAD-India and carried out by staff from the Centre for Environment Education (CEE): Kandasami, Prakash, Radha and Sowmya. Students from Mount Carmel College generously volunteered their time: Priya, Sophia, Shabreen and Kavitha. DEEDS (Development Education Society) and TIDE (Technology Informatics Design Endeavour) gave valuable technical and organisational assistance. The Children's Hour Helping Fund of the Norwegian Broadcasting Corporation made it possible to construct a children's centre in Sathyanagar, as a small measure of appreciation for the contributions of the children of Sathyanagar themselves.

NORWAY: Research in Trondheim was funded by the Norwegian Housing Bank and based at the Norwegian Centre for Child Research. Additional funding and support were given by the Municipality of Trondheim. Research assistance was provided by students from the Geography Institute of the Norwegian University of Science and Technology: Cecilie Danielsen Skare and Barbara Rogers. The research team was ably served by Alexandra Beverfjord, Trude Nordal, John T. R. Johansen, and Kjell Inge Stelander. The research analysis was completed during a Research Fellowship at the Oslo School of Architecture. Mary Bjaerum prepared the chapter translation and Helene Stub helped with the final version.

POLAND: Research in Powisle was funded by the Jacobs Foundation of Switzerland. Professors Andrzej Eliasz and Krystyna Skarzynska of the Institute of Psychology at the Polish Academy of Sciences — participants in the original Powisle study — gave help and encouragement; and Professor Skarzynska made an initial summary of the research on participants' perceptions of change and attitudes toward politicians. Anna Cieslicka and Annelise Carleton translated the manuscript of the Polish chapter into English, and Annelise also served as a very thoughtful reader and critic of the work. Arrangements for interviews were made with extensive help from the local school principal. The students Marta Wieczorek, Magdalena Wroblewska and Mariola Pietron served as research assistants. The boys and girls of Powisle generously shared their experiences and hopes for the future; and last but not least, Kuba Zylicz shared his insights.

SOUTH AFRICA: Research at Canaansland was financed by the MOST Programme of UNESCO, UNICEF, and the HNRE Programme (Human Needs, Resources and the Environment) of HSRC (Human Sciences Research Council of South Africa). The Mayor of Greater Johannesburg, Isaac Mogase, supported GUIC in South Africa from the project's inception. Peter Rich, architect, served as co-director of the initial research phase. The research team was ably served by Greg Jacobs, Lineo Lerotholi, Maurice Mogane, Melinda Swift, Moeketsi Langeni, Nondumiso Mabuza and Zenzile Choko. After Canaansland residents were moved to Thula Mntwana, Peter Rich designed the Ubuhle Buyeza Children's Centre (for which he received an architectural prize) and supervised its erection, and Mike Sarakinsky trained members of the Canaansland Development Committee. Jill Swart-Kruger has continued to provide support to the Committee and individuals with problems, as well as serving as a mediator between residents and the outside world. Funding for Ubuhle Buyeza and an adjoining playground was provided by the Children's Hour Helping Fund of the Norwegian Broadcasting Corporation and the Embassy of the Netherlands. Carien Engelbrecht, Chief Director of the Gauteng Department of Housing and Land Affairs, served as an invaluable advisor.

UNITED STATES OF AMERICA: The research in Oak Park was supported by the FAAR Foundation (Fondazione Architetto Augusto Rancilio) of Milan, by the MOST Programme of UNESCO, and by IURD (Institute of Urban and Regional Development) at the University of California-Berkeley. Precious encouragement, support and advice were given by: Professors Randolph Hester and Marcia McNally of the Department of Landscape Architecture, University of California-Berkeley; Josh Kirschenbau and Victor Rubin of IURD; and Michael Schwab, then at the Children and Environment Program of the Wellness Foundation. Alice and Christine, Dan and Russell from the Oak Park Ministry opened the doors of their wonderful community. The work would not have been possible without the dedicated assistance of Rath Pahl. University of California graduate students Martha Martinez, Lara Zureikat and Tetsu O'Hara shared both the exciting and difficult moments of research. A special thank you goes to Enrico Moretti for his enthusiastic help at all stages of the work.

Contents

Foreword

I take great pleasure in offering *Growing Up in an Urbanising World* to the development, practitioner and academic communities around the world. This book is about giving a genuine voice to children and youth; it is about participation and the design of participatory methods; and it is about lending an adult ear to the views of young people on their needs, and on the quality of the physical and social environment in which they live. It is also about human rights and the rights of the child as enshrined in the principles of the 1989 United Nations Convention.

The authors will lead you from an impoverished squatter camp in Johannesburg, South Africa, to a low income neighbourhood in Melbourne, Australia, to an immigrant Hispanic community in Oakland, United States, to a peri-urban slum skirting the city of Bangalore, India. Norway, Argentina, the United Kingdom and Poland complete this journey, a journey that captures the essence of what it is like to grow up in today's cities.

While moving through this volume, listen to the voices of the young people as they open up their thoughts, insights and views to the teams of architects, anthropologists, developmental psychologists and other facilitators and rights activists who generously donated their time and expertise to this endeavour. Listen also to the voices of the authors whose accounts resonate with authenticity as they depict the lives of young people in environments inherited from their elders, where the adage "children should be seen but not heard" commonly applies.

This book comes at a time when development theory and practice are embroiled in a storm of criticism. International financial institutions, development aid and donor agencies, and non-governmental organisations are seeking new formulas and partnerships to reduce poverty in a lasting way, to overcome processes of impoverishment and move toward an international framework that humanises globalisation. UNESCO is openly confronting these mutating human needs via its Intergovernmental Social Science Programme entitled Management of Social Transformations (MOST). *Growing Up in an Urbanising World* is the outcome of a MOST international comparative research project which aims to strengthen research and international cooperation and contribute to the exchange of knowledge and human capacity building.

As Assistant Director-General of UNESCO, as former Secretary General of Amnesty International, as a human rights activist and in my own name, I invite you to open your minds and hearts to the young generations who offer here the gift of their vision. It is with them that we will build the foundations for a more egalitarian and peaceful world.

Pierre Sané
ASSISTANT DIRECTOR-GENERAL FOR
SOCIAL AND HUMAN SCIENCES, UNESCO

Introductory Note

Growing Up in an Urbanising World is the culmination of a journey that began in 1995. It started when a group of researchers, activists, urban planners and architects from eight countries decided to overcome disciplinary barriers and join hands to launch a comparative research project on how young people from impoverished communities around the world assess their urban environment. The purpose was to provide recommendations for increasing the genuine participation of young people in community development projects, so that they may be heard as full-fledged agents of community change, rather than, as is more generally the case, muted passive recipients of social transformation dictated by others.

UNESCO has a long history of achievements in social science, and its support of research worldwide is well known. An important step was taken in 1993, when an Intergovernmental Programme in the Social and Human Sciences, entitled the Management of Social Transformations (MOST), was established, thus providing an international platform for supporting high quality comparative, interdisciplinary and policy relevant research. This was what drew Louise Chawla, a Fulbright Scholar and International Coordinator for Growing Up in Cities, to present the project to UNESCO on behalf of the eight country teams. It was her enthusiasm and commitment as well as the excellent quality of the international teams, that ensured the ultimate success and relevance of the project.

A number of high profile international events during the 1990s provided a pertinent backdrop for the objectives of this study: the entry into force of the Convention on the Rights of the Child; the Rio Summit for Environment and Development; the Beijing Summit which stressed the rights of women and of the girl child; the World Summit for Social Development; the Habitat Conference; and their respective follow-up meetings. The conferences established action plans that explicitly point to the importance of environmental preservation, sustainable and liveable cities, poverty reduction and the need to focus development aid on projects that improve the living conditions of the most vulnerable groups, notably children, youth and women.

In this same period, another feature of the development shift came to light, through the 2000–2001 World Development Report by the World Bank and the introduction of the debt relief initiative for Heavily Indebted Poor Countries. Debt relief was to be contingent on the preparation of "nationally owned" poverty reduction strategy papers founded on the full participation of civil society. However, there is little evidence yet that the principles inscribed in the Convention on the Rights of the Child (notably Article 12 which states that children have a right to express their views on matters that affect their lives) are respected in the preparation of these national action plans for poverty reduction. Of course, it is not an easy challenge to meet: how can young people be involved in the design of these poverty reduction plans — even at the municipal, community or neighbourhood level? It is through the participatory experiences presented in this volume that we hope to offer a response to this question, and convey the message that excluding young people from their own development cannot but hinder the efficiency of programmes designed to reduce inequality and poverty — particularly with a rights-based approach to development and poverty reduction. The practitioner manual that is the companion to this book, entitled *Creating Better Cities with Children and Youth* (by David Driskell), provides a user-friendly, step by step explanation of how municipalities, communities, aid agencies and non-governmental organisations can effectively include young people in project design.

As I noted above, this book is a journey into collaboration across social science fields and practices. It is also an adventure in inter-agency cooperation. There is a great deal of discussion about the need for United Nations agencies to work together within the UN System, to create partnerships with bilateral agencies, private foundations, major research think tanks and non-government organisations. Putting this into practise is often difficult. That is why I wish to dwell on how such collaboration developed within the framework of the project and express my particular gratitude to all those who made it a cooperative venture. First, the Norwegian Centre for Child Research, under the direction of Per Egil Mjaavatn and in alliance with Childwatch International, has my gratitude as the initial institution that supported the development of the Growing Up in Cities research proposal that was subsequently submitted to UNESCO. UNICEF South Africa, notably represented in this project at the time by Mr. Admassu Tadesse, has been a source of inspiration, an unflinching defender of children's rights and a model for inter-agency cooperation. Many other organisations and individuals, too numerous to name here but who are listed in this volume's acknowledgments, came forward with their contributions.

Of course, this endeavour would not have been possible without the invaluable work of the contributors to this volume. Suffice it to say that the personal contact we have shared as an international research team has been a rewarding and enriching experience, and my heartfelt gratitude is extended to each and every one of the team members. It is important to recognise that many of them worked on a volunteer basis, using their precious time and resources to invest in this project because of their commitment to its ideals and principles. And many of them are continuing their work in this area, spreading the message enshrined in the Convention on the Rights of the Child, the Habitat Summit, the Earth Summit and the World Summit for Social Development. In addition to being academics, these people are activists and community leaders, and many spearhead non-governmental organisations focused on the needs of children and youth. It is through the personal motivation, dedication and hard work of people like them that the lives of young people around the world will gradually be improved.

Looking inward toward UNESCO, I wish to express my appreciation to a number of people who have contributed to forming a support network for the Growing Up in Cities project within the Organisation. First, my appreciation goes to those UNESCO regional offices that have disseminated the principles of this project, and who are continuously building new initiatives around its findings. I thank my assistant, Tamara Blondel for her dedication to this project and her encouragement, enthusiasm and professionalism.

UNESCO's Youth Unit and the Programme for Coastal Zones and Small Island States (CSI) have contributed to spreading the findings of this project to Youth Forums and to the inhabitants of environmentally fragile coastal zones around the world, and I appreciate their collaboration. Appreciation is extended to my colleague Brigitte Colin, who, through her expertise in rehabilitating world heritage and historic city centres, has invested particular attention in the needs of children and youth living in these areas, thereby spreading the recommendations and participatory methods described in this volume to new sites around the globe.

Philippe Ratte, then planning officer for the Social and Human Science Programme, has provided intellectual and administrative impetus, encouragement and continuity to this initiative, and on behalf of the Growing Up in Cities team, we wish to express our deep appreciation for his acuity and support.

Finally, on behalf of the whole International Growing Up in Cities network, I wish to express my deep gratitude to the Executive Secretary of the MOST Programme, Dr. Ali Kazancigil, who, from the outset, has been a steadfast supporter of this project. His unfailing confidence and optimism have been instrumental in achieving the outcomes of this endeavour.

One cannot sufficiently recognise the debt we have toward the children and youth around the world who took time from often very busy study and work schedules to engage with the research team in participatory processes. In turning the following pages, you will meet these remarkable young citizens, and will hear them tell you the stories of what life is like in a squatter camp in Johannesburg, a low income suburb in Melbourne, an immigrant housing site in California, or an impoverished district of Buenos Aires. You will learn, from their own insights, what they perceive to be a decent living environment — one that is free from insecurity, fear, impoverishment, violence, dis-crimination and inequality. You will understand what the objective of a decent livelihood and future may mean from a young person's perspective, and you will gain an alternative perspective on the meaning of the social, economic, and cultural rights of future generations.

On a more personal note, I would like to pay tribute to the children who gave their time to participate in this project. They were at once generous, candid, enthusiastic and honest, and taught us many valuable lessons in team spirit, equality and cooperation. We are immensely grateful to them.

Nadia Auriat
UNESCO MOST PROGRAMME

© LOUISE CHAWLA

CHAPTER ONE

Cities for Human Development

Louise Chawla

The accelerating process of urbanization and its consequences for children are placed in the context of social, economic and environmental trends at the beginning of the 21st century. Growing Up in Cities, a project that seeks to understand the urban environment from children's perspectives, is presented as one means to address international agreements about children's right to a voice in environmental planning and decision-making. The project's origins in the advocacy planning movement of the 1970s are described, along with an overview of the results of the project's 1990s revival with children in low-income urban areas around the world, in industrialised countries of the North and in developing countries of the South.

The world is always changing; but a defining characteristic of the present is its unprecedented rate of change in an increasingly interdependent world that is undergoing profound restructuring of societies, economies, human settlements and people's relationship with the planet. This book examines the interrelationship of five of these patterns of change: urbanisation, growing populations with high proportions of children, evolving ideas about childhood, increasing disparities between rich and poor, and intensifying pressures on the earth's resources. Building on ideas about children's rights, it describes processes designed to understand children's own perspectives on the places where they live as a basis for partnerships between children and adults to improve urban conditions. These processes are relevant to all communities with children, but with growing urbanisation and the rising number of people who live in poverty, the focus here is on children from low-income families in cities. The values that these children express point to a model of development that can respond to human needs for friendship and place, and provide social support as well as physical necessities. These values are in harmony with the requirements of sustainable development.

An Urbanising World

This book focuses on cities because one of the major patterns of change at the beginning of the 21st century is urbanisation. Regionally, the history of cities may show periods of expansion and decline, but with the Industrial Revolution in the 19th century urbanisation rapidly accelerated.[1] What is new now — and a momentous change — is that most of humanity is projected to inhabit urban areas by the first decade of the 21st century.[2]

Nations use widely varying definitions of 'urban', and the scale and nature of urban growth vary from nation to nation. Taken as a whole, however, global census data show an irregular but general trend toward urbanisation. In North America, Latin America and Europe, approximately 75 percent of the population already lives in urban areas. In Africa and Asia, this figure is about 37 percent, and rising. In some Pacific Rim countries, it is more than 90 percent.[3] There has been much talk about 'mega-cities' (10 million inhabitants or more), but only 4 percent of the world's population currently lives in them, and their rate of growth has slowed since 1980; most growth is in smaller cities or regional centres[4]. Despite regional variations in patterns of urbanisation, it can be generalised that more and more people are moving into denser settlements as fewer and fewer make their living directly off the land.[5]

> *This book is motivated by a vision of engaging children in practical projects to realise the priniciples of the Convention on the Rights of the Child and Agenda 21 in urban environments.*

New Conceptions of Childhood

Another momentous change that human society is undergoing is that more attention is being given to children and there are new attitudes about childhood. This is not to say that parents did not recognise that their children had special capacities and vulnerabilities in the past, but this 'discovery of childhood', as it has been called, represents a qualitative change.[6] With modern science and industrialisation have come new techniques in medicine and public health, and a corresponding fall in child mortality rates. The major consequence has been a proportionate increase in child populations, resulting in societies where 40 to 50 percent of the population is under 18.[7] In Northern Europe, these two trends of urbanisation and population increase combined in the 19th century to create city streets teeming with young life, as memorialised in the London of Charles Dickens and the Paris of Victor Hugo.

When there is a rising standard of living, including rising levels of education and paid labour for women, societies enter a 'demographic transition' where life spans increase, birth rates fall and the proportion of the young declines. During the 20th century, the urbanised and industrialised nations of Europe, North America and the Pacific moved into balanced population structures in which the young under 15 and the old over 65 each constitute roughly one-fifth of the population.[8] This phenomenon of proportionately fewer children, who can be expected to live long lives and support social services for the elderly, has encouraged a new degree of emotional and economic investment in children as individuals. These were the conditions that emboldened the Swedish advocate for children, Ellen Key, to proclaim the 20th century the 'Century of the Child.' There was a new scientific understanding of human development, she believed, that brought with it a new obligation to provide for health, education, respect, nurturance and leisure for play as basic entitlements of childhood.[9] With the United Nations' adoption of the Convention on the Rights of the Child in 1989, this vision was officially endorsed by the world community.[10]

While the societies of the industrialised nations of the North are faced with the challenge of balancing the needs of roughly equal numbers of the elderly and the young, several nations in Africa, Asia and Latin America are in a different 'population time zone', characterised by early industrialisation. In Kenya, for example, 44 percent of the population is under 15, in Malaysia 37 percent, and in Ecuador 35 percent.[11] Globally, 40 percent of the world's population is under 20.[12] Combined with urbanisation, this has resulted in new concentrations of the young in Third World cities, informal settlements and squatter camps.

A World of Ecological and Social Imperatives

If contemporary civilisation is to remain viable, the 21st century must become the 'Century of Limits.' Where the 20th century began with discussions about *child development* — about scientific methods of child rearing and psychoanalytic origins of the adult personality — the discourse that dominates the 21st century is *economic development*. Since the end of the Second World War, when the United States began to seek postwar markets for the output of its factories, the meaning of 'development' has been centrally associated with the increasing production and consumption of material goods and with increasing returns on business investments. By these terms, the world has been developing even faster than it has been urbanising or increasing in population. For example, the burning of fossil fuels has increased almost fivefold since 1950, the world's marine catch fourfold, and the consumption of fresh water twofold since 1960. The result is severe stress on the planet's capacities to absorb all of the pollution and waste produced, as well as a rapid deterioration of fresh water reserves, soil, forests, fish and biodiversity.[13]

Along with this expanding exploitation of the earth's resources, there has come a greater awareness that human life depends on the fragile life support systems of a finite planet. One of the unifying images of late 20th century public media is a satellite view of the earth: a planet of modest size, alone in the darkness of space, unique and lovely in its blue-green, cloud-filmed shell of biosphere. In 1992, the nations of the world acknowledged the planet's limits at the United Nations Conference on Environment and Development (UNCED) at Rio de Janeiro, when they adopted a new definition of 'development' — *sustainable development* — that balances development with the protection of the environment 'so as to equitably meet developmental and environmental needs of present and future generations.'[14] Agenda 21, the plan of action that the assembled governments endorsed, identified children and youth as a major group who must help make this vision a reality.[15] (The Convention on the Rights of the Child defines 'children' as all people under 18, and 'youth', in United Nations' practice, refers to 15–25 year olds.) If articulating this vision has been a great achievement of the 20th century, realising it will be the great necessity of the 21st. In 2002, the world's nations are assembling for the Rio +10 Conference in Johannesburg to renew their commitment to this goal.

If the nations of the world were evaluated on the basis of sustainable development and on how much of the earth's resources their citizens consume, the rankings of most-developed and least-developed nations — which now emphasise gross domestic product and per capita income — would have to be reassessed. The United Nations Development Programme estimates that the richest fifth of the world's people, who primarily inhabit the North, possess almost 86 percent of the total world wealth, with its corresponding purchasing power, compared to about one percent for the poorest fifth. On average, a child born in a high-income industrial country will consume and pollute more in his or her lifetime than 30 to 50 children born in low-income countries.[16]

> *Despite the diversity of the countries and places where they live, there is a remarkable consensus about the qualities that create places where children and adolescents can thrive, versus conditions that cause them to feel alienated and marginalised.*

In response to these disparities, the governments from the North and South assembled at UNCED agreed to the opening principle of the Rio Declaration and the statement of principles underlying Agenda 21: 'Human beings are at the centre of concerns for sustainable development. They are entitled to a healthy and productive life in harmony with nature.'[17] Other principles emphasise that social equity and the eradication of poverty, as much as the protection of the environment, must be integral dimensions of future development practices (Principle 5), and that environmental issues are best handled with the participation of all concerned citizens (Principle 10). In all the years since the first UNCED Conference in 1992, the latest global statistics show ever-rising rates of consumption of the earth's resources and ever-widening gaps between rich and poor, while most high-income nations that promised increased aid to low- and middle-income regions have cut their overall aid budgets.[18] Whether there are limits to this perpetuation of poverty by the rich, or to its endurance by the poor, has yet to be seen.

When these trends of urbanisation, growing populations with large numbers of children, environmental degradation, and intensifying disparities between rich and poor are taken together, they signify that more and more children live in urban areas under conditions of poverty and environmental risk. Here, where these trends converge in children's lives, is the focal point of this book and its main concern.

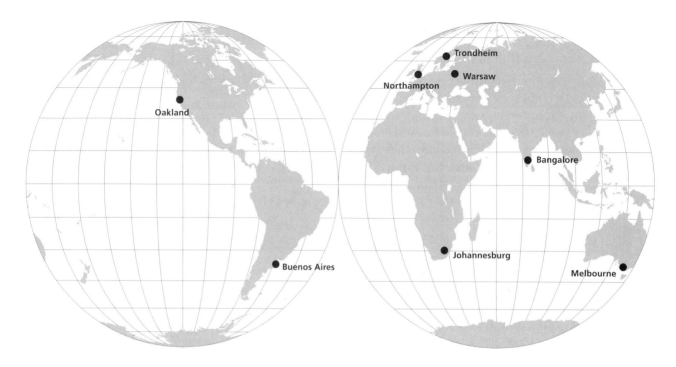

Figure 1.1 An increasing number of the world's children grow up in urban areas. The eight Growing Up in Cities sites featured in this book are marked above.

This may appear a bleak place, with little scope for hope. For some of the sites and situations that this book describes, the horizon *is* bleak. But the subject of this book is children, with all their energy and resilience. Specifically, its subject is children and adolescents from the ages of 10 through 15, who combine energy with considerable ability and maturity. This book is motivated by a vision of engaging children of this age in practical projects to realise the principles of the Convention on the Rights of the Child and Agenda 21 in urban environments. As much as it is a book about children's perspectives and ideas about the places where they live, it is also a book about processes for bringing together researchers, child advocates in local communities and city governments, urban planners and designers, and families, in order to work with young people to improve urban conditions and, in the process, build their collective confidence in their abilities to effect progressive positive change. This is a location of hope.

NEW LIFE FOR A VISIONARY PROJECT

The environmental and demographic trends described above were already perceptible by the 1970s. Apollo Mission photographs of the earth as seen from the moon imprinted an image of the planet's self-containment on people around the world, while public media carried pictures of fish kills in polluted rivers and cities submerged in smog. In the North and the South, the dominant postwar equation of development with unlimited economic growth and consumption was being challenged. People sought alternatives, such as at Habitat I, the first United Nations Conference on Human Settlements in 1976, where urban visionaries proposed new models for community and nature in the city. This search for more sustainable settlements continues intently today.[19] How cities can foster healthy child development — which is the fundamental question of this book — must be part of this larger discussion about the best forms of social, political and economic development for people as a whole.

One approach would be to assemble what is known about children's needs for optimal development at different ages, and on this basis recommend child-friendly policies for city planning. To a considerable degree, this has been done in recent books, such as *The Environment for Children, Cities for Children,* and *Children, Cities, and Psychological Theories.*[20] Another approach — on which this book is based — is to learn from children themselves how they evaluate the places where they live and how they would like to live, and then use this dialogue to bring children and adults together in participatory programmes to improve the urban environment.

There are strong justifications for this approach. The above mentioned books argue that the conditions for optimal child development include the kind of creative, constructive, and collective activities that participatory processes involve. In the chapters that follow, several authors describe children's increasing self-confidence, self-expression, awareness of others' perspectives and awareness of a larger world in the course of processes of this kind. They also document how children can learn democratic skills by working together to bring about positive changes in their environment. As other books observe — notably *Children's Participation, Children as Fellow Citizens, The Participation Rights of the Child, Changing Places, Children in the City* and *Creating Better Cities with Children and Youth* — children need experience with this kind of practical democracy in order to grow into responsible citizens.[21] Finally, for urban planners, designers and other urbanists who want to build better cities, working with children has the advantage of providing them with a moral high ground in negotiations with city governments, because few mayors or other officials will overtly oppose the reasonable requests of a group of children who want to cooperate to improve their environment. Reliably, the priorities that children express are conditions for making cities more liveable for all ages.

This book reports on the revival of the Growing Up in Cities project of UNESCO that was first conceived by the urban planner Kevin Lynch in the 1970s, was reintroduced by the Norwegian Centre for Child Research and Childwatch International in 1994, and is currently spread-ing to cities around the world. This book reports on three years of fieldwork (from 1996 through 1998) in eight cities: Buenos Aires, Argentina; Melbourne, Australia; Northampton, United Kingdom; Bangalore, India; Trondheim, Norway; Warsaw, Poland; Johannesburg, South Africa; and Oakland, California, in the United States of America. Together, the project sites represent old working-class neighbourhoods, peripheral suburbs, a self-built settlement and a squatter camp, located in countries that range from rich and powerful established democracies to newly emerging democracies that are struggling to meet their populations' basic needs.

> **BOX 1.1**
>
> ### Project Guidelines
>
> The research phase of the 1990s Growing Up in Cities has followed the general guidelines that Kevin Lynch summarised in the 1970s, with some variations and usually working with larger numbers of children:
>
> *'In brief, they called for interviews with a group of twenty children in early adolescence, all living in one locality. They were to be asked how they used, conceived of, and felt about their surroundings. Investigators were to observe how the children actually used the setting, make a careful physical description of the place, and conduct comparative interviews with parents and with officials concerned with the public planning of the locality.'*
>
> **LYNCH** (1977, p 2)

This new vision of Growing Up in Cities has progressed through three phases:

- A research phase that gathers qualitative and quantitative information about the conditions of children's lives in representative urban environments;
- Wherever possible, an action phase when the research results are applied to urban policy-making and to creating programmes, curricula and environmental improvements in response to children's needs;
- A dissemination phase, when project achievements in

one city or region of the world are used as the basis for workshops, publications or other media to increase public awareness about urban issues for children and the possibility of engaging children themselves in research and action for change.

With some variations and adaptations, the project sites that this book describes have followed the general research scheme proposed by Lynch in the 1970s. (See Box 1.1 and the Research Guidelines at the back of the book.) Through words, drawings, photographs, neighbourhood tours and other means, the 10–15 year olds who are the subject of this book evoke their lives in their communities and their own priorities for improvements. Despite the diversity of the countries and places where they live, they show a remarkable consensus about the qualities that create places where children and adolescents can thrive, versus conditions that cause them to feel alienated and marginalised. First there is a presentation of the research phase, and then five chapters describe different

> *Those who were committed to ideals of community and individual self-realisation, saw participation not just as a means to economic ends but as an intrinsic good, and thus an end in itself.*

degrees of success with the action phase of the project that has created alliances of officials, urban planners and designers, child and youth workers, researchers, community leaders, journalists, parents and other adults who have been willing to work with young people to help them realise some of their ideas for change. Drawing on this experience, the final chapter makes recommendations for urban policies that will be more responsive to young peoples' needs. This book, its companion manual *Creating Better Cities with Children and Youth* that details the project's principles and methods, numerous other publications, a website and workshops to spread these processes to other cities are part of the project's ongoing third phase.[22]

This approach has grown out of the ferment of ideas of the 1970s. As an introduction to the methods and goals on which this book is based, the following section reviews the origins of Growing Up in Cities some 30 years ago: the Man and His Environment Programme of UNESCO, the concerns of Kevin Lynch, and the larger context of debates about public participation in planning. Rather than forming a background that can be relegated to the past, the decade of the 1970s represents a period of radical analysis and experimentation that in many ways is still relevant today.

THE LEGACY OF A SEMINAL DECADE

The Participation Debate

The revival of Growing Up in Cities has depended upon the support of many agencies and institutions, as the acknowledgements at the beginning of this book make clear. The ability to maintain such a coordinated project over the years, however, has been primarily due to the UNESCO's MOST Programme (Management of Social Transformations), which was established by the General Conference of UNESCO in 1993 in order to facilitate international and interdisciplinary research cooperation. The programme's priorities include sustainable human settlements and a human rights approach to development and poverty eradication. The Growing Up in Cities project's involvement of children and youth in improving urban environments, with an emphasis on low-income communities, falls directly within its sphere.

In promoting a view of young people as potential agents in community development, Growing Up in Cities remains an innovative model for the 1990s and beyond. The *Human Development Report 2000* on human rights and human development of the United Nations Development Programme and the year 2000 version of the World Bank's *Poverty Reduction Strategy Sourcebook,* for example, stress the necessity of citizen participation for the realisation of human rights and successful development, yet never mention children's capacity to contribute to participatory processes.[23] That Growing Up in Cities remains on the frontier of development ideas in this respect is ironic — considering that its roots extend back to the 1970s. This testifies to the depth of adult prejudice against any view of children as independent and responsible actors. To understand the principles that have motivated the project and how barriers to recognising children's roles in their communities were first overcome, it will be helpful to revisit the historical context in which the project first took form.

In the 1970s, whether development planners and aid agencies defined the *ends* of development as more wealth and material goods, or as an increasing spirit of community and individual well-being, a key word in their discussions about the *means* to development was 'participation.' From those who equated development with Western-style industrialisation and modernisation, as well as those who emphasised community cooperation and alternative technologies, a vocabulary of 'people's participation' and 'people-centred development' emerged.'[24] Those who were promoting increased industrialisation and consumption saw participation as a means to gain people's compliance with new products and technologies, and to ensure the social and political stability that continuous economic growth requires. Those who were committed to ideals of community and individual self-realisation, saw participation not just as a means to economic ends but as an intrinsic good, and thus an end in itself.

Development workers observed that these different goals implied different approaches to participation. In 1969, Sherry Arnstein, an advocacy planner, ranked various forms of community engagement in the influential article 'A Ladder of Citizen Participation.'[25] On the bottom rungs of the ladder she placed coercive measures designed to secure people's apparent support for predetermined ends, such as manipulation and tokenism. Through gradually increasing degrees of power, the steps of the ladder rose to partnership, delegated power, and citizen control at the top. Ten years later, the United Nations Research Institute for Social Development (UNRISD) categorised all forms of participation as either 'systems maintaining' or 'systems transforming.'[26] According to UNRISD definitions, the purpose of systems-maintaining participation is to make people more receptive to the development policies of authorities, whereas systems-transforming participation seeks to engage people in significant decision-making, even when it challenges existing structures of authority and involves genuine transfers of power.

Figure 1.2 Children at the Argentine site of Growing Up in Cities in the 1970s — a project initiated by the urban planner Kevin Lynch under the sponsorship of UNESCO.

During this same period, strong voices argued that only a systems-transforming approach could solve the world's growing problems of poverty. In the field of education, 1970 saw the publication of Paolo Freire's *Pedagogy of the Oppressed.*[27] Building on a long tradition of resistance to colonialism, he argued that teachers and students, as well as leaders and their people, become more fully human by working together with a critical eye to confront reality and transform it. In the field of health care, 1978 saw the International Conference of Alma Ata, convened by the World Health Organization and UNICEF, which articulated a model of primary health care based on the 'three pillars' of equity, citizen participation and collaboration among different sectors of government. The Declaration of Alma Ata declared that health — in the full sense of well-being — requires community participation 'in a spirit of self-reliance and self-determination.'[28] Participation was identified as a necessary means to achieving the goals of eradicating poverty as well as realising human dignity and well-being. More than 20 years later, the struggle to realise these goals in practice continues, and incorporating children into these processes remains a bold challenge.

Man and His Environment: An Opportunity for Children and Their City

In the spirit of these discussions about the ends and means of development, the 1968 General Conference of UNESCO established a 10-year programme on 'Man and His Environment' in order to increase understanding of potential people-centred solutions to environmental problems. ('Man and His Environment' was later absorbed into the 'Man and the Biosphere Programme.') In proposing that the search for solutions to environmental problems must include enabling people to pursue beauty and dignity in their lives, the mission of the new programme remains provocative to this day. (See Box 1.2.) In order to create policies that could promote this end, the programme plan recommended new forms of environmental assessment that would include human perceptions, values and behaviours. From the beginning, the Man and His Environment Programme sought to create interdisciplinary alliances of social researchers with natural scientists, architects, planners and other environmental practitioners.

Among the experts who attended the initial symposium on programme planning was Kevin Lynch, a humanistic professor of urban design and planning at the Massachusetts Institute of Technology. By 1970, Lynch was concerned by questions about how different forms of urban development facilitate human development — just as human thought and action in turn shape cities. Best known for his book *The Image of the City,* which focuses on adults' perception of different types of cities and movement through them, he had come to consider this early work published in 1960 as limited to 'a static image, a momentary pattern.' As he himself later criticised *The Image of the City,* 'There was no sense of development in it — of how that pattern came to be, nor of how it might change in the future, as the person matured, her or his function changed, her or his experience enlarged, or the

city itself was modified.'[29] To understand how city images develop, he was eager to work with children. Therefore he proposed to UNESCO that he direct a pilot project with children for the Man and His Environment Programme. His plan was accepted under the title 'Children's Perception of the Environment', a title that changed over time into 'Growing Up in Cities.'

BOX 1.2

The Mission of the Man and His Environment Programme of UNESCO

'The focus will be on man as a whole, the creation of favourable social relationships in a human environment, the prevention of alienation and attention to social and mental health on the community scale. The positive aspects of man's control of his environment will be explored with a view towards determining the most effective means of achieving a design for living that would encourage the pursuit of beauty and the enhancement of dignity in human relationships'.

(UNESCO, Report of a 1970 symposium that was convened in Helsinki to launch programme planning, p1.)

At the same time as he was working on Growing Up in Cities, Lynch summarised his thinking about development in the following general question: 'What interchange between people and the environment encourages them to grow into fully realised persons?'[30] Then, as now, the breadth of Lynch's concern extended beyond the conventional theory and practice of urban planning and design. He argued that it is not enough to evaluate human settlements according to their aesthetics, or function, or cognitive legibility, or cultural identity or any other single dimension. Rather, analysis needs to be conducted at the level of people's actions and perceptions as they inhabit and shape the environment, and are shaped by it — the level where all other dimensions converge. Here, the measure becomes whether or not the environment facilitates the development of the best human qualities. Lynch's question also implied that human development cannot be understood apart from interactions with the environment, and that fully realising human potential must involve exchanges with life-fostering environments.

To this sense of human development Lynch brought a sense of the environment as a complex whole. In the 1960s and 1970s, Lynch was one of a group of researchers and practitioners who were defining the 'environment' as a functional whole that includes physical features, cultural meaning, the behaviours that a place affords, and the social roles and relationships that it supports. Therefore people's interactions with a place have to be understood through multiple disciplines and research methods. Lynch, in urban design, along with Roger Barker, David Canter, Harold Proshansky, Leanne Rivlin and others in ecological and environmental psychology, agreed on these principles and rejected any notion of the environment as a purely material setting external to the inhabitant.[31] In this intellectual climate, it made good sense to ask how people are shaped by their interactions with the places where they live, from childhood on.

The Growing Up in Cities Model

Growing Up in Cities pursues several simultaneous goals. It seeks to document how children use local environments and how they evaluate local resources and restrictions, and then apply these insights to understand how the urban environment affects children's lives, formulate indicators of enabling environments, and create child-sensitive urban policies. The material gathered can also

> *The project can also expose the misperceptions of planners and other officials about how their policies affect the lives of children and their families.*

serve as a baseline for charting changing urban conditions for children, as this book's chapters on Australia and Poland, which revisit original project sites from the 1970s, demonstrate. The project can also expose the misperceptions of planners and other officials about how their policies affect the lives of children and their families. Project outcomes are communicated as widely as

possible in order to increase public awareness about these issues, and the process of working with young people to implement some of their ideas provides an occasion for building alliances of support for improved conditions, from the local level to municipal and even national levels. Finally, as project teams gain experience, they can offer training to a widening circle of communities and child and youth advocates who are interested in participatory action-research of this kind.

Growing Up in Cities identifies urban communities that typify the conditions of many children's lives, or that represent issues of particular significance for urban policy-making. The research phase at each location falls into four parts:

- **Objective descriptions** of each location's physical and social features via maps, census data, photographs and observations.

- **Observations** of people's use of public and semi-public places, with attention to all generations, but with a particular focus on the presence of children, recorded via behaviour maps, photographs, written descriptions and, at some sites, film.

- **Extended interviews** with a sample of girls and boys at each site, usually between the ages of 10 through 15, that include asking the children to draw and describe the area where they live. Additional insight into the children's lives may be gathered through group discussions, photographs taken by children, child-led tours through the area and other methods.

- **Interviews** with a small number of parents and urban officials to understand their perceptions of the children's environmental needs, of environmental changes that have occurred since they were children themselves and, in the case of officials, how they believe that their policies affect the quality of children's lives.

This information is used to engage children and their communities in planning improvements for the local environment and increase public awareness about urban issues for children, as well as a foundation for more child-friendly policies. These methods, including different ways to analyse and present results and involve children in taking action in their communities, are described in

© LOUISE CHAWLA

Figure 1.3 Growing Up in Cities works with children at locations which embody critical urban issues — in this case, with children in a South African squatter camp.

detail in this book's companion manual, *Creating Better Cities with Children and Youth.*[32] They closely follow the research guidelines that Kevin Lynch presented in his 1977 book *Growing Up in Cities*[33], except that most of the contemporary project teams interviewed more than 10 girls and 10 boys which Lynch recommended as a minimum number, and they have extended the original sample of 11–15 year olds to ages 10–15 (or at the Norwegian site, 9–15).

From the beginning, Growing Up in Cities was intended to focus on low-income communities undergoing rapid change, where children were particularly dependent on the resources of their immediate environment and where the findings could have the most immediate effect on urban policies. Both Lynch and UNESCO were especially interested in working in the developing world,

and for a while a site in Tunis was under discussion. The project's implementation, however, was dependent on funding from national UNESCO committees and, in the end, four countries participated in the project's first round. By 1972, work was underway in Salta, Argentina, and Melbourne, Australia. By 1973, Poland had joined, with an ambitious study that included inner-city and peripheral sites in Cracow and Warsaw, as well as a rural village. Two sites in Mexico were added in 1975 — a neighbourhood in Toluca, the provincial capital of the State of Mexico, and a *colonia* of largely self-built housing on what was then the periphery of Mexico City.[34]

Lynch noted in his introduction to *Growing Up in Cities* that the project's original intention was to emphasise the settlements of the immigrant poor, as these were the people who were presumably most exposed to environmental stress yet, in the end, all but one of the sites were relatively stable working-class settlements. He expressed a hope 'that future studies will turn more often to those areas and nations with even more critical problems.'[35] There were, however, no further studies, until the project was picked up 25 years later in the new form reported in this book.[36] To Lynch's regret, he never saw the project extended to new countries in the developing world or saw it proceed to the second stage of participatory urban design and policy-making involving children. Nevertheless, he believed that the project showed great promise: it could be completed using simple means; it could be easily modified to fit local conditions; it produced information relevant to local planning decisions; and it could initiate further policy-linked research.[37]

Based on the results of this first set of project trials, Lynch made several specific urban policy recommendations. Observing that much of children's play and socialising takes place in public places close to home, he noted that the regulation of local streets and small open spaces is a critical issue, and he made several recommendations to diminish or divert traffic from areas where children live. He recommended the rehabilitation of underused or abandoned rights of way, wastelands and other 'left-over' spaces that could be used for children's recreation and creative play. Observing that 'the hunger for trees is outspoken and seemingly universal', he emphasised that landscaping 'is not window dressing', and needs to be recognised 'as essential a part of the basic infrastructure of a settlement as electricity, water, sewers, and paving', and, whenever possible, that children should be enlisted in the landscaping work. He also noted children's preference for places with a clear social and spatial identity, the importance of community celebrations, as well as the need to conserve natural resources and historical landmarks in which children can take pride. At the same time, he recommended that: 'The city should open out to these children.' Therefore, he made several suggestions to make city services and cultural and environmental resources accessible. Finally, as a general rule for practice, he recommended that observation and research with children needed to become part of the environmental planning, design and management process, and that 'for-

mal bodies concerned with children's welfare at the local and national levels' needed to be instituted to ensure attention to children's rights and needs.'[38]

Twenty-five years after Lynch wrote this, the realities of most urban areas are that traffic dominates the streets; waste places and public open spaces are often barren or dangerous; children's hunger for trees does not appear to be shared by most developers and city officials; communities still have to fight to maintain their heritage and identity in the face of development pressures; most children have narrowly limited ranges of movement; and research with children and attention to their needs are emphatically not part of most urban policy, planning, design and management practices.

> *The Convention on the Rights of the Child contains 41 articles that are designed to ensure protection from harm, provision of basic needs and children's participation in decisions that affect their lives.*

Nevertheless, the following chapters of this book show that there is more support for participatory research and planning with children today than at the time when Lynch and his colleagues first envisioned this work. Between 1970, when Lynch conceived Growing Up in Cities, and 1994, when it was reconceived, there have been watershed events related to a greater awareness of children and their participation, which have created opportunities to realise more fully Lynch's original vision and goals.

CHILDREN AND ENVIRONMENTAL CHANGE

Between 1970 and the present, the defining historical event related to children's participation has been the Convention on the Rights of the Child. Since its adoption by the United Nations in 1989, the convention has moved through rapid ratification by almost all member nations.[39] With ratification, a nation commits itself to make the Convention widely known to its citizens — adults and children alike — and to submit regular five-year reports on the progress that it is making to ensure children full enjoyment of their rights. These reports are reviewed by the Committee on the Rights of the Child within the United Nations, which may ask for further review by UNICEF or other advocacy organisations for children. As a convention, the agreement is legally binding.[40]

Defining children as all human beings below the age of 18, the Convention contains 41 articles that are designed to ensure *protection* from harm, *provision* of basic needs and children's *participation* in decisions that affect their lives, followed by 13 articles related to implementation. Many of these articles are relevant to the quality of

human settlements, including Article 3, which specifies that 'in all actions concerning children (…) the best interests of the child shall be a primary consideration', and, centrally, Article 6, which requires that '(…) States Parties shall ensure to the maximum extent possible the survival and development of the child.' UNICEF and other advocacy groups for children have been construing these articles broadly; and according to such an interpretation, health, safety and social integration in the living environment, as well as access to education, recreation and other local services, are instrumental to ensuring a child's well-being and survival.[41]

A cluster of articles are directly relevant to participatory approaches involving young people in evaluating and planning their living environment. Article 12 provides that children have a right to express their views in all matters that affect them; and a broad interpretation of this principle recognises that children need opportunities to give input into government and institutional policy-making and planning that affect their life quality, and thus their living environment, as well as judicial and administrative matters related to individual and family concerns. Article 13 recognises the child's right to freedom of expression, Article 14 to freedom of thought, conscience and religion, and Article 15 to freedom of association and peaceful assembly. (See Box 1.3.)

Other articles are also relevant to the quality of children's environments and the principle of participation. Article 27 requires that, 'States Parties recognise the right of every child to a standard of living adequate for the child's physical, mental, spiritual, moral and social development.' As the following chapters of this book show, children have strong ideas about the environmental conditions that support adequate development. Article 29 advises that education should be directed to the full development of the child's personality, talents and mental and physical abilities, a respect for human rights and freedoms, respect for a child's own cultural identity as well as those different than its own, respect for the natural environment, and preparation for 'responsible life in a free society.' As several succeeding chapters show, many of the processes in which children engage in the course of participation address these ends, and can

---

BOX 1.3

'Participation Clauses' in the Convention on the Rights of the Child

Some of the key passages of the Convention that are relevant to children's participation in environmental decision-making and planning include:

'States Parties shall assure to the child who is capable of forming his or her own views the right to express those views freely in all matters affecting the child, the views of the child being given due weight in accordance with the age and maturity of the child.'
(Article 12.1)

'The child shall have the right to freedom of expression; this right shall include freedom to seek, receive and impart information and ideas of all kinds, regardless of frontiers, either orally, in writing or in print, in the form of art, or through any other media of the child's choice.'
(Article 13.1)

'States Parties shall respect the right of the child to freedom of thought, conscience and religion.'
(Article 14.1)

'States Parties recognize the right of the child to freedom of association and to freedom of peaceful assembly.'
(Article 15.1)

UNICEF (1990)

be applied to community-based curricula for formal and nonformal school systems.

Article 30 ensures that children of ethnic, religious or linguistic minorities have a right to enjoy their own culture, and Article 31 recognises children's rights to leisure, play, recreation and participation in cultural life and the arts. Provision for these rights requires places for their realisation within the local environment. Article 32 seeks to protect children from economic exploitation and harmful or hazardous work, in home or community workplaces.

Children in the Habitat Agenda

'The needs of children and youth, particularly with regards to their living environment, have to be taken fully into account. Special attention needs to be paid to the participatory processes dealing with the shaping of cities, towns and neighbourhoods; this is in order to secure the living conditions of children and of youth and to make use of their insight, creativity and thoughts on the environment'.

(Paragraph 13) Preamble to the Habitat Agenda of the Second United Nations Conference on Human Settlements (1996)

UNCHS (1997)

Subsequent international conferences have built upon this foundation. As previously noted, Agenda 21 and the Programme of Action which came out of the United Nations Conference on Environment and Development in 1992, includes a chapter on children and youth as a major group who must be involved in decision-making concerning the environment and development. The Agenda provides, specifically, that governments should take measures to 'ensure that the interests of children are taken fully into account in participatory processes for sustainable development and environmental improvement' (Paragraph 25.13.b).[42] Similarly, the Copenhagen Declaration from the World Summit for Social Development in 1995 reaffirms that people should be at the centre of development, that equity among generations and the integrity of the environment should be respected, and that the rights of children and youth should be observed.[43]

The Habitat Agenda — signed at Habitat II, the second United Nations Conference on Human Settlements held in Istanbul in 1996 — is particularly relevant to Growing Up in Cities. The Preamble recognises the special needs of children and youth with regard to their living environment. Other sections recommend that governments institutionalise participatory approaches to sustainable human settlements and provide for the representation of intergenerational interests, with special attention to children and other vulnerable groups (Paragraphs 113.1, 182.m).[44] (See Box 1.4.) In 2001, nations reaffirmed the principles of the Habitat Agenda at the Habitat + 5 Conference in New York.

Given this international movement to give children a more visible, active role in environmental planning at all levels, the goals and methods of Growing Up in Cities are getting a more encouraging reception from governments and international agencies today than they did 25 years ago. Although the way ahead is far from clear, a wide range of people in funding agencies, public media, municipal offices, nongovernmental organisations, community-based organisations and, not least of all, parents, have given their support to the project's contemporary revival.

GROWING UP IN CITIES IN THE 1990s

New Research Conditions

The preceding international agreements have created a momentum for participatory action involving children and the environment that was unattainable in the 1970s. From the beginning, Kevin Lynch intended the research stage of Growing Up in Cities to serve as a foundation for programmes that would involve young people in maintaining and improving their urban communities and for more child-friendly policies related to urban planning, design and management. However, the original project never progressed beyond this research stage. In the

1990s, project sites in Argentina, Australia, India, South Africa and the United States had different degrees of success in moving from research to the creation of participatory programmes. The story of these successes, and the barriers that they have faced, forms an important record of contemporary efforts to transform the language of international agreements into action.

Figure 1.4 One of the goals of Growing Up in Cities is to form networks of people who are committed to improving urban conditions for children. Here, Argentine project members join forces with a mobile environmental education unit.

Partly through design, partly through necessities that appear advantageous in retrospect, and partly through fortunate accidents, the contemporary version of Growing Up in Cities differs from the original project in several ways. This section reviews the conditions that have contributed to its success.

Broad international representation. From the beginning, there was a determination that the new Growing Up in Cities should include Asia and Africa. As a result, India and South Africa have been included. Because the project was revived in preparation of a conference on Urban Childhood to celebrate the 1000th anniversary of Trondheim, Norway, this city has been added. Trondheim brings the distinctive environment of a Scandinavian country with a strong social welfare tradition to the project. By serendipity, young researchers in England

and the United States were beginning projects with goals in harmony with Growing Up in Cities, and therefore they have brought their work into the project's fold. There was also an intention to revisit the original countries, and funding to do this was found for Argentina, Australia and Poland. As a consequence, the final count of core countries in this second round of the project is eight rather than four. This has proved an optimal number for international collaboration: manageable to coordinate; rich in diversity and opportunities for comparison; small enough for personal cohesion and exchange; and large enough to allow for the formation of subgroups with particular common concerns.

Commitment to child advocacy. Another difference between the 1990s and 1970s projects is that most of the contemporary project leaders are committed to child research, education or advocacy as their long-term professional focus. Every contemporary site has at least one person who is anchored in issues related to children. As international coordinator, I work on topics involving children and the environment where my disciplines of developmental psychology and environmental psychology overlap. Others focus on children within the fields of anthropology, geography, environmental education or urban design. The result is a long-term investment in the project's goals.

Personal exchange. Another critical advantage of the contemporary project is that all of the research leaders have had opportunities to meet each other face to face, beginning with an initial workshop in June 1996 at the Norwegian Centre for Child Research and again at the centre's Urban Childhood Conference in June 1997. In the course of the original week-long workshop, people formed personal as well as professional bonds, which opened the way for a regular exchange of questions, answers, observations and advice during fieldwork, analysis and programme development. For this purpose, e-mail — the communication lifeline of an international project of this kind — has been an enormous technological advance of the 1990s over the 1970s.

Broad funding base. Another difference appears to be an advantage in hindsight only. The original project was funded by UNESCO through the national committees of the four participating countries. When I sought to reinitiate Growing Up in Cities with the support of the Norwegian Centre for Child Research and Childwatch International of Oslo, I hoped that a large donor would take over general sponsorship. Instead, it quickly became apparent that each individual country would have to find its own funding. As the acknowledgements at the beginning of this book demonstrate, the project has been supported by a mosaic of public and private agencies at international, national and local levels. While the process of raising funds was slow and laborious, and budgets were limited at some sites, the overall result has been a broad base of support. As a consequence, many organisations have an investment in the project's success and future development.

> *The goals and methods of Growing Up in Cities are getting a more encouraging reception from governments and international agencies today than they did 25 years ago.*

Extensive networking. Forewarned by the history of the original project, contemporary project leaders have invested extensive time in identifying a network of child-friendly allies in city government, universities, media, child welfare agencies and community-based organisations in order to ensure that there will be a broad base of support for moving forward from research to implementation. Where implementation has been most successful, networking has involved more time than fieldwork. As a result, this second version of Growing Up in Cities has had two equally important, overlapping research phases: first, to understand how young people use, value and seek to improve their urban communities; and second, to understand how to move governments and leaders in civil society to enable young people to participate in constructive urban change. As a result, several of the following chapters are case studies of action research with young people, from the initial phase of gathering information to the later phase of developing and implementing a plan of action and reflecting on its effectiveness.[45]

An international agenda for children's participation. The Convention on the Rights of the Child, Agenda 21 and the Habitat Agenda have created a new international context for participatory work related to children and the environment from which the contemporary version of the project has undeniably benefited. While work of this kind is still far from easy and still faces formidable challenges, these international commitments have opened doors and created a new climate for sympathy and support.

Long-term support for coordination. The investment of the MOST Programme of UNESCO in project coordination and dissemination, beginning in 1995 and continuing through the writing of this book, with commitments to the future, has made it possible for project members to build upon each other's experience and to cooperate in providing advice and encouragement to an expanding number of new sites.

Research Goals

Research at the eight contemporary Growing Up in Cities sites has pursued three main goals: to collect information about young people's contemporary urban experience; to develop models for participatory urban planning with children and youth; and to compare the project's present and past results.

Goal One. Collect comparative international information about the urban experience and ideas of low-income 10–15 year olds as a means to evaluate contemporary urban resources and risks for young people of this age.

Growing Up in Cities was never intended to result in broad generalisations of the type that *this* is children's urban experience, but to represent some of the very diverse settings in which urban children live. Although the project has followed similar research methods at different sites, within each site researchers have sampled children who represent the diversity of the local population in terms of age, sex, ethnicity, residential location within the community, housing type and any other characteristics that are locally important. Not only is the urban world multifaceted, but so are the children's points of view regarding their experience.

To these diverse children in diverse places, the research teams have posed common questions, such as: 'Which places are most important to you?' 'Are there places where you don't like to go?' 'Are there places where you aren't allowed to go?' 'Where do you most like to be?' 'If you could make changes in your place, what would they be?' (For a complete list of interview questions, see the Research Guide at the end of the book.)

Based on the interviews and other research methods that have been described, this book explores whether, under different urban conditions, 10–15 year olds differ in their behaviour, feelings and ideas related to their local environment. Conversely, across different sites, do children this age express common responses? Across a range of places and cultures, do they express similar basic needs in terms of environmental resources?

Goal Two: *Develop a set of models for research-based, participatory urban planning, design and community development with children and youth.*

Growing Up in Cities is action research. It is directed to gathering information that can inform urban decision-making and help in developing programmes to engage young people in improving their environments and thus the quality of their lives. It also seeks to refine effective strategies for action through experience and reflection. To some extent, strategies have to be situation specific: each site presents a unique combination of resources and restrictions. To a great extent, however, the barriers encountered and the means to success at different sites can be generalised. The concluding chapter of this book synthesises the most successful principles and practices that evolved across sites to secure political commitment and organise community events that involve children and highlight their needs.

Goal Three: *Compare urban conditions today with conditions 25 years ago by revisiting project sites from the 1970s.*

Because work for the project in the 1970s collected extensive material about urban children's lives, it presented a rare opportunity for longitudinal research that would compare children's experience now with their experience then. When the project was revived, this historical dimension was expected to be dominant. For several reasons, it has played a small though still important part. First, only two of the present sites have this historical dimension: Braybrook in Melbourne and Powisle in Warsaw. Funding was not found to revisit Mexico; and in Argentina, opportunities to apply the Growing Up in Cities model in Buenos Aires, where there was a large supportive grassroots network and opportunities to attract national attention, made this coastal city a more compelling investment for money and energy than distant Salta. Therefore, this comparative dimension of the

> *Across all eight countries, the young people involved in the project doubted that adults in power would really listen to them or take their ideas seriously.*

project is reported in only two of the following eight chapters. Second, the physical forms of both Braybrook and Powisle have remained generally stable over the intervening 25 years, as has the pattern of children's lives in space and time. The main changes in these locations have been political, economic and cultural. For each site these historical changes have been sketched in broad strokes; but in Braybrook a historical focus has been pre-empted by the practical problem of how to motivate the municipal government to engage children in participatory programmes to improve the environment now. In Powisle, the transition from a Communist government and centrally planned economy to a capitalist democracy has been so dramatic that the children's reactions to this major political change in their lives, and its implications for their participation in the local community, have been the main concerns from a historical perspective.

The eight chapters that follow concentrate on bringing each of the contemporary project sites to life in their diversity and similarity: the children who dwell there describe where they live in drawings, photographs and words, and the research teams observe them in their fieldwork, notes and photographs. A common thread running through each description is a focus on how each site functions, or fails to function, to fulfil children's needs for place, people, identity and activity. How well parents' and officials' assumptions coincide with children's perspectives has been a secondary concern. How to create the most effective strategies to engage children in improving their lives has been an important issue in some accounts.

Before this trajectory through eight cities begins, a map of major findings may help to tie the following chapters together.

COMMON VOICES

In their answers to individual interview questions, the children in Growing Up in Cities often showed distinct differences according to culture, gender and environment. In answer to a question about favourite places, for example, the children in Oakland, California, spoke almost exclusively about their housing site and internal courtyard, fenced off as they were from their neighbourhood by fear of crime. In Boca-Barracas, Buenos Aires, children took researchers to a range of places in a proud display of community identity. In Canaansland, the Johannesburg squatter camp, the children were bemused by the question: no matter how it was worded, the possibility of choosing a place according to preference appeared beyond their comprehension. Different sites often gave radically different responses to questions. However, with regard to adults' attitudes about children, or what makes for good and bad places to live, the children spoke with remarkably united voices. This section reviews some main points that have revealed converging attitudes across the different sites.

Across all eight countries, the young people involved in the project doubted that adults in power would really listen to them or take their ideas seriously. This was true whether the country was a newly restored democracy, like post-Communist Poland, post-apartheid South Africa or post-junta Argentina, an established democracy like England, Australia or India, or a socialist democracy that particularly prides itself on its care for children, like Norway — and despite the fact that all of these countries, except the United States, have ratified the Convention on the Rights of the Child. A 13 year old boy in England expressed this disbelief: 'People like politicians and stuff don't really know what we want to do... and just think we're like stupid and a bit of a waste of a time really... They just think, "Oh, he's just a little kid, what does he know?"'

> *In all countries, North and South, this study found a large gap between the rhetoric of international agreements and the reality of authorities' provisions for children.*

In interviewing city officials and attempting to build child-friendly coalitions, project leaders found much evidence to confirm this response: everything from officials' failures to respond to communication, to direct dismissal, to an administrator's 'reappropriation' of the funds designated for community-based planning in Bangalore, to the violence of batons and police dogs when the children of Johannesburg and their families were suddenly evicted from their squatter camp without fair negotiation. For alliances of the poor and for organisations that advocate for them, all of these are familiar tactics by which the powerful control the powerless. Within this hierarchy of inequality, the children in this study are doubly stigmatised: they are poor, and they are children, within cultures that tend to dismiss them as 'just a little kid.' Yet if world governments are to honour their international agreements related to human rights, children's rights, social equity and sustainable development, they must recognise that it is the poor who carry the weight of the world's numbers and children who carry the seeds of the future. In all countries, North and South, this study found a large gap between the rhetoric of international agreements and the reality of authorities' provisions for children.

If such resistance to children's participation were universal, this book would never have been written. Warned by the fate of the 1970s version of Growing Up in Cities, contemporary project leaders began with a determination to move beyond research to action. On the positive side, when they looked for cooperation in government, media or organisations that advocate for children or the environment, they found numerous allies who have understood the potential of children and youth and the obligations of society. Several sites have demonstrated how, together, these intergenerational alliances can lead to limited but vital triumphs.

Also on the positive side, the children in each country have shown that they have serious, well-considered ideas to contribute. As soon as they understood the nature of the project in which they were engaged, they responded with realistic recommendations for community improvements. Most of these recommendations were small scale: to clean up trash, renovate a plaza, reopen a teen centre, build a place for quiet studying, protect or plant more trees. Some went beyond possible improvements for the immediate neighbourhood: to clean up a polluted river, reduce traffic or provide jobs for full employment. These large-scale suggestions can be dismissed as impractical only if the concepts of sustainable development and social equity are dismissed as well.

> *As soon as they understood the nature of the project in which they were engaged, the children responded with realistic recommendations for community improvements.*

Basic fairness means that the present generation of adults owes future generations a world as liveable and resource-rich as that which they inherited. Prudence requires that they should carefully nurture and educate those who will carry the earth's cultural and environmental heritage forward into the future. Beyond these common justifications and the reality that children, as representatives of future generations, have a central role in sustainable development, the voices of the children in this book demonstrate that they merit being heard also for this reason: in order to improve the places where they live. They call for the same radical reorientation of development goals as the concept of sustainable development necessitates. If we imagine these children as being the

subject of the opening principle of the Rio Declaration on Environment and Development, then its words acquire a hopeful ring. 'Human beings are at the centre of concerns for sustainable development.' This principle reflects the resolution of a debate between the nations of the North and the South, in which the South maintained that high-consuming Northern nations must not expect the South to protect its natural resources at the expense of its people.[46] Cast in these terms, the statement may appear a license to give human interests priority over environmental protection...but if the children in this book are taken as guides to people-centred development, then this principle becomes not a cause for concern but a reason for hope.

For what the children talked about were predominantly social and psychological needs and places where they could fulfil them: needs that make small demands on natural resources and large demands on their societies. To say this is not to diminish the importance of basic material provisions; when these were lacking, the children felt the stigma of their absence perhaps as keenly as their physical deprivation. As the chapter on South Africa so poignantly shows, the children of Canaansland understood the absence of water pipes and toilets in their camp to be a message from their society that they were not worth water or shelter from shame.

Beyond this level of basic physical provisions, what the children talked about was less quantifiable. They expressed satisfaction with their community when it had a positive self-image, friendly adults, available playmates, accessible and engaging public spaces where interesting activities could be found and places that children could claim as their own for socialising and play. When these elements were lacking, they expressed high degrees of alienation.

The communities where the children expressed the most happiness with their place were Boca-Barracas, one of the poorest districts of Buenos Aires; Sathyanagar, a self-built settlement on the periphery of Bangalore; Powisle, an old working-class district of Warsaw; and the two locations in Trondheim. Children expressed high degrees of alienation in the United States, England, Australia and South Africa.

In material terms, Boca-Barracas and Sathyanagar fall below all of the other project sites, except the squatter camp in South Africa. To observe that children were contented with many dimensions of these places is not to suggest that their material needs can be dismissed. It is not to excuse their governments from providing piped water, sanitation, secure housing, education, employment for their parents, and protection from pollution. The thrust of this observation is that along with having material needs, children also need the 'shelter' of a cohesive and friendly local culture. As the following chapters show, community characteristics that create such a culture, and those that destroy it, can be specified, and means to protect and foster the beneficial characteristics can be recommended. According to the children in this study, policies to do so need to be high on the development agenda.

These characteristics that children value highly are similar to those that sociologists identify with 'urban villages.'[47] Although urban villages are not necessarily poor, many of those used as examples in the literature of urban sociology are. In the past, however, research that has distinguished urban villages from neighbourhoods that are merely poor and lacking in social cohesiveness, has focused on how these places serve the needs of adults. The following chapters demonstrate how important these community characteristics are from the perspective of children as well.

At this point, the chapters that follow need to speak for themselves: each one recreating a unique yet representative place through images and words. Each site-based chapter describes a particular physical, social and historical geography — and the children's place within it — and locates it within the larger context of its city and nation. Together, these chapters reveal the resources and barriers that this project's efforts to improve children's urban conditions have encountered. In conclusion, a final chapter weaves these site descriptions together into an international perspective on urban development and children's needs.

ENDNOTES

1 Davis (1973).
2 United Nations Population Division, *World Urbanisation Prospects: The 1999 Revision,* and *The World at Six Billion.* Fifty-three percent of the world's population is projected to inhabit urban areas by 2015.
3 Ibid.
4 Ibid.
5 Satterthwaite (1996).
6 For childhood as a modern discovery, see Aries (1962); for premodern views of children, see Pollock (1984).
7 Kennedy (1993, chapt 2).
8 Ibid.
9 Key (1909).
10 Mower (1997), UNICEF (1990).
11 United Nations (1999, Table 7).
12 Annan (2000).
13 United Nations Development Programme (1998, pp. 2-4).
14 United Nations, 'Rio Declaration' (1992, Principle 3).
15 United Nations, 'Agenda 21' (1992, chapt. 25), UNICEF (1992).
16 United Nations Development Programme (1999, p. 3).
17 United Nations, 'Rio Declaration' (1992, Principle 1).
18 United Nations Development Programme (1998, 1999).
19 Satterthwaite (1999).
20 Satterthwaite et al (1996), Bartlett et al (1999), Gorlitz (1998).
21 Hart (1997), de Winter (1997), Flekkøy and Kaufman (1997), Adams and Ingham (1998), Driskell (2001), O'Brien and Christensen (forthcoming).
22 For updated project developments, see www.unesco.org/most/growing.htm.
23 United Nations Development Programme (2000); World Bank (2000).
24 This review of participation in development policy is indebted to Macdonald (1994, pp. 86-98).
25 Arnstein (1969).
26 Pearse and Steifel (1979).
27 Freire (1970).
28 Macdonald (1994).
29 Lynch (1990, p. 252).
30 Lynch (1976, pv).
31 Barker (1968), Canter (1977), Proshansky, Ittelson and Rivlin (1974).
32 Driskell (2001).
33 Lynch (1977).
34 Project history drawn from Kevin Lynch Collection, M.I.T. Archives.
35 Lynch (1977, p. 2).
36 Lynch's liaison in UNESCO, Jose Villegas, left the agency in 1975, and Lynch himself moved on to other commitments.
37 Lynch (1977, p. 1).
38 Ibid., pp. 56-59.
39 As of the year 2000, the Convention on the Rights of the Child has been ratified by all member states of the United Nations except Somalia and the United States.
40 UNICEF (1990).
41 Hodgkin and Newell (1998); UNICEF (1996).
42 United Nations (1992, chapt. 25).
43 United Nations (1995).
44 United Nations Centre for Human Settlements (1997).

[45] For discussions of action research, see Fals-Borda and Rahman (1991), Kemmis and McTaggart (1988), Greenwood and Levin (1998).

[46] Grubb (1993).

[47] Gans (1962), Ley (1983, chapt. 5), Schorr (1964).

REFERENCES

Adams, E and Ingham, S (1998) *Changing Places,* The Children's Society, London.

Annan, K (2000) *We the Peoples: The role of the United Nations in the 21st century,* United Nations, New York.

Aries, P (1962) *Centuries of Childhood,* Baldick, R (trans.), Jonathan Cape, London.

Arnstein, S (1969) 'A ladder of citizen participation', *American Institute of Planners Journal,* vol 35, pp. 216-224.

Barker, R (1968) *Ecological Psychology,* Stanford University Press, Stanford, CA.

Bartlett, S, de la Barra, X, Hart, R, Missair, A and Satterthwaite, D (1999) *Cities for Children,* Earthscan, London.

Canter, D (1977) *The Psychology of Place,* St. Martin's Press, New York.

Davis, K (1973) *Cities,* WH Freeman, San Francisco.

Driskell, D (2001) *Creating Better Cities with Children and Youth,* UNESCO Publishing/Earthscan, Paris/London.

Fals-Borda, O and Rahman, MA (eds) (1991) *Action and Knowledge,* Apex Press, New York.

Flekkøy, MG and Kaufman, NH (1997) *The Participation Rights of the Child,* Jessica Kingsley Publishers, London.

Freire, P (1970) *Pedagogy of the Oppressed,* Ramos, MB (trans.), Continuum, New York.

Gans, HJ (1962) *The Urban Villagers,* Free Press of Glencoe, New York.

Gorlitz, D, Hasloff, HJ, May, G and Valsiner, J (eds) (1998) *Children, Cities, and Psychological Theories,* de Gruyter, Berlin.

Greenwood, D and Levin, M (1998) *Introduction to Action Research,* Sage Publications, Thousand Oaks, CA.

Grubb, M (1993) *The Earth Summit Agreements,* Earthscan, London.

Hart, R (1997) *Children's Participation,* UNICEF, New York/Earthscan, London.

Hodgkin, R and Newell, P (1998) *Implementation Handbook on the Convention on the Rights of the Child,* UNICEF, New York.

Kemmis, S and McTaggart, R (eds) (1988) *The Action Research Planner,* Deakin University, Victoria, Australia.

Kennedy, P (1993) *Preparing for the Twenty-first Century,* Random House, New York.

Key, E (1909) *The Century of the Child,* GP Putnam, New York.

Ley, D (1983) *A Social Geography of the City,* Harper and Row, New York.

Lynch, K (1976) 'Foreword' to *Environmental Knowing* in Moore, GT and Golledge, R (eds), Dowden, Hutchinson and Ross, Stroudsburg, PA, ppv-viii.

Lynch, K (1977) *Growing Up in Cities,* MIT Press, Cambridge, MA.

Lynch, K (1990) 'Reconsidering "The Image of the City"' in Bannerjee, T and Southworth, M (eds), *City Sense and City Design,* MIT Press, Cambridge, MA, pp247-255; reprinted from Rodwin, L and Hollister, R (eds), *Cities of the Mind,* 1984, Plenum Press, New York.

Macdonald, J (1994) *Primary Health Care,* Earthscan, London.

Mower, Jr., AG (1997) *The Convention on the Rights of the Child,* Greenwood Press, Westport, CT.

O'Brien, M and Christensen, P (eds) (forthcoming) *Children in the City,* Falmer Press, London.

Pearse, A and Stiefel, M (eds) (1979) *Enquiry into Participation— A Research Approach,* United Nations Research Institute for Social Development (UNRISD), Geneva.

Pollock, L (1984) *Forgotten Children,* Cambridge University Press, Cambridge.

Proshansky, HM, Ittelson, WH and Rivlin, LG (1974) *Environmental Psychology,* Holt, Rinehart, and Winston, New York.

Satterthwaite, D (1996) *The Scale and Nature of Urban Change in the South,* Human Settlements Program International Institute for Environment and Development, London.

Satterthwaite, D (1999) *The Earthscan Reader in Sustainable Cities,* Earthscan Publications, London.

Satterthwaite, D, Hart, R, Levy, C, Mitlin, D, Ross, D, Smit, J and Stephens, C (1996) *The Environment for Children,* Earthscan, London.

Schorr, A (1964) *Slums and Social Insecurity,* Department of Health, Education, and Welfare, Washington, DC.

United Nations (1992) *Agenda 21, Rio Declaration, and Statement of Forest Principles,* United Nations, New York.

United Nations (1995) *World Summit for Social Development: The Copenhagen Declaration and Programme of Action,* United Nations, New York.

United Nations (1999) *Demographic Yearbook: 1997,* United Nations, New York.

United Nations Centre for Human Settlements (UNCHS) (1997) *The Istanbul Declaration and The Habitat Agenda,* UNCHS, Nairobi.

United Nations Development Programme (1998) *Human Development Report 1998,* Oxford University Press, Oxford.

United Nations Development Programme (1999) *Human Development Report 1999,* Oxford University Press, Oxford.

United Nations Development Programme (2000) *Human Development Report 2000,* Oxford University Press, Oxford.

United Nations Population Division (1998) *World Urbanization Prospects: The 1996 Revision,* T/ESA/SER.A/170, United Nations, New York.

UNESCO (1970) 'Final Report: Interdisciplinary symposium on man's role in changing the environment', Helsinki, Finland (8-13 June), Kevin Lynch Collection, MIT Archives and Special Collections.

UNICEF (1990) 'Convention on the Rights of the Child', *First Call for Children,* UNICEF, New York, pp. 41-75.

UNICEF (1992) *Children and Agenda 21,* UNICEF, Geneva.

UNICEF (1996) *Children's Rights and Habitat: Working Towards Child-Friendly Cities,* UNICEF, New York.

de Winter, M (1997) *Children as Fellow Citizens,* Radcliffe Medical Press, Oxford.

World Bank (2000) *Poverty Reduction Strategy Sourcebook,* World Bank, Washington, DC.

CHAPTER TWO

Our Neighbourhood is Like That!
Cultural Richness and Childhood Identity in Boca-Baraccas, Buenos Aires

Nilda Cosco and Robin Moore

Young people in Boca-Barracas, the historic port district of Buenos Aires, described their lives and neighbourhoods through a variety of Growing Up in Cities methods. They revealed the 'paradoxical poverty' of an area of low material resources that is nevertheless rich in settings where its young people can play a vital role in the social and cultural life of their community. A community action programme was created based on the children's insights and priorities, which has inspired reflection on issues of governance related to the rights of children in the urban environment, as well as a discussion of the importance of a 'holding environment' where children have freedom to assimilate and transform their culture through play and exploration.

One day, best friends Cecilia and Fabiana invited us to see the monthly musical performance in *Pasaje Bardi* near their home. The *Pasaje* (Passage) was a small, elongated open space recently developed in the neighbourhood, adjacent to the railway station. Both girls had shown the space in their drawings during their interview and had included a visit there during the field trip. They told us how they liked it because of the paintings (a tango mural) and all the different community events that happened there. The *Pasaje* evidently held much meaning in their lives.

We went to pick the girls up on a Sunday afternoon. They were eagerly waiting for us, dressed in their best freshly laundered and pressed clothes, proud to be taking us on a trip to one of their special haunts in the neighbourhood. As we walked the several blocks to the *Pasaje* they were very sociable, telling us stories about different

places in the area, where they could go on the train and the fact that they lived in houses built under the arches of the elevated tracks (see *Cooperativas*, Table 2.2).

While we were walking, we heard clinking sounds coming from the bag Fabiana was carrying. We arrived at the *Pasaje* to discover that the jazz programme had been cancelled. We decided to sit down anyway and spend some time together. Fabiana opened the bag and we found that the sounds we had heard came from chinaware for a picnic. The girls carefully laid out a tablecloth on the elevated grassy patch where we were sitting and arranged the cups and saucers, silverware, plates, napkins, a homemade cake and thermos of coffee.

The girls' enjoyment was obvious as they conducted the ritual of preparation and serving their guests. The 11 and 12 year olds had planned and executed the whole event with great care, with the assistance and support of their mothers. Their sense of hospitality was remarkable. We had a very enjoyable party, sitting together on the retaining wall of the small terrace that served as a sitting area for performances. The whole experience impressed us as an example of high quality childhood, even though the material circumstances of the girls' families were extremely modest.

> *We began to see that at least for the group of Boca-Barracas children we were working with, low material resources had two very different faces — one the joyful, mature face of culture, the other the daily struggle of material survival.*

There was a quality of cultural richness here in this place and in the lives of these children that was striking. Similar experiences with other children and their families before and after our trip with Fabiana and Cecilia pushed us to overcome our initial commonplace assumptions about poverty (or as we prefer to say, 'low material resources'). We began to see that at least for the group of Boca-Barracas children we were working with, low material resources had two very different faces — one the joyful, mature face of culture, the other the daily struggle of material survival. For the parents, one made the other bearable. For the children the reward was fundamental. The richness of their cultural lives gave them a critical dimension of healthy development: a sustaining self-identity as individuals and as participants in community life.

This discovery caused us to dramatically shift our thinking by the time we completed our fieldwork. We had not been prepared to learn that many aspects of these children's lives were so positive in ways we had not considered prior to starting the Growing Up in Cities project in Buenos Aires. Even though these children lived in deprived environments, they gained a strong personal identity and sense of belonging from the cultural richness and social density of their daily lives. This shared identity with the neighbourhood and community helps explain the impressive ethical development of these chil-

dren. Repeatedly during the interviews, field trips and photographic activities, we observed their feelings of solidarity, cooperation and care for each other.

For many years, conventional wisdom has perpetuated the idea that children living in low resource communities are poor in all aspects of their individual and social lives. One reason for this, as John McKendrick has discussed, is that we do not have a child-focused understanding of poverty.[1] For children, experiential richness in urban neighbourhoods is not readily correlated with income level.[2] The enormous range of contexts of family and community life conditioned by geography, climate, culture and political economy make us wary of generalisations. In the face of such complexity, how can one attempt to explain the dynamics of the quality of life of children as they age and develop? This is the question we found ourselves addressing as the project progressed, and the provocative results of our observations and field experiences with the GUIC children unfolded.

Our insights reflect our interdisciplinary backgrounds, as one of us is a design researcher of children's urban habitats (Moore) and the other an educational psychologist practised in working with children in low resource communities (Cosco). To do justice to our findings, we

TABLE 2.1	
Boca-Barracas Community Profile	
LAND AND POPULATION	
Land Area	967 hectares (2389.5 acres)
Population	126,000
Density	130 persons/hectare (53 persons/acre)
Number of blocks	576
Area of plazas and parks	26 hectares (0.2 ha/1000 population) (64.25 acres) (0.49 acres/1000 population)
Number of plazas and parks	26
Ratio of blocks to plazas and parks	22/1 approx.
RELIGION	Official national religion is Catholic. Minorities of other Christian and non-Christian religions exist, but they are extremely small.

will attempt four things in this chapter: first, to reflect on and interpret selected findings from the interviews of children and other standardised components of the GUIC project; second, to describe and comment on the results of the special Boca-Barracas community action components; third, to reflect on the issue of governance in relation to children's rights in urban planning policy and practice; and finally, to interpret the findings using the concept of the neighbourhood as a 'holding environment' according to the theories of Donald W. Winnicott.

BOCA-BARRACAS

Boca-Barracas, one of the oldest and lowest income sections of Buenos Aires, is located near the centre of one of the world's largest cities.

Shelter conditions in Boca-Barracas range from living in the street to residing in apartment buildings, and include many squatted houses and *conventillos* (see Table 2.2)

La Boca (the mouth) dates from the beginning of the 19th century. It was the original port area of the city and by mid-century was one of the most important immigrant settlements in Argentina. It was the birthplace of the tango and attracted many musicians, poets and painters to settle there. This has given a special identity to the area, both physically and politically. Here, the immigrant groups (especially Italians from Sicily) founded diverse social and political organisations which gave rise to a feeling of local solidarity unique in the city. As a consequence, La Boca has retained a strong sense of community identity and independent spirit, while at the same time influencing city power in its favour.

As Argentine trade grew, Barracas (which means warehouses) accommodated the increased port function up the Riachuelo River. Related industrial development expanded away from the river, stimulating a period of economic prosperity and an elevated quality of life. This era continued until the new *Puerto Madero* was built in the 1930s on the Plate River to accommodate larger cargo vessels. Then began the gradual decline of Boca-Barracas until implementation of the flood control public works

Figure 2.1 This aerial view of Boca-Barracas shows the characteristic grid street pattern of Buenos Aires and the fine grain texture of high density, low-rise residential buildings. 'La Boca' (the mouth) of the Riachuelo river can be seen far right. The 'Boca Juniors' soccer stadium is labelled 'CABJ'.

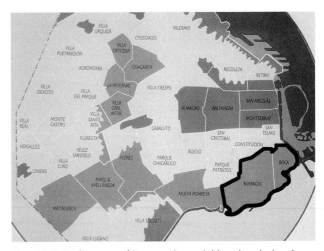

Figure 2.2 Outline map of Buenos Aires neighbourhoods showing low income areas in dark tone. La Boca and Barracas (bottom, right) are part of a band of the lowest income communities along the Riachuelo River.

and first trickle of reinvestment in the mid-1990s — coinciding with the GUIC project.

The tradition of solidarity and activism remained strong through the decades of military rule in the 1960s and 1970s. With the rebirth of democracy in Argentina in 1983, the area was able to rapidly rebuild its social infrastructure through community participation, reflected in

TABLE 2.2

Housing Types in Boca-Barracas

TYPE	CHARACTERISTICS	COMMENTS
1. *Calles y plazas.* Streets and plazas.	Streets and plazas where the homeless *(los sin techos)* live.	Local informants said some *sin techos* lived in Boca-Barracas. Informal observation suggested fewer people live this way in Buenos Aires than in cities in the USA.
2. *Asentamientos.* Settlements. Literally 'settling'.	Initial stage of a *villa* (cf. 3). Land is squatted and people construct 'emergency shelters.' Community feeling of solidarity is limited. People act as individuals to resist being pushed off the land.	To negotiate effectively with the owners, it is important to organise into a cohesive group, as for example the housing cooperative (cf. 9)
3. *Villas.* Villages.	*Villa* is the term used in Argentina for infor-mal, self-built housing areas, along with *villa de emergencia* (emergency village) and the disrespectful *villa miseria* (misery village). Initially, structures are built from scrap and slowly improved with more substantial materials. The *villa* eventually becomes an organised community with political clout and street addresses. Outdoor space affords opportunities for social contact.	*Villas* date from the 1930s coincident with the greatest wave of European immigration. They provide basic shelter for very poor families but without security of tenure. Sites are often built on marginal, low-lying land and are liable to flooding. Some *villas* are over 30 years old. Boca-Barracas had two small *villas* where two GUIC children lived. The social and psychological impact of living in such a chaotic environment was apparent in their behaviour.
4. *Casas tomadas.* Squatter houses.	Literally 'taken houses'. Reliable information difficult to find.	As in other countries, squatter residents face problems of lack of basic utilities, insecurity, etc.
5. *Hoteles.* Hotels.	Former hotels that rent one room per family. High rents with several families sharing one bathroom.	No security of tenure.
6. *Conventillos.* Literally, 'little convents'.	Traditional La Boca housing. One family per room but with the advantage of a shared interior courtyard.	Tenure same as *inquilinatos* (cf. 7). Woodframe construction and oil stove heating cause high risk of fire.
7. *Inquilinatos.* Tenant houses.	Legal form of tenure introduced by Juan Peron to replace *conventillos (cf. 6),* makes tenants more secure. Rent of whole house sometimes shared by extended family or friends.	Currently, to evict a tenant, a landlord will refuse to take rent until the legal deadline is passed and through no fault of their own the tenants become 'illegal residents'.
8. *Hogares.* Homes.	Homes for children without families, such as orphans and former street children. Exist in many forms in Latin America, usually supported by the Church.	Two GUIC children lived in a Boca-Barracas *hogar* for school-aged boys. It was a typical two-story house, managed by an outspoken priest and wonderful, caring staff.

TABLE 2.2   (continued)

TYPE	CHARACTERISTICS	COMMENTS
9. *Cooperativas.* Housing cooperatives.	*Cooperativas* have the great advantage of being organised, legal entities and therefore support long term sweat equity investment.	A Boca-Barracas example was founded in 1994 by homeless people under railway arches. They invaded the area, resisted police eviction, eventually negotiated permanent lease with the railway company, and converted the arches into houses. Two GUIC children lived in the *cooperativa*.
10. *Departamentos tipo casas.* Apartments like houses.	Duplex/triplex/quad apartments built as row houses with street entrances to separate units.	Residents rent or own as part of a condominium.
11. *Departamentos.* Multi-story apartment buildings.	The bulk of Buenos Aires residents live in highrise apartments but few such buildings exist in Boca-Barracas.	Apartments can be rented or owned as a condominium.
12. *Casas.* Houses.	Typical houses are one or two stories high and are entered through a doorway directly from the sidewalk, Spanish style, often into a small private courtyard.	Few Boca-Barracas residents lived in either a rented or owned house.
13. *Loft* (anglicised). Lofts.	The newest housing form, similar to that found in older industrial cities in Europe and the USA where old, disused inner city warehouse buildings have been recycled and converted into living space.	Buenos Aires *lofts* are the domain of young, upper middle class professionals. Some are close to Boca-Barracas in the redeveloped *Puerto Madero* (former main port that replaced La Boca; the new port moved downstream to accommodate container vessels).

the Boca-Barracas Solidarity Network of more than forty local community organisations. This history provided a compelling reason for implementing Growing Up in Cities in Boca-Barracas, as the Network's objectives for children and families coincided with the project's philosophy, giving us a sense of assurance that the project would result in permanent changes beneficial to children. This turned out to be a somewhat naive assumption.

Although this chapter will focus on the cultural richness of the lives of the Boca-Barracas children, our intention is not to paint a simplistic, rosy picture that ignores the negative side of community life there. Children in Boca-Barracas, as in many other Buenos Aires neighbour-

hoods and in Argentina as a whole, face many problems. In 2001, four years after the completion of the field work, the socio-economic situation for working class families remains desperate. It is difficult to avoid slipping into a level of poverty from which there is no escape. Day-to-day survival is a major preoccupation.

OPEN SPACE AND QUALITY OF LIFE

Buenos Aires, like other large dense cities in South America, has a low level of open space provision: less than three square metres per capita, whereas the World

Health Organization recommends ten square metres per capita.[3] Furthermore, most of the city's open space is concentrated in two huge parks: the mature Palermo Woods (134 hectares) in the middle class residential centre of the city, designed by Argentina's first landscape architect, Carlos Thays; and a newly designated, but un-developed, open space (130 hectares) in the working class southern part of the city. Boca-Barracas was better endowed with neighbourhood space than many other districts in the city because of the relatively large number of small plazas and parks for public use (see Table 2.1).

There is also the unique *Reserva Ecológica* (Ecological Reserve), a magnificent 350-hectare wetlands extending into the Plate River, used by thousands of people of all classes each weekend as an escape from the city. The Reserve is the most important environmental education resource in the city, serving about 30,000 school children

Figure 2.3 GUIC children interview an older resident of the neighbourhood to record his ideas for redeveloping the vacant lot behind the group as a park.

each year. Located less than two kilometres from the centre of La Boca, the Reserve was a very special resource for older children and their families as it was easy to get to by *colectivo* (public bus) or even by foot, bicycle or moped. Several GUIC children mentioned this special resource during their interview or included it in their draw-

ing. However, the Reserve and other major open spaces were mostly not accessible to children on their own.

As the global economy advances, the material quality of life of many families in Argentina — as in a great number of other countries — is falling below minimum living standards. Environmental quality is becoming de-graded and indigenous cultural richness is under siege.[4] The physical environment is becoming less and less friendly towards children. The stability of the Argentine economy, which in the 1980s and 1990s produced rising incomes in middle and upper middle class families, making loans and long-term credit possible, resulted in a dra-matic rise in car ownership in a very few years. In Buenos Aires, almost overnight, city streets became clogged with traffic, heavily polluted (in 1997 leaded petrol was still in use) and physically very dangerous because of the undis-ciplined traffic. Argentina is reputed to have one of the highest traffic accident rates in the world. Already in 1988, in a study on *Children and Play in Large Cities,* spon-sored by the newspaper Clarín, urban planner Ruben Gazoli warned that the streets of Buenos Aires had be-come mere traffic corridors. He was concerned that they were rapidly losing their social function especially for children, the primary users of streets in urban residential neighbourhoods.[5] As the global economy extends its reach, children living in the world's major cities, includ-ing Buenos Aires, are suffering an unfair share of negative impacts to their primary outdoor space, urban streets.

The plazas and public open spaces in Buenos Aires offer little respite from the conditions of the streets. The municipality has no money to take care of open spaces. They are dirty and polluted, and the needs of children tend to be ignored. Children are never involved in the re-design of a park or new management procedures spon-sored by private enterprise. Nonetheless, as no other choices are available, children must play and so adapt their needs to these inadequate physical conditions. In Boca-Barracas, as in many Latin American city neigh-bourhoods, there were a few far apart but highly-prized small neighbourhood plazas that provided alternative spaces for play and hanging out.

Children in Boca-Barracas probably suffered less from the impact of traffic than in most other neighbourhoods in the city. Certainly the neighbourhood was traversed by several major arterial boulevards which were uncrossable 'rivers of metal' for younger children. The many factories in the area generated noisy truck traffic. However, the location of Boca-Barracas along the Riachuelo on the edge of Buenos Aires meant that there was not as much through traffic as in more central city neighbourhoods. The number of children observed outdoors, moving around the neighbourhood in non-school hours and on weekends, was impressive.

This observation contrasted with some middle class neighbourhoods of Buenos Aires where children live in restricted high-rise apartment buildings with little chance to get outside to play freely. These children's time is over-occupied, as they attend school from 8:00 am to 5:00 pm and then take classes in computer skills, martial arts, English and sports. On the weekends, they participate in programmes at private clubs. In contrast, children in Boca-Barracas led a rich daily life in a physically and socially diverse environment, over which parents asserted a relaxed territorial control. These children roamed farther from home than their North American and European counterparts (most walked to and from school, for example, and went on domestic errands and family visits many blocks away). As a result, they appropriated a wide range of local spaces.[6]

Although children in Boca-Barracas criticised the general level of litter, untidiness and lack of repair and maintenance of the plazas, streets and sidewalks in the area, they still used these spaces as there was nowhere else to go. Although these spaces might have seemed undesirable to an outsider, they harboured community life in the form of small neighbourhood industries, cafes, stores and the ubiquitous *kioscos* where a child might purchase something sweet for a few *centavos* (cents).

One of the most extreme examples of polluted open space in the whole city of Buenos Aires constituted one edge of the Boca-Barracas neighbourhood: the Riachuelo River corridor forming the *boca* of the old port of La Boca before flowing into the Plate River. The stinking Riachuelo, laden with industrial poisons from many unregulated plants upstream, had been an environmental *cause célèbre* for years, with successive governments promising to clean it up, but lacking the political will to do so. In 1998, the Buenos Aires government completed construction of a massive flood control system to keep the Riachuelo from flooding the neighbourhood. The objective is to protect the residents from the filthy waters entering their homes from time to time, but it will not change the pollution. As the flood problem appeared solved, the new threat of 'gentrification' became very real. Suddenly, La Boca has become a fashionable place to live because it is close to the centre of the city, has a strong local identity, a rich history and inexpensive housing — up to this point.

TABLE 2.3.			
Boca-Barracas Participants Profile (N=32)			
Male, 14 Female, 18			
AGE	# OF PARTICIPANTS	AGE	# OF PARTICIPANTS
10	8	13	8
11	8	14	8

THIRTY-TWO CONSULTANT CHILDREN

Fabiana and Cecilia were two of the group of 32 'consultant' children who were selected to work with us in the Boca-Barracas neighbourhood and brought together by Virginia and María, two social workers we had met at the local municipal offices. The selection criteria included half girls and half boys, spread from ages 10 through 14 (Table 2.3), evenly distributed across the residential zones of the neighbourhood, and representative of the forms of shelter listed in Table 2.2.

The children were knowledgeable about conditions in the neighbourhood and were willing to discuss them. The search for decent housing was a constant preoccupation, and the fear of losing their home was a constant cause of anxiety for many children. As one of the social workers commented, 'They don't live a deceived life… they know what is lacking or wrong.' When the GUIC children talked about dangers such as drugs, for example, they did not label the situation simplistically as 'bad' but analysed it from a more mature point of view, explaining the 'war' between different drug dealing groups as a 'struggle to survive.'

> *'Don't worry', they told the Gringo researcher (Robin Moore) before setting out on a field trip through their territory, 'we'll take care of you'. This was their domain and they knew every square metre of it, who lived there, who their friends were, and areas to avoid because of drug dealing and violence.*

Pedro and Claudio were two of these neighbourhood experts. They were best friends who lived in a group home run by the Catholic parish as part of the *Hogar Don Bosco* system.[7] The traditional masonry domestic building housed 13 boys ages 9 through 16.[8] Later in the project, the *Hogar* became a great place for subgroups to meet to work on projects in the common room in the front of the building, with shutters opening on to the street. It was the most neutral meeting place in the neighbourhood.

Pedro and Claudio were both 14 and therefore 'senior' members of the *Hogar* and as such accorded considerable freedom to come and go and to be responsible for their own lives. This was a deliberate policy on the part of the *Hogar* staff to prepare the members of the *Hogar* family to live independently in separate accommodations after the age of 17. Because of their knowledge of the neighbourhood and their interest in the project, Pedro and Claudio soon became key members of the GUIC group. Pedro's drawing was an accurate rendition of the street plan extending for many blocks around the *Hogar*.

'Don't worry,' they told the Gringo researcher (Robin Moore) before setting out on a field trip through their territory, 'we'll take care of you.' This was their domain and they knew every square metre of it, who lived there, who their friends were, and areas to avoid because of drug dealing and violence. During the trip we stopped outside the fire station. La Boca had had a volunteer fire department for many years, as the traditional portside houses in the neighbourhood were timber framed, sheathed in corrugated iron, and heated by a variety of open oil and gas heaters. Fires were common and firemen had high status in the community. As we viewed the fire station, Pedro explained that he wanted to join the force as he was a few months away from the minimum age of 15. There was only one problem: he wore an earring, which was strictly forbidden by the fire team. He was still considering this difficult teenage dilemma.

We looked upon each of these carefully selected children as a consulting 'expert', in the sense of someone who has acquired special skill or knowledge from experience: in this case, knowledge of the physical space of the neighbourhood and an understanding of the community dynamics. GUIC opened up a new dimension to their lives. Several of them commented about how good it felt to be asked for their opinions about their experiences in the neighbourhood and their ideas for improvement. Most of them had never been asked this type of question before — at least not in such a genuine way. After the interview with Pedro and Claudio, one of them thanked us for the exercise, saying how much he had learned from answering the questions. The two boys had an impressive capacity to explain themselves articulately. They were able to analyse aspects of their lives in the neighbourhood, answering questions that no one had asked them before. Most likely for this reason, like most of the GUIC children, they expressed a strong commitment to the project, gave carefully considered answers to the questions and participated creatively in the activities.

Pedro and Claudio were clearly aware of their knowledge of the neighbourhood. From them and most other members of the group of 32, we felt we got reliable information, often expressed with uncompromising clarity. Although these children felt immersed in a harsh reality, most of them were able to discriminate the reasons for their difficult lives and analyse the causes. They knew they lacked material resources and, at the same time, they were able to describe unforgettable, fulfilling events in their lives. We learned that behind the hard reality and struggle against adversity, there was plenty of logical thinking and objective understanding of reality — the mark of an 'expert.' Another reason for their expertise is being *rooted* in a particular place, feeling part of that place, knowing that 'this is where I live so I know what I'm talking about.' To learn what children have to share simply requires letting them express themselves and listening respectfully.

FIELD TRIPS AND OTHER METHODS

Like the GUIC programmes in other countries, the Argentine programme had two main components. First, there was the standardised protocol with the selected group of children like Pedro and Claudio, Fabiana and Cecilia. In Argentina, it consisted of interviews with the children and some parents. During the interview, each child was asked to make a drawing of the part of the neighbourhood where she or he lived and to include the most important places in it. The methodology was similar to that employed by Moore in earlier research on the role of the physical environment in urban childhood.[9] Each child was also given a camera loaded with a 24-exposure roll of film and asked to photograph important places in the neighbourhood. As a final step, each child took one or two members of the research team on a walking tour around her or his neighbourhood 'domain' to share first-hand the places that had been described in the interview and photographed (Figure 2.6). This research was organised by the authors and conducted on the ground by them and three local social workers, and complemented by the authors' observations of public life.

The trips around the neighbourhood reinforced the value of favourite places such as the *Caminito,*[10] plazas, parks and schools, as well as landmarks such as the transporter bridge, churches and railways. Our additional independent observations of public life in the streets, plazas and parks made it possible for us to interpret the children's drawings more accurately. Many of the drawing elements were colourful renditions that, in the words the children used to describe them, expressed positive social values. By the same token, the drawings downplayed aspects that adults might have perceived as

Figure 2.4 (ABOVE) The old transporter bridge across the Riachuelo — a highly visible, landmark and significant source of identity for the area.

Figure 2.5 (LEFT) Child drawing the transporter bridge.

strongly negative, such as disrepair and litter.

Children mentioned the social dangers of some of these places after dark or when no one was around, but they emphasised the extent to which these places afforded freedom of action for their peer group. Although limited in size and widely scattered geo-graphically, the public spaces afforded children critical freedoms: to be together, to act. Without this, the quality of life would have been greatly diminished. Most children were part of an extended family peer group, usually with a few younger brothers, sisters and cousins in tow. From an early age, children walked every day around their *barrio.*

The way many children spoke with pride about the places that we visited during the field trips, and their bold confident body language as they moved around, indicated their strong sense of ownership of their environment. This sense of the children's affiliation with their surroundings was supported by the interview results. All the children, except four, identified a 'favourite place' in the neighbourhood (14 different places in all, five of them parks or plazas) and all, except three, said they felt they 'owned' these places. The Boca-Barracas children lived a socially integrated life that was radically different from that of more affluent children in other parts of the city, whose time, space and social relations were restricted by

Figure 2.6 Claudio and Pedro take the 'researcher' (Moore) on a tour of the neighbourhood.

the demands of after-school activities. Those children — and those in other cities around the world — are losing the depth of feeling expressed by Gabriel when talking about 'the good memories' of Plaza Colombia (occupying one city block), which, he said 'was my whole life.' Cecilia and Fabiana added cultural insight to Gabriel's sense of satisfaction. On our trip back home, we were reflecting on their life in the neighbourhood. 'I love the neighbourhood,' Cecilia commented. 'If someone took out La Boca from the city, it wouldn't be Buenos Aires anymore.' 'Here is where culture matters,' Fabiana added.

The field trips showed us that the children really knew their neighbourhood and genuinely appropriated the places they used. The girls especially were proud to show us how well they knew the neighbourhood and how

competent they were to lead us through it. Most children did not take us into their houses as they were ashamed of the condition or size or both. Cecilia and Fabiana were exceptions. They lived in a housing cooperative which had gained legal rights to land that was originally squatted: a victory won through strong community solidarity. The owner-occupiers were justly proud of their accomplishments and this was reflected in the pride of the children. Most of the other children could not share this feeling. Possibly, this partly explains their strong feeling of identity with the neighbourhood which substituted for the home as a source of identity. As Nicolás bluntly put it, 'I don't like the house where I live but I like the neighbourhood'.

COMMUNITY ACTION

The second component of our work addressed the GUIC objective of involving the children in developing a participatory community action process, designed to take advantage of local opportunities for giving visibility to children's issues in urban planning. As much as possible, we tried to add to the children's cultural and ethical strength by developing an action programme that would provide an educational opportunity for the children and their families, to strengthen their capacity for understanding and to prepare them for community action in the future. It was a way of giving back something valuable to the children and their parents in return for their time, energy and ideas. These activities were designed to motivate the children to create solutions to their own problems in the context of a realistic awareness of both constraints and opportunities. At the same time, we also tried to create a partnership with community and governmental organisations to influence policy and create permanent change.

The community action process was further extended and used as a vehicle for exploring ways to build a governance process that would involve young citizens permanently in decision making about development of the urban environment. Our strategy in Boca-Barracas was to conceptually merge these components, hoping that syn-

© NILDA COSCO AND ROBIN MOORE

Figure 2.7 Gulliver's Mapping (LEFT TO RIGHT): carrying the base map to the plaza; rolling it out; everyone joins in, sharing their memories and opinions.

ergistic links would grow between them and guide progress. This 'action component' of the project was organised by the authors and implemented by the *Móvil Verde* (the Mobile Green Unit, a non-formal education team affiliated with the urban environmental education programme of a labour union organisation).

Three community actions were included in the programme. First, a Gulliver's Mapping[11] (Figure 2.7) event was implemented as part of the Winter Vacation Festival in La Boca. Second, the children organised an exhibition of their photographs of Boca-Barracas which was also launched at the Winter Festival and presented at the Cultural Centre of Buenos Aires, *La Recoleta*. Third, a series of design education workshops involved children living in a sub-area of La Boca in implementing action projects in their neighbourhood.

Gulliver's Mapping

The 1997 Winter Festival in La Boca provided an ideal opportunity to involve people of all ages in a Gulliver's Mapping event. The map was constructed from the standard survey sheets prepared by the city (some of them unrevised for 40 years!), generously provided by the Urban Planning Department, taped together on sheets of cardboard backing. The day of the Festival, the map was assembled by our *Móvil Verde* colleagues at the *Teatro de la Ribera* as part of a public presentation of the whole GUIC project. After the presentation, a group of GUIC children helped roll up the four-metre-long map and carry

it on their heads through the streets to *Plaza de los Bomberos*, where it was laid out on the sunny side of the space. The *Móvil Verde* was parked alongside to help facilitate interaction. It was not long before a couple of dozen participants of all ages had taken off their shoes and were sitting or kneeling on the map, coloured markers in hand, discussing their comments (neighbourhood memories, anecdotes and criticisms of present conditions) with each other and the *Móvil Verde* facilitators. A lady who appeared to be in her 50s was talking about a well known jazz trumpeter who had lived down the street. A lively discussion got underway between several neighbours and Móvil Verde staff about the polluted conditions of the Riachuelo — and what, if anything, the city was doing about it. Most people were sceptical if not apathetic, as there had been news stories, TV programmes and political debates for years without success in cleaning up the river. However, the city was installing a large scale ambitious flood control scheme that some participants valued and recorded.

After about three hours, the map was rolled up and stored overnight at the *Mutual Esperanza* neighbourhood club. The following day, Sunday, the map was unfurled at a different location, next to the *Biblioteca Popular de la Boca* where the children's photographic exhibition had been launched the previous day. Again, dozens of people of all ages expressed their observations, memories and opinions on the map. It was entertaining and informative for everyone. At mid-afternoon, the *Murga* festival[12] came leaping by the Gulliver's site, which drew more participants into its spell: they just *had* to add their contributions. The completed map was later used in a public exhibition as an annotated reference map of the area, and in design workshops with the children.

Children's Photographic Exhibition

The photo exhibition was possibly the most successful activity we did with the children in terms of the public relations benefits and the modest cost of materials. In total, 13 children in nine teams participated in taking photographs of their environment. Some of these volunteered to help produce the catalogue and organise the exhibition. We acted as overall curators, while leaving the children as much creative freedom as possible.

Simple, inexpensive cameras were used to take the photographs. After a few minutes of instruction, most children had no problem using them. Each was loaded with a 24-exposure film. Most children worked in pairs, sharing the available shots. After a few days, each camera was returned, the film processed and the prints brought back to the child photographers for them to write captions. After analysing each picture the children made a final selection of the best shots. They were encouraged to explain why they took each picture, what it meant to them, and what they wanted to show to other people. They were asked to choose five or six of the most

© NILDA COSCO AND ROBIN MOORE

Figure 2.8 Preparing exhibit catalogue

representative pictures and write captions for the general public.

This process obliged the children to analyse the life of the neighbourhood more deeply by highlighting aspects they found positive or negative. By taking photographs, they documented their social lives (friends, siblings), the polluted environment, their favourite places, their homes, and the landmarks of Boca-Barracas (Caminito, Parque Lezama, Riachuelo, and the old transporter bridge[13]). The girls especially photographed aesthetic objects such as paintings and statues. The captions helped reveal the meaning and intent of the photograph to both photographer and viewer.

An enjoyable part of the process were the three sessions organised with the children to design the exhibition catalogue. The workshop sessions were held at a local café and in the meeting room at the Hogar where Pedro and Claudio lived.

The children invented the title of the exhibition (from which the title of this chapter is taken), slogans to promote it, designed the layout of the catalogue and compiled the list of photograph titles. The exhibition opened in the *Biblioteca Popular de La Boca* on the first day of the Winter Festival, blessed by the priest from the *San Juan Evangelista* Church, and with refreshments provided in the form of bread freshly baked by Cecilia and her mother. It was interesting to observe the children from different parts of Boca-Barracas discussing their photographs with each other for the first time. The exhibition and the Gulliver's Mapping both encouraged a stronger feeling of solidarity among the group. This had been impossible to achieve during the interviews that were mostly one-on-one.

Creating Place From Space

La Boca contained many *baldíos* (vacant lots) and vacated buildings — the residue of bad economic times when many industries left the area and local businesses went under. From the community's perspective, the vacant land and buildings reinforced a negative image of economic neglect and abandonment. For children, however, they were places to explore, mess around in or play football. As in any city, the vacant lots offered space for a limited range of activities; nevertheless, this space was more than mere square footage. As we discovered through the initial phase of standardised investigation, children attached identity and meaning to the vacant lots. They were spaces with a 'sense of place' as defined by Kevin Lynch in his book *The Image of the City.*[14]

We decided to continue working on the theme of creating place from space as part of the community action programme with the children. As a step towards exploring the development of a governance structure for children's participation, we organised a series of participatory design workshops with the children in a section of La Boca where the Solidarity Network was already working. Representatives of the Network said they were interested in the children's proposals, as they had identified the area as a priority for physical improvement.

Two fortunate coincidences enabled the design workshop initiative to be launched and rapidly move ahead. First, our search for space to work with the children in the immediate area (nearly always a problem in neighbourhood participatory work) led us to the grandfather of one of the children in the group. He was the president of *Mutual Esperanza,* a neighbourhood housing rehabilitation cooperative[15] that owned a large meeting room on the ground floor of one of their rehabilitated buildings. He was happy to let us use the space during the four-week programme. The second fortuitous circumstance was the availability of the *Móvil Verde* group to implement the programme.

Apart from our research interest in exploring processes of creating place, the purpose of the workshop series was to deepen the children's perceptions and understanding of the problems and opportunities in the neighbourhood through a hands-on approach to playful environmental exploration, learning, programming and design. Overarching themes included consideration of the neighbourhood as a child's habitat, children's rights and habitat (especially Article 12 of the Convention on the Rights of the Child), imagining a child-friendly neighbourhood and the extension of the participatory process into the realm of governance.

A critical artefact at the first session was the Gulliver's Map generated during the Winter Festival some weeks earlier. Many of the children were at the festival, which celebrated the winter vacation from school, and participated with their peers and family members in annotating the Gulliver's Map. The huge map was hung on one wall of the meeting room and immediately provided a means for the children to see that the much larger area

> *It was interesting to observe the children from different parts of Boca-Barracas discussing their photographs with each other for the first time. The exhibition and the Gulliver's Mapping both encouraged a stronger feeling of solidarity among the group.*

of Boca-Barracas contained their immediate neighbourhoods and to explore their neighbourhood by identifying the locations of their homes.

At the first session, children engaged in an exercise called 'Place as a Person'[16] where they had to work in small groups and role-play different places in the neighbourhood as if these places had human history and personality. The rich, expressive drawings and dramatic presentations of the children created an upbeat spirit for the sessions to follow.

In the second session, with the *Móvil Verde* staff acting as facilitators, small groups went out into the neighbourhood (the child's habitat) to explore it as a multisensory environment. They recorded smells (noting their location on paper), sounds (with tape recorders), sights (with cameras), tactile characteristics (pretending to be blind) and taste (visiting a couple of *Kioscos* on the way!). This research information was brought back, shared and discussed. In this way, children were helped to more consciously understand the multi-sensory reality of their environment and to practice recording (objectifying) it. The session ended with a decision about specific design projects the group wanted to work on. Two vacant lots were chosen for renovation.

With the *Móvil Verde* staff continuing to facilitate the process, the third session started with groups visiting each of the sites to record and evaluate the existing conditions. These included typical items any site designer would look at such as size and shape, solar orientation, wind exposure, microclimate, access, boundary conditions, natural features and cultural artefacts. The children also interviewed local residents about their ideas for the sites. They returned back to base and again shared the results of the field investigation, with the *Móvil Verde* staff prompting discussion by asking questions about the children's discoveries. This led each group into the challenging phase of deciding what they wanted to propose for their site and then developing the design programme to support the proposal, just as a professional designer would.

One group chose to design a neighbourhood chapel to replace one that had been destroyed by fire. The other group identified a large lot that they wanted to develop as a park. The third session ended after some initial discussions of the design programmes for each site.

The fourth session started with the completion of the programmes, which were then used as the basis of schematic designs on paper. Three-dimensional models were built from the designs, shared in the group of children, and presented to parents and some members of the Network during the final workshop session. Later, the models were displayed as part of the governance effort (discussed below) at the Buenos Aires Cultural Centre. *Móvil Verde* continued working on the Neighbourhood as a Child's Habitat programme for the rest of the year with some of the same GUIC children and others from the area as part of the Saturday programme sponsored by *San Juan Evangelista* Church. The Network also continued working in the area. Only time will tell if the children's designs for the new chapel and plaza will have an influence on renovations.

REFLECTIONS ON GOVERNANCE

In the GUIC project and in the field of policy development for children, recent attention has been focused on the issue of governance: the structure and process that are necessary for both developing and implementing policy. [17]

Figure 2.9 *Móvil Verde* staff working with neighbourhood children.

This is the realm of social action. Certainly governance is a function of local government, but to be effective in implementing children's rights, the process must include collaborative relationships with many other organisations and institutions within civil society working with children at the local level where they live. Throughout the GUIC project we devoted almost obsessive attention to trying to establish these organisational connections and to make them work in favour of children. In reality, putting these principles of governance into practice was extremely difficult. It was relatively easy and very rewarding to work with the children and to engage them in actions to improve their environment. But finding ways to have their ideas taken seriously and to influence urban planning policy in favour of children's participation were enormous challenges. GUIC provided a vehicle for wrestling with these issues by testing different types of strategies and actions at local and city government levels. To try to understand the mystifying web of political nuances and personal allegiances and conflicts that dominated the domain of governance, we kept a running record of actions and our reflections on the (mostly frustrating) consequences.

The GUIC project was initiated at the beginning of a new democratic era of Buenos Aires city government and was officially adopted by the Secretary of Urban Planning and Environment, who expressed much interest in training and replication in other neighbourhoods in the city. His department organised a public exhibition of the children's photographs, models and the Gulliver's Mapping results in the *Recoleta* Cultural Centre of Buenos Aires — *the* place for local visibility and for best exposure in the national press.

At the local level, the GUIC project was recognised by the 'Boca-Barracas Solidarity Network.' *Móvil Verde* agreed to partner with GUIC to help implement the Gulliver's Mapping project and the Neighbourhood as a Child's Habitat programme.

At face value this record looks promising. In reality, at both city government and local levels there were major problems. Among the most severe were the attempts at both ends to coopt the GUIC project. After some excellent initial cooperation in the supply of base maps and aerial photography, cooption was deftly achieved at government level with promises of further cooperation and joint programme development. The Urban Planning Department took the GUIC project on board, then created an umbrella initiative called *Buenos Aires Ciudad Nueva — Construir la Ciudad con los Chicos y los Jóvenes* (Buenos Aires New City — Constructing the City with Children and Youth), and added their name beside the names of UNESCO and Childwatch International. The city had already conducted an environmental education project with young people and appeared to be committed to adding new participatory projects to their programme. Readers may understandably assume that it was good that the Department of Urban Planning promised to continue working in other parts of the city to add to the GUIC success. Whether that happened or not, we do not know as it was very difficult to track the actions of the city. The GUIC team, a small group of independent researchers, lacked leverage in a situation where all the power was on the other side.

In theory, children's rights should be non-partisan. In practice, political conflict was the dominant brake on progress. Every action was filtered by politics. At the local level, the mesh was very fine. The political stripe of newcomers was heavily scrutinised. However, as the objectives of the Boca-Barracas Solidarity Network and GUIC overlapped, we were initially welcomed to a meeting of the whole Network. As a group of independent organisations, the Network shared the common goal of working cooperatively for the community using member resources. Being diverse and decentralised was their strength but also a weakness. Problems of coordination of action and reconciling individual political interests were the most serious challenges they faced. We were thankful to those who cooperated for the children's sake, putting political ideologies to one side and accepting with humorous tolerance the English accent of one of us (the 'language of capitalism'). After contentious discussions driven by a suspicion of outsiders from an international project, several members of the Network supported GUIC, although still with reservations.

This led each group into the challenging phase of deciding what they wanted to propose for their site and then developing the design programme to support the proposal, just as a professional designer would.

All the Network member institutions were desperately looking for funds to implement their own missions. At the same time, the Network itself was struggling to secure space in the community and to project itself as a worthwhile option to the people. In the background one could notice political aspirations expressed by some of the community leaders, although it was difficult to evaluate the real motivations behind their actions. Meanwhile, neighbourhood institutions, cooperative groups, day care centres, volunteer firemen and the Church, all participated in the Network's activities in an attempt to stay together and not lose opportunities — or perhaps to exercise a measure of control over each other's actions.

In 1998, when the Children's Hour Aid Fund of the Norwegian Broadcasting Corporation offered GUIC a grant to set up a toy 'library' in La Boca, it was difficult for us to decide which institution was best qualified to implement this international project and administer the funds transparently. At that stage of the GUIC project we had a pretty clear view of the neighbourhood groups, and we invited the YMCA to take charge of the project. Surprisingly, the Network leaders claimed their right to the grant, at the same time expressing their support of GUIC. It took several months of confusing discussions to resolve the situation so that the project could be successfully implemented. Through this experience, we discovered that without a lot of care, the local struggle for resources can spoil even very good programmes for families and child development.

In the descriptions of both the governmental and local situations, we have omitted much detail that added greatly to the level of frustration and a sense of wasting time to no ultimate advantage. One benefit that came out of facing so many difficulties was that we were forced to recognise the strength of political barriers to the process of governance at all levels. Even though the GUIC project achieved short term success, with good press and public visibility, in the longer term it could not succeed without committed political advocates at all levels; and even then, if their parties were voted out of power, the chain of governance would still be broken.

> *Finding ways to have their ideas taken seriously and to influence urban planning policy in favour of children's participation were enormous challenges. GUIC provided a vehicle for wrestling with these issues by testing different types of strategies and actions at local and city government levels.*

An important assumption in the practice of effective governance is that city government and community-based organisations are able to collaborate to achieve common objectives. During the period of the GUIC fieldwork, the Solidarity Network was a substantial innovation in governance. Potential for action at the local level was considerable. The Buenos Aires Department of Urban Planning was aggressively reinventing itself, embracing the new technology, tackling the capital city's long neglected major environmental planning issues, and launching an environmental education programme in the city's schools. The problem was that the city government staff and the Solidarity Network seemed to have little interest in working with each other. Mostly this was because the party in power at City Hall was different from most of the political ideologies represented in the Network. This ideological contrast was an insurmountable barrier to collaboration, even though both sides supported the GUIC mission and were openly committed to children. The situation most likely changed as a result of the political alliance that moderate and leftist parties formed in their successful bid to wrest power from the *Peronistas* in the 1999 presidential election.[18] With the nation and city controlled by the same alliance, one may hope for a more fruitful dialogue between City Hall and the local community — and more substantial interventions supporting children's rights.

Another — positive — reality is that leaders move on, taking experiences with them to new positions of potential influence. For example, the former director of urban planning is now dean of a university school of architecture. The GUIC ally in the labour movement was elected to the city government. Leaders of the Solidarity Network have surely risen up the political ranks. Each may have new opportunities for promoting GUIC-related issues.

GUIC worked directly with children to help them speak for themselves and propose changes to their environment. In reality, children cannot vote so they will always be dependent on wise adults to facilitate processes of democratic participation, to find resources, to open doors to influence. Even though the Convention on the Rights of the Child is embedded in the Argentine national constitution and the new constitution of the City of Buenos Aires contains strong paragraphs about the rights of children, an adult lobby and leadership will always be required to create action.

Where can such trustworthy individuals be found? In which type of stable, influential, non-political institution? We discovered that such individuals and institutions did exist in Boca-Barracas, for example in the Catholic Church and the Christian Association for Young People

BOX 2.1

Taking Action

- Participate in existing festivals and community celebrations.

- Create opportunities for children to present their points of view in creative ways (drawings, photographs, drama, role-play, street theatre).

- Network with pro-child organisations (churches, youth organisations, Girl and Boy Scout groups, YMCA/YWCA, neighbourhood associations, parent and teacher associations, women's organisations, worker's unions).

- Foster media attention by creating newsworthy events with and about children.

- Provide politicians with information about children and children's participation that can be used in their political campaigns.

- Encourage community groups to prepare a set of questions about children's needs for local politicians and gatherings of community leaders.

- Facilitate direct contact between children and local politicians and leaders.

- Create engaging, interactive public events that promote intergenerational interactions and communication (Gulliver's Map, *murgas*).

- Engage children in field-based design workshops, including presentations of proposals to municipal authorities.

- Collaborate with radio/TV children's stations and individual programme producers.

- Collaborate with university departments of journalism to facilitate children expressing themselves through newsletters and journals.

(the YMCA in the English-speaking world). Results of the GUIC experience in Buenos Aires point to the critical importance of local institutions (school, church, community centres) in helping children survive in an unfriendly environment of overcrowded housing, fast moving traffic, flooding from the heavily polluted Riachuelo River and scarce public open space.

These types of institutions are governed by strong long-term missions that are deeply embedded credos in organisational psyches. Constancy of mission and non-political, stable leadership make them trustworthy. They work to alleviate daily problems and to help people to organise themselves to change negative structural constraints on their lives. They are therefore much appreciated and respected by the community. (The main church in La Boca was involved in defending squatters' rights, for example.) Furthermore, they organise themselves so that residents see that every activity and event reflects the mission of the institution (not necessarily the case in overly politicised organisations which can lose sight of their main purpose). Yet, even in such organisations, it is

always good to have young people remind us of primary goals. A YMCA leader told us about a boy's first visit to their recreation programme. 'Everything is very nice here,' he said, 'but when do we eat?'

Another valuable institutional resource we found was the social work team based at the municipal neighbourhood centre. This cadre of trained professionals committed their time to solving the innumerable problems families face. As impartial professionals who knew all the available community resources in the city, they were able to give critical support to families and children. For many women in the community, the social workers were their best ally. They helped women to get jobs, to solve problems with their alcoholic husbands, to take care of disabled children or to continue their education by attending evening courses. Social workers can be a remarkable community resource. The GUIC fieldwork would have been impossible without their help.

Clearly, local government has an important role. However, to be more effective, it needs to collaborate with recognised neighbourhood-based non-governmental organisations and community-based organisations. Such an association could be the starting point for solving the most urgent family needs. Argentine labour leader and GUIC supporter, Victor Santa María, addressed the issue as follows:

'The high level of mistrust means that it is almost impossible for governments to intensify their communication with neighbours as they must do in order to take effective local action. To fill this void, many NGOs have developed missions that target specific issues and problems. These new, non-government social action entities have the capacity to communicate with neighbourhood associations and have the ability to unite people by implementing their objectives through actions. The government could become far more effective if they were willing to partner with NGOs to take care of the big priorities — employment and nutrition — as well as other important issues related to children, like spaces for play and recreation.'[19]

CHILDHOOD, CULTURE AND ENVIRONMENT

Through the GUIC intervention in the lives of 32 carefully selected consultant children in a densely developed urban district in Buenos Aires, we discovered that despite the low material resources of their domestic environment, these children lived in a culturally rich environment which added much value to their lives and sense of identity. How did such an economically stressed area manage to provide such rich cultural resources?

As co-authors with a strong professional grounding in the field of children's urban play, in addressing this question we thought about the probable lives of these children in the neighbourhood in their earlier years. From observations of the GUIC children and children in general in Boca-Barracas, we discovered that by age 4 or 5 many children were out and about in the neighbourhood in the

Figure 2.10 Group of children playing table soccer (for a small fee) on the pavement opposite the Boca Juniors stadium.

care of older siblings. From an early age they are exposed to the extended neighbourhood environment through play and through the interpretations of their older sisters, brothers and cousins.

Because the children live in such small cramped houses, neighbourhood social spaces (pavements, street corners, plazas, vacant lots, *kioscos*) become an extension of daily domestic life just beyond the range of parent intervention. These children grow up with a much higher degree of spatial freedom than more affluent children living in more spacious highrise apartment buildings. Boca-Barracas housing is dense but close to the ground. One

> *What are the qualities of the world of children that make it a potential space where they can play creatively and build culture?*

can readily conclude, as research has shown in cities in the Northern Hemisphere, that this housing form (often with business on the ground floor and living accommodations above) results in more social contacts per block than other forms of urban neighbourhood.[20]

From an early age, children in Boca-Barracas spend much time outdoors interacting with their peers, neighbourhood adults and the physical surroundings that embody the history, culture and ethos of the place called Boca-Barracas. We saw the neighbourhood as a vessel that supported the subtle process of childhood culture, driven by children's intrinsic motivation to play. The theories developed by Donald W. Winnicott with respect to play in the lives of babies and young children help us understand the significance of this process of culture building. According to Winnicott, the true significance of play is that it is a *transitional phenomenon* linking the child's internal life to her or his physical surroundings and *culture*. He considered play as a transitional phenomenon because 'it is not inside; nor is it outside' of the individual. Winnicott postulated play as a 'potential space' between the baby and the mother.[21] He beautifully articulated this transitional world that exists as a kind of magic hologram embracing child, mother, others and the physi-

cal world. The latter is crucial in providing a grounding for the growth of an authentic culture. For Winnicott:

'The place where cultural experience is located is in the potential space between the individual and the environment …The same can be said of playing. Cultural experience begins with creative living first manifested in play…For every individual the use of this space is determined by life experiences that take place at the early stages of the individual's existence.'[22]

The richer and more diverse the world is socially and physically, the richer this potential space will be, and the greater the possibilities for developing a rich culture rooted in place. Other writers, such as Edith Cobb and Joseph Chilton Pearce, drawing on other sources of information, have postulated similar processes of development.[23]

How does this process of developing identity through play move beyond infancy? In a socially rich environment, additional adults extend the parenting role beyond the mother. As children develop spatial competence, they move out into the world around them, exploring and discovering its treasures and building culture. Every place, every component of a place, has a history, a personality, a substance — in short, a meaning. GUIC children were very eloquent in this respect. Defining La Boca, Pedro said: 'It has two sides: one good, one bad. Poverty, sadness, but it is nice to visit Caminito, Costanera, Lezama Park, and the Don Bosco Home soccer field.' He pointed to the yin-yang medal hanging around his neck that seemed to epitomise his feelings and concluded: 'Everything is here; everything good, everything bad; the best and the worst.'

What are the qualities of the world of children that make it a potential space where they can play creatively and build culture? This has become a key question as we try to interpret the GUIC findings. Through play, children explore and discover places, transforming them as potential spaces to create culture. At the deepest personal and social levels, each place resonates with the local culture. For a place to be lived in as a potential space, various conditions that were present in Boca-Barracas seem paramount. Places should be stable and predictable, discovered at an early age through play, and contain features that provide a strong identity that is the essence of the place. At the same time, places should be flexible enough to accommodate creative exploration. They should be highly differentiated into component parts that stimulate many different creative relationships for all types of children. They should support children's needs, especially in terms of scale and diversity. Places should be sufficiently safe physically, socially and psychologically. These conditions facilitate the emergence of popular culture and collective expression as a natural out-

Figure 2.11 Three boys enjoying being out and about in their 'holding environment'.

come of playful exploration that for Johan Huizinga is transformative: *'In the twin union of play and culture, play is primary. The relationship between play and culture is not static; time helps the elements [of play] to be absorbed in the 'sacred sphere,'* and the remaining elements are transformed into *'knowledge: folklore, poetry, philosophy, or in the various forms of judicial and social life.'*[24]

From the GUIC children we learned that a culturally rich neighbourhood supports healthy development and helps children gain positive identification and higher self-esteem. Conversely, creative play and free individual expression enriches the culture. This was easy to see in the many different artistic expressions in Boca-Barracas: street theatre, *murgas,* painting exhibitions and the tradi-

tional *picados.*[25] The challenge is to discover how community workers, child caretakers and other significant adults can become active agents to promote this kind of creative play, and therefore create the basis of culture.

Some insights about this issue were provided by the mothers of the girls and boys participating in the GUIC project. When asked how they would like their children to spend their time in the neighbourhood, most mothers responded in terms of their children's need for diverse opportunities for a creative life:

'Doing creative things'…'Playing, taking advantage of her childhood'…'More possibilities and spaces for leisure, like workshops, and courses. I am working in the neighbourhood to help develop these possibilities'…'I would like her to enjoy her age and not grow up too fast.'

These wise words from mothers expressed their intuitive understanding of child development. Notice too, the equal focus on play and enjoyment of life. Although living in very poor conditions, almost 30 percent of the GUIC children said they would like to live in the same place in ten years, and more that 50 percent said they felt that some places in the neighbourhood felt like they were their own. These expressions of GUIC children helped us to understand that children living in poor conditions can still have a sense of fulfilment if they live in a supportive environment where creativity is the precursor of culture.

Winnicott also questioned the conventional wisdom of putting a negative mark on 'poverty' and 'slums' — which so often stereotypes the residents negatively. He suggested that 'for a small…child a slum family may be more secure and 'good' as a *facilitating environment* than a family in a lovely house where there is an absence of the common persecutions' [by persecutions, Winnicott means 'pursuits,' or doing things together as a family].[26]

He defined a 'holding environment' as a necessary condition for healthy psychosocial development and offered what can be called an ecological conception extending from mother's arms to locality and beyond. In Winnicott's words, 'One can discern a series — the mother's body, the mother's arms, the parental relationship, the home, the family including cousins and near relations, the school, the locality with its police stations, the county with its laws.'[27] Using the experience in Boca-Barracas, we have attempted to understand children's healthy development in relation to the facilitating or 'holding' environment of the family and community, and especially the influence of physical factors on its quality.

> *From the GUIC children we learned that a culturally rich neighbourhood supports healthy development and helps children gain positive identification and higher self-esteem. Conversely, creative play and free individual expression enrich the culture.*

Through creative relationships, children develop a sense of belonging and self-esteem. They acquire a resilient shield of survival which, on the one hand, comes from their environment and, on the other, is a protection against it. The Boca-Barracas environment provided rich experiential material for the children to work with, to elaborate, to differentiate themselves as individuals from both the good and the bad aspects of their surroundings …and to understand and appreciate the difference.[28]

The 'holding environment' of the neighbourhood can be a nurturing space for expanding creativity and establishing a sense of belonging. It contains the products of collective imagination — in other words, culture. In the case of Boca-Barracas at its best, the 'holding environment' resembled the mothering role in offering a nurturing environment for child development. A GUIC mother, who had had a traumatic childhood with a violent father, expressed this combination of physical and social dimensions when comparing her childhood with her daughter's in Boca-Barracas. 'The physical environment is not better but the social and family environments are,' she said, thus acknowledging the many sides of the holding environment. Mothers intuitively understand this complexity. Answering a question about what her child would need to be successful as an adult, a mother said, 'Material and spiritual support.' She later explained that by 'spiritual' she meant emotional support, tolerant understanding

and sense of companionship, rather than something provided by organised religion.

Our conclusions point to the critical importance of the holding environment of extended family and child friendly institutions (school, church, community centres) in helping children from low-income families to experience the transitional space of play and culture, and therefore to survive the lack of material resources in their lives.

Constant exposure to stable cultural expression gives children a sense of belonging and self-identity. Culture gives structure to children's identities that are constantly reflected in their relationship with their surroundings. As a child, you feel that you belong to that place and that place belongs to you. Familiar surroundings leave no doubt that you are in your place, the place that others share with you in a collective culture. In such a place, children become socially fluid and do not have to waste energy decoding strange territory. They simply enjoy living there with both its good and bad sides. In Winnicottian terms, we might consider Boca-Barracas a 'good enough' neighbourhood and a successful 'holding environment' for child development.

Our professional responsibility, then, is to find ways to conserve and create cultural richness by providing opportunities for a creative life through which families and their children can reach fulfilment as human beings. The results of the Growing Up in Cities project in Buenos Aires have taught us that the creation of revitalised 'holding environments,' where culture can develop through play, is a process that must come about through long-term systematic, participatory community development involving both children and adults. Local government members, community workers, caretakers, educators and artists will need to find ways of responding creatively to the social demands of the present day. This seems to be the path of wisdom towards a more equal, supportive and culturally rich society that supports personal growth.

ENDNOTES

1 McKendrick (1997).

2 Moore (1990).

3 Study conducted by the *Instituto Pro Buenos Aires,* coordinated by environmental expert, Daniel Luzzi. Results published in *Clarín,* 28 April 1997.

4 UNDP (1999); Korten (1995).

5 Gore and Cosco (1988, p. 27).

6 The chapters by Malone and Hasluck, Percy-Smith and Salvadori in this volume document the trend towards restriction of children's spatial freedom, as does Hillman and Adams (1992). See also Moore (1997) for a recent review of the issue.

7 Don Bosco was an Italian priest who came to Argentina in the 1940s to establish a network of social institutions, including homes *(hogares)* for homeless children.

8 The children had different backgrounds. Some had no family. Others could not live at home, as was the case with Pedro and Claudio.

9 See Moore (1990).

10 *Caminito* (little walk) was a well-known place in Buenos Aires. In the 1950s a group of artists and tango composers persuaded the city to remove a disused rail line and redevelop the space as a strolling street curving diagonally across a single block. Overlooked by brightly painted houses, Caminito is a place where artists exhibit their work and tango musicians entertain passers-by. It was a favourite place for local children to hang out and enjoy watching visitors from all over the world.

11 Gulliver's Mapping is a hands-on technique developed by Japanese architect Junzo Okada and colleagues to engage resident participation in community development. Okada first brought the technique to Buenos Aires in 1994, giving an opportunity to try it out. See Driskell (2001) for full details.

12 *Murga* is a rhythmic form of street dancing for all ages, accompanied by drumming and athletic kicking-style dancing. *Murga* groups perform around carnival time with 60 to 400 dancers from individual neighbourhoods. They each have their own costume designs and colour schemes, invent their own emblems, have funny names and write their own ironic protest songs. This vital form of popular culture is very much alive in Buenos Aires.

13 The tall, steel framework structure, now abandoned, had provided the means of transporting motor vehicles across the river before the high level road bridge was built.

14 Lynch (1960).

15 *Mutuals* are a specific type of legal entity common in Argentina. *Mutual Esperanza* was a cooperative organisation dedicated to raising funds for the rehabilitation of residential buildings in La Boca. Housed on the ground floor of such a building, it provided programme space for children, families and elders.

16 'Place as a Person' was an interactive workshop designed to help participants understand the characteristics of the place where they lived through creative personification.

17 For a recent discussion of governance in the context of children's rights and urban development, see Bartlett et al (1999).

18 The moderate *Radicales,* who were already in power in the Federal Capital of Buenos Aires, under Mayor Fernando de La Rua, created an alliance with the more left-leaning *Frepaso* party. The resulting *Frente Solidario* (Solidarity Front) was created to take on the *Peronistas,* solidly ensconced under the ten-year rein of Carlos Menem. In September 1999, de La Rua was elected president of the Republic.

19 Interview conducted 24 August 1999.

20 Excellent sources for research on housing form and social contact are Cooper Marcus and Sarkissian (1986) and Van Vliet (1983).

21 Winnicott (1971, p. 100).

22 Ibid. (p100).

23 See, for example, Cobb (1977, p. 100) and Pierce (1977).

24 Huizinga (1955, p. 46).

25 A *picado* is a soccer game played by whichever players show up, usually in a vacant lot.

26 Winnicott (1971, p. 142).

27 Winnicott (1975, p. 310).

28 Vickers (1972).

REFERENCES

Bartlett, S, Hart, R, Satterthwaite, D, de la Barra, X, and Missair, A (1999) *Cities for Children: Children's Rights, Poverty and Urban Management,* Earthscan, London.

Cobb, E (1974), *The Ecology of Imagination in Childhood,* Columbia University Press, New York.

Cooper Marcus, C and Sarkissian, W (1986) *Housing as if People Mattered,* University of California Press, Berkeley, California.

Driskell, D (2001) *Creating Better Cities with Children and Youth,* UNESCO Publishing/Earthscan, Paris/London.

Gore, E and Cosco, N (1988) *Children and Play in Large Cities,* Clarín, Buenos Aires.

Hillman, M and Adams, J (1992) 'Children's freedom and safety', *Children's Environments,* vol 9(2), pp. 10-12.

Huizinga, J (1955) *Homo Ludens: A Study of the Play Element in Culture,* Beacon Books, Boston.

Korten, D (1995) *When Corporations Rule the World,* Kumarian Press, West Hartford.

Lynch, K (1960) *The Image of the City,* MIT Press, Cambridge, MA.

McKendrick, J (1997) *'Paradoxical poverty: Poor communities and children's poverty',* Paper presented at the Urban Childhood Conference, Trondheim, Norway, 9-12 June, 1997.

Moore, R (1997) *'The need for nature: A childhood right',* Social Justice, vol 24(3), pp. 203-220.

Moore, R (1990) *Childhood's Domain: Play and Place in Child Development,* MIG Communications, Berkeley, CA (first published, 1986, Croom Helm, London).

Pearce, JC (1977) *Magical Child,* E.P. Dutton, New York.

UNDP (1999) *Human Development Report,* Oxford University Press, Oxford.

Van Vliet, W (1983) 'Families in apartment buildings', *Environment and Behavior,* vol 15, pp. 211-234.

Vickers, G (1972) *Freedom in a Rocking Boat: Changing Values in an Unstable Society.* Penguin Books, Harmondsworth, Middlesex.

Winnicott, D (1975) 'The antisocial tendency', in *Through Pediatrics to Psycho-Analysis,* Basic Books, New York.

Winnicott, D (1971) *Playing and Reality,* London, Routledge.

CHAPTER THREE

Contested Worlds

Constraints and Opportunities in City and Suburban Environments in an English Midlands City

Barry Percy-Smith

Young people's views of Semilong, a working-class district of Northampton (United Kingdom), are compared with their peers' views of life in nearby Hunsbury, a recently developed suburb on the edge of the city. Despite the differences between these two environments, the experiences that each group relates raise many similar questions about what it means to be a young person in contemporary England, society's attitudes toward the young, and the quality of the environments in which children grow up. Sources of conflict between young and old over the use of community space are explored, and ways to reduce conflicts by bringing young people into local decision-making processes are suggested.

ENCOUNTERING THE HIDDEN WORLDS OF YOUNG PEOPLE

In the early stages of the Growing Up in Cities research in Northampton (United Kingdom), I met a group of young boys along Semilong Road, the main street running through the inner city neighbourhood. Some of them were disappearing up a long driveway to what appeared like a piece of wasteland. I asked one of them where they were going and he told me about a den they had up there and asked if I would like to go and see it. The den was in an abandoned lock-up garage with piles of garbage lying around (Figure 3.1). Given this sight I was nervous about what I might encounter inside. As I struggled to get in through a gap where the metal door had been pulled away, I felt as if I were entering into these young people's private world. This was indisputably their place. What I saw was a place rich in meaning and purpose created within the margins of the adult world, hidden from the adult gaze, and a source of pride for the young people. They busied themselves tidying up and invited me to sit down on one of the pieces of furniture they had acquired. We talked about why the lock-up was important to them. For some it was a quiet refuge to come and be alone, for others it was a discreet place to sit and have a cigarette when it rains, but for all it provided a place to get away and hang out far from adults.

After some time we emerged to find an adult couple walking down the drive to their car. They immediately started reproaching the young people about what they were doing hanging around there, about how dangerous it was, about why they didn't have anything better to do. Their assumption was clearly that the boys were up to no good and that this was not a place for children. Yet I had just experienced the importance of this place for these young people!

© BARRY PERCY-SMITH

Figure 3.1 The lock-up garage which the main street boys had colonised as a den

This incident was to prove typical of the stories and experiences encountered in the course of the research for this chapter. It raises a number of questions and paradoxes about what it is to be a young person in Britain in the late 1990s, about society's attitude towards young people and the quality of neighbourhood environments for children to grow up in. For example, what characteristics of a neighbourhood are important for young people and in what way? How do young people respond to, and negotiate, the social and environmental contexts in which they find themselves? What can be learned from the relationships young people have with their environments which might inform how urban neighbourhoods are planned and managed? What assumptions about childhood and children's social and environmental needs underlie the rationale for local decision making? What are the implications of not involving young people in the development of their neighbourhoods and communities? These are the questions explored in this chapter.

The Changing Context of British Childhoods

This study is set within the context of social and economic changes which have altered the urban landscapes of British towns and cities. Many of these changes have been brought about through piecemeal efforts to regenerate inner urban areas (for example through the Central

Government's Single Regeneration Budget) and, at the same time, a continued emphasis on private investment in suburban residential developments. This process of suburbanisation is also characterised by the relocation of retail and leisure functions to out-of-town areas. Macro social and economic changes are also modifying the socio-cultural context of childhood: for example there are increasing pressures of consumerism on the developing identities and lifestyles of young people, as manifested by the electronic media explosion and the commercialisation of children's play places.[1]

The widening gap in social inequalities in Britain throughout the 1980s and 1990s has given rise to concern about the increasing number of young people growing up in poverty.[2] Given that social identities are increasingly being constructed around modes of consumption, these young people are being excluded from the rites of citizenship and left with feelings of disaffection and alienation. As traditional social affiliations are being fragmented and gradually replaced by an ethos of individualisation,[3] childhood is becoming increasingly differentiated around cultures and lifestyles which may cut across conventional social divides of class and gender.[4] At the same time there is a growing moral panic about young people in public places, which has resulted in new attempts to control and regulate young people, for example through the imposition of curfews.[5] There is a fallacy here whereby, despite the increasing emphasis on individualisation, State intervention into young people's lives is becoming more invidious. These are some of the contemporary social and economic contours which shape the landscape of childhood in England at the beginning of the twenty-first century.

A Comparative Study of Childhood

This chapter is based on a comparative study of young people's experiences growing up in inner and outer neighbourhoods of Northampton, a city in the English Midlands. Such a comparison is distinctive in that it provides insights into the similarities and differences in young people's experiences growing up in low-income and middle-income neighbourhoods.[6] The inner city area of Semilong is characterised by a dense network of gridiron streets lined with Victorian and Edwardian terraced properties that have small backyards and access directly onto the streets. These are fringed with local authority apartment blocks constructed in the 1970s. The neighbourhood contains few open green spaces and is bounded by three main roads.

Semilong falls within the eighth most deprived ward (district) in Northampton (out of a total of 21 wards),[7] with a significant proportion of the population who are in some way socially disadvantaged. The area is host to high rates of alcoholism, drug abuse, prostitution and a significant transient population (see Table 3.1 for community profile).

Semilong is typical of poor inner city neighbourhoods in Britain in which many young people grow up with limited life chances in a context of social and material disadvantage.

The suburban location of Hunsbury, by contrast, consists of a more extensive sprawl of modern housing estates providing a mix of largely private family homes with gardens, but also starter homes and flats for older citizens. Although the houses are close together, there are numerous open green spaces between the estates. In contrast to Semilong, Hunsbury falls within the third least deprived ward in Northampton[8] (see Table 3.2 for community profile).

Hunsbury is typical of the growth in suburban residential developments that has occurred in Britain since the 1970s.

Investigating the Lives of Urban Young People

This chapter will focus on the main issues and themes which emerged in the course of doctoral research in geography undertaken by the author between 1996 and 1998 concerning the lifeworlds of young people growing up in these two neighbourhoods of Northampton.[9] A range of participatory and ethnographic methods were used to gain insights into young people's lived realities and explore possibilities for change. Initial semistructured interviews were conducted with a total of 181 young people aged 10 through 15 who were identified using a snowball sampling method (see Table 3.3 for participants profile). Subsequent case study work was then

---

TABLE 3.1

Community Profile of Semilong

Land Area	40 hectares (99 acres)
Number of households	1,613
Privately rented households	35%
Total population	3,451
Total aged 10–15 years	131
Unemployment	12%
Employment (professional and managerial)	27%
Children receiving free school meals *	20%
Households with no central heating	40%
Households without a car	48%

Source: OPCS (1992)

* Free school meals are available for children whose families are in receipt of income support and therefore are an indicator of poverty. (Data from school secretary).

TABLE 3.2

Community Profile of Hunsbury

Land Area	248 hectares (614 acres)
Number of households	2,837
Privately rented households	9%
Total population	8,664
Total aged 10–15 years	504
Unemployment	4%
Employment (professional and managerial)	47%
Households with no central heating	3%
Households without a car *	5%

Source: OPCS (1992)

* Approximately 50% of households have more than one car.

TABLE 3.3		
Participants Profile (N=181)		
Semilong: Male, 44 Female, 36		
Hunsbury: Male, 58 Female, 43		
AGE	# OF PARTICIPANTS IN SEMILONG	# OF PARTICIPANTS IN HUNSBURY
10	21	11
11	10	18
12	12	16
13	9	18
14	7	20
15	21	18

undertaken with 12 boys and 12 girls in both locations using a mix of techniques, including in-depth interviews, children's drawings, child-led neighbourhood tours, photographs taken by the children, and focus groups. This data was then supplemented with behaviour observation surveys in key locations. Interviews were also conducted with parents and local officials, including youth workers, planners and parks managers.

This chapter uses young people's voices to illuminate some of the multiple realities, tensions, paradoxes and possibilities that they experience while using neighbourhood space. It recognises the multiple ways in which childhood is experienced and at the same time acknowledges the commonalities that young people may share as a generational group. It focuses on young people in the inner city, but draws comparisons with the suburban site to provide insights into similarities and differences in young people's views and experience growing up in each location. Emphasis is placed on understanding how children mediate the disjunctions between their own desires and intentions and the social and environmental contexts that influence and constrain them. In this way, children's experiences are understood as a composite outcome of the way they respond to social and environmental opportunities.[14]

YOUNG PEOPLE'S VIEWS OF THEIR NEIGHBOURHOODS

Walking through each neighbourhood, it would be easy to make judgements about the different areas as places for young people to grow up in. Semilong lacks the open space and environmental quality that characterise Hunsbury and as such appears less attractive. These differences are borne out by the fact that only 39 percent of young people in Semilong said they liked living there compared to 78 percent in suburban Hunsbury. Young people in Semilong typically talked of their area in terms of poor environmental quality and a lack of opportunity.

'It's a bit of a rough area...people going round picking on other kids and smoking and all that...and there's always weirdoes about.' (13 year old boy)

'In some places it's scary, like the park...at night it turns into a horrible place because of all the...drunken people ...there's been people bashed in the park and...killed so, it's a bit of a weird area...and there's nothing really around here, just the park. That's all there is, so it's quite boring.' (12 year old girl)

'There should be more for us to do...and there's too much pollution and there's loads of bottles that are broken...it's just not a healthy environment to grow up in.' (13 year old boy)

'It's not a very good area really, it's only good because of the people we know...the best thing about the area is it's close to town and all your mates are here...that's all.' (15 year old boy)

(Multiple perspectives from inner city young people)

In contrast, suburban boys and girls commonly spoke positively about their area, highlighting its aesthetic quality and the availability of open space.

'I would say it's very pretty...it's quiet...and it's not like a really rough area or anything.' (14 year old girl)

'It's quite a pleasant place...and grass areas to muck about on and stuff.' (12 year old boy)

'It's safe because it's like a cul-de-sac.' (10 year old girl)

'I'd like to stay living round here...yeah...it would be nice ... It's a nice area.' (11 year old boy)

(Voices from suburban young people)

However, within these general trends differences emerge: for example, in terms of gender, with a higher proportion of girls than boys who liked living in Hunsbury (81 percent compared to 74 percent boys), and with boys more likely to be enthusiastic about the inner city neighbourhood (48 percent compared to 28 percent girls). Despite these locational differences, a comparison of what young people think is good about their area reveals many similarities (Table 3.4).

Young people tend to evaluate their area predominantly in terms of environmental opportunities and having friends around. In both locations young people most readily identified parks as the best thing about their areas. Local amenities (such as shops) and youth clubs were also commonly noted as being positive aspects of their areas. However, despite these common expressions of what young people most value, those in Hunsbury appear more advantaged by virtue of having one of the town's sports centres within their locale.

Alongside 'good things about their area' young

people voiced concerns about environmental hazards and the poor quality of local opportunities (Table 3.5).

Common concerns — in particular heavy traffic — contrast with significant locational differences. Whereas the suburban young people are preoccupied with dealing with boredom and a perceived lack of facilities, young people in Semilong expressed greatest concern about environmental hazards and pollution.

The Blight of Urban Hazards

Poor environmental quality affects young people's sense of well-being as well as their use of neighbourhood space. Young people in the inner city commonly talked of their area as being 'dirty' or 'polluted' by urban detritus such as litter, discarded refuse and dog excrement, of the dangers posed by traffic, used syringes and broken glass, and of social dangers such as bullies, drunks, druggies and weirdoes.

'You can't do a lot down the parks because...it's dirty and dangerous...and you...find tramps and syringes and things down there so...you have to really restrict yourself down the park to where you go...so I play in the street...football or kerby...we put a coat down for a goal, but cars keep

TABLE 3.4			
What young people think are the 'good things about their local area' (% SITE SAMPLE)			
INNER CITY	PERCENTAGE	SUBURB	PERCENTAGE
Parks/open green space	60	Parks/open green space	51
Having friends/young people around	11	Sports facilities	45
Local amenities	10	Local amenities	19
Youth club	10	Lots to do	19
Friendly people	10	Youth club	14
Nothing	9	Having friends/young people around	13
Safe	6	Safe	10
		Quiet	7
		Friendly people	7
		Nice area	6

TABLE 3.5

What young people think are the 'bad things about their local area' (% SITE SAMPLE)

INNER CITY (N = 80)	PERCENTAGE	SUBURB (N = 101)	PERCENTAGE
Traffic/too many cars	20	Lack of facilities for young people	30
Rubbish/pollution/dirty streets	20	Boring/too quiet/not much to do	22
Social dangers	18	Traffic/too many cars	15
Lack of facilities for young people	16	Vandalism/crime/fear of attack	13
Bullies/gangs/other young people	16	Bullies/gangs/other young people	9
Poor quality playgrounds	10	Poor quality playgrounds	6
Crime/fear of attack	10	Adults complaining	4
Boring/too quiet/not much to do	1	No friends about	4
		Rubbish/pollution/dirty streets	3

coming round…We can go to the play area…but that's all covered in glass.'
(Views from three inner city boys aged 10–12)

Of the photos inner city young people took of 'what was important to them in their local area', 43 percent were of litter, rubbish or pollution in places such as parks, the river, alleys and play areas which they use most in their daily round to play, hide, take short cuts or explore. Apart from a shared concern about traffic problems, suburban young people rarely mentioned environmental hazards and social dangers. Instead, these young people talked of their suburb as a 'nice' place to live.

For young people in the inner city, the quality of their neighbourhood environment is particularly pertinent given the lack of domestic space for children to play in and the consequent reliance on street space. The archetypal inner city environment of terraced housing, which offered safe streets for past generations of children to play in, poses significant problems for young people in the 1990s.

The war between kids and cars

Although traffic was also the most frequently mentioned environmental problem in suburban Hunsbury, the more compact and congested nature of the inner city locality, the reliance on street space, and the location of the local green spaces outside of the three main roads that bound the neighbourhood, make Semilong a more hazardous environment for young people.

'The main road at the top…is…very, very, busy in the morning and in the evening. And the road down the bottom is quite dangerous…needs another crossing really…my brother nearly got run over on it….' (15 year old inner city girl)

During the research, one of the 13 year old boys, Carl, who had become an enthusiastic research partner in this project, was killed crossing one of these roads. High levels of car use within the area place restrictions on young people's safe use of neighbourhood space and heighten the potential for conflict with car owners. These insights highlight the impact of the growing problem of car ownership in British cities, but also the lack of commitment to addressing this planning dilemma. On a number of occasions young people suggested that cars should be left at the top of the street to create safer places to play.

'They could…make the cars park at the top of the street …then we would have more space…we could play in the street and it would be better then.' (12 year old inner city boy)

While this may be a reasonable solution from the child's perspective, the feasibility of such a scheme is open to question. However, it highlights the need for young people to participate in collaborative community planning processes which explore ways of addressing competing demands on neighbourhood space.

The threat of social dangers

After traffic and issues concerned with poor environmental quality, young people in Semilong most frequently talked of social dangers within their neighbourhood. Many young people, in particular girls, recounted stories of the way social dangers limit their use of the neighbourhood, for example, by being 'flashed at', of being propositioned by kerb crawlers, or of being fearful of walking through parts of the neighbourhood where adults hang around drinking.

'It's just like drug use and the drunks walking round and while you're walking around…it's just weird people around and you want to stay in for safety but you wanna go out and play and be adventurous too.' (11 year old inner city girl)

Whereas girls are clearly constrained by these social dangers, boys were less threatened or restricted by them. They can turn them into opportunities to have fun, as Carl (aged 13) related:

'We sometimes go and take the mick out of [make fun of] the prossies [prostitutes] on the corner. That's really funny…and then sometimes these blokes that keep an eye on them…sometimes leg [run] after you…it's fun.'

There is an irony here in that, despite moral panic and media coverage about young people hanging around in public places, young people are more likely to be at risk from adults than adults are from young people.[11] There is also a paradox: in spite of the higher levels of real social dangers in inner city Semilong compared to suburban Hunsbury, young people in Semilong expressed lower levels of fears of such dangers than suburban young people. In this respect, locational differences were far more significant than gender variations (Table 3.6).

This data suggests that these types of environmental fears may be magnified in situations where the reality of

their occurring is minimal. In contrast, in the inner city, by being constantly aware of dangers and hazards, young people's perceptions are based on real experiences rather than imaginary fears, and they can learn to cope with the problems. The implications of these hazards are reflected in the fact that after parental controls, young people stated they were most restricted in where they went by the presence of strangers and fear for their own safety.

TABLE 3.6		
Specified social dangers perceived by boys and girls (% GENDER/SITE SAMPLE)		
	FEAR OF ATTACK	FEAR OF STRANGERS
Inner city boys	16	16
Inner city girls	25	25
Suburban boys	71	57
Suburban girls	93	72

Despite large locational differences in young people's fear of social dangers, 48 percent of young people in Semilong (compared to 58 percent in Hunsbury) mentioned at least one place they were afraid of visiting in their local area. Two out of three of the places mentioned were open green spaces or play areas. The most common reason for being afraid of these places was fear of being attacked or mugged. Twenty-five percent of the remaining cases mentioned the main road through the neighbourhood, because of the 'weird people who sit outside the houses along there' and bullying by older teenagers.

These initial insights provide a sense of how young people growing up in inner and outer areas of Northampton view the quality of their neighbourhoods. Young people's sense of place, however, is also intertwined with feelings of belonging and acceptance, as well as opportunities to engage in social and recreational activities.

Boredom and Engagement: Young People and Environmental Opportunities

For many young people, views about their local area are informed to a large extent by their experiences of social and environmental opportunities in their neighbour-hoods. For example, being with friends, having fun, mess-ing about, playing sports, doing something different, hanging around chatting and 'doing stuff', are all impor-tant priorities for young people when they have free time.

'Just want to have a good time...just have a laugh...do things you haven't done before.' (14 year old boy)

'Have fun, forget about school, relax and have a good time with friends...just letting my hair down, not being worried about what I've got to do. Especially after school when you've been told what to do all day. You just wanna go somewhere where theres no rules or nothing...just doss about.' (14 year old girl)

Catering for young people's local environmental needs is therefore not simply a matter of providing one or two to-ken opportunities (such as a playground or youth club), but providing an environment in which young people are free to engage in a range of activities and place uses ac-cording to their own values, needs and creative potential. In this way, neighbourhoods act as a potential social and environmental resource for young people, providing opportunities for recreation, relaxation, stimulation, new experiences, social encounters and place identity.

At first sight suburban Hunsbury, with abundant green space and a leisure centre located within its bound-aries, seems to provide many more advantages for young people in relation to inner city Semilong.

'I just sort of like growing up here...you get to play in the street...there's quite a lot of things to do...because you've got three or four parks...and it's got Danescamp (leisure centre), I go there sometimes...and there's lots of areas for biking around.' (13 year old suburban boy)

'I think it's a good place for children to grow up because there's plenty of areas to just muck about and not be told off.' (14 year old suburban girl)

In contrast, young people in Semilong typically talked of a lack of local opportunities:

'There's nothing to do round here, it's boring really, all you've got is the park and after a while you get tired of it, so you stop going there, then you get bored not going out.' (12 year old inner city girl)

'I don't find my area very interesting...not that many places to go...it's just...not very exciting.' (13 year old inner city boy)

In spite of these differences, when asked what they didn't like about the area, the most frequent response of boys and girls in both locations was that it was boring with not much to do.[12] Suburban young people were twice as likely to complain about the quality and availability of opportu-nities and more likely to say the area was boring. These contradictory perspectives suggest that despite different levels of environmental provision, young people in both the inner city and suburbs share similar experiences and frustrations about local opportunities, about a lack of possibilities for stimulation and new experiences in the neighbourhood. In the inner city, 83 percent of young people said they wanted a wider variety of things to do, compared to 78 percent in Hunsbury. Whether it is because of these limited possibilities or because of the inclination and capacity of young people in responding to their local contexts, it appears that both localities fail to provide adequate opportunities to engage young people.

Three sets of recurring issues about local environ-mental provision emerged from discussions with young people: the inappropriate range of formal and informal play and recreational facilities, limited options for meeting up and hanging out with friends, and problems of access to commercial facilities outside of the neighbourhood.

Inappropriate recreational provision

Young people in both locations valued the recreational facilities (parks, sports and community facilities) that exist, but at the same time talked of their frustrations with the general inadequacy, poor quality and lack of appeal of these facilities. They also talked about having a limited variety of things to do and about problems they encountered in their attempts to make use of local places.

Parks and play places. Although parks and play areas were highly valued, many young people were at the same time critical of the poor condition they were in and the inappropriate nature of the play equipment for older children.

'There is only the little parks for babies, but if they put a few more things like a bigger slide for the older kids...a few rope things or something.' (15 year old inner city girl)

Recreational facilities for young people tend to involve the token provision of a restricted range of play equipment. Yet even for the age group they are designed for, these hold only limited attraction. Recreational needs appear to be either devalued or misunderstood by local authorities and based on simplistic and undifferentiated notions of their needs. The poor levels of provision and the lack of a voice for young people in the local planning process suggest that there is little commitment to meeting their real needs.

'I'd be wrong if I said yes we do fully take account of all the needs of that particular age group (10–15 years). Apart from policies regarding provision of children's play areas...it (facilities for young people) doesn't get there unless we bang on the table and say it should be there.' (Local Planning Official)

In contrast to local decision makers' limited provision for 10–15 year olds, an important facet of young people's environmental behaviour is having the opportunity to engage in a diverse range of activities such as messing about with friends, sitting and chatting, playing games, exploring, interacting with nature, running about, making rope-swings, making jumps and circuits for bike riding or simply sitting and reflecting. Environmental needs are not static but change according to what motivates young people at the time: for example, to play sports and games or just mess about with friends. How different places are used will also vary according to age and gender, such that a park may be used by older teenagers as a place to meet and sit and chat, or by younger adolescents as a place to play. In this way, young people's use of open space is characterised by a mosaic of heterogeneous place uses (see Figure 3.2).

Places for sport. Playing sports is a popular activity for many young people, especially boys (56 percent of the boys and 20 percent of the girls in the combined sample). A higher proportion of inner city boys (68 percent), compared to suburban boys (47 percent), like to do sport activities in their free time. The apparent advantage for young people in Hunsbury of having one of the town's major sports and recreation centres is diminished by the limited appeal of this type of facility for some young people and its limited ability to satisfy all the needs of even the most keen sports enthusiast.

'I'd rather be playing football...but there's no football pitch here... there's nothing round here to do it on...the nearest place is up the school field and then the caretaker chases you off.' (15 year old suburban boy)
'There is the leisure centre but that's...that's okay, but there's not much to do apart from swim or go to the gym. Sometimes we don't want to do those things.'
(15 year old suburban girl)

There is a paradox here in that the local planning department acknowledges young people's need for playing fields:

'Apart from the necklace of open space running through the (suburban) area...I fully accept there is no 'kick-around space.' (Local planning officer)
'The adoption of a 'dual use' approach to community and open space facilities means that 50 percent of community playing field allocation for public use is accounted for by existing school playing fields.'
(Northampton Borough Council 1984)

Yet the planning department fails to recognise that in reality young people do not have access to many of the facilities that do exist.

In Semilong, there is no formal sport and recreational provision and limited open space within the neighbourhood. There is one park with a small flat green space, a small 'play area' with an enclosed hard surfaced area for ball games, and a pocket of green space located next to a busy main road. These spaces are blighted by social and environmental hazards (strangers, broken glass, used syringes, litter), and a lack of proper sport equipment.[13]

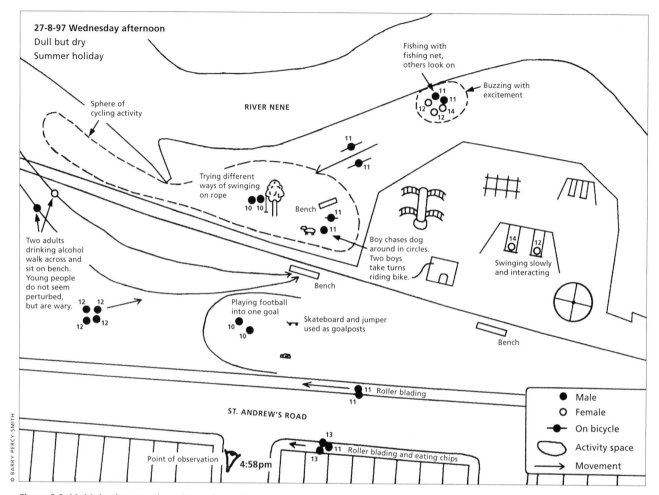

27-8-97 Wednesday afternoon
Dull but dry
Summer holiday

Sphere of cycling activity

Fishing with fishing net, others look on

Buzzing with excitement

RIVER NENE

Trying different ways of swinging on rope

Bench

Boy chases dog around in circles. Two boys take turns riding bike.

Swinging slowly and interacting

Two adults drinking alcohol walk across and sit on bench. Young people do not seem perturbed, but are wary.

Bench

Playing football into one goal

Skateboard and jumper used as goalposts

Bench

11 Roller blading
11

ST. ANDREW'S ROAD

Point of observation   4:58pm

13
13   11 Roller blading and eating chips

Male
Female
On bicycle
Activity space
Movement

© BARRY PERCY-SMITH

Figure 3.2 Multiple place uses in an inner city park

'There's not really like any football teams, or anything, round here. I'm really into basketball at the moment but there's nothing...I have to go all the way up to the race-course.' (14 year old inner city boy)

'There's nowhere to play football...Basketball I like, but you can't play basketball round here. The play area you can but there's no rings...and there's loads of bottles and glass...if it was a bit bigger so there was...a football pitch and a few rings for a game of basketball...everybody would enjoy it round here...instead of going round causing trouble.' (12 year old inner city boy)

The Local Authority's response to the inadequacy of recreational facilities in Semilong is that there is a large municipal park adjacent to Semilong where young people can play. What is not taken account of, however, is the major road separating the park from the neighbourhood, the bad reputation the park has for muggings and assaults, parental restrictions on young people's environmental range, and issues concerning territoriality between different groups of young people.

Despite government initiatives to increase participation and achievement in sport and physical recreation, and to increase the quantity and quality of sports facilities,[14] improvements in sports and recreational facilities have yet to benefit either Semilong or Hunsbury. In response to the lack of formal sports opportunities, but also because young people need spontaneous 'kickabout' space, they use whatever space they can find to play sport such as the street, isolated patches of green spaces, the spaces between industrial units after work hours and car parks (Figure 3.3). While this type of place use reflects the way young people are able to creatively adapt their environment, it often brings them into conflict with residents and car owners and compromises their right to play safely.

These insights raise important questions about the type of environments young people are growing up in, about commitment of local authorities and communities in providing a range of appropriate opportunities for young people according to their needs and desires, and the extent to which young people can use their own creativity in spending free time in the neighbourhood. There also appears to be an implicit assumption in the young people's comments that opportunities should be provided by adults rather than created by themselves.

All the neighbourhood's a playground: the search for fun, excitement and new experiences

The popularity of parks masks the fact that much of young people's use of neighbourhood space takes place in the fourth environment[15] — beyond the home, school and playground. Parks are an important resource, but cannot possibly satisfy all young people's needs, especially during school holidays when they have a lot of time on their hands. For many young people, a large part of their outdoor activities does not involve predictable place behaviour, but instead is characterised by creating their own random and spontaneous amusement. They may use whatever they may find in the course of their movement through the neighbourhood, such as discarded supermarket trolleys, pieces of rope or car wheels, or adapt the environment itself. In this way all the neighbourhood is a potential play area. Hence streets are used for skate boarding, or as racetracks or arenas for play. Street furniture is used for bases or reference points for games. Walls, lampposts and railings are used as climbing frames. Building sites offer sand-pits to jump

into. Apartment blocks become adventure playgrounds. Hidden corners of the neighbourhood, disused land and derelict buildings provide opportunities for exploration and adventure, as places to go wild and let off steam or to build dens.

'We go out exploring new places…take all these short cuts and see where we end up…sometimes we go through this fence to where the railway is and go up the side of the track and wave at the train drivers.' (12 year old girl)

'I climb onto the green box, through the barbed wire and into this back yard…no one lives there now…there's like this pile of old newspapers behind this shed thing…and sit there and just like…if I want to get away from my sister and everything.' (11 year old boy)

(Voices of inner city children)

In their search for fun, excitement and new experiences young people often discover hidden corners of their environment, places abandoned by adults but invaded by

> *Young people's sense of place is intertwined with feelings of belonging and acceptance, as well as opportunities to engage in social and recreational activities.*

children, to which they attach their own meanings and values. Although young people in both locations demonstrate this type of environmental behaviour, those in the inner city appear to benefit from fewer parental restrictions and a more heterogeneous environment with a plethora of abandoned, derelict or liminal public spaces which enhance environmental possibilities. In this way young people in the inner city appear to derive a richer environmental experience from their neighbourhood than suburban young people. This has been referred to as 'paradoxical poverty' in similar research by McKendrick.[16] For young people growing up in the suburb, the tightly planned landscape offers a more homogeneous and sterile landscape with fewer possibilities for environmental (re)creation.

Young people are often seen hanging around waiting for something to happen, or for someone to come up with an idea for something to do, or just messing about having a laugh.

In some cases this may involve their transgressing boundaries, compromising the moral order of the street or breaking the law. For example, one 11 year old inner city boy talked of how they use the post office vans in a nearby car park as a trampoline.

Figure 3.3 Kids versus cars: street play in the inner city

Interviewer: 'What do you most like to do when you're out?'
Daren: 'Jump on them vans.'
Interviewer: 'Why do you jump on the vans?'
Daren: 'It's entertainment.'
Interviewer: 'Do you think it's all right to do that?'
Daren: 'No, but it's more fun than walking round bored getting into trouble.'

Young people frequently talk of a range of exploits, such as climbing over people's walls, throwing eggs at passing taxis, garden hopping and setting off car alarms as they seek stimulation and excitement from their neighbourhood. These types of activities provide a 'thrill of transgression',[17] heightened by the possibility of being chased off, which they call 'getting a leg.' They say that if they

get told off they just 'give the person lip.' Crossing boundaries may thus constitute acts of deviance, but for young people they are a way of creating amusement. These activities may be fun, but they are also aggravating for other residents and indicate a breakdown and lack of respect between generations.

Restrictions on young people's use of neighbourhood space: for whose benefit?

Young people in both Semilong and Hunsbury related how their use of open spaces is often thwarted by controls laid down by adults or by competition with other place users. The role of parks as a recreational resource for young people is, for example, contested by the desire of dog owners to use the same spaces as a dog's toilet. Yet in terms of what is deemed appropriate place use, it tends to be young people who lose out as a result of the way places are regulated, for example, through local by-laws prohibiting ball games or as a result of hostility from local residents. Conflicts appear to arise as a result of the ambiguous status of neighbourhood space and contested assumptions about young people's right to use these spaces. These are often semi-public or transitional spaces, sandwiched between public and private realms: for example, open grassed areas and neighbourhood streets around community buildings, or routeways through local authority housing.

'I play on this patch of grass and this lady doesn't like us playing on it. It's a big patch of grass, it's got quite a few trees on there...to play football...and she didn't like us playing on it. So we're not allowed to play on it anymore. I don't really think it's very fair.' (10 year old boy)

These types of restrictions are especially hard for young people otherwise faced with a limited range of alternative spaces to use, and hence they become marginalised as neighbourhood place users. They often use these spaces all the same, but in so doing get into trouble. The unintended effects of marginalising young people are fewer possibilities for integrating children's play into the everyday life of the community and increased feelings of alienation and animosity between young people and adults. The implications of failing to provide suitable opportunities for young people is summed up by the following comment from a 15 year old suburban boy:

'Until they make new things and new places for young people, there is always going to be trouble…'cause when you get bored, if you get really bored constantly, you start getting angry, you want to take your anger out on something.'

Instead of responding to this boredom, anger and frustration through collaborative community development exercises with young people, local planning and decision making tends to take scant account of their perspectives. There is a paradoxical situation here where there is growing public and political concern about young people hanging around the streets getting bored, but a tendency for political priorities to reflect powerful business interests rather than a commitment to addressing social problems and the needs of the young.

Problems of access to commercial facilities

A common feature of many British cities is the movement of recreational and retail services to out-of-town locations, with a corresponding closure of in-town facilities. This is no less typical for Northampton and poses significant problems for young people. Many are disadvantaged in their ability to use out of town facilities, such as cinemas and sports centres, as a result of geographical inaccessibility and the cost of the transport to get there. This was particularly a problem in the inner city where nearly 50 percent of the households did not own a car.

'They could bring a cinema back over 'cause, if mum can't take me I can't go. Like when it was near in town, I liked it when it was there and I could just go and watch something, but now I can't just walk to Virgin (cinema). It's miles away.' (11 year old inner city girl)

The problem of geographical inaccessibility is compounded by the high cost of many leisure and recreational facilities. As a 13 year old inner city boy noted about an amusement arcade: 'When Zapatak opened it was something like 50p for half an hour, but now it's well over £2.50 for 15 minutes. They're ripping you off.' For many young people, the commercialisation and privati-

sation of recreation are placing local opportunities out of their reach. There is a tension here in that on the one hand young people are being lured into the economy as consumers, but on the other hand many young people are restricted in their means to participate as a result of growing social inequalities.

In contrast, while the suburban young people face similar problems of accessibility, their parents are more likely to be able to pay their entry fees and drive them around or encourage alternative programmes of activities, for example, in sports or drama clubs.

'We've got a policy of "keep the children busy and they keep out of trouble"…but everything our children do tends to be fairly structured…so we try and make sure they're always doing something.' (Suburban parent)

In this way young people may benefit from opportunities, but at the same time not all parents (especially many of those in Semilong) are able to provide this type of support, giving rise to inequalities in life chances. However, institutionalising young people's activities in this way can undermine young people's autonomy and exacerbate their separation from their own community. It is also based on an instrumentalist view of young people's use of free time and fails to address their desire to simply spend time hanging out with friends.

> *There appears to be an implicit assumption in the young people's comments that opportunities should be provided by adults rather than created by themselves.*

Between the home and the youth club: the search for a 'third space' to hang out

For a majority of young people in this study, when they have free time their primary motive is to meet up and spend time with friends (72 percent inner city, 62 percent suburb). They also stated they were happiest 'when they were messing about with friends' (40 percent inner city, 57 percent suburb). Nine out of ten young people in both

© BARRY PERCY-SMITH

Figure 3.4 Using the street as a skate boarding track

locations stated they prefer to be outside if they can. When asked what they liked most about being outside, young people in both locations most frequently stated that they had more freedom outside.

'It's just the freedom we want…to make as much noise as we want so that other people don't complain…that's why we normally go to the park…because we can dance, sing, do what we want 'cause there's…hardly no houses around …and we can just do whatever we want…without nobody saying "oh you can't do this, you can't do that" ….'
(14 year old suburban girl)

However, young people in Semilong and Hunsbury are faced with the reality of having few places to spend time with friends outside of the home.

'I think there is…not enough for young people…That's why a lot of the time we're just walking about and things… Really we don't have anywhere to go where it's warm in winter…There's only the youth club on Thursday nights and that's about it really.' (14 year old suburban girl)

Traditionally youth clubs have been relied upon to fill this gap but they tend to be open for only a few hours a week and do not necessarily appeal to all young people. Only 26 percent of inner city young people and 35 percent in the suburb said they attended a youth club. Nevertheless, 65 percent of inner city young people and 54 percent in the suburb said it was important to have a youth club. What this suggests is that young people look to a youth club as a possible solution to having nowhere to go, but are not attracted by what is available. The most frequent reasons given for not attending a youth club were lack of information about what was available, lack of appeal, or because of others that attend.

'There is a youth club…, but my friend used to go there and says it's not very good at all. They hardly do anything.'
(12 year old suburban girl)

'I know there is the youth centre but I went up there, but there doesn't seem to be very much up there…it's a good idea but it's not been sort of thought through very much as to what we want…if they had a few more discos and things like that…and a few things like just for girls…because sometimes the girls get intimidated by the boys.'
(15 year old inner city girl)

In many cases young people simply want somewhere they can sit and chat with friends and to have the freedom to relax and mess about without hassle from adults.

'We just sit and talk…about stuff that has happened, what we've done in the day, what everybody's doing tomorrow, where we are going to meet next time, who's walking who home.' (15 year old suburban girl)

Young people often respond to the lack of social venues by hanging out on the streets, around the community centre (see Box 3.1), sitting on garden walls or in local parks and play areas.

Hanging out at the suburban Blackymore Community Centre

The area round the Blackymore Community Centre is one of two major hangouts in the suburban area. Every evening between 7.30 and 8.00 pm young people start to gather, with as many as forty young people on one night. Young people freely associate around the open field by the centre, especially when it gets dark, standing or sitting on the ground, by the play equipment, on the solitary bench, or round the side of the centre where it is sheltered from the wind. In a bid to discourage young people from congregating in this area, the bench has been taken away. There are few other place users at this time, so this area temporarily becomes an outdoor youth club. The youth club housed in the centre only opens for two hours a week due to a lack of financial resources. Even when the youth club opens, there is not much for young people to do, with the result that they often hang around outside anyway. The young people readily admit they are bored, saying that if they had some money it would be different. So strong is their desire to spend time with friends that they hang around outside even on cold winter nights, huddling close to the sides of the centre. Although they are congregating in public open space, they are accused of trespassing by the secretary of the centre. As a result of graffiti and vandalism to the centre, fencing has now been erected to keep young people away. All the same, the lack of alternative places to go, the centrality of this location, the proximity of the shops, and the relative autonomy and shelter it provides are reasons why young people continue to hang out here and consequently have identified this place as their patch.

Hanging out has tended to be interpreted as an aimless pursuit with 'nothing better to do',[18] posing a threat to the moral order of public life.[19] These views undermine the integrity of hanging out as a meaningful activity and young people's need for this kind of socialising. Participant observation revealed how the actions and behaviour of young people hanging out is, in fact, little different than the activities of adults in social settings such as a pub or club. Yet because of limited social provision for young people, they are forced to socialise outdoors.

Changing cultures of childhood: the retreat indoors

Despite the continual attraction of being outdoors for many young people, there is simultaneously a growing tendency for many of them to spend time in indoor activities. Contrary to previous studies[20] which identified a 'bedroom culture' of young girls, evidence in this study suggests that boys are just as likely to hang out indoors as girls. Patterns of indoor leisure culture of young people emerge from the interplay between gender and locational factors, with suburban boys most likely to spend time engaged in indoor activities, but few differences for inner city boys and girls (Table 3.7).

These trends appear to be in part due to the boom in computer games, videos and satellite television.

'Just sit in my mate's bedroom...play computer games and stuff every night from about 7 pm until about 9.30 pm...it's warm and comfortable and you can have a laugh there.'
(14 year old suburban boy)

Computer games, in particular, are played more frequently by boys than girls (18 percent compared to 4 percent). This is especially so in the suburb where 21 percent of boys and no girls said their favourite activity was playing games on the computer. Boys in the suburb are also more likely than girls to choose watching TV as their most favoured free time activity. Differences were marginal in the inner city. The locational differences in these 'new' cultures of childhood appear to be due to greater levels of affluence of suburban families. On one level this suggests that suburban boys are more advantaged: however, the impact of electronic-based leisure activities on the well-being of young people is open to question.

TABLE 3.7			
Proportion of boys and girls who most like to spend their time doing indoor activities in the home (% GENDER/SITE SAMPLE)			
Suburban boys	72	Inner city boys	30
Suburban girls	47	Inner city girls	33

This section has exposed the lack of environmental opportunities for young people and has provided insights into their heterogeneous needs. At the same time it demonstrates how the perceived problematic nature of some young people's use of neighbourhood space may be a result of a lack of opportunities for stimulation, amusement and spending time with friends. If young people are to be considered equal citizens, then the existing inequality in providing them with social venues needs to be addressed. There is, however, a danger in assuming that a good environment is one in which young people have everything provided in a structured way. On the contrary, young people articulate a need to participate in different ways within the everyday life of the community. In particular, they demonstrate both an inclination and capacity to create their own activities and places of meaning. The extent to which young people are able to participate in different ways in their communities depends partly on the attitudes of adults.

YOUNG PEOPLE, COMMUNITY AND CONFLICT: BELONGING AND ALIENATION

A sense of belonging is an important facet of individual well-being and is necessary for developing a sense of self in relation to the world.[21] For many young people, an important aspect of how they feel about where they live is their sense of belonging within the community,[22] which accrues from their social interactions with peers and adults in the course of everyday life. However, some young people may have ambivalent feelings towards their community.

Community Cohesiveness and Fragmentation

Young people, on the whole, articulated a strong sense of attachment and identification with their neighbourhoods, although the sense of community was stronger in inner city Semilong than suburban Hunsbury. Young people in Semilong are part of a long established neighbourhood with often three or more generations of the same family still resident in the area. It is a compact neighbourhood with clearly perceived boundaries, within which daily pedestrian flows to and from local amenities continually nourish social networks and keep the sense of community alive. Karen (15 years old) expressed her feelings of community in Semilong by stating: *I think Semilong is a really close knit community. There are a lot of people you can talk to…I often talk to the people around the shops… 'cause my mum knows the people that work like in the post office…and a lot of people I know around this area…and it's a really nice place.*

Hunsbury, on the other hand, has only been developed during the last twenty years, and in contrast to the hive of activity in the streets of Semilong, has comparatively little pedestrian movement, due to the size of the suburb, higher levels of car ownership and less developed community networks. Young people in Hunsbury tended to identify with different areas within the broader catchment of the suburb. Hunsbury therefore consists of a mosaic of interlinking neighbourhoods, each with a different identity which young people variably relate to according to their own activity range. These are not static, but constantly changing communities. As the new estates in Hunsbury become established and children grow up together, a sense of shared identity and attachment to Hunsbury appears to be developing. In contrast, Semilong appears to be witnessing a gradual fragmentation of community, as Karen (15) relates:

'I think it's okay, but it could be better. People could come together a bit more to make it better. When people move out to quieter places it breaks up the community. …My brother used to live in Norfolk Street but now he's in Spinney Hill. My aunty used to live in Semilong Road next to the post office and my sister used to live in Baker Street, but now lives in Duston (another part of town).'

Despite the evident sense of community in Semilong, outside of their homes, feelings of alienation within these spaces serve to exclude young people from a sense of community. These ambivalent feelings of community and belonging are in part due to the hostility of adults toward young people over their use of neighbourhood space, but also result from fears and anxieties young people have about 'stranger danger' posed by alien 'others' — those in the significant transient population who get filtered down into the cheap rented accommodation the neighbourhood provides. Feelings of being unaccepted, however, may also arise out of problems posed by other young people in the neighbourhood in the form of bullying.

Figure 3.5 Hanging about on the street looking for action

Neighbourhood bullying

In this study, 57 percent of young people in Semilong and 42 percent in Hunsbury said that they had experienced bullying while out in their neighbourhood.

'There are too many bullies around. Older kids on West Street...they take your ball away and kick it where you can't get it.' (12 year old inner city boy)

'At the top of Craven Street there's Adam and Luke...and there's like their friends...if you've got a football they'll come round and say 'let me kick the ball'...and if you say 'no' you're beaten up. You get no choice.'
(13 year old inner city boy)

'The big kids, Adam and Luke, ...ask for money and sweets and chase you.' (11 year old inner city boy)

'Once I was in the shop and Adam and Luke were banned from the shop...and they sneaked in and asked us to steal for them. When you try and walk away they follow you and say I'll batter you if you don't.' (13 year old inner city boy)

As illustrated by the repeated reference to the same individuals[23] in the narratives above, young people's use of neighbourhood space is controlled by the tyrannical rule of a few notorious individuals. Evidence suggests that these individuals are likely to come from families that are materially less well off, have experienced some kind of family breakdown, and are educational underachievers, school excludees or unemployed.

Although boys are most likely to experience bullying (64 percent), girls may also be victims (36 percent). Whereas boys were most likely to be bullied by boys, girls reported being bullied by both boys and girls, suggesting a complex gender dynamic to bullying. In 87 percent of the cases, young people were bullied by older teenagers or gangs. The places where they reported being bullied mirror the places that they use most. In Semilong, 68 percent were bullied in the street and 20 percent in parks and play areas. Bullying adulterates the quality of young people's neighbourhood experience and gives rise to a fragmented activity space within the neighbourhood. Nicole (aged 10) recounted her own story of the effects of bullying on her use of neighbourhood space.

'Well we went down to 'the field' once...so that Katie (younger sister)...because she has cerebral palsy she can play on the grass, but the Riordan gang came down and threatened to throw her in the water...and Daren (gang member) picked Ricky (younger brother) up by the throat and threatened him. We don't go down there no more. Anyway we're going back to Ireland soon.'

The irony is that the boy (11 years old) being implicated here, in turn, also talked of the problems he had of being bullied by older teenagers: 'I get picked on by Adam and Luke…in West Street…when I'm walking along they just pick on you and nick your fags.'

Bullying is one way in which young people experience community disharmony. However, for a significant number of them, their experience of place and sense of community are weakened by conflict with adults which they commonly referred to as 'getting grief.'

'Getting Grief': Conflict Between Young People and Adults Over Neighbourhood Space

The extent to which young people are either integrated into, or alienated from, their community determines the quality of their social environment. In Semilong, the strong sense of community gives rise to well-developed social support networks around younger children, for example through play groups, after school clubs, and mums and tots groups. However, as dependency on parents decreases throughout the teenage years, support and commitment for young people changes.

> *These young people exist in a culture which fails to value them as place users and citizens in their own right, and instead prioritises the social values, norms and concerns of adults.*

Whether hanging out in a group, playing games or moving through their neighbourhood, young people in both Semilong and Hunsbury frequently voiced their frustration with what they commonly termed 'getting grief' from adults. 'Getting grief' involves getting told off or accused of behaviour perceived by adults as socially unacceptable, but which young people considered as being 'normal' or 'reasonable', such as laughing, shouting, running or hanging about. In many cases they are hassled simply because they are young rather than for any misdemeanor.

'You get hassle off people, because there is nothing to do, we all walk around and all you get is, "You're doing this wrong, you're doing that wrong". No one ever comes round

and says, "You're not a bad bunch of kids" or anything. It's always putting us down or something. Adults think we're pains in the ass, vandals, that we're no good and all that…just causing trouble all the time… You see… documentaries on youth today, …and they see all the vandalism and under-age drinking and all that, that's all they show, so naturally if you are a group of kids, that's what they think you are going to be doing.'
(15 year old suburban boy)

These comments reflect an apparent mistrust and suspicion of young people based on adult stereotypes of young people as irresponsible, likely to engage in socially unacceptable behaviour and therefore in need of socialisation and control to maintain the 'moral order of the street.' As a result, young people's use of public space may be further regulated by police activity which may be experienced as unnecessarily punitive or restrictive by some young people.

'Everywhere you turn the police are giving aggro. Like my mate David I don't know if you've seen him, he's quite tall and he's black and they pulled him over the other day, and just started questioning him thinking he had drugs on him, for no reason. We get it all the time, if you walk down the road in a big group, they will pull us over and then like, we will all have to empty our pockets and all that because they think we are up to no good, just because we are in a big group, and the police just don't like it. …They break us up now if there's more than three of us in a group.'
(15 year old suburban boy)

These scenarios expose the sense of alienation many young people feel with respect to their community. The fact that their use of public space is frequently not tolerated suggests that young people themselves are not tolerated or understood. These young people exist in a culture which fails to value them as place users and citizens in their own right, and instead prioritises the social values, norms and concerns of adults.

The comments in Box 3.2 illustrate the way in which moral panics about young people in public places are constructed on the basis of a perception that they are 'other', that they are untamed savages out of control, run-

No automatic right to play: conflict between adults' and young people's use of the 'Play Area' in inner city Semilong

The play area is one of the few places that is specifically allotted for young people to use in the neighbourhood, and it has become one of their most popular places. However, local residents frequently complain about young people being around there, the way they use the available space and the poor condition of the area. Young people have frequently asked for the play area to be improved but no one has listened. On the contrary, when local residents complained about young people being there, the response was immediate in the form of police patrols. Some of the intolerance and lack of acceptance of young people playing in urban space is captured by these comments from local residents, which emerged in the course of a commu-

nity consultation exercise seeking support to improve the play area:

'There are already too many noisy, abusive and uncouth children running loose in this vicinity... The thought of encouraging them into an area that should be dedicated to the care and safety of the elderly seems outrageous'.

'With all the trouble we're tolerating, this so-called play area should be demolished and replaced with O.A.P.* bungalows. There are plenty of parks nearby where young and old can play...'

(Comments from local residents)

*Old Age Pensioner

---

ning feral through the neighbourhood. It also illustrates the way in which social constructions of childhood are reproduced spatially in terms of geographies of exclusion as adult residents seek to control and contain young people according to their own conceptions of childhood and 'acceptable' behaviour and attempt to control public space in a way that legitimises dominant adult views and interests.

While they recognise the rights of adults in the community to live peaceably, putting those rights above their right to use public space is likely to appear unjust to young people who are already faced with a limited range of environmental opportunities. Because of the unlikelihood of constructive dialogue in which the views of both parties could be reconciled, boundaries are drawn between adults and young people, giving rise to spiralling 'relationships of mistrust and mutual antagonism'[24] which exacerbate the separateness of young people and adults.

'I get really angry about people always having a go at us... Where we play footie against the wall the old biddies come out and have a go at us. An old bloke just has a go at you for no reason. To get on his nerves we throw stones at the garage...Adrian doesn't help much by taking the mick and

shouting out and kicking the ball back at the flats, at the old biddies and one of the old ladies once took the ball, so he went over and started firing stones at her door and says "Give us our ball back or I'll get my mum over" and she goes "Get your mum over then cause you shouldn't be playing there" ...and she says "I'm using this as evidence" and so we just have a go at her....' (13 year old inner city boy)

For young people, however, the cumulative unresolved injustice and frustration of these confrontations give rise to the perpetuation of intergenerational hostility as they actively contest adult constructions of them as a problem and struggle for their right to use neighbourhood space. Experiences such as this are symbolic of the everyday conflict between many adults and young people over space. It suggests that part of being young is about negotiating the politics of position within the social and generational hierarchy and the systematic and repetitive marginalisation of young people within their neighbourhood.

Although young people may learn to negotiate the hostile social terrain of the neighbourhood, conflicts such as those reported here raise questions about the impact this type of social environment has on them and their developing sense of self within the community, and also about the effects these types of tensions have on the community itself. Young people's response may be seen by adults as being disrespectful and disobedient, as they fail to fit into adult conceptions of the world and young people's place within it. What may be seen as deviance or defiance could alternatively be interpreted as young people responding to their marginalisation by simply reflecting back the hostility and lack of respect they have experienced, as they struggle for the space to play out their own agenda.

> *A major problem underlying conflicts between adults and young people is the assumption that because children are minors they must be in the wrong.*

A major problem underlying conflicts between adults and young people is the assumption that because children are minors they must be in the wrong. Yet, in reality, both young people and adults are complicit in creating these tensions as they mutually engage in a continually reflexive process of constructing, contesting and reconstructing childhood and youth around notions of rights, participation and citizenship, from different sides of the generational divide. However, it is also within this 'encounter space' that opportunities for integrating young people in society may be realised through processes of collaborative social learning.

YOUNG PEOPLE, PARTICIPATION AND ENVIRONMENTAL PLANNING

This chapter has provided insights into the complex and multi-faceted experiences of young people growing up in different locations. The views and experiences of young people in this study suggest that popular assumptions of suburbia as an 'ideal' place to bring up children are open to question. The inner city area of Semilong is clearly blighted by a congested built environment, a shortage of open space and a multiplicity of environmental and social

dangers. However, young people's views and experiences of their neighbourhood can not be understood simply in terms of the attributes of the locality, but also in terms of the diverse ways in which young people make sense of, and respond to, their particular social and environmental context. What emerges from this study is that, despite locational differences in environmental quality and opportunities, young people in both locations voice similar frustrations about their neighbourhood.

Responding to Young People's Local Environmental Needs

Urban planning and leisure and recreation provision appear to take little account of young people's interests and perspectives or their varying social means. And little account is taken of this situation when young people are criticised for hanging around with nothing to do. The ineffectiveness of communities in facilitating the engagement of young people in meaningful and self-determined ways leads to a sense of boredom, alienation, apathy and frustration for many. The extent to which young people are provided for within their neighbourhood can be seen as a reflection of the extent to which young people and their place needs are valued in the community.

However, while it is important to provide some opportunities, young people also need time and space to create their own amusement. Addressing problems of local provision for young people is therefore not just about structuring and 'curricularising'[25] their time in formalised activities, but is also about providing a neighbourhood environment in which their needs are integrated into the community through the use of wild, informal or 'transitional' places where young people can be in charge of their own time and space. Instead, many local environmental opportunities are 'planned out' of neighbourhoods in the course of urban development.

The disjunction between what young people would like from their neighbourhood and what is actually provided poses a local planning and policy dilemma, which, it would seem, can be appropriately addressed by policy makers and planners only if young people are engaged as partners in the community development process. However, young people's views and experience of their

Figure 3.6 Play areas provide a place to sit around and talk in a large group.

environment are not homogeneous, but vary according to their own interests, orientations, capacities and inclinations. Hence, while some may become bored and apathetic, others may actively create their own opportunities. The experiences of young people growing up in different neighbourhoods can be characterised as a mosaic of different 'microgeographies': that is to say, local spatial cultures which emerge out of 'particular combinations of personalities, interests and shared experiences' which young people move into and out of over time.[26]

Their use of neighbourhood space, however, is also set within the context of unequal social relations between children and adults and the way neighbourhood space is structured to reflect dominant adult uses. In this way the boundaries which demarcate 'being adult' from 'being young' are reproduced spatially in the course of local neighbourhood geographies, giving rise to geographies of marginalisation, conflict, transgression and

exclusion.[27] What is commonly interpreted as a 'youth problem' appears on closer reflection to be a societal problem arising out of the inequalities in citizenship status, mistrust and intolerance of young people by many adults, and a lack of suitable places to go. There will undoubtedly be some young people who will be troublesome. However, to stereotype all young people in this way commits a status offence since there are also adults who cause problems. It also fails to acknowledge the difficult social and environmental contexts in which some young people grow up. Despite these disjunctions and dilemmas there is ample evidence to suggest that involving young people in local decision making processes is an effective way of enhancing their opportunities while at the same time helping to alleviate community tensions.

The Participation of Young People in Local Decision Making

Young people possess an intimate and detailed knowledge of their local environment, yet despite their ability to actively shape their own social and spatial identities, to evaluate their neighbourhood and prioritise changes, they express frustration about having insufficient account taken of their views and interests in local decision making.

'People like politicians and stuff don't really know what we want to do...and think we're like really stupid and a bit of a waste of time really I suppose. Think we just stay in all day watching telly. They just think, Oh he's just a little kid what does he know.' (13 year old suburban boy)

> *There is ample evidence to suggest that involving young people in local decision making processes is an effective way of enhancing their opportunities while at the same time helping to alleviate community tensions.*

The marginalisation of young people in local decision making processes appears to be the result of exclusionary structures and processes in local governance giving rise to a 'culture of non-participation.'[28] Only 19 percent of young people in Semilong and 14 percent in Hunsbury said they had previously made suggestions about improving their local area, mostly to friends, parents or youth workers. In almost all cases they either did not know what happened, never had a response or found that nothing happened. This suggests that even when ideas are proposed, young people are often not heard, not acknowledged or possibly not taken seriously.

There are three sets of reasons given by young people for not making suggestions about improvements to their area. First, the whole concept of participation and having their say does not appear to have been enculturated into their mindsets, such that it never occurred to many of them that they could contribute. However, when provided with the opportunity, many responded positively. When I evaluated young people's experiences of taking part in this research, 52 percent said they felt good about having the chance to say what they felt, be involved and be listened to. A second set of reasons related to young people's not knowing how to go about being involved. There are clear implications here for ongoing debates about citizenship education, not just in schools as is being emphasised currently in England, but in the way communities value and integrate young people into the everyday lives of their communities. In this way notions of children's participation are extended beyond decision making to embrace participation in everyday life.[29] Young people will only become responsible place users if they have their specific place needs accommodated and are provided with opportunities to participate and learn as equal citizens in the everyday life of their community.[30] The third set of factors underlying young people's lack of participation relates to apathy and cynicism among some young people.

Despite these barriers, young people demonstrate a keen sense of wanting to be involved in local development processes. On average, 75 percent of young people in both Semilong and Hunsbury stated they would like an opportunity to be involved in making improvements to their areas, with little variation across the age range. Many young people were vociferous in arguing why they should be listened to.

TABLE 3.8

Young people's views of how they could be more involved in local developments

Local discussion meetings	10
Youth councils/committees	7
Interview/surveys	5
Council consultation with young people	5
Get involved in local groups	2
Talk to the council	3
Self initiated action (e.g. litter picking)	2

'It's important to listen to kids because kids have got their own ideas and they can have some good ideas about things to do, but I mean, it could be the youngsters that change things around here and get new places up and running and things.' (14 year old inner city girl)

'Young people should be involved because it's us that have to play round here.' (10 year old suburban girl)

'It's always adults talking for young people, you feel like …can't I just have a little say in something. They say no, no, you're too young to have a say, and you think, I really wanted to say something about that but I can't because adults rule the world.' (11 year old suburban boy)

'Children deserve a say just the same as adults do…adults think they don't need a say just because they're just children, they're too young to speak, but we're not, we can speak…you never know, some children could make…the world a lot better.' (10 year old suburban boy)

Although young people showed a strength of feeling about participation in local development processes, they were uncertain how this might best be accomplished. However, this is hardly surprising since many had had little experience of developing such views. Nonetheless, young people suggested a common range of possible modes of participation in both Semilong and Hunsbury (see Table 3.8). The variety of responses suggests that there is not just one way of enhancing opportunities for young people, but rather a range of possibilities.[31]

'I reckon at the community centre they should have like some teenagers on the committee so they could…say what they wanted. At least they'd feel as if they're being involved in something.' (13 year old inner city girl)

'I mean we were asked…what things we would like to do in the youth club but we weren't actually asked our opinions about putting together a youth club.' (15 year old inner city girl)

'I think they should have like a young people's spokesman …something so they'd have an idea what young people want to do.' (13 year old suburban boy)

'A youth council would be good…'cause if we were allowed to discuss about things, and they actually listened…if they would just listen for once…that would be great.' (12 year old inner city boy)

'The smallest opportunity you would get everyone down, just…to make better things to do, everyone will come down…it's just that there ain't no opportunities at the moment.' (15 year old suburban boy)

The evidence provided here reveals the strength of young people's desire to participate in local decision making and capacity to contribute in a variety of ways. Despite this, few young people have experience of being involved in local decisions. While some remain apathetic, others feel thwarted by the lack of opportunities to be involved. Young people appear to be caught in a systemic culture of non-participation in which democratic structures and processes remain exclusive, dominated by powerful interests such as development corporations, restricted by entrenched bureaucratic structures and paternalistic assumptions about young people's role in local decision making. If the marginalisation of young people in urban communities is to be addressed, young people themselves need to be supported in reflecting on their own conditions and provided with opportunities to engage more fully in the everyday life of their communities and in local decision making as equal citizens.

ENDNOTES

1 McKendrick *et al.* (1998).
2 Kumar (1993) notes that in 1991 poverty was affecting one in three children in the UK.
3 Naesman (1994); Furlong and Cartmel (1997).
4 Percy-Smith (1999).
5 Jeffs and Smith (1996); Matthews *et al.* (1998).
6 Studies of this kind are rare, but see Valentine and McKendrick (1997) and Woolley, Spencer, Dunn and Rowley (1999).
7 Northamptonshire County Council Policy Division (1991).
8 Northamptonshire County Council Policy Division (1991).
9 This research is in turn part of a broader cross-section of geographical research projects within the Centre for Children and Youth at University College Northampton concerned with investigating children's environments and the participation of young people in local development processes.
10 See Percy-Smith (1999) for an elaboration of this conceptual framework.
11 Davis and Bourhill (1997).
12 These contradictory perspectives are based on two different lines of quesitoning.
13 Football goals have now been installed in the 'play area' as a result of a community development exercise with young people undertaken during this study.
14 See for example Sports Council (1993).

[15] Van Vliet (1983).

[16] McKendrick (1997).

[17] Sibley (1995).

[18] Corrigan (1979); Marshland (1993).

[19] Cahill (1990).

[20] McRobbie and Garber (1976); Frith (1984).

[21] Hummon (1992).

[22] Chawla (1992).

[23] Names of individuals and streets have been changed to protect the identity of the people concerned.

[24] White et al (1996, p. 5).

[25] Ennew (1994).

[26] Matthews, Limb and Percy-Smith (1998).

[27] White (1993); Sibley (1995); Valentine (1996); Percy-Smith (1998).

[28] Lansdown (1995).

[29] de Winter (1996).

[30] Hart (1992, 1997).

[31] Fitzpatrick, Hastings and Kintrea (1998).

REFERENCES

Cahill, S (1990) 'Childhood and public life: reaffirming biographical divisions', *Social Problems,* vol. 37, pp. 390-402.

Chawla, L (1992) 'Childhood place attachments' in Altman, I. and Low, S.M. (eds) *Place attachments,* Plenum Press, New York.

Corrigan, P (1979) *Schooling the smash street kids,* MacMillan, London.

Davis, H and Bourhill, M (1997) 'Crisis: the demonisation of children and young people' in Scraton, P. (ed) *Childhood in Crisis,* UCL Press, London.

De Winter, M (1997) *Children as fellow citizens: participation and commitment,* Radcliff Medical Press, Oxford.

Ennew, J (1994) 'Time for childhood or time for adults' in Qvortrup, J. et al. (eds) *Childhood matters: social theory, practice and politics,* Avebury, Aldershot.

Fitzpatrick, S, Hastings, A and Kintrea, K (1998) *Involving young people in urban regeneration,* The Policy Press, Bristol.

Frith, S (1984) *The Sociology of youth,* Causeway Press, Ormskirk.

Furlong, A and Cartmel, F (1997) *Young people and social change: individualisation and risk in late modernity,* Open University Press, Buckingham.

Hart, R (1992) *Children's participation: from tokenism to citizenship,* Innocenti essays no. 4, UNICEF International Child Development Centre, Florence.

Hart, R (1997) *Children's participation: the theory and practice of involving young citizens in community development and environmental care,* London, Earthscan.

Hummon, DM (1992) 'Community attachment', in Altman, I. and Low, S.M. (eds) *Place attachments,* Plenum Press, New York.

Jeffs, T and Smith, MK (1996) 'Getting the dirtbags off the streets: curfews and other solutions to juvenile crime', *Youth and Policy* 53, pp. 1-14.

Kumar, V (1993) *Poverty and inequality in the UK: the effects on children,* National Children's Bureau, London.

Lansdown, G (1995) *Taking part: children's participation in decision making,* IPPR, London.

McKendrick, J (1997) 'Paradoxical poverty: poor communities and their children', Paper presented at the *Urban Childhood Conference,* University of Trondheim, June.

McKendrick, J *et al.* (1998) 'From play space to play spots: 21st century challenges for children's play', paper presented at the *Launch of the ESRC's 5-16 programme,* Church House Conference Centre, Westminster, London, January.

McRobbie, A and Garber, J (1976) ' Girls and subcultures – an exploration', in Hall, S. and Jefferson, T. (eds) *Resistance through rituals,* Hutchinson, London.

Marshland, D (1993) *Understanding youth: issues and methods in social education,* Claridge Press, St. Albans.

Matthews, H, Limb, M and Percy-Smith, B (1998) 'Changing worlds, changing places: the microgeographies of teenagers', *Tijdschrift voor Economische et Sociale Geografie* 89, 2, pp. 193-202.

Matthews, H *et al.* (1999) 'Reclaiming the street: the discourse of curfew', *Environment and Planning A,* 31 (10), pp. 1713-1730.

Naesman, E (1994) 'Individualisation and institutionalisation of childhood in today's Europe' in Qvortrup, J. *et al.* (eds) *Childhood matters: social theory, practice and policy,* Avebury, Aldershot.

Northamptonshire County Council Policy Division (1991) *Census Atlas of Northamptonshire,* section 30.

OPCS (1992) *General Household Survey 1991,* London: Her Majesty's Stationery Office.

Percy-Smith, B (1998) Marginalisation of children and youth in urban neighbourhoods: implications for citizenship', Paper presented at the *Children and Social Exclusion Conference,* Hull University, March.

Percy-Smith, B (1999) *Multiple childhood geographies: giving voice to young people's experience of place,* unpublished doctoral thesis, University College Northampton.

Sibley, D (1995) *Geographies of exclusion,* Routledge, London.

Sports Council (1993) *Young people and sport: policy and frameworks for action,* The Sports Council, London.

Valentine, G (1996) 'Children should be seen and not heard: the production and transgression of adults' public space', *Urban Geography* 17, 3, pp. 205-220.

Valentine, G and McKendrick, J (1997) 'Children's outdoor play: exploring parental concerns about children's safety and the changing nature of childhood', *Geoforum* vol. 28, 2, pp. 219-235.

Van Vliet, W (1983) 'Exploring the fourth environment: an examination of the home range of city and suburban teenagers', *Environment and Behaviour* vol. 15, no. 5, pp. 567-588.

White, R (1993) 'Youth and conflict over urban space', *Children's Environments* 10, 1, pp. 85-93.

White, R et al. (1996) *Negotiating youth-specific public space: a guide for youth and community workers, town planners and local councils,* Youth Programs Unit, East Sydney.

Woolley, H, Spencer, C, Dunn, J and Rowley, G (1999) 'The child as citizen', *Journal of Urban Design,* 4, 3, pp. 255-282.

© KAREN MALONE

CHAPTER FOUR

Australian Youth
Aliens in a Suburban Environment

Karen Malone and Lindsay Hasluck

Growing Up in Cities returned to Braybrook, a suburb of Melbourne (Australia), 25 years after the project was first carried out in this 'underclass' community. The physical environment and the frustrations of its young residents remain largely unchanged, although the composition of its population reflects a new ethnic diversity. The community is revealed by its young people through the lenses of gender, ethnicity and age. The initial research phase of Growing Up in Cities was used to create Streetspace, an innovative school-based project that uses participatory design to reduce young people's marginalisation and increase their access to public spaces.

'Local encounters or the fear of encounters with another are informed by images of alien other worlds...'[1]

alien, n. *stranger; non-naturalised foreigner; one excluded from.*[2]

CHANGING TIMES

Neighbourhoods are living entities constructed over time. How a place is experienced is relative to its history. Physically, time can be recorded by the enlarging cracks on the footpath or the growth of the trees — in social terms, time is recorded through the stories of people in places, their experiences and perceptions. In this chapter we compare young people's perceptions of a neighbourhood in Melbourne, Australia, at two different junctures during a 25 year period between 1972 and 1997. This research reveals that a developing climate of fear, suspicion and tension has resulted in conflicts over the legitimacy of young people using public places. The conse-

quences of these conflicts are geographies of exclusionary practice determined by location, class, ethnicity, gender and age.[3] This phenomenon of exclusion, appearing predominantly in late modernity and which is most prevalent in Western or industrialised nations, positions the child and the young person as the 'other' and contributes to an emerging hierarchy of spatial access and mobility. If providing supportive environments where children and youth can develop and experience a growing sense of self and place is the responsibility of adults, then it is critical to consider what a youth inclusive space might be like. This longitudinal study provides a rare opportunity to explore these questions over time.

In addition, this chapter discusses the construction of youth subcultures and groupings as they emerge from the social and spatial lives of young people. These groupings provide an entry point for discussing the complexity of youth environmental behaviours rather than providing a framework for constructing a universal or stereotypical youth identity. The groupings are explored through the stories of four young people growing up in the 1990s. Following these stories the chapter then provides an insight into the participatory action phase of the research project. The programme of action was to provide a forum where young people could initiate shared dialogues and make contact with other members of the community. 'Streetspace', the environmental design project undertaken by the authors in conjunction with the city council, a local secondary school and the community, celebrated the ideal of inclusive communities while highlighting young people's skills and expertise as participatory planners. This project showed how some of the issues identified through our longitudinal study could be addressed.

GROWING UP IN BRAYBROOK

'My children grew up in Braybrook; although I had to take them out of Braybrook for recreation, they have grown up without problems. Braybrook has always been an under-resourced suburb but we are all poor together so we all cope together. I have friends who live outside Braybrook and they ask me how I can live in Braybrook and is it as bad as they say. Well, this is where my home is and I live here.' (Mrs Betty Wilson, Braybrook elderly resident)[4]

For many outsiders like Betty's 'friends', Braybrook represents social decay and 'underclass' morality. Underclass as described by McDonald is:

'a social group or class of people located at the bottom of the class structure who, over time, have become structurally separate and culturally distinct from regularly employed working class and society in general [and are] almost permanently confined to living in poorer conditions and neighbourhoods.'[5]

Images of the irresponsible welfare-draining single mother and feckless, dangerous youth have come to represent the underclass. Cycles of disadvantage, constructed historically, become manifest in the physical and social domain of a neglected neighbourhood. Conservatism and demands for the purification of public space have helped to fan these images of the underclass as a means for justifying 'containment' and 'social exclusion'.

These hierarchies of desirable and undesirable locations feed moral panics and mask diversity and difference by simplifying the complexity of community experience. The following statement by a local resident in a community interview in 1996 clearly makes this point: 'We get it rammed down our throats by the newspapers that the western suburbs are deprived, illiterate and breed crime and are full of no-hopers. If you live in the area you're lumped with it'.

How do these cultures and hierarchies of places come to exist? What does this mean for young people growing up in these so-called 'underclass' neighbourhoods? The following brief introduction positions the neighbourhood of Braybrook within the context of the Growing Up In Cities project and its origins as a postwar impoverished housing estate.

Path to Poverty

Melbourne was one of the four original case study sites in the book Growing Up in Cities by Kevin Lynch.[6] Called 'Children's Perception of Space', the research was conducted over a six-month period in 1972 by Peter Downton, an architecture masters student from the University of Melbourne. Guided by the criteria provided by Lynch in the research guide for country directors, Downton decided to study an area typical of suburban development throughout Australia. He chose Braybrook, a low-density suburb (rather than a high density inner city neighbourhood) due to the relative absence of studies of these areas. He decided on a location in the western suburbs of Melbourne because this part of the city was generally of lower socio-economic status than the area east of the Central Business District. According to Downton there were many social indicators of this lower status.[7] For example, the average per capita expenditure on new education buildings from 1966 to 1972 throughout Melbourne was 130 US$, but in the western suburbs, the average was 69 US$; and the average value per capita of health building approvals for the year ending June 1971 for areas other than the western sector of Melbourne was $1.94 US$, but for the west the value was $0.07 US$.

The borders between suburbs and cultures in Australian cities are blurred because of the history of their settle-

ment and development. Nevertheless, real and visible distinctions have evolved, creating hierarchies of desirable addresses.[8]

Braybrook, again a GUIC site in 1997, is a 488-hectare housing estate in the western suburbs of Melbourne. Couched between a train yard and a polluted river and divided by a major road, Braybrook is juxtaposed between the inner and outer suburbs of Melbourne. Built at the start of Melbourne's 20-year postwar public housing boom[9] over a five-year period between 1951 and 1956, the estate has four distinctive streetscapes: residential, industrial, commercial and arterial. According to Powell, during this period housing demand often outstripped supply: 'The suburban developments that accompanied changes after the war throughout Australia were not smooth and well-planned exercises but often hurried and fitful responses to meet overwhelming and urgent needs after years of "making do".'[10] The consequence of this unplanned public housing boom was a number of 'fibro frontiers.' Fibro cement sheeting was the building material used inside and outside during this period of estate construction in Australia. According to Winter and Bryson, these estates were 'built by government; of a large scale and uniform appearance; constructed of poor quality cheap materials; home to relatively high percentages of public renters; comprised of predominantly working class families; adjacent to manufacturing employment; and stigmatised.'[11] Powell describes them as 'a shadowy miniature version of the dream houses depicted in the many new glossy home magazines and in newspaper features'.[12]

The greater part of Braybrook estate housing consisted of semi-detached and detached houses, and flats up to three storeys high, constructed from prefabricated concrete slabs and fibro cement sheeting. Because the buildings were constructed of this cheap material and were situated on reclaimed wetland, the residences suffered from chronic and rising water damage. This was characteristic of many houses built by the Victorian Housing Commission during this period: 'The concrete houses were cold in winter and hot in summer, and a problem in their construction was the difficulty in joining walls. In later years many developed horrendous

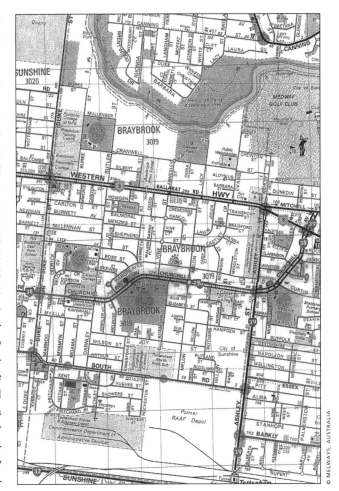

Figure 4.1 Map of Braybrook

cracks.'[13] For this reason a considerable number of these houses have sat vacant and in disrepair.

Lack of maintenance has been an issue in the estate since its development. According to a youth worker in a 1997 interview, 'The rate that they are improving the flats is not keeping up with the needs'. In regard to similar estates in Melbourne, Winter and Bryson[14] have argued that it was these poor quality materials and construction that set these estates on a path to '...becoming a site of urban poverty'. Large quadrants of industry and commercial zones were also characteristic of estates built during this time. These manufacturing industries would have provided employment for the estate occupants; but by the time Downton began the UNESCO Growing Up in

Cities study of the neighbourhood in 1972, most of the industry had been relocated and the factories abandoned.

'"Flat, brown and not dissimilar to the table top I am speaking from". That was how I described the area to the general assembly of UNESCO in 1973.' (Peter Downton, 1996 interview)

In a summary of Downton's work in Braybrook, Lynch described the community in the following terms relative to other project sites: 'In Melbourne people think themselves as being at the bottom of society, even though their way of life in material terms is substantially higher than in Argentina, Mexico or Poland. If these Australians have hope for themselves or their children, it is to be somebody else and to get away.'[15] When describing specific problems of the area, Downton wrote in his country report: 'There is one primary fault in the outdoor public space in the study area — it is boring.'[16] In his final report to UNESCO, Peter Downton noted that the interviews with young people revealed a sense of boredom with the social, physical and educational environment. He also explained that the total area of open space locally available needed to be doubled to meet government standards.

Forgotten People

Twenty-five years after Downton, our project team returned to the original site of Braybrook. The focus of this visit was to replicate data collection methods and to put into practice participatory research methods involving young people in neighbourhood urban renewal.

When comparing Australian Bureau of Statistics data, it was evident the population profile of the 6425 people who now lived in Braybrook had changed dramatically in the time between the studies.[17] At the time of the original study, one in every ten residents was 10 through 15 years of age, whereas in 1997 this had substantially decreased to one in every 14. The number of young people between the ages of 10 through 15 in the neighbourhood was 450 at the time of the study, and 33% had parents whose place of origin was outside Australia. Comparison of ethnic diversity in 1972 reveals the local residents' place of birth was predominantly Australian (80%), with a small number of residents having been born in the United Kingdom (15%) and Mediterranean coun-

Figure 4.2 Braybrook community space: Skinners Reserve

© KAREN MALONE

tries (5%) . In contrast, by 1997 the origins of the residential population were approximately 67% Anglo-European Australian, 23% Asian, 4% South/Central American, 2% African and 4% from other locations. In 1972, demographic data also revealed that one-third of the population was classified as 'in poverty' with nearly half the male income earners in unskilled occupations. A similar picture emerged in 1997, with one-third of adult residents of working age unemployed, and of those with incomes, half earned less than 50% of the national average wage. Of the Braybrook unemployed, one-quarter were sole-parent families and 36% lived in rented public housing. These figures suggest that two-thirds of the residents of

Braybrook were living in poverty. This figure is supported by the 1996 socio-economic disadvantage index, which classified this community as the most disadvantaged neighbourhood in the state of Victoria. Disadvantaged status is measured by the residents' level of employment, qualifications, secondary school completion, individual and family income, and accommodation. In Victoria, the average socio-economic disadvantage index score is 1019; Braybrook scored 803[18]. The stigma of living in the estate as expressed by residents in the original study still prevails as this comment by one of the young people living there today reveals: 'Everyone thinks we're trash 'cause we live 'ere' (15 year old boy, 1997).

When the team replicated and analysed a historical photo-grid of the streetscapes, they found that other than deterioration due to age, the occasional fence and the maturing of trees, the core of the estate had changed

Figure 4.3 Photogrid reference 1972

Figure 4.4 Photogrid reference 1997

very little during the 25-year period. The types of outdoor places available in the estate in the 1970s, such as treeless flat parks or reserves, sporting ovals, and wild places such as the river, remained undeveloped and under-utilised. What had changed, however, were the surrounding commercial areas. A variety of commercial outlets now ringed the estate, adding to traffic and urban congestion, and air, visual and noise pollution. These outlets included video shops, large warehouse-style stores, car dealers, petrol stations, an entertainment centre, poker machine venues and a number of fast food stores.

According to local residents, the physical deterioration of the study area can be explained by two major factors. First, the Housing Commission Victoria[19] neglected to maintain the housing stock, and second, local city councils hesitated to invest in the development and maintenance of community infrastructure. Many community members believed inequitable distribution of monetary and human resources by the previous local council

TABLE 4.1

Community Profile Braybrook: 1972 and 1997

LAND AND POPULATION (1997 ONLY)

Land Area	488 hectares
Population	6425

PLACE OF BIRTH REGIONS	PERCENT OF POPULATION	
	1972 (1966 CENSUS)	1997 (1996 CENSUS)
Australia/Oceana	80%	56%
UK/Europe	15%	11%
Middle East	5%	1%
Asia	—	23%
South/Central America	—	4%
Africa	—	2%
Other	—	3%

AGE STRUCTURE	PERCENT OF POPULATION	
0–9 years	21%	14%
10–19 years	22%	14%
20–29 years	14%	14%
30–39 years	14%	15%
40–49 years	14%	12%
50–59 years	10%	8%
60+ years	3%	19%

TABLE 4.2

Participants Profile: 1997

NUMBER OF PARTICIPANTS

Female	18
Male	26

AGE (YEARS)	FEMALE	MALE
10	2	1
11	1	4
12	6	8
13	4	6
14	4	4
15	1	3

TIME LIVING IN NEIGHBOURHOOD		
0–6 months	1	0
6 months – 1 year	—	2
1–3 years	3	6
3–6 years	2	6
6–10 years	4	5
10 years plus	8	7

PLACE OF BIRTH	YOUTH		PARENTS	
	FEMALE	MALE	FEMALE	MALE
Australia	15	20	27	20
British Isles	—	—	3	8
Somalia	—	1	4	4
Vietnam	1	3	4	4
Mediterranean	—	2	2	3
South America	1	—	1	2
Tonga	—	—	1	1
New Zealand	1	—	1	1
Unknown	—	—	1	1

has meant that the community would maintain the stigma of being both fringe and marginal for a long period of time. As residents explained, both of these government bodies neglected the needs of the community over a period of 40 years,

'I am very unhappy about the historical neglect of the area. I have lived here for many years and I know what was promised for this community'...'We were the forgotten people in this area.' (Interviews with elderly residents, 1997)

Researching Youth

Understanding the reality of young people's lives is not just a question of identifying who they are and where they live. 'Children', 'youth', 'young people' are socially constructed concepts which, depending on young people's social, cultural and political circumstances, have different meanings in space and time. Young people as a cohort within society have very different needs and aspirations than other members of the community, and as a group their experiences are also very diverse and complex. Therefore, research design when working with young people needs to be flexible and interactive so it can respond adequately to these specific needs.

There were twenty 14 year old participants — 11 girls and 9 boys — in the original Braybrook study. All participants were students in their third year of secondary schooling (Year 9) at Braybrook High School (now Braybrook Secondary College). Based on the research guidelines set down by Lynch, Downton used multiple methods to gather data. He used objective measures of the economic, demographic and environmental features of the selected neighbourhood; the observations of young people's use of public and semi-public places; and phenomenological measures of young people's perceptions of their communities and their priorities for future change and improvement. The study also compared young people's perceptions with those of parents, municipal planners and officials. According to the final report compiled by Downton, '...The findings provided extremely practical and valuable information regarding young people's perception and use of the local environment — information that often countered official perceptions regarding young people's environmental needs and preferences.'[20]

Having a balance of ethnicity, age and gender was imperative in selecting the sample of participants for the 1997 Braybrook study. This was due to recent research in Australia and abroad which clearly identified that significant diversity in youth environmental behaviour was determined by age, gender and ethnic differences.[21]

A broad range of approaches was adopted when inviting young people to participate in the study. These approaches included contacting young people through the local schools, the neighbourhood temple, local shop-keepers, parents, and the manager of the recreation centre, as well as 'hanging' around the neighbourhood, putting up posters and running an article in the local newspaper. Following this process, a group of 44 young people were invited to participate. While these core 44 participants took part in all facets of the research, during the two-year research study over 100 young people between the ages of 10 and 15 participated in various phases of the study. Forms of participation included being interviewed, doing behaviour and spatial mapping exercises, photographing and videoing, drawing neighbourhood maps and pictures, creating time schedules, participating in workshops, and conducting city and neighbourhood tours. To ensure confidentiality and safety, young people were encouraged to select a site where they felt most at ease for the interviews. Most chose the local secondary school, with a small number being interviewed at a local community youth centre during a school holiday break. Table 4.2 provides a demographic profile of core participants.

While an attempt was made to replicate the original study as closely as possible, 25 years of shifting academic ground (including methodological, ethical and substantive issues) meant some of the data were not directly compatible for rigorous analysis. Most of the longitudinal analysis was based on determining changing patterns rather than alluding to specific trends. It is interesting to note also, in terms of 'generational trends,' that the timing between the original and the replication was 25 years, which meant that the parents of the children we spoke with in the replication could have been 14 year olds in the first study. We did attempt to locate children (now adults) from the original study but without success.

GEOGRAPHIES OF YOUTH

'Vandalism of trees and buildings is a result of alienation. Young people have been disenfranchised by the lack of access to recreational and support facilities: this has resulted in alienation and a lack of respect for the area.'
(Betty, an elderly resident who had lived in Braybrook for 38 years, community interviews, 1996)

Positioned as aliens in the social and physical architecture of our cities, young people in Australia are portrayed through media and police campaigns as deviant, barbaric and unclean — a threat to social order.[22] The visibility of youth and their competing use of street space has led to public demands for greater policing power to marginalise, exclude and remove young people from public view through the construction of imaginary boundaries.[23] There is concern that a focus on social order acts as a red herring that leads social discussions away from the core issues faced by young people and the poverty-stricken — the inequitable distribution of social resources.[24]

> *When asked to draw or map their neighbourhood, they often responded by creating images that were based on social rather than physical characteristics of the area.*

The politics of repressive interventions that accompany moral panics about underclass youth, such as media campaigns and policing practices to move on young people in streets, represent a response to public fear and an underlying attempt to eliminate ambiguity between categories of adult/child and public/private spaces. Through the categorisation of young people as intruders, they are located in a liminal zone — too old for playgrounds, too young to be valued consumers.[25] The geography of youth is complex. The following section represents the changing geography of youth by drawing on the data across the two study time frames to provide a picture of how living in Braybrook has changed for many young people.

Favourite Places

'Places constitute the basis for the discovery of the self, and caves or trees or even a corner of the house may be claimed as "my place". These childhood places frequently take on great significance and are remembered with reverence...both remembered and currently significant places are essential concentrations of meaning and intention within the broader structure of perceptual space.' [26]

Figure 4.5 Drawing by Anna (13 years old) of her neighourhood

Generally, young people in Braybrook described the neighbourhood as boring and dangerous, although this could be relative to neighbourhood experiences, as Sam's story reveals:

'My street is boring and quiet and 'nothin' much 'appens except well yesterday when a firebomb was thrown from a passing car at the house next door. I saw it from my lounge room window. And do you know it only took the fire brigade 15 minutes to arrive but the police didn't come for over 30 minutes.' (Sam, 15 year old, 1997)

Consequently, one of Sam's recommendations for neighbourhood change was faster police response time. Young people often described their neighbourhood through these stories or incidents — the child abducted from the street, the house that was burnt down, the hotel owner who was shot by drug dealers, the person who con-

tracted HIV/AIDS from stepping on a syringe. How do these stories of the neighbourhood compare with our imaginings of childhood spaces as places where children engaged in spontaneous play and adventure with their friends — as in the epigraph by Relph at the beginning of this section?

To determine if these young people had favourite places such as those expressed by Relph, the participants wrote a list of every place they knew and circled their favourite and most frequented places. The data were then interpreted using place categories of home and home sites, streets and associated spaces, formal developed open space, informal undeveloped open space, commercial places and community facilities. The home and home sites were most often nominated by girls as their favourite place, with boys nominating commercial places (video stores, shopping centres). Favourite and most frequented places correlated for girls — both were the home and home sites. Most girls interviewed fitted into the two groups of either carers or homebodies: that is, they either stayed at home or the home of friends so they could care for a sibling or because they had purposely retreated from the public domain.

'...well I have to look after my sister every night so I just stay home and watch television. Sometimes I might play in the street outside my house.' (15 year old girl, 1997)

The boys' favourite destinations were commercial facilities and their most frequented places were community centres, with the local community sports centre being the most likely destination. In all our discussions with young people, not one identified a 'natural place' as a favourite place — although a small group of roaming young boys often visited 'wild places' on the periphery of the neighbourhood. Owens,[27] in her 1992 study at a site close to Braybrook, also reported that the teenagers she interviewed did not frequently mention natural areas. Nature wasn't such a 'cool place.'

The 1997 results were not dissimilar to the responses of children interviewed by Downton in 1972, with a focus on home and friends' homes as the main site for socialising. Young people also specified sporting and social centres as favourite places in 1972 and 1997, with an emphasis on the social rather than physical aspects of the sporting endeavour.

'Sporting and social centres are the best place to be, because we meet our friends there.' (Composite answer, 14 year old boys, 1972)

In addition, there was evidence that a select group of young people in the 1970s study also favoured the river site (even though it was polluted) and the abandoned industrial sites. The river wilderness area and the abandoned building sites were used for unregulated play and risk taking. This was seen as a valued endeavour, and although considered dangerous by young people and their parents, it meant the young people had adopted a sense of ownership over these leftover neglected spaces in the neighbourhood.

As Relph[28] and others have explained, one indication of a sense of place is a person's ability to represent it in images, whereas an inability reflects 'placelessness.' In our story, the young people's placelessness could be described as a sense of apathy or ambivalence about their role in placemaking. When asked to draw or map their neighbourhood, they often responded by creating images that were based on social rather than physical characteristics of the area. In the majority of drawings, and the subsequent photographs they were asked to take of 'special places' in their neighbourhood, they showed very few public or natural spaces. Most drawings and photographs illustrated elements close to or in their homes (pets, family, friends, bedroom, and backyard); and in their drawings the icons that represented issues for them were things such as syringes, drugs, beer cans, cigarettes, and fast cars.[29]

Although they often portrayed the neighbourhood negatively, when one young woman heard negative comments about the neighbourhood, she was obviously affronted: 'Yeah, people call it a trashy place, but I love it, its me 'ome.' This comment exemplifies another tension many young people expressed about their neighbourhood — to portray it negatively but also to defend it if others spoke of it harshly. It illustrates that although often despondent and ambivalent about the neighbourhood's significance in their lives, the young people had a

shared meaning of what it meant to grow up in Braybrook and had claimed it as their place. This was further evident in the Streetspace project, which will be discussed in the final section of this chapter.

> *As our research revealed, the young people were frequently excluded on the grounds they 'could' be disruptive to others.*

Activity Spaces

In both the 1972 and 1997 studies young people were asked to provide a time schedule which included everything they did in a typical day. The 1972 data revealed that most of spare out-of-school time was taken up watching television. Many of the children spoke about feeling 'bored.' One of the least identified activities was 'messing around outdoors' in public spaces.

'It is boring, there is nothing to do.' (14 year old boy, 1972)

From an open list of favourite activities developed from time schedules in 1997, boys nominated playing sport six times as often as any other activity. The favourite activities of girls were (in order of preference) playing sport, messing around with friends and watching television. An analysis of the girls' time-use schedules revealed that the activities they spent most time doing included messing around with friends, watching television and hanging out in the streets close to their homes. Lack of safety limited the capacity for many young girls to access places for activity.

'Trashy and there's nothing for kids to do, 'cause there's needles everywhere. Everyone, nearly everyone does drugs.' (13 year old girl, 1997)

'I [with my friend] go into the backyard and just talk.' (14 year old girl, 1997)

When analysing the boys' time schedules, it was evident that even though many of them spent time at the community sports centre and listed playing sport as a favourite activity, very few of them actually played a sport. In fact, the boys spent most of their time watching television, messing around with friends or hanging around in the street. When asked what they did when messing around with their friends they replied, 'hung around outside the sports centre' or 'stayed at home'.

Considering that playing sport was an activity often nominated by participants and that a large sports complex existed in the neighbourhood, it seemed inconsistent that many of the time-use schedules revealed that most young people did not use this facility. Exploration of this discrepancy revealed complex issues in regard to the facility. First, many girls were afraid to walk to the facility. In addition, young people had to pay an entrance fee even as spectators, and once inside could not use the facilities unless they were a bona fide member of a team. Hence the only place to socialise and be playful was the spectators stand, which was noisy and congested. The best option it seemed for most young visitors to the facility was to hang around outside and watch young people from other neighbourhoods coming and going. The management saw this activity as inappropriate and was concerned that these young people's presence deterred other visitors to the centre, made the place look untidy and encouraged possible 'criminal' activity. Consequently, the young people were often 'moved on', causing animosity and occasional violent outbursts between them and the management.

> *Moving around and taking up space in the neighbourhood was a much easier task in the early 1970s.*

Without legitimate user status as consumers, young people are often harassed or labelled as troublemakers if they hang around community facilities. Yet in this neighbourhood the sports facility was one of the few places where young people felt safe and stimulated. It potentially offered shelter from the streets, adult supervision, and a vibrant and playful environment to interact with others. As our research revealed, the young people were frequently excluded on the grounds they 'could' be disruptive to others.

To add further substance to the analysis of young people's time use, the research team in 1997 asked young people to identify with whom they spent time. The results illustrated that gender and ethnicity were a determining factor in social interaction. Most young people nominated 'friends' but a large percentage (around 40%) of boys chose 'alone.' Of the boys who spent time alone, most were from non-English-speaking backgrounds and of Asian origin. Asian girls, on the other hand, were perceived to be 'at risk' when left alone after school and were often billeted with grandparents or other relatives in neighbouring suburbs. In contrast to these minority youth, African boys tended to congregate in groups. Because of the limited space in their homes (many African families had up to 12 members), they used the streets as their communal point and as a cultural and symbolic marker of masculine dialogue. The boys told us they met on the street to talk about family issues, share experiences and build alliances. Many of the boys were the male head of their family unit and carried the burden of this responsibility. Because of this visibility and the perception that a group of young people constitutes a 'gang', they evoked fear in the local community. Consequently many of them experienced verbal abuse and harassment from police, as the following story written by a young African boy reveals:

'Coming to Australia is not bad but there is still lots of discrimination against black people. Police often discriminate against us. Once we [a group of Somalian boys] were walking on the street and a police car stopped and asked me for my name and address for no reason. He said to me "don't speak in bloody African language." This made me feel really angry because he didn't respect my language or culture. He pushed my friend over when he came to help.'
(16 year old Somalian boy, personal newsletter entry, 1997)

Moving around and taking up space in the neighbourhood was a much easier task in the early 1970s. Two-thirds of young people interviewed in 1972 considered that they were able to go wherever they wished in their neighbourhood and the city. Their movements were not inhibited by such contemporary constraints as policing or regulation, but rather by lack of money, sibling responsibility, not many places to go to, and nothing to do when they got there. Downton wrote: 'Most spaces are rendered almost unusable for children by lack of development on the one hand and restrictions limiting their use to "polite" activities only — walking, standing and talking are allowed.'[30] Even though young people generally felt more able to move freely in their neighbourhood in 1972, the most frequent recreational activity was watching television.

'I can go where I want to provided I tell Mum and there is somebody with me — mostly though I stay home and watch television.' (14 year old girl, 1972)

Roaming Range

'… to be a child outside adult supervision, visible on city centre streets, is to be out of place.' [31]

Public spaces can provide young people arenas in which to experience and explore their world or they can become sites of conflict and struggle. Young people 'doing nothing' on a street corner can be seen by adults as unproductive and dangerous. Yet it would be wise for adults to realise that young people hanging off a lamp post, playing soccer with a discarded soft drink can, or sitting in the open area of a shopping centre are engaging in a complex alternative narrative: narratives of self-display, assessing of themselves in relation to others, and developing cultural codes. These 'antics' are essential if young people are to construct a spatial identity and be enabling agents of their environment, instead of victims of it.[32] These activities have their own internal logic — a logic often ignored by the policing agents, the shopkeepers, or the passers-by who view their play as an intrusion into the order and structure of public space. Constantly 'moved on', these young people can only question the rationale of secular and exclusive societal values — aren't we public too?

Young people in the revisited GUIC study were asked to construct maps of their normal activity space to illustrate the extent of their roaming range.[33] Their use of the neighbourhood environment generally included no more then one or two blocks from their homes. During mapping exercises, they described places in the environment

Over 80% of both boys and girls commented in interviews that they believed there were dangerous places in their neighbourhood.

that they avoided, such as certain streets where house occupants were identified as potentially dangerous or reserves where syringes were likely to be found. As a 14 year old girl observed, 'Parks are dangerous…because sometimes you find needles…I don't go there.' (1997)

Over 80% of both boys and girls commented in interviews that they believed there were dangerous places in their neighbourhood. One in every 10 girls stated that everywhere in the neighbourhood was dangerous:

'Everywhere is dangerous especially at night — I can hear the drunk people yelling and that up at the flats when I'm in bed and I get scared.' (13 year old girl, 1997)

Streets were recognised by one third of the young people as the place where they felt most in danger. Both boys and girls listed drugs, alcohol, and physical and verbal abuse as the primary cause of fear in the streets. This was due to adults or adult activities (drug taking, drunkenness, policing). For girls, verbal abuse was normally related to incidents of sexual harassment, and for young people from non-English-speaking backgrounds, it was racial abuse and discrimination. Young people talking about dangers in the streets said:

'Normally we cut through the flats to come to the shops… I'm a bit scared, in case someone's there in the alleyway… People who take drugs and stuff, they don't know what they're doing once they've taken them.' (14 year old girl, 1997)
'When walking back from YCW[34] at night, 'cause it's all dark near there, so I just carry a stick.' (14 year old boy, 1997)

In contrast, in Downton's study it was physical and natural elements of the environment that were most likely to be identified by young people as a danger for them. Roads and railway lines were often mentioned due to their large volumes of traffic, and the river because of its isolated location and the risks of getting a snake bite or being swept away by the river current. These places represented possible physical risk — the very attribute that attracted many boys to them. Girls in 1972 spoke of a similar fear as their counterparts in 1997 — the fear of the unpredictable or unknown person in the streets at night:

'Anything can happen to you! Hoods — people — out to get you. You can't be safe anywhere really! People jump out at you in the dark.' (14 year old girl, 1972)

Although young people presented drug use and trafficking as major concerns in 1997, according to local police statistics these were no longer problems. Despite reassuring statements by police in the media, we were hesitant to dismiss the young people's fear of the streets. Staffing cutbacks and delayed police responses (as noted by Sam, above) had meant many crimes went unreported or undetected in the neighbourhood. We were also aware that a history of tension between young people and police could influence perceptions of what constitutes harm to youth.

'Acting Detective Inspector John Johnson said… "there is nothing in our statistics to reflect that crime against young people is a major problem in Braybrook" …He said he was surprised by the results of the UNESCO study… "We have had times, in years gone by, where there have been problems with crimes against youth but that is very much resolved".'[35]

This focus on drugs and the influence of a fear of crime on young people's spatial range was not evident in Downton's original study. Street dangers and fights were mentioned by the young people in 1972, particularly around the local football club on a Saturday night after a big match, but most young people stated it was easy to avoid these places so it didn't really impact their own activities. In the original study, young people still felt able to use the neighbourhood as an environment to explore and play in — even though mostly they didn't bother! For young people in 1997 the picture was very different. Most young people living in the neighbourhood feared being victimised in public spaces and either limited their movements to specific times of the day and locations or only moved around in large groups.

Changes for the Future

During the interviews, young people were asked to express their views about how they thought the neighbourhood might change in the future. In 1972 some young people thought it would get better, others thought it would get worse; while half were not sure how the changes would impact the area, they acknowledged there

Figure 4.6 During interviews most young people said they needed safe places that would allow them to get away from their families and socialise with friends.

would be changes. Many expected that families of different nationalities would occupy the area, and some hoped conditions would improve with better facilities, improved buildings and services. Most of the young people expected increased crowding, pollution, noise and traffic. Young people 25 years later generally felt that the neighbourhood was going through a period of transformation. The advent of new medium density housing replacing the abandoned factories and houses, the projected doubling of the population due to this new housing, and the development of a large shopping complex on the estate's perimeter may be some of the reasons why many young people in Braybrook felt unsure of the future. Many others, however, expressed the view that any changes in the historically stagnant and neglected environment would be an improvement.

When asked for ideas for changing the neighbourhood, young people in 1997 focused on both social and physical changes. For instance, changes included cleaning up the physical dangers in the neighbourhood such as broken glass, syringes and rubbish, as well as evicting people who were likely to be the cause of these problems, such as prostitutes, drug dealers and users. On a more personal level, most young people said they needed places that enabled them to get away from their families and socialise with friends in a safe environment where they wouldn't be hassled.

CONSTRUCTING YOUTH

'Analysis of youth subcultures explores the ways in which young people attempt to resolve contradictions of their age and situation, often producing distinctive perspectives and behaviour.'[36]

To perceive Braybrook youth as one homogeneous culture, a single 'youth' stereotype, would be to reiterate the same mistaken assumptions of the media and authorities and gravely underestimate the complexities of the young people's lives.[37] This is especially true in the 1990s, with the high ethnic diversity of the neighbourhood and the impact this has from a cultural and social perspective. To understand their behaviours, universal images of youth need to be put aside. This is not to say that young people defy all classification and that there are no points of similarity in their behaviour. When grouping and naming distinct aspects of youth culture, it is imperative to be mindful that behaviours are fluid and transitional, just as identity is never static. Being 'young' is a temporary time in a person's life, and the analysis of youth culture highlights the ambiguity of being positioned as child, youth and adult.

To begin our discussion on the construction of youth identities, we start with an exploration into the influence of gender, ethnicity and age. Supporting earlier research findings, gender, ethnicity and age turned out to be deciding factors in young people's ability and desire to use specific facilities in the neighbourhood. Using their stories, we grouped together loosely young people who

exhibited similar environmental behaviours. There were four main groups that represented the constructed identity of youth in Braybrook: roamers, carers, homebodies and groupies. To illustrate these groupings of Braybrook youth, four stories have been compiled from interview transcripts. Meg (girl, 15) and Butler (boy, 12) are from Anglo-Saxon descent and have been living in the neighbourhood most of their lives. In contrast, Lu (girl, 14) and Ali (boy, 16) come from non-English-speaking-background families. Lu is Vietnamese, Ali is Somalian. The final discussion is an analysis of the changing geographies of youth and their influence on identity construction.

Gender, Ethnicity and Age

Gender, ethnicity and age are deciding factors in young people's ability to use recreational time and facilities — where they go and what they do. These three controlling factors and their real life combinations can clearly be seen in the young people's personal stories. The one aspect under which all the young people suffer is age. There is not a lot of entertainment specifically for young people, as they are not a section of society with great economic resources. With the privatisation of sport and entertainment facilities, their access has become even more limited. In addition, adults often complain if older children use playgrounds designed for the younger children. Competition over leisure resources means tension between adults and young people, and between groups of young people.

> *There were four main groups that represented the constructed identity of youth in Braybrook: roamers, carers, homebodies and groupies.*

Because of their age and the lack of physical resources, most young people in Braybrook had a limited capacity to find alternative spaces when tensions arose. In fact, very few young people knew or used facilities in neighbouring towns. In the original report, Downton commented on journeys by young people outside of their neighbourhood:

'The usual means of transport are cars, or some form of public transport. Neither type is conducive to increasing the children's knowledge of other areas, cars because only limited attention is paid to the route taken and the surroundings are seen in a limited fashion and at speed, and public transport because set routes are followed and new knowledge is not gained.'[38]

The same comment is applicable today. Most of the young people's parents are either very poor, working long hours or single, and therefore unable to provide their children with opportunities for extended discovery. Consequently, young people in Braybrook are growing up with limited environmental experiences. This point was really evident when the students from the local secondary college were taken on a bus tour of different playgrounds and facilities around Melbourne. Most of the 13 year olds had never been over the bridge that separates the industrial west from green leafy eastern suburbs. As a consequence of the tension in their own neighbourhood and the lack of exploration into other neighbourhoods, children retreat to what is becoming teenage space — the lounge room or den.

> *Most of the 13 year olds had never been over the bridge that separates the industrial west from green leafy eastern suburbs.*

The retreat to their homes and reliance on home-based resources has meant entertainment such as video, computers and electronic games have become their major leisure pursuits. These results conform to the results of Lawrence and colleagues which found that, 'Time devoted to watching television has usurped time previously devoted to other mass media and has eaten into portions of time previously spent on other activities.'[39] These young people, like other young people around the world, have connected with the global community through chat-lines on the World Wide Web or with American icons such as basketball heroes and McDonalds. Many parents may complain of the sedentary lifestyles of their teenagers,

but until public spaces become socially cohesive and integrated, many young people will continue to find the reclusive and safe environments of their homes a much more appealing alternative.

Ethnicity accounted for many differences in environmental behaviour and, along with age, seemed to influence young people to become *homebodies*. Braybrook has changed from being a homogeneous Anglo culture to having great ethnic diversity, including many Vietnamese and Africans. Asian boys in particular were a small group who were evidently leading much more reclusive lives than other young people. In the competition over public space and recreational resources, most of the Vietnamese youth have opted for home entertainment, leaving street resources to the Anglo and African groups. Many of the Vietnamese youth told stories of being subjected to racial torment, and other than going to and from school, opted to stay indoors. As Lu's story in the next section illustrates, Asian girls are closely protected by their families and are rarely seen in public. Even the boys tend to spend more time with their computers and television than with friends. In our interviews, it was the Vietnamese boys who most often stated that the person they spent most time with was themselves, 'alone'. Many of the Vietnamese youth spoke of connections with the Vietnamese cultural community, either through the Buddhist temple or by visiting relatives in nearby Footscray, which has a large Vietnamese community and is often referred to as 'little Vietnam'.

The African boys, whatever age they may be, were active street users. They frequented the streets as inclusive mixed-age groups. Older boys assumed responsibility for the young boys and socialised them in the ways of the masculine African culture. The Africans were specific about the role of the streets as a place for discussing family business and sharing the burden of being the male head of the family. In situations where the home environments were very crowded, the street became a sanctuary. Although this identity as *groupies* helped maintain cohesive bonds between the African families, these street meetings caused a lot of anguish for locals who saw the clusters of boys as a threat to public safety. Because of their physical presence and their predisposition to loitering on street corners, groupies were constantly under the gaze of the community and policing agencies. The police were often called to disperse them, which meant ongoing conflict.

Gender was another significant factor in determining patterns of spatial behaviour. Girls, also in need of equal opportunities for play and socialisation in community life, were often more restricted than the boys. Many of the girls spent most of their leisure time in the family home or in the homes of friends. In part, this was due to the demands placed on them to be *carers* of siblings in the absence of adults. In the case of the African and Asian girls, spatial restrictions were also a formal element of cultural customs. In addition, safety and danger were significant restraining factors in girls' spatial mobility — with many of them staying close to their home because of fears of sexual harassment. Our research revealed that these differences in environmental behaviour due to gender were significant, and that because girls are often invisible in public space, special attention must be given to involve girls in the evaluation of their neighbourhoods. In contrast, those with the widest range of movement through Braybrook — the *roamers* — were typically young boys.

Roamers

Roamers are young people, generally Anglo boys between the ages of 12 and 14, who wander at large over their own and other neighbourhoods, either alone or in small groups of twos or threes. The street offers them opportunities for discovery and exploration, and the street and its associated spaces are their playgrounds. It is this group that had the most extended roaming range. This range was attributed to their lack of parental constraints and because, being so young, they weren't a threat to the older street frequenting boys. Although some girls also used the streets, they tended to restrict their movements to specified times and places and did not hang around the streets or socialise with the street frequenting boys. Butler's story illustrates the playfulness of the roamers, who are constantly moving on and 'looking for action.'

Figure 4.7 Butler's neighbourhood drawing

Butler

'The best fun is to throw stones at rabbits and goannas[40] but you have to be careful of drowning in the river, or of snakes in the long grass of the vacant land. Broken glass, used needles and rubbish are pretty bad. Druggies and weirdos too, they're everywhere around here. Nothing much happens around here 'cept a few weeks ago the deli got held up by an armed robber. They should make it so the cops come faster. But you've got to watch the cops too, 'cause they hassle ya. Even if you're just walking along or standing around in a group. I always watch TV in the morning before I walk to school. I ride my bike to a friend's house and leave it there so it doesn't get nicked at school. I like to play footy but I didn't make the local team. Anyway it costs too much. I do a few chores around the house but that doesn't affect my amount of hanging out time. Most of the time I spend roamin' around streets with my mates, at the Youth Centre or sometimes I go play video games at the Go-Kart track. But usually I haven't got any money. I feel comfortable wherever I am, as long as there are no Chinese [Asians]. Braybrook is much better now that the new video superstore has come. On most nights we get fish and chips or pizza and watch videos. Mum and Dad work late so I'm at home alone. I could stay till late at a friend's house but it's too dangerous getting home after dark. I can always play on the computer. I eat at McDonalds as much as I can but I wish it was closer to my house — you have to cross a really busy road to get to it.'

Groupies

Groupies are the older youth, generally male but not necessarily so, who use the street space for recreation but in a different manner than the younger children. As visible entities on the streets, they generally move and gather in collectives. Unlike their younger counterparts who are involved in a process of exploration, their primary purpose of hanging out is to socialise and take up territorial ownership of the streets. These sociable young people have usually been roamers and are therefore reasonably comfortable and familiar with the street environment.

Ali

'I left Somalia when I was thirteen and after spending almost a year in refugee camps in Kenya and Queensland, my family ended up in Braybrook with my parents and ten brothers and sisters. We all live in a house. Like the other African boys, we stand out because we're tall and have black skin. So we are often hassled by police and Anglo youths. They got no respect. So we hang together in a large group, even the young ones, but some of the locals find it intimidating. In a group we go where we want, we stick together and make decisions. But I think Braybrook is fun. There are basketball and soccer fields near my home. Braybrook is not dangerous, me and my friends we know each other from the refugee camps. We know how to stop fights. We like the Youth Centre, but sometimes we have to be strong to get the basketball equipment. People are jealous because we play the best, we're the tallest. We can't use the Recreation Centre much because of the cost, and all the sport is teams. Also there are so many rules at the Recreation Centre that they always get angry at us for not behaving normally. They don't like us hanging around. If I have money I like to go and eat KFC fried chicken. We're all Muslim and on the weekends we go to a special school to maintain our own culture. I also play soccer for an African team in a neighbouring suburb. It's hard for us to get into the Aussie way of life, since even when we have money to go to the movies or play video games people won't let us and use us as the scapegoats for any local trouble. When we enter shops the shop owner he treats us with great suspicion. We don't have much to do with the Anglos. But we do with the Anglo girls, 'cause we're cool. The African girls you don't

see. Because they are good Muslim girls and stay at home, covered up. I can go anywhere I want, but it is better to go with friends. Some of the other kids don't like Africans, especially at the Youth Centre and the Recreation Centre. I prefer to 'chuck hoops' with friends at some of the local school yard basketball courts. Unfortunately we have to climb over high fences to get in and there is always the chance of being chased off. Then the adults think we are bad and blame us for everything. One day I'm going to leave here.'

Figure 4.8 Ali's neighbourhood drawing

Carers

Carers are usually girls who spend much of their free time looking after younger siblings either because their families have broken up or because of cultural expectations. In their free time and sometimes with younger siblings in tow, they join in the street activities of the boys. There are also those carers who remain invisible, such as the African and Asian girls who take on a caring role in extended families. These girls remain invisible (physically and socially) for cultural and religious reasons, and if encountered in the streets they shy away from entering into dialogue with others. Some of the carers may also simultaneously be homebodies if they choose to spend their free time at home alone or at a friend's house rather than in the public domain. Meg's story is typical of a young person in this group. Her story illustrates how, because she is a girl who has taken on a caring role in the absence of her parents, she has limited time for leisure activities.

Meg

'My house is just behind Skinners Reserve. My mum works until late in the evenings and after school I've got to go home to look after my younger sister and my grandmother who lives in a flat at the rear of the house. I have to cook the meals while I babysit. I usually watch TV or talk to my friends on the telephone. Heaps of my friends also have to stay at home to babysit. There's nothing in Braybrook to do. It would be good if there were some seats and playthings, rollerblade stuff in the park, in the shade, then we could talk there and mind the others. I only feel safe in the parks when other people are using them and I only go with friends. Too many weirdos and junkies — there's needles and bongs everywhere, especially in the abandoned houses. There's heaps of broken glass. Even when I'm free

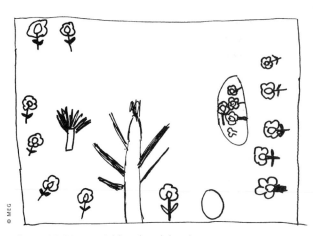

Figure 4.9 Meg's neighbourhood drawing

there's nothing much to do so mainly I just hang out at the local Youth Centre with some of my mates, but it can be pretty rough with some of the boys. My mum worries about where I am and prefers me to stay close to home. There are no organised activities anymore at the Youth Centre. I just go there to meet up with friends and because it is close to home. On the weekend me and my girlfriends go and watch the guys play footy and basketball at the local ovals and Recreation Centre. Footy, cricket and basketball, that's all

there really is to play around here and since I don't like to play any of those we just go and watch. I like to go to the cinema at the local shopping complex but it seems a long way to go so we don't go too much. The best would be if they had dances and raves here, so we could have somewhere to meet people. Usually they're held in a neighbouring suburb so they're hard to get to and mum says no. Even if we walked, everywhere in Braybrook is too dangerous after dark. People jump out at you from behind bushes and alleyways. When I'm walking around I don't go very far and not near the old abandoned houses. I always use streets I know — sometimes that means taking longer to get there but it's safer. Braybrook's getting worse for sure, especially recently with more trucks, fast cars and the abandoned homes. You have to watch out for strangers and we all know stories about dangerous strangers and crime around here. I know where to avoid, you've got to. Even which houses, like the druggies' houses or where they got big dogs. It's better to be at someone's house where you can watch TV.'

Homebodies

Some older youth choose to move away from their earlier youthful roaming behaviour and retreat to their home space where television and computer games become their main activities. Other young people often affectionately refer to them as homebodies. They are no longer part of the visible street frequenting youth.

Lu

'I don't like staying home all the time like most of my Vietnamese girlfriends. Their parents say it is dangerous but since we came from Vietnam five years ago I think it's quite safe. When I'm feeling adventurous and with friends we will visit the park by the river where I have a favourite spot near what I call the waterfall, but it's really the drainage pipe from the factory overlooking the park. My house is an average household with a large garden and a white fence in a friendly neighbourhood. It's sort of green vegetation, um, lots of wildlife like birds and things like that and people generally. To me Braybrook is a good place to live, but there are not many good parks for us to enjoy. Going to the city to window shop and have dinner in a restaurant when

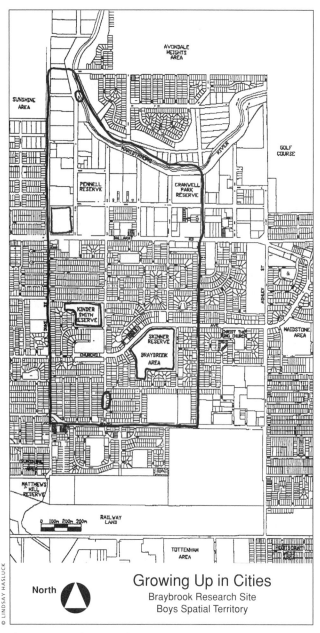

Figure 4.10 Butler's spatial map

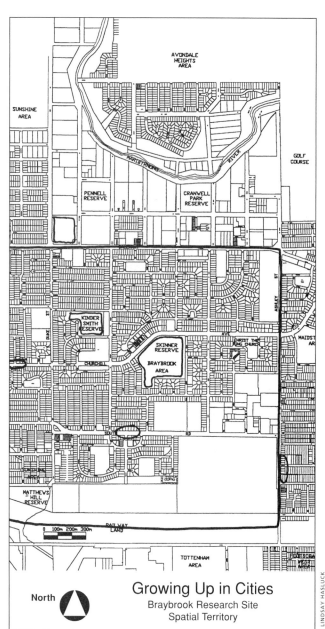

Figure 4.11 Ali's spatial map

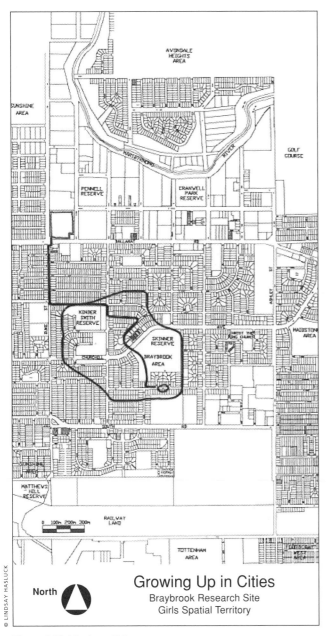

Figure 4.12 Meg's spatial map

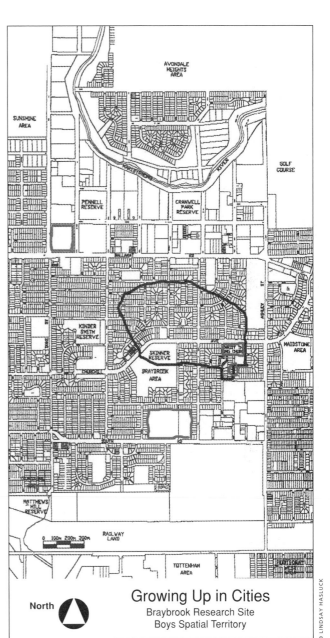

Figure 4.13 Lu's spatial map

my cousin is driving — that I like. I like the shops and busy streets, especially around Chinatown, so different from the quiet emptiness of Braybrook. The quiet streets, especially the back streets and around the public housing flats, seem really scary to me, especially if I'm alone.[41] My main fear is people, all people. The area just doesn't feel safe, so my friends and me use the parks and avoid hanging out on the street. The play at the Youth Centre is too rough and my parents have too many concerns about it. I'm Buddhist, so is Mum and Dad, so we often go to the temple. On Saturdays I have to go to a Vietnamese school where I learn about my own culture and language. The school is located in Footscray nearby, but we always drive. I find it tiresome and boring, then Sundays I have to spend with my sister and parents, which is good but sometimes I want to do my own thing. Like I like to read a book or visit my relatives, even though many of them (one grandmother, five uncles and four aunties) live only a few streets away. Until recently we all shared two houses in the same street, but it became too

Figure 4.14 Lu's neighbourhood drawing

crowded and my parents moved to another house close by. I go to Grandma's after school until Mum and Dad get back from work in the evening. I always do my homework there, or in the morning because Dad has to drop us off really early on his way to work and I walk my sister to her school on the way. I suppose though mostly I spend time at home.'

Inversion and Retreat

'I would there were no age between ten and three and twenty, or that youth would sleep out the rest; for there is nothing in between but getting wenches with child, wronging the ancientry, stealing, fighting.'
William Shakespeare, *The Winter's Tale,* Act III: Scene iii

Youth hanging out and the fear it evokes are not new phenomena. Shakespeare's lament mirrors much of contemporary discourse on the idleness and deviancy of youth in the streets. In the current climate of fear of crime and the subsequent fragmentation of the public sphere, evidence suggests that young people are being extradited to the margins of our public spaces. Loukataitou-Sideris believes the current fragmentation of the public sphere is caused by fear, suspicion, tension and conflict between social groups and is resulting in an attempt to segregate space in terms of legitimate and illegitimate user groups.[42]

Contrary to media hype and community perceptions, young people in Braybrook are not taking over the streets: the majority of young people in this neighbourhood spend very little time in public spaces. The invisible youth — the carers and the homebodies — spent most of their time close to or in their homes and the homes of friends. Their retreat from the public domain is a direct consequence of exclusionary factors in the social and physical environment. In contrast, visible youth were in the minority, had wider and more diverse territorial ranges and were more indifferent to the impact of repressive interventions and exclusionary narratives. The visible youth fit into the two categories of roamers and groupies. The roamers, although visible, posed less of a threat to the community because of their age, lack of physical presence and mobility. This group was often identified as being a public nuisance with their mischievous criminal acts of vandalism and graffiti. When found in public places they were often harassed and accused of causing damage. For these reasons most chose abandoned or out of way places to meet and plan their antics.

Tensions over the social and physical boundaries can cause changes in the dynamics of the street. Inversions, caused by the retreat of those who would normally occupy the streets, can recast the neighbourhood residents as spectators and allow those normally hidden to take up ownership. Morgan provided an interesting recent elucidation of these phenomena: 'An ironic contrast can be drawn between the fear of a dense public sociability at the turn of the century and the contemporary fear of urban crime which is based on a lack of sociability in street spaces that are not occupied or controlled.'[43]

> *The team realised that, even when given the opportunties to create a 'youth' space, young people want to be integrated into community life.*

Influenced by the exaggeration or 'beat up' of youth- and drug-related issues by the media and the police, parents feared that if young people were in public spaces, they were likely to get caught up in deviant behaviour, either as victims or perpetrators. 'Hanging out' or even just 'going out' was determined not to be a safe option for many young people. Witness this extract from a girl's letter to a friend outside the neighbourhood:[44]

Dear Jessica Trinh,
Hi how's it going? It's been a while you haven't visited my place. So I think I'll inform you of all the glory and traumatic changes that happened in my neighbourhood. The crime rate is really high. Last night my next door neighbours had burglars attack…Mate, the most traumatic thing is that all the young guys in my neighbourhood are turning into drug addicts. These issues are turning my parents into freaks. Believe me it's worst on me because my freedom percentage is zero at the moment. Gosh I can't even take the dog for a walk. (14 year old girl, 1998)

Parents also recited stories of violence, based on local history or imaginary, to dissuade their children from hanging around the streets. To negotiate fears, young people either limited their movements or only moved around in groups. Adopting the strategy of staying in groups often meant that they were targeted as 'gangs.' To prevent this outcome, they hung around in dangerous

places (for example behind shops or in secluded areas of parks), thus increasing the likelihood of becoming a victim. Polzot, in her study of young people in Sydney, found similar behaviours: 'Young people felt they were getting mixed messages about how they should behave in community spaces from police, security guards, the media and parents. For example, young people were told to stay in groups for safety whilst at the same time being asked to disperse and move on.'[45]

Fortunately the story of Braybrook represents the extreme rather than the norm in Australian society, yet many elements of it are replicated in communities around the nation. Fear of young people and the consequential sanctioning of measures to regulate and exclude them have resulted in a form of self-policing. The groupies, the dangerous youth, were thought to stalk the streets seeking innocent youngsters who might fall prey to their influences. Therefore, even these youth retreated to less visible public spaces. In Braybrook we find a situation not dissimilar to Foucault's panopticon phenomena.[46] Young people, such as Foucault's imaginary inmates of the panopticon, do not know when they are under surveillance; they may or may not be watched. In reality they are watching themselves. James, Prout and Jenks echo this sentiment when they exclaim: 'modernity's child, at school, on the street and even at home, becomes its own policeman.'[47] Responding to the outcomes of the research and these interpretations, the focus for the action phase of the project inevitably became street behaviour and street space.

Campaigns in Australia to alleviate the tensions between different public space users have mostly focused on the removal of young people from the streets to designated youth spaces. These spaces often take on the form of leftover or marginal areas, such as a corner in the basement of a shopping mall or an open space on the outskirts of town. In addition to these areas presenting a series of safety and mobility problems for young people, their appeal is contrary to the very attraction of public space — the opportunity to partake in community life. These solutions only reinforce perceptions that young people are undervalued and illegitimate users of public space — out of sight, out of mind. For this reason, and to provide an opportunity to be active in the reconstruction and design of their neighbourhood, the GUIC project team developed a proposal in conjunction with a local secondary school and the state Arts Council to conduct the 'Streetspace' project.

STREETSPACE

Think of a city and what comes to mind? Its streets.[48]

Youth Needs

Participatory workshops conducted after the interview phase of the 1997 GUIC project reinforced findings that many young people were experiencing a sense of disconnection with their physical, natural and social environment. To respond to these feelings, over a length of time the GUIC group developed a comprehensive list of the resources young people need in their local environment in order for them to feel good about themselves. The list is presented below.[49]

Responding to the list, an issues paper was sent to the local City Council highlighting what we had prioritised with the children as being the most significant issue

for them — *secure and safe corridors for moving around the urban environment without harassment, regulation and surveillance.*

Unfortunately, the Council had already initiated a community development process which, although participatory and community-oriented in rhetoric, was pragmatically constructed in terms of community needs as adult needs and youth as a problem. To provide a more positive outcome for the research and one which involved the young people in an authentic change process where they actually had power over its direction, the team applied for funding from the Arts Council of Victoria and the Ministry of Education under the Artists and Environmental Designers in Schools project (AEDIS). The project was to conduct a school-based environmental design project with 50 young people from ages 12 through 14. Called Streetspace, the project commenced in 1998 during the second semester at Braybrook Secondary College. The proposal submission stated:

'Streetspace is an environmental design project engaging young people and an environmental designer in a creative, innovative and community driven urban street design project. The project will give the opportunity for the envi-

---

BOX 4.1

A List of What Young People Need:

Unregulated places, whether privately or publicly owned, where they can congregate without undue harassment, surveillance or intervention by adults.

Diversity of public spaces ranging from their immediate environment to places for them to meet in neighbouring communities, thus expanding their spatial range, lived experiences and interaction with other young people.

Safe and secure meeting places which are well lit, private, diverse (to be able to meet individual needs and respect gender and ethnic differences) and accessible via private or public transport.

Flexible places in terms of shelter, indoor and outdoor areas.

Authentic input into decision-making over the use of public places and choices about the ways and times for utilising these areas.

Variety in the dimension, size and malleability of places, ranging from large and small commercial areas and community facilities, to informal undeveloped open spaces and formal developed open spaces.

Secure and safe corridors for moving around the urban environment without harassment, regulation or surveillance.

Facilities which encourage, consolidate and allow identification and connection with the surrounding physical, social and natural environment of their community.

Opportunities to engage in discussions with others about their concerns, needs and aspirations and have their views listened to and acted on.

A list compiled by the young people of Braybrook while engaged in participatory workshops with the Growing Up in Cities project team, October 1997.

*ronmental designer to share with young people her exper-
tise and experiences in working on landscape, streetscape
and installation designs.*

*Streetspace focuses on urban space and how streets play an
important role in people's movement and flow around urban spaces.*

*Streetspace is about capturing the spirit and essence of
movement and flow in creative and physical forms (built
and natural).*

*Streetspace is about designing and creating streetscapes
that encourage young people, and others, to venture out
into the streets and enjoy the urban environment.'*

Youth Action

While Streetspace was presented as a formal curriculum
subject in a school setting, it was ultimately about creating resources and opportunities for the 50 young people
to embark on a physical and intellectual exploration of
their urban environment.[50] The local neighbourhood
became the outdoor classroom, resource centre and library. The young people became designers, educators
and researchers. While the task was challenging and the
students anything but easy, the teachers and the project
team decided to attempt as much autonomy as possible
for individual student learning. An important aspect of
this approach was opportunities for dialogue between
the project team members and the students. For this an
online e-mail link was developed between the project
team and the school. At the beginning of the project, students were asked to send a message to the team describing their neighbourhood:

*Hello, we go to Braybrook Secondary College in a special
suburb called Braybrook. Our neighbourhood is special
because there are a lot of Multi-cultural children. ...We are
working on a project for Streetspace. We are having a lot of
fun and enjoyment at our school, from all of us.*

(Age, Stacka, Jacky Chan and Woody)

*Hi, my area is very busy and loud. I have moved here five
years ago. There are lots of trucks, trees, cars and shops. I
don't like it because it is too noisy.* (Kimberlee)

The students were involved in a number of activities

Figure 4.15 Streetspace bus tour of the city

throughout the ten-week project. As an initial exercise
they took a bus tour around the city. The trip exposed the
young people's limited environmental literacy and persuaded the team to explore even further possibilities of
enriching the environment both in terms of structured
content and unstructured exploration. It also reminded
us that when tough kids are given the opportunity to be
stimulated, they forget to be bullies. Consider an extract
from the researcher's journal:

*Acland Street, St Kilda, cosmopolitan, loud, colourful and
extroverted, boasting its pleasures for diversity and difference, is next stop on the city tour. For Maggie (the environmental designer), Acland Street is home. The street represents years of devotion and labour — an experience she attempts to share and celebrate with our troupe. But the congestion, the extravagance, the colour...unsettles the young
people. Used to wide, empty streets they cluster together,
warding off any intrusion, and quickly move through the
streets, leaving Maggie behind.*

*Meandering on foot through the back streets of St.Kilda, on
their way to our lunchtime destination, the young people
marvel at the majesty of the homes. Do people actually live*

© KAREN MALONE

Figure 4.16 Streetspace city tour: St. Kilda Adventure Playground

in these houses? Arriving at St Kilda Adventure Playground they press up against the wire fence with excited anticipation. And in a flurry of boisterous abandonment, not unlike a scene of shoppers at a department store stocktake sale, when the gate is opened they pour into the playground. For one and a half hours the playground is alive with the sound of shrills and laughter — many forget to eat their lunch. For Maggie, who had doubted the attraction of a 'child's' playground for these tough adolescents, a realisation of the ambiguity of youth.

An e-mail from two of the students after the city tour illustrates the importance of exposing children and youth to a variety of environmental experiences as a way to prepare them to be critical consumers and designers:

Hello Karen, this is Jackie and Sara. We went on the Streetspace excursion with you to St. Kilda. We found that the features that make an environment attractive are parks that are well looked after, unpolluted rivers and lakes, shops with neat appearances, colourful and comfortable street furniture, clean and unlittered streets and places for children to play safely in. The things that make an environment safe are needle bins, well-lit streets, working streetlights and police stations with police that actually listen. We had lots of fun, and we hope we can do it again.[51]

When Streetspace began, the plan was to design a pathway through the neighbourhood. Instead, the City Council decided to engage the young people in the participatory design of Ash Reserve, a space earmarked for youth.

BOX 4.2

Streetspace Activities: Young People *in* Places, Designing Youth Spaces

YOUNG PEOPLE *IN* PLACES

WEEK	THEME	GUIDING QUESTIONS/ ACTIVITIES
1, 2	My place – tuning in	**How do people choose where they live?** • Draw plan of my house and street • Create a mosaic house number • Neighbourhood drawings • Create individual spatial maps • Local area community survey
3	Places in the world	**How is my place different from other places?** • Describe eight international Growing Up in Cities sites • World map: find GUIC sites and mark in places I have been or where parents have come from • Research GUIC Australian, South African and UNESCO website • Demographics: map population trends in the neighbourhood
4, 5	Our place	**How do places and their uses change over time?** • Guest speaker: Mark Grist, indigenous archaeologist • Our place: Interviewing each other about neighbourhood use and perceptions (favourite places, dangerous places) • Collate data and make comparisons

DESIGNING *YOUTH* SPACES

WEEK	THEME	GUIDING QUESTIONS/ ACTIVITIES
6, 7	Youth-friendly spaces	**How are spaces designed for different uses by different people?** • Neighbourhood tour • 'Gulliver's Footprints' mapping activity • Develop photogrid of neighbourhood • Guest speaker: Adrian Weedon, City Council Urban Planner (Trails) • City tour – Westgate Park; Southbank, City; Acland Street and Adventure Playground, St Kilda; Pipemakers Park.
8, 9, 10	Youth designed spaces	**What would 'youth-designed' spaces look like?** • Guest speaker: Jenny Lee, City Council Playground Designer in charge of Ash Reserve • Skill development in reading and constructing designs • Excursion: Local design company • Site visit to Ash Reserve • Brainstorming ideas in groups • Draft 2D design: presentation to class • 3D Model construction • Photographing model • Generating computerised image of model • 'Celebrating Streetspace': presentation to City Council and community members

This shift illustrated the nature of working with governments that are dynamic and sometimes quite fickle. Although local government railroaded the young people into the design of this predetermined youth space, the team with the students decided the shift was the most effective way to achieve our primary aim — a tangible outcome. With the help of Maggie, the students moved from developing two-dimensional maps of the neighbourhood pathway to creating designs for the redevelopment of the reserve and finally creating three-dimensional scaled models. Students incorporated all facets of community activities into the designs of their park. This brought home to the team that, even when given the opportunities to create a 'youth' space, young people want to be integrated into community life. Designs included elements such as barbecues, shaded eating areas, play equipment,

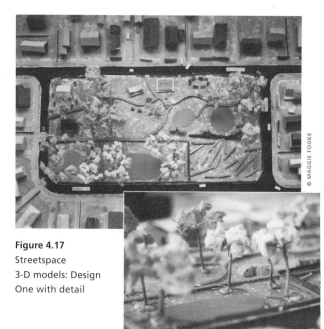

Figure 4.17
Streetspace
3-D models: Design
One with detail

The young people learned valuable skills of personal development such as articulating and sharing ideas, working as a team, peer assessment, reflection and active citizenship.

rose gardens, ponds, garden beds, pathways lined with trees. These areas were integrated with more youth-focused elements such as skate ramps, bike tracks and basketball hoops. The students selected six designs and constructed scale-size elements of their park. Each of these elements was arranged on a base model of the park and the surrounding streetscape, then photographed. Using three-dimensional scale models was an important educational step in the students' development of environmental and spatial cognition. Students were able to manipulate elements of their design and make judgements about their designs' viability.

The final designs and models illustrated that the students had learned fundamental design and geographical skills such as the use of legends and scale, drawing, mapping, model-making, and the integration of model pieces into a comprehensive site design. They also learned observation skills and verbal and visual presentation skills by doing historical analysis, writing research reports,

sending email, creating computer images, making graphs and taking photographs. They learned valuable skills of personal development such as articulating and sharing ideas, working as a team, peer assessment, reflection and active citizenship. By the end of the project, students had developed a sense of commitment and pride in the work they had been doing. They spent lunchtimes cleaning up and helping Maggie prepare for classes. They took students from other levels through the workspace and explained to them the importance of the work they were doing. When the mosaics and the models were displayed in the hallway of the school, they stood by them and pointed out their significance to passers-by.

When the time came for the final presentation of the streetspace models, designs and report[52] to members of City Council, Youth Services and AEDIS at the conclusion of the project in November 1998, the young people bustled with excitement and enthusiasm as they attempted to make 'everything perfect' for the occasion. During the presentation they spoke clearly, sat quietly and graciously and received their certificates of achievement with great pride. 'Celebrating Streetspace' provided an opportunity for the young people to share their ideas and to illustrate the value of their experiences as participatory planners of their street spaces:

'Our local area desperately needs more facilities for young people. Streetspace allowed us the opportunity to design spaces for the youth of Braybrook. We only hope that the Council will now seriously think over our ideas and allow us to have more facilities and useable space. The Council and planners always think about facilities for toddlers such as playgrounds but now we would like them to think about facilities for older children and teenagers.'

(Emma, 14 years old)

'Young people should have a say in what their area looks like. I think the Council should listen to what young people have to say because they live in the area and they are future taxpayers.'

(Amanda, 14 years old, Celebrate Streetspace presentation, November 1998)

REFLECTIONS ON PARTICIPATORY RESEARCH WITH YOUTH

The diversity of young people, their experience, and the context of their lives are issues that need considerable reflection when planning with or planning for young people. First and foremost it is important to recognise that public space is not neutral. Geographies of power, resistance and control are mapped out in real and imaginary boundaries across the landscape.[53] If neighbourhoods are to become youth-friendly, young people need to be part of the evaluation and planning process. To participate constructively though, young people need to be skilled and have experiences to draw on. Young people who have limited access to different urban environments need environmental exposure, so they can read the environment and be critical consumers of designs and plans. Participatory planning means addressing these power relationships through changes in the policing, regulation, monitoring and planning of public space.

Planning with young people is not just about changing or designing physical forms or structures for them. It is about understanding the culture of a community and young people's role within it. To do this, rigorous research, rather than superficial consultation, needs to be conducted with and by the young people about their lives. But it cannot be assumed that young people are going to be willing to participate until a commitment is made to value their contribution. Would adults ask any

> *Following on foot a group of young people on bicycles during a neighbourhood guided tour while taking notes and photographs has been the most successful research method we have used.*

less? For planners, planning with young people means changing the types of community consultation processes they have become accustomed to conducting. Young people like to be pragmatic, mobile and stimulated by their involvement. Following on foot a group of young people on bicycles during a neighbourhood guided tour while taking notes and photographs has been the most successful research method we have used. Alternatively, conducting community meetings often leads to apathy, disinterest and silence. Planning with young people means reading the neighbourhood from the lives of young people and embarking on participatory processes with them.

The role of neighbourhoods for supporting young people has changed throughout Australia during the 25 years that have elapsed between the original Growing Up in Cities study in the 1970s and its revival in the 1990s. Neighbourhoods, previously the site of spontaneous and exploratory play, are becoming less supportive and consequently less appealing for young people. This is due to a lack of resources and maintenance, urban planning centred on adults and an escalating climate of fear of youth, especially those identified as 'underclass.' In Braybrook the impact of these changes over time has served to reinforce the already marginalised and disadvantaged position young people found themselves in

25 years ago. The fear adults have of youth — constructed from media hype, stereotyping and moral panic — has diverted attention from the collective disadvantage of the community to a focus on youth as prime suspects in a fight for social order. Braybrook youth find themselves caught in this climate of fear and suspicion. Twenty-five years ago they were members of a neglected community. Now they find that they are marginalised in broader society and in their own community — *truly aliens in a suburban environment.*

ENDNOTES

1 Sibley (1995, p. 112).
2 The Concise Oxford Dictionary.
3 James, Prout and Jenks (1998).
4 From Gough (1997, p. 7).
5 Macdonald (1997, pp. 3-4).
6 Lynch (1977).
7 Downton (1973).
8 Powell (1993, p. xiv).
9 Winter and Bryson state: 'In Victoria, between 1945 and 1960, the government built 47,000 dwellings on 231 estates, comprising 15 percent of all dwellings built during this period' (1998, p. 62).
10 Powell (1993, p. 53).
11 Winter and Bryson (1998, p. 64).
12 Powell (1993, p. 72).
13 Howe (1995, p. 81)
14 Winter and Bryson (1998, p. 73).
15 Lynch (1977, p. 11).
16 Downton (1973, p. 73).
17 Comparisons were constructed from demographic data obtained from the Australian Bureau of Statistics (ABS). The ABS data are obtained from Australia-wide surveys conducted every four years. The 1972 study used data from the 1966 ABS survey and the 1997 project used ABS data from 1996.
18 Information on Braybrook's disadvantage index was obtained from the Maribrynong City Council (1995) and from statements by council officers in Gough (1997, p. 7).
19 Housing Commission Victoria was a department of the state government whose role was to supply public housing in accordance to the demands.
20 Downton (1973 , p. 77).
21 See Massey (1994), Pe-Pua (1996), Valentine (1996), James, Prout and Jenks (1998).
22 Sibley (1995), Malone and Hasluck (1998).
23 See Macdonald (1997) for further discussions on youth and underclass ideology.
24 Sibley (1992, p. 109).
25 Sibley (1995).
26 Relph (1976, p. 113).
27 Owens (1994, p. 299).
28 Relph (1976).

29 Image 4.5 is an example of this style of neighbourhood drawing.
30 Downton (1973, p. 71).
31 Connolly and Ennew (1996, p. 133).
32 Spencer, Blades and Morsley (1989).
33 See images 4.10, 4.11, 4.12, 4.13 as examples of spatial maps illustrating the differences in young people's roaming range.
34 YCW – Young Christian Women. The YCW was a recreation facility developed in the 1970s on council land and run by the church as a community recreation facility. By the time of the 1997 study, the facility had been taken over by the local council and was being developed as a commercial facility.
35 Archer (1998, p. 18).
36 Wyn & White (1997, p. 149).
37 Hasluck and Malone (1999).
38 Downton (1973, p. 26).
39 Lawrence et al. (1986, p. 431).
40 Goannas are large indigenous Australian reptiles found in the wilderness and desert locations. A lizard will often be called a goanna by children — meaning it was a large lizard. It is very unlikely a goanna would be found in an urban setting like Braybrook.
41 This comment is contradictory to statements made by Lu earlier about feeling safe in the neighbourhood, but it was not unusual for the young people in Braybrook to have a variety of contradictory feelings about their neighbourhood.
42 Loukataitou-Sideris (1996).
43 Morgan (1994, p. 80).
44 Writing a letter to a friend to describe the neighbourhood was a Streetspace project activity.
45 Polzot (1997, p. 31).
46 Foucault (1979).
47 James, Prout and Jenks (1998, p. 56).
48 Jacobs (1961, p. 39).
49 As reference material, the young people used the guide by White, Murray and Robins (1996).
50 See Malone (1999) for an extensive discussion of the philosophy of participatory planning underpinning the Streetspace project.
51 The young people were encouraged to send e-mail messages to the research team reflecting on their experiences. This message was dated 21/8/1998.
52 Streetspace, a report on the curriculum and youth design project, is available from chapter author Karen Malone.
53 Morgan (1994), Sibley (1995).

REFERENCES

Archer, M (1998) 'Crime against youth "under control"', *Footscray Mail*, 20 July, p. 18.

Connolly, P and Ennew, J (1996) 'Introduction: Children out of place', *Childhood*, vol. 3, pp. 131-147.

Downton, P (1973) UNESCO: *Children's Perceptions of Space Project, Melbourne Study*, Unpublished research report, University of Melbourne, Melbourne.

Foucault, M (1979) *Discipline and Punishment: The birth of the prison*, Vintage Books, New York.

Gough, D (1997) 'The forgotten people', *The Mail,* 14 May, p. 7.

Hasluck, L and Malone, K (1999) 'Location, leisure and lifestyle: Young people's retreat to the home environment', in C Shehan (ed) *Through the Eyes of the Child: Revisioning children as active agents of family life,* JAI Press, Stamford, pp. 177-196.

Howe, R (1995) 'The concrete house frontier: The Victorian Housing Commission and the Planning of Melbourne in the 1940s and 1950s', in G Davison, T Dingle and S O'Hanlon (eds) *The Cream Brick Frontier: Histories of Australian Suburbia,* Monash Publications in History no 19, Monash University, Clayton, Melbourne.

Jacobs, J (1961) *The Life and Death of Great American Cities: The failure of town planning,* Penguin Books, Harmondsworth.

James, A, Prout, A and Jenks, C (1998) *Theorising Childhood,* Polity Press, London.

Lawrence, F, Tasker, G, Daly, C, Orhiel, A and Wozniak, P (1986) 'Adolescent time spent viewing television', *Adolescence,* vol 21 (82), pp. 431-436.

Loukataitou-Sideris, D (1996) 'Cracks in the city: Addressing the constraints and potentials of urban design', *Journal of Urban Design,* vol 1, pp. 91-104.

Lynch, K (1977) *Growing Up in Cities,* MIT Press, Massachusetts.

Macdonald, R (1997) *Youth, the 'Underclass' and Social Exclusion,* Routledge, London.

Malone, K (1999) 'Growing Up in Cities as a model of participatory planning and 'placemaking' with young people', *Youth Studies Australia,* vol 18, (2), pp. 17-23.

Malone, K and Hasluck, L (1998) 'Geographies of exclusion: Young people's perceptions and use of public space', *Family Matters,* vol 49, pp. 21-26.

Maribrynong City Council (1995) *Braybrook Community Centre Feasibility Study,* unpublished report, City of Maribyrnong.

Massey, D (1994) *Space, Place and Gender,* Polity Press, Cambridge.

Morgan, G (1994) 'Acts of enclosure: Crime and defensible space in contemporary cities, in K Gibson and S Watson, *Metropolis Now,* Pluto Press, NSW, pp. 78-90.

Owens, P (1994) 'Teen places in Sunshine, Australia: Then and now', *Children's Environments,* vol 11 (4), pp. 292-299.

Pe-Pua, R (1996) *'We're just like other kids!' Street Frequenting Youth of Non-English-Speaking Background,* Australian Govern-ment Publishing Services, Canberra.

Polzot, L (1997) 'Young people and police in public space', *Youth Issues Forum,* Winter, pp. 30-32.

Powell, D (1993) *Out West: Perceptions of Sydney's western suburbs,* Allen & Unwin, St Leonards, Australia.

Relph, E (1976) *Place and Placelessness,* Pion Limited, London.

Sibley, D (1992) 'Outsiders in society and space', in K Anderson and K Gale (eds) *Inventing Places: Studies in cultural geography,* Longman, Melbourne, pp. 107-122.

Sibley, D (1995) *Geographies of Exclusion,* Routledge, London.

Spencer, C, Blades, M and Morsley, K (1989) *The Child in the Physical Environment: The development of spatial knowledge and cognition,* John Wiley, Chichester.

Valentine, G (1996) 'Children should be seen and not heard: The production and transgression of adults' public space', *Urban Geography,* vol 17, pp. 205-220.

White, R, Murray, G and Robins, N (1996) *Negotiating Youth-Specific Public Space: A guide for youth and community workers, town planners and local councils,* Australian Youth Foundation, Sydney.

Winter, I and Bryson, L (1998) 'Economic restructuring and state interven-tion in Holdenist suburbia: understanding urban poverty in Australia', *International Journal of Urban and Regional Research,* vol 22 (1), pp. 60-75.

Wyn, J and White, R (1997) *Rethinking Youth,* Sage Publications, London.

CHAPTER FIVE

Children in a South African Squatter Camp Gain and Lose a Voice

Jill Swart-Kruger

Young people in Canaansland, a squatter community in Johannesburg (South Africa), shared their hardships and challenges as well as their sources of happiness and hope through the Growing Up in Cities project. Their experiences form the first published account of the lives of children in a squatter community as they seek to survive in the city, only to suffer eviction and resettlement on remote peri-urban land. At the same time, their story illustrates how participatory processes with children can serve as a catalyst for community development with all ages, and outlines steps that municipal governments can take to support disadvantaged families' own efforts to improve the conditions of their lives.

A MEETING

Saturday, 17 November 1998, was a warm and sunny autumn day in the Thula Mntwana informal settlement south of Johannesburg. I dusted a chair for myself and glanced at the men and women, boys and girls, sitting and chatting companionably around the plastic table set up outdoors in the stippled shade to one side of a row of corrugated iron shacks. A breeze popularly known in South Africa as the dust devil swirled by, rapidly covering everything with a layer of grit.

As people wiped their eyes and dusted off the table once more, I marvelled at the difference in composition between this meeting and my first meeting with committee members from the Canaansland squatter settlement almost three years earlier and before their relocation to Thula Mntwana from the city. At that time the committee consisted of five men only. Women were excluded on the basis that they spoke too much and were always drunk,

while the notion that children's representatives might be present to voice their opinions was inconceivable. The chairman had been the person who had built the first shack on site, and four other middle-aged men who had settled there soon afterwards with their families comprised the rest of the committee.

The years between these two meetings were not easy for the residents of Canaansland. There were many interventions in their lives, not all of which were welcome. During that time they had moved from acceptance of a closed patriarchal committee system, legitimated primarily by sequence of shack ownership, to endorsement of an open committee system where men and women were elected to membership in equal numbers and children were asked to send representatives when issues affecting them were to be discussed. In attempting to explain the mechanisms which led to the women and children gaining a voice, I shall return to Canaansland before its relocation and chart the transitional process, including the role of researchers from the Growing Up in Cities project. This project has been the most extensive history yet of life inside a squatter camp from children's perspectives[1]. As the only published study that has followed squatter camp children from life in an initial settlement through eviction and resettlement, it will place the story of these children and their families in the context of policies to manage informal housing within South Africa and the international community. Later in this account I will return to this meeting, and will then move beyond it.

GROWING UP IN CITIES AND THE SOUTH AFRICAN HOUSING CRISIS

In its White Paper on Housing, the first democratically elected government in South Africa made a strong commitment to alleviate the housing crisis in the country.[2] This crisis is rooted in the racially restrictive employment and settlement policies of the apartheid era, which resulted in millions of African people being left homeless or in small overcrowded township houses, backyard shanties and huge shack settlements.[3]

> *One of the most important features of the project was that it required practical outcomes. It aimed to create opportunities for the chidren themselves to present their views to urban policy makers and planners.*

Housing problems have been particularly acute in the Gauteng province where Johannesburg is located. As a mining and industrial city, Johannesburg draws people in need of work from neighbouring provinces and countries. The 1996 census[4] shows that Gauteng is the country's smallest province but that it has the second largest population and is the most densely populated. Almost a third of its 7.3 million residents were not born there and only 3 percent live in non-urban areas. One in seven is not South African by birth. Since immigrants to

Figure 5.1 Children at home

Gauteng rarely realise their intention to become financially secure and to move to suburban homes, informal housing proliferates.[5]

Almost half of the South African population is made up of children under the age of 18 years. Their lifeworlds are varied and views into them are presented largely in the form of statistics or graphic images in the media. We know from details presented in the report on poverty and inequality in South Africa[6] that three of every five South African children live in poverty, in homes where they are vulnerable to public and domestic violence as well as environmental problems. They have no easy access to basic services or educational and health facilities. An unknown number of these children are not constantly parented or schooled and are malnourished. In 1998, the total expenditure on children and families amounted to only 13–14 percent of provincial welfare outlay since the focus in spending was on the elderly and disabled. In South Africa, 13 percent of all homes are located in informal or squatter settlements. The views of children about their daily lives in these environments are largely unknown.

For the above reasons, involvement in the international GUIC project seemed particularly appropriate to a South African context. This project has created opportunities for data collection from children in socio-economically disadvantaged urban areas, including their views on the benefits and shortcomings of these neighbourhoods and their recommendations on how to make improvements. To be of use to urban officials, the project needed to focus on pressing urban issues. Since squatting was a widespread problem in South Africa, it seemed sensible to work with children at the Canaansland squatter camp in inner city Johannesburg, as the data would yield useful applications to the design of further investigations at other squatter sites. Research was to include both spatial and social science analysis and was undertaken by a small team of researchers and university students.

One of the most important features of the GUIC project was that it required practical outcomes. It aimed to create opportunities for the children themselves to present their views to urban policy makers and planners. For this to be more than just a token exercise, the involvement and commitment of various adults would be necessary: those in the children's immediate environment, local and regional government officials and other stakeholders who would be identified in the course of research.

I knew from previous experience as an anthropologist researching children that they welcome the chance to discuss their lives — if they know that this will serve some useful purpose. As founder of the Street-Wise South Africa project for street children, I also knew that work with children living in difficult circumstances was not easy but that it could be done. I was able to place the GUIC project under the management of Street-Wise, which aims not only to help children on the streets, but also to attend to problems in the areas from which street children come. Squatter sites are an important source of street children.

CANAANSLAND IN JOHANNESBURG

Canaansland is a biblical name popular among squatters in South Africa. Sites that seem completely inhospitable to people with their own homes can appear a haven to the homeless. The Canaansland of this narrative, on the periphery of the central business district in Johannesburg, was such a haven. One water tap served over a thousand people and there was no sanitation or electricity on site, but it was close to the city centre and bordered on residential and shopping areas. This enabled residents to find piece-jobs and to collect cardboard or waste metal for recycling. The Braamfontein railway station yielded a constant flow of customers for the vegetables, sweets, cigarettes and other small goods that women sold from roadside stalls. Women also sold home-brewed and commercial liquor at four *shebeens* (informal bars) on site, or from home.

The main languages spoken at Canaansland were IsiZulu and Sesotho, although all nine official African languages could be heard on site. The personal circumstances of residents were varied. People who had lived in cramped conditions and paid relatively high rentals found it a relief to live at Canaansland. Some families had been ousted from their homes when breadwinners were retrenched; others had lost breadwinners through death from violence or illness. There were male immigrants from neighbouring countries who had married South African women and were working and saving to purchase their own homes, and families from other South African provinces who hoped to find better incomes and educational opportunities in Johannesburg.

The ethnic and linguistic diversity of residents seemed to hinder the creation of a strong sense of community. On the other hand, even same-language speakers did not form distinct groups that worked together. The children on site seemed to have a greater communal

TABLE 5.1	
Community Profile	
Site	0.6 hectares (1.48 acres)
Shacks	230-250
Density	± 13 shacks (about 55 people) per 250 square metres
Residents	± 1000
Languages	IsiNdebele, Sepedi, Sesotho, SiSwati, Setswana, Xitsonga, Tshivenda, IsiZulu, IsiXhosa, and a few languages from elsewhere in Africa

spirit than the adults: they shared the same problems and many of the same pleasures, and a number of them went to the same school. Age, gender and common pursuits seemed to draw them together rather than a common ethnic identity or language.

Although density on site was high, women pointed out that the alternative was to live on city pavements. Being housed in a shack meant that they could shelter their children from extremes of weather and from street violence, cook meals, do laundry and store personal belongings. People stretched their meagre incomes by shopping at cut-price outlets and scavenging at commercial rubbish bins and local dumps. Occasionally church committees and local shopkeepers brought food for the children. Many parents were unable to send their children to schools of their choice due to the cost of school fees, uniforms and bus tickets; but there were no such costs at the New Nation School for street children where most of the children were enrolled. They walked a kilometre and a half to and from the school daily, and received a nourishing midday meal.

The insignificance of Canaansland relative to other environmental features around the settlement are clearly illustrated in a boy's drawing of the area (see Figure 5.2). An architectural map (Figure 5.3), the first ever to-scale map of a South African squatter camp, reveals the density on site. Attractive features of the Canaansland encampment were a hedge along the western boundary, while a line of plane trees on the eastern and northern perimeters offered shade and greenery in the summer.

The triangular piece of land on which Canaansland had mushroomed belonged originally to the Department of Public Works, which fell under the authority of the Gauteng Department of Housing and Land Affairs. A police station with holding cells lay on the southern periphery; the rest of the site comprised its parking lot and a small bus depot. In 1993 the police station closed and the site was given to the Indian House of Delegates to extend a vacant plot of land across High Street which they already held. The police station was converted into an Indian-owned funeral parlour, but the parking lot was quietly invaded by African people in need of a place to live.

The streets to the north, south and west of Canaans-

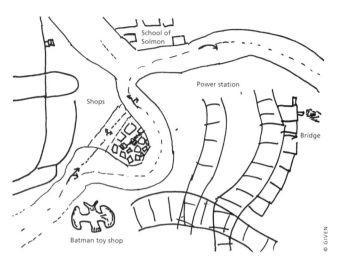

Figure 5.2 Canaansland panorama (Given, 14 years old)

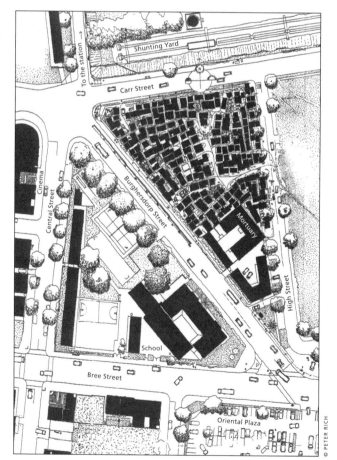

Figure 5.3 Canaansland site map

land carried a heavy flow of traffic, while High Street on the East was little used and children played there for the greater part of the day. People relieved themselves on the vacant plot across High Street, given the lack of toilets. It held a rubbish skip that was emptied fairly regularly by the municipality, but refuse was also strewn over the site. On cold, wet days, girls were sent there to collect sticks and other flammable materials. Toddlers played on the verges during the day under the eyes of adults, who used this space to sort waste materials for recycling, with sporadic assistance from their children and their children's friends.

On the southern boundary, along Bree Street, was a row of buildings which housed shops and the offices of the Central Islamic Trust. The Oriental Plaza shopping mall lay directly across Bree Street.

The Canaansland residents knew that people who lived on land which was not their own could be moved unexpectedly. In its efforts to address housing issues at local, regional and national levels, the South African government had introduced a number of reforms, including housing and land policies as well as a democratised planning process. This included the formation of local development objectives (LDOs) to be defined in consultation with local people. The LDOs span five-year periods, subject to annual reviews during the first five-year period.

During the GUIC research there was no indication that Canaansland residents had been included in the local LDO process. They seemed to be aware, however, that land would be restored to people from whom it had been wrongfully seized in the apartheid era, and that haphazard land settlement was going to be stopped. From time to time officials reacted strongly against land invasion by having squatters evicted violently, in the manner of the previous apartheid government.[7] Canaansland residents were anxious not to be treated in similar fashion.

It has been said that poor housing leads to feelings of despair, apathy and shame,[8] but unless outsiders take a close personal interest in shack dwellers, they will not know how proud people feel of the distinctive personal character which they have vested in their shacks.[9] They will also find it hard to envisage that such shacks offer the greatest possible comfort while families wait and work for something better. Some of their neighbours presumed that people at Canaansland lived in squalor and survived largely through criminality; others were sympathetic and tried to help with gifts of food. Yet others behaved as if the Canaansland site and its people were invisible. Enough people thought they were a blemish on the neighbourhood to tell government officials that they wanted the people to be relocated.

Figure 5.4 Children playing on High Street

WORKING WITH THE CHILDREN

Building Trust

Since the congestion on site meant that work with the children would be constantly interrupted, an offer of vacant office space by the nearby Central Islamic Trust as a base for project activities was gladly accepted. Work with the children commenced in February 1997 after a series of formal and informal meetings had been held with the all-male Canaansland residents' committee and GUIC objectives had been explained at a public meeting.

Residents said that they appreciated these introductions and explanations since it showed a degree of respect not commonly accorded to them. Often people arrived on site, walked about, asked personal questions, took photographs and made recordings — all without permission. They entered homes uninvited and, when asked to explain their presence, replied that they were government officials or researchers. Since residents were left in suspense regarding the purpose of the material collected and received no feed-back from such visits, the presence of unknown persons on site generated considerable anxiety.

From the first, Canaansland residents felt that it would be appropriate for GUIC researchers to liaise with women, since matters concerning children fell within the domain of women's responsibilities. The chairman underscored this point by refusing to officiate at the public meeting in January 1997 at which the research team explained the purpose of the project to residents. Two women volunteered assistance at this meeting, and many more assisted during later stages of the work.

Members of the research team had varied backgrounds and although they observed protocol, not all of them felt comfortable on a squatter site. Two research assistants felt that residents were hostile, but it is a moot point whether their personal reserve and body language contributed to the generation of this reaction by residents who were highly sensitive to negative responses. When on site, most GUIC researchers were courteously welcomed and offered refreshments as well as a safe place off the street to park. Some team members developed warm, long-term friendships with people at Canaansland.

Research Workshops

An open invitation was issued to all girls and boys at Canaansland who were ten to fourteen years old to take part in the GUIC research. Of the twenty-three children who decided to take part, fifteen were present for all data collection procedures. Three were absent from one procedure during a workshop, four from two and one from a full workshop. Absences were due mostly to parents' requiring their help at home or to run errands.

At three Saturday workshops, held in February, March and April 1997, girls and boys worked individually and in groups to evaluate their neighbourhood and to

TABLE 5.2				
Participants Profile (N=23)				
Male, 10 Female, 13				
AGE	# OF PARTICIPANTS		AGE	# OF PARTICIPANTS
10	7		13	3
11	7		14	3
12	3			

suggest practical solutions to problems there. Between data collection sessions, they had meals, games, free play, singing, and dancing. The simple meals of hot dogs or chicken, salad, fruit and peanuts were seen as feasts by children whose daily diet was mostly dry bread, tea, mealie-meal porridge and cabbage. The children and adults of Canaansland legitimated the research process as an educational initiative and called it 'Saturday school.' Although the researchers explained that it was they who were learning from the children, this was difficult for the adults and the children to credit.

The participatory nature of the workshops[10] generated a spirit of companionship between the boys and girls who attended. They set their own behavioural boundaries by agreeing on rules for each day and writing them on flip charts. They shared insights generated in individual interviews, displayed and discussed the work done in small groups and brain-stormed together. Although group discussions were sometimes chaotic when everybody wanted to speak at the same time, a home-made imitation microphone helped to prevent forceful children from dominating. Only the person holding the microphone was permitted to speak.

Sometimes children hit out at others when they were annoyed and occasionally girls were hit very hard by boys: this behaviour reflected that of drunk adults in Canaansland and of men there who beat their women-folk. Such bullying is widely reported for children in the age group studied by GUIC.[11] Researchers were usually able to dispel the aggression by reminding the children to restudy their rules and by giving them a break for an energetic game.

Before work began with the children, three full-day workshops were held to plan the participatory research process. A workshop was then held at the Street-Wise locale, where the children enjoyed acting as guinea pigs for members of the research team to test their skills. Subsequently, the procedure for using specific methods was practised with research assistants before each data collection workshop with the children at Canaansland.

© MELINDA SWIFT

Figure 5.5 Preparing for the morning's activities

Despite this careful preparation, the first Saturday workshop with the children began in a disorderly way. Although only 10–14 year olds had been invited, virtually all the children from Canaansland arrived, shining clean and dressed in their best clothes. The crisis of having so many children of all ages milling about was resolved by involving them all in a game, distributing refreshments, then asking the mothers who had come with the children to take all except the 10–14 year olds home again. The unhappiness this generated was alleviated by a promise to host one morning playgroup for the younger children after data collection with the older children was complete. Only games, songs and refreshments were planned for this playgroup, but halfway through the morning many of the children asked when they were going to start work. They insisted that they wanted to do what the older children had done and were satisfied only when paper and crayons were produced and their drawings were pinned on the wall.

Some of the research assistants found the mass influx of children to the first workshop nerve-wracking. Evaluation at the end of the day included a heartfelt: 'More training should have been provided to prepare researchers for the *worst*.' However, the team did agree that, after the younger children had left:

'All the children were happy and enjoying themselves... prepared to provide us with relevant information...in a playful manner; they enjoyed the exercises and felt happy in the company of their friends.'

Many residents were curious about what the children might communicate. A few women always came to the workgroups, although the research assistants escorted the children to and from Canaansland. During games the women would tell the children what to do, and during discussions they would speak for the children. Their presence hampered data collection, but it was difficult to persuade them to leave without causing offence. It was usually necessary for a research assistant to walk back to Canaansland companionably with them and to take leave of them there. In time, these initially annoying interruptions were found to have value since the women conveyed what was happening with the children to other residents and verified that the activities were not only respectable but informative concerning site conditions.

Data Collection

A number of researchers have noticed that children share information in a spontaneous and playful way and readily explore their own responses when research environments are non-threatening and personally accepting.[12] The children from Canaansland were intrigued by the research process and marvelled that there were adults who found their ideas and opinions of importance.

On the very first day, while agreeing on the day's rules, one of the girls said that they should draw for the researchers. Others agreed and also said that they wanted to talk about their lives. Without prior information from the research team, the children themselves proposed some of the planned methods of data collection.

Although a core set of data collection methods was to be used at each GUIC site, research teams were encouraged to collect data in other appropriate ways as well. In South Africa, a number of supplementary methods were used. In getting-to-know-you sessions, for instance, everyone sat in a large circle on the floor and members of the research team told something of interest about themselves, after which the children did the same. A Venn diagram enabled the children to chart their places of origin in relation to the squatter camp and to comment briefly on differences in their past and present locations. At this session, the children voiced their disgust at the stench from decaying rubbish, stagnant water and human waste, as well as their dislike and fear of the rats that destroyed food supplies and infested rubble. These reactions to degraded environments are common among children around the world.[13]

> *Research showed that the children's daily lifestyles were structured in much the same way as those of children in suburban homes, except that special features of the squatter site had to be taken into account.*

Spontaneous role-plays by the children during one recess led to the suggestion that they show the researchers how they interacted on site with their parents and guardians. When the girls had acted out their role-play, the boys said they were too shy to do theirs. After whispered discussion and hilarity, the children announced that the girls would act out the boys' play for them. They promptly did so while the boys called out instructions from the side.

From time to time the children would exhibit an unexpected vulnerability, as happened on the first day when they were asked whether their drawings could be put up on the wall. They were afraid that their drawings would be laughed at. They were assured that all the drawings were valuable for their content and also that they would not be shown to others without permission. Subsequently the children were encouraged to share the products of the research outside the group and were pleas-antly surprised at their good reception. In small ways such as these, support for the development of self-esteem and self-efficacy was built into the research process. When the formal research report had been written, some of the children wrote an epilogue with the help of a research assistant, and included ideas gleaned from the other children. Later, they helped create a video to present their lives.[14]

RESEARCH FINDINGS

Initially the lives of the children appeared to be unstructured and they seemed to come and go as they chose. Specific children could seldom be found even if prior arrangements had been made to meet with them, and their caretakers were seldom able to say where they were at any particular time. Personal experience has shown, however, that this is not uncommon in urban areas such as Johannesburg and Soweto today, and that it is exacerbated when people have no access to telephones, as in Canaansland.

Research showed that the children's daily lifestyles were structured in much the same way as those of children in suburban homes,[15] except that special features of the squatter site had to be taken into account. Boys and girls were expected to look after their own belongings, to do home chores, to attend school and not to roam beyond the neighbourhood boundaries set by their caretakers. Showing obedience and respect to parents and elders, helping them in times of need and working to keep the family intact, are values so widespread in Africa that they are written into the African Charter on the Rights and Welfare of the Child.[16]

One of the children's main chores was looking after younger siblings. Boys helped with babies and toddlers only if they did not have sisters to do this, but adult residents also kept an eye on toddlers, as they were inclined to stray off the site because there were no fences. Other regular chores included fetching water and running errands for their families, and most girls and boys also washed dishes, cleaned shacks and helped with the family laundry.

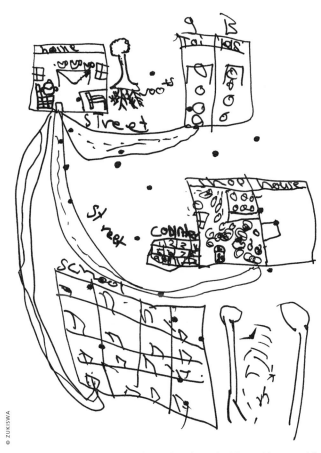

© ZUKISWA

Figure 5.6 Home and other favourite places (Zukiswa, 10 years old)

Although parents preferred their children to be indoors when night fell, girls and boys tried to stretch their time outside by lingering on the streets with their peers. A number of boys rambled about the neighbourhood at night, either alone or with a friend or two. Children who were indoors watched battery-operated television, listened to the radio (especially to sports matches), told and listened to stories, and played cards with their families and friends.

The lack of outside lighting created pools of darkness between shacks at night and made it impossible to identify people passing by. This alone was enough to scare the children, who said that criminals fled into the camp when they were being pursued by the police. They feared attack when fetching water in the dark, or were afraid that flimsy shack walls might be breached by rob-

bers. The nocturnal activities of the adult residents also concerned and frightened them. In one group discussion a passionate wish was voiced:

'We would like the people of Kanana to sleep at night, not go about stealing each other's property and not walking around and shouting and fighting with each other.'

The noise outside and poor visibility indoors led many children to neglect their homework. Conscientious children found it hard to work in peace. Drunken adults lurched against the walls of shacks located on main pathways through the camp, but children who lived in cul-de-sacs were able to work at small tables outdoors, before most adults returned at twilight.

The girls and boys thought of 'home' as the places they had originally come from. They remembered these as safer and more comfortable places with a network of caring relatives. They made the best of things at Canaansland, and valued being with other members of their families, but hoped to move on to something better:

'I hope not to be here in ten years' time and I don't want to know what it would look like here, then.'
(Christopher, 14 years old)

Despite these problems, most of the children spoke of their shacks in Canaansland as safe and happy places. Figure 5.6 shows one girl's shack in relation to her other favourite places in the area. There is a shade tree with roots where she sits when it's hot, the toilets at Braamfontein station, the shop where she is sent on errands by her mother, and netball poles in Mayfair where she and some of the other girls play.

Numerous activities could be enjoyed on site. Games of hop-scotch, various skipping games and catch were played on High Street. Vacant shacks awaiting sale or rental were fun sites for pre-adolescent girls and younger children to play 'house' or 'school', without having to worry about knocking over stoves or getting in the way of adults. Girls, who spent more time on site than boys, particularly appreciated features of the natural environment, such as the trees on the eastern side of the camp, where they sat in the shade to think and rest, or to play with pets or chat with friends. Even the small veld flowers, which sometimes bloomed on the vacant plot across the road that was used for garbage and sanitation, were noticed and appreciated.

Boys and girls returning from school visited their favourite spots in the neighbourhood before going home and seldom remembered the boundary limits set by parents. They did not return home first since this would mean having to walk all the way back to the play sites. It would also mean that they would forfeit their time to roam and play, since parents were strict in insisting that they do chores before they could begin play or homework.

The most popular site for both boys and girls was a park with play equipment and large grassy mounds. They were completely at ease there, knowing that it was a place designated for the use of children. They often lost track of time while engrossed in their games and returned home to a scolding. Boys tried to swing high enough 'to get into the sky' and rough-housed on the grass. When they tired of the roundabout and swings, girls played 'stories.' This required a search for stones that reflected distinctive characters. They would name their characters and draw a location on the ground with sticks. Some characters were done away with and others drawn in as the story progressed. The plots were often those of

favourite stories heard at school, such as Cinderella or Sleeping Beauty, but when stories were created and played out on the spot, they were mostly about children.

The Oriental Plaza close to Canaansland offered window-shopping, rides on escalators and video games, but many children went there only with parental permission. It was so close to home that adults from Canaansland who were shopping or scavenging, used to admonish them to go home, believing that they were shirking chores. Each adult knew only a few other adults well, but active children became widely familiar. It has been said that in African communities, and especially at squatter sites, 'people interfere in everybody's business *when that business is a child'.*[17]

Favourite activities of the boys were swimming in a local pool in the summer, watching the trains at the shunting yard or practising their soccer skills on the playing field of a neighbourhood school when the staff and students had left. Some of the girls spent time after school at a large garage in Mayfair where cars were repaired. They were welcome and safe there and could watch the mechanics or the television, which was on all day. Most of all, they enjoyed drinking clean, cool water from the water dispenser. Others enjoyed practising netball on the field of a girls' school in the area. Like the boys, they did so after everyone else had left. Girls spent a lot of time playing on the pavement along Burghersdorp Street or on High Street. Parents said that the girls were safer close to home, and that they needed to be on hand to help with tasks at home or to look after younger children.

Despite their clear vision of the shortcomings of their dwellings, both girls and boys spoke with appreciation of the effort that their male relatives had put into building for them and that their mothers had made to make indoor space habitable. Older boys took pride in helping in the construction or renovation of their shacks, and both boys and girls decorated the corners where they slept with posters or pictures cut from magazines. Few shacks had enough space for a bed for each person and many children slept on the floor. Not every shack at Canaansland had courtyards — a traditional feature of indigenous South African housing — but the homestead

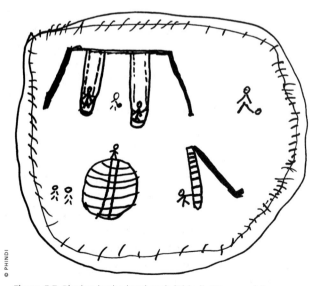

© PHINDI

Figure 5.7 Playing in the local park (Phindi, 10 years old)

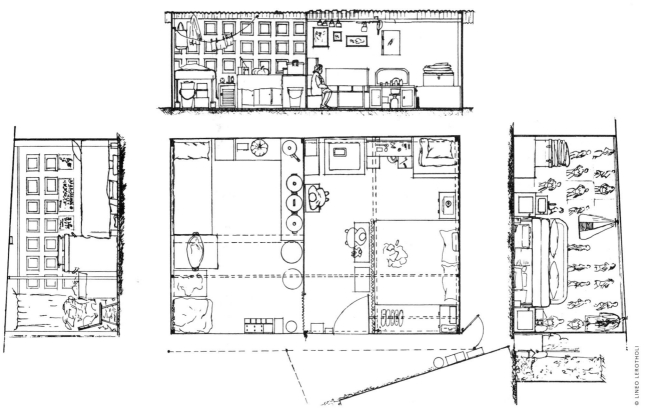

© LINEO LEROTHOLI

Figure 5.8 Shack floor plan (centre). The shack is divided into a small kitchen on the left with a bed for the teenage son. His parents and two daughters sleep in the bedroom on the right.

shown in Figure 5.8 had two. The back courtyard was a storage and toilet area containing a bucket. Pickings from dumps were stored here for mending or making furniture and utensils. There was a brazier in the side courtyard where people could warm themselves, cook and sit with visitors.

Awareness that the children at Canaansland were victimised and abused by outsiders emerged gradually during the research process. First one of the older boys asked that photos should not be printed in the local newspaper because his peers and teachers would no longer treat him well if they knew where he lived. Then children said that when people knew they were 'squatters' they were blamed for anything that was wrong in the area. They and their parents were followed about in shops by the staff, in case they stole anything. Often children were rudely asked if they had money when they ar-

rived at a shop. When friends went to the shops together, those without money were often refused entry and had to wait outside on the pavement.

One research assistant experienced this prejudice personally. As she entered a shop at the Oriental Plaza she caught the attention of the shopkeeper, who began to flirt with her. Having heard the children's accounts she decided to test his reaction:

'The shop owner…started telling me how much he loved me and that he would like me to be his girl-friend. I pretended to seem very optimistic about his proposal but it was a complete turn-off on his side when he asked me where I lived and I answered: "Canaansland squatter camp"!'

When children drew and discussed their neighbourhood, they included public places that Indian people forbade them to enter. Boys who went swimming told of being beaten up by white boys their own age or older at the pool. Mothers said that they were prevented from enrolling their children at neighbourhood schools and pre-schools, even if they could afford the fees. They detailed instances of rudeness and other forms of obstruction.

Two professional women living in the area, who were sympathetic to the problems of Canaansland residents, suggested that the rejection of people from Canaansland was probably due to religious and racial factors. They had also heard people say that toddlers from Canaansland were unhealthy and might spread diarrhoea, lice and infections, possibly even HIV, among other children.

These were not the only ways in which the children were humiliated. Even on their home territory they were abused verbally, physically and emotionally. While playing on the pavement on busy Burghersdorp Street, they could be thrown onto the road, slapped, spat upon and cursed by pedestrians, most of whom were African. Their playthings were vandalised: small stones selected carefully for the game of *diketo* were scattered and footballs were punctured. On High Street, which was hardly ever used by motorists, people of all race groups amused themselves by driving at high speed to scatter children skipping or playing hopscotch and catch, and to upset mothers who had to snatch up their toddlers who were quietly playing with toy cars or sticks and twigs. The speeding drivers would often stop at the end of the road, look back at the disruption they had caused, and laugh. From time to time Canaansland residents were injured by drivers who did not bother to stop and see how seriously people were hurt.

In an emotional interaction[18] some of the children discussed the problem of rejection:

Mandla: *'Those who go to the station badger us when we play games and sometimes they say we are dirty as well as the shelters. They make fun of people from the camp who sell food; they say the food is dirty because of us…'*

Bongani: *'Yes, what Mandla says is true. When we make fires to get warm, they say we will make them smell of smoke and they will get dirty because of the fire and their clothes will smell. They say our shelters are smelly and we*

are not respectful. They say whatever they feel like saying.'

Mandla: *'They say…our shelters have faeces and that these even get into the food for sale. Some of us ask why they keep on going this way…they should change their route.'*

Lindiwe: *'The passers-by say that we are always dirty and we don't ever wash ourselves!'*

Nondumiso: *'People who walk past our shelters talk about the dirtiness and the dirty [stagnant] water [emptied out into the gutters] and that's true. Some of the people do crime; that's why people don't like the place.'*

Tshepo: *'People…do robbery and other criminal things and then they run to our shelters where they hide and people think it is us.'*

As noted earlier, although some of their neighbours were kind and considerate, the people of Canaansland seemed, as a whole, to be a target for hostile discrimination. The children, who were most powerless, appeared to carry the greatest burden of this discrimination.

> *In the long-term, the girls and boys all wanted better housing with basic services, in a location where they would be treated with dignity.*

The children agreed on the short-term improvements they would like on site. They wanted toilets, piped water, better garbage disposal, stronger shacks and fencing to keep criminals at a distance. Electricity was also a priority, and not only for light. Girls who helped to cook knew that overturned paraffin stoves could cause fires to sweep through squatter camps, and all the children knew the anguish of not being able to warm themselves in cold weather because toxic fumes from burning coal in braziers indoors could be fatal. The girls and boys longed for a sheltered place, at a distance from adult interference and noise, where they could do homework, socialise, play and read. Children and teenagers in low-status or problem areas in other parts of the world have also spoken of a deep-seated need for a place they can call their own.[19]

The girls and boys disagreed on the location of these

improvements, so they were listed and colour-coded (blue for taps, red for toilets, green for a safe place to play, and so on). The girls and boys were then given two large draft maps of Canaansland, and they withdrew to separate rooms to mark their recommended placing of improvements in colour on these maps, before discussing them together.

In the long-term, the girls and boys all wanted better housing with basic services, in a location where they would be treated with dignity.

MAYOR'S WORKSHOP

When data collection was complete, the mayor of Greater Johannesburg co-hosted a one-day workshop where GUIC researchers and the children were able to present research findings. Participants included local and regional government officials and representatives of nongovernmental organisations, community based organisations, and child-focused national and international agencies.

In order to prepare for this, the research team held pre-workshop meetings separately with the Canaansland adults and children. Adults were asked not to bring inebriated residents and they took this request, as well as the meeting, very seriously. They identified issues which they believed were problematic for the children, and elected two women and two men to attend the workshop and to present their viewpoints.

At their meeting, the children agreed that those who presented their views should:
• behave well
• be clever
• know what to do there
• be beautiful and good-looking
• speak fluently
• be honest and truthful
• speak well

It was suggested that since they all met these criteria, all should go. They agreed, but said that it would be impossible for them all to have a voice. A discussion on the voting process followed and two boys and two girls were elected to speak. The topic of democracy was then intro-

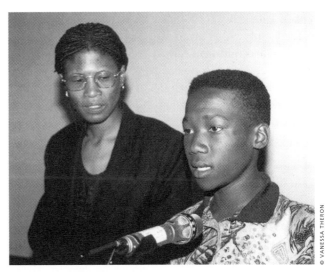

Figure 5.9 Christopher speaking as a children's representative

duced. After an intense and somewhat heated discussion, the children concluded that the representatives could not say whatever they liked. They had to present points agreed to by their peers. The children then decided upon points for presentation.

The adults and children of Canaansland found the workshop immensely supportive and they valued the acceptance and concern of the mayor and other officials. The children were initially awed by the number of persons present and the grandness of the venue. They especially liked the 'beautiful toilets' and tasty food. They used graphic examples from their own experiences to illustrate four issues: the urgent need for sanitation on site, the importance of proper housing, the need for a place to do their homework and the importance of being treated with dignity. One of the girls brought many in the audience to tears when she described the humiliation that the children suffered on a daily basis.

The children were delighted to find primary and high-school pupils from the Mini and Junior City Councils present. When the time came to debate matters jointly in a children's commission, however, they found this too taxing in addition to the long morning of presentations. They were restless, but the other young people eagerly debated issues of concern and drew in responses from the Canaansland children. Adult workshop participants were divided between five other commissions, which discussed not only the needs of the children from Canaansland, but also how to develop better informed plans for squatter settlements throughout the city and how to make Johannesburg as a whole a more friendly city for children. Plenary reports were followed by a summing-up period in which the way forward was outlined by a UNICEF representative.[20]

At the workshop, two main priorities were established for Canaansland:

- Local government should address problems concerning the access to potable water, sanitation, schooling and health services, crime prevention on site, refuse removal and safety measures in children's play areas;
- The GUIC team would seek donor funding for structures to create a play and study area to be used by the children after school hours.

> *Adult residents were proud that their children presented their own evaluations to urban planners and other officials.*

The mayor then activated procedures to stimulate a formal resolution in the Greater Johannesburg Metropolitan Council to enable problems on site to be addressed. The Norwegian Children's Broadcasting Corporation *(Barnetimefondet)* offered funds to GUIC to set up the children's play and study area and finance was also received from the Netherlands Embassy. At this time the children agreed that they would like the centre to be used as a creche for toddlers in the mornings.

Barriers between adults and children can be created quite unwittingly. Adult residents were pleased and proud that their sons and daughters presented their own evaluations to urban planners and other officials. An offshoot of this presentation, however, was that the mother of one of the young presenters felt shamed by her son's public exposure of his and his siblings' discomfort in wet weather when pools of water prevented them from sleeping on the floor and they had to spend wearisome nights trying to sleep sitting upright in chairs. He was unhappy about this until the situation was resolved; when his mother told her employer of her shame, the employer bought a bed for the children.

Neither the mayor nor the GUIC team knew at the time of the workshop that procedures were already in place to relocate the residents. Months passed and nothing could be done to improve the children's living conditions until Council approval was received. Then in mid-November 1997, the people of Canaansland were relocated to Thula Mntwana, 44 kilometres from the city centre.

RELOCATION OF CANAANSLAND TO THULA MNTWANA

From 1993 when the first shacks were erected at Canaansland, key members of the residents' committee were warned by government officials that they might be moved one day. After the election of the African National Congress to power in 1994, however, and in view of promises by the new government that those without homes would be accommodated, most residents appeared to believe that low-cost housing units would be built for them on the vacant stand across High Street.

Therefore Canaansland residents were shocked when informed by officials on Wednesday, 12 November 1997, that they would be relocated on the coming weekend. They claimed that they were not told where they would be taken, and said that they refused to accept leaflets with official notification of the relocation when these were brought the next day, since the period of notice was insufficient. A resident who felt that this injustice should be made public reported it to the South African Broadcasting Corporation. The relocation, which began early on Saturday 15 November, was publicised in television news broadcasts.

Outsiders were forbidden entry to Canaansland by armed guards, behind whom were posted a small number of uniformed and armed men with dogs, and a large phalanx of men clothed in red overalls and carrying shields and *sjambokke* (Afrikaans for rawhide whips). The Central Methodist Mission issued a press release to publicise the hostile nature of the action. Eyewitnesses agreed that residents were treated badly and, in many cases, brutally. Houses were knocked down while breakables were still inside. Children's pets were confiscated, to be lodged at the SPCA. Personal belongings became mixed up, damaged or lost, and personal property was burnt in the presence of owners and despite their protests.[21] On Sunday 16 November, all material remaining on site was burnt.[22] Residents were concerned that people who were absent would return home to find their homes were charred rubble.

School examinations were to start on Monday 17 November. Provision had been made for an open truck to transport the children from their new location to their former schools until the school term ended. The circumstances were, however, far from optimum for writing examinations. The comments made by a ten-year-old girl reflect the experience of many other children:

'We only heard on Saturday morning [that we would be moved]. When they were breaking down the shacks some of the security [people] set dogs on the people of the camp…I saw whites with guns and dogs. I was afraid. I thought they were going to beat us.'

GUIC researchers and Methodist workers who took food to the people at the new site found that no shelter, food or potable water had been provided. Roads were still being scraped. Few people were able to erect their homes completely; some could find none of their building materials and some materials were delivered just before sunset, when it was too late for people to set up their shacks. Many people at the old site and the new slept in the open that night. A fierce storm soaked them.

It takes time to settle into a new home, even when conditions are comfortable. Research shows[23] that children can suffer intensely through forced eviction. Viewing the destruction of their homes and the careless handling of their personal belongings, being exposed to harsh acts by people in uniform, witnessing the helplessness of their parents and other adults — all these experiences can affect children's emotional and physical well-being. Long-lasting effects can include difficulties

in concentration and feelings of insecurity. Although the violation of economic, social and cultural rights does not affect all children equally adversely, there can be no doubt that many children do suffer intensely at such times.[24]

The warm relationships built up during the GUIC research made it impossible for members of the original GUIC team to view the relocation with composure. It was considered costly, inhumane and contradictory to the human rights principles enshrined in South Africa's new Constitution. Therefore the GUIC team — and later the Canaansland residents — lodged a complaint with the Public Participation and Petitions Office of the Gauteng Legislature.[25] When informed in May 1999 that the matter was still pending, the residents wrote to the Regional Premier to bring their grievances to his notice. One and a half years later, they had still received no reply.

Local and regional government officials maintained that the relocation was consensual, but residents denied that this was so. It seems surprising that, if the Canaansland residents had been aware of the plan, they had never mentioned it to the GUIC or Methodist personnel. Three years later, the mother of two of the girls who worked with GUIC, reflected on the whole issue:[26]

'If we had cared about each other more and been better neighbours, maybe we would have known about the government's plan to move us and maybe we would have been able to discuss it and agree on our rights in this matter. But people were too jealous and suspicious of each other. Also, we did not trust certain people on the residents' committee… And Mandela said we can go to a place in Johannesburg where they are planning low-cost housing for poor people. We heard that low-cost housing would be built right there, near where we were staying, so we thought these things were coming to us.'

MOVING FORWARD

In this way the people of Canaansland became part of the larger settlement of Thula Mntwana, where about 3,000 shacks already housed relocated people, pending re-

© PETER RICH

Figure 5.10 The relocation of Canaansland

settlement elsewhere. Loosely translated from IsiZulu, 'Thula Mntwana' means 'hush my child.' Some people say the name was coined by parents who reassured their children that they now lived in a better place than the city, where they had cried constantly. Others disagree. They say that Thula Mntwana is a place where you are put out of the way until the authorities have decided what they are going to do with you. When you ask for better conditions or what the future holds, you are scolded and told to be silent and not to complain, as if you were a child.

At the new site there were things to enjoy, such as the extra space — shacks were not jumbled together as before. Children were safe from traffic, since there was none. But people relocated from Canaansland suffered great hardship, since all their back-up supports had been removed. Without donations of food from shopkeepers and churches, and with no means of making a living, there was very little to eat and everyone was desperately hungry. Travel to and from Johannesburg used up any small payment earned from recycling waste materials or doing piece-jobs. People said that the chemical toilets

supplied were insufficient for their needs. Water was often not delivered regularly by tanker, as promised:

'I think they just go to sleep and forget about their job and about us. They forget that we have to wash our clothes to go to work or school, especially on Sunday.'
(Nokuthula, 12 years old)

The mayor of Greater Johannesburg visited the children just before Christmas in 1997, taking gift packs of food, utensils and playthings for each of their families. He assured them of his concern but told them that he could not 'press buttons' to make things happen for them since his position was ceremonial. His gestures of caring were warmly appreciated.

Staff of the Nelson Mandela Children's Fund offered emergency food supplies for the children for three months. Since the Fund worked only through local committees, residents were motivated to reconvene the Canaansland committee. They decided that former committee members would have to stand for re-election, since their positions would not be guaranteed. Chief office-bearers should be literate to enable them to deal with paperwork and financial statements; this led to the demotion of some of the former key figures on the committee, who had not been trusted.

After many weeks' debate, four men and four women were approved as officers of the Canaansland Development Committee. At their request, the ABET Institute[27] at the University of South Africa ran a workshop for committee members, where routine committee procedures were explained, as were financial planning, the arrangement and recording of meetings, and the writing of a constitution. The Department of Indigenous Law provided legal advice.

A shipping container was bought with some of the money collected for the play and study area. It served as a food storage and distribution depot and quickly became a central meeting place for the girls and younger children, since it was a main feature in the barren settlement and it cast shade. The children said that what they missed most about the city was the playground which they had all visited regularly. It was clear that they needed the play and study area, which had been previously agreed upon, more than ever before. Officials at the Gauteng Department of Housing and Land Affairs were sympathetic to the children's need and allocated the site on which the storage container stood, as well as a number of other areas alongside it, as a play and study site.

The nutrition scheme and the delivery of the container sparked intense anger in greater Thula Mntwana, even though many of the toddlers there were also given food from the container. The residents said that they should be first in line for benefits and that the people from Canaansland had jumped the queue. Sporadic small fights broke out, especially on weekends when people had been drinking at the local taverns, and some of the Canaansland committee members feared for their lives. Many months of meetings[28] were necessary to help the residents of greater Thula Mntwana come to terms with the fact that the container was only one part of a larger structure that donors had earmarked for the children of Canaansland.

When the play and study area began to take shape, hostilities resurfaced. In December 1998 the children of Canaansland found that neighbours were still hostile: *'People here are just as horrible to us as they were in the city although they are living like us'* (Zukiswa, 11 years old). The children said that they were not welcome at the rough playing fields in Thula Mntwana and that they did not want children from Thula Mntwana in their living area. If a wide range of people in Thula Mntwana, including the children, had been able to participate in the process of setting up the centre, this would probably have helped to develop a sense of ownership, but there was no funding for a participatory process of such magnitude.

Other ways were, therefore, sought to work towards greater unity in the area. Early in 1999, an impact assessment[29] was undertaken with the children from Canaansland to find out how taking part in the GUIC research had affected them. It was decided to use some of the children from Thula Mntwana as a control group — if they and their caretakers would agree to this. When the impact assessment workshops for the children from Canaansland were over, they were asked to invite neighbouring children to a workshop a fortnight later and to help with the games. Some children refused angrily but others liked the

---

At the new site there were things to enjoy. But people relocated from Canaansland suffered great hardship, since all their back-up supports had been removed.

---

idea. Only nine of the thirteen children who were formally invited did come, but the day passed happily. This opened the way for the children's peer group to be extended to neighbouring children.

By this time, one member of the Canaansland Development Committee had been elected to the Thula Mntwana Residents' Committee and the people of Canaansland had been largely reconciled with their neighbours. The Canaansland committee routinely sought the viewpoints of the children's representatives in matters affecting them, such as the use of the study and play area and schooling issues.

UBUHLE BUYEZA, AND BEYOND

We now return to the meeting described in the opening of this chapter. It was a time of great excitement since the mayor had agreed to open the play and study centre. Arrangements had to be made for the opening programme and celebrations, and a name agreed on. After consulting with the chairman, one of the girls suggested shyly that it be named *Ubuhle Buyeza* (IsiZulu: good things are about to happen). The name was unanimously accepted, and in May 1999 a huge crowd of people ululated as the mayor of Greater Johannesburg and the mayor of the Southern Local Council jointly unveiled the naming plaque.

The centre could not be fenced since the whole of Thula Mntwana was to be re-measured and declared a township. This decision had been announced at a mass meeting in Thula Mntwana. People were overjoyed since this meant that their difficult living conditions would be rectified. Until the children asked that a small fence be erected on one side, however, the water tanker continued driving through Ubuhle Buyeza when children were at play.

The use of the area was redefined by the children in consultation with the Canaansland committee. They no longer needed the structure for schoolwork since there was now enough space for them to study at home. Girls and boys of all ages used the outdoor courtyard and seating area for games and to meet socially; adults used it for meetings. Mothers set up an informal hairdressing salon so that they could use the outdoor seating to watch their young children at play on the swings, slide and climbing frames, while their hair dried in the sun.

The indoors was used only for occasional children's meetings and when they worked in groups on educational projects. Mothers were anxious to set up a creche, as agreed with the older children. They needed guidance and training, but the long drive to the site put off people who might have offered this help.

By March 2000, the quality of life for people at Canaansland who did not have steady jobs or small businesses on site had deteriorated. Competing for scarce resources with over 10,000 other people was personally disabling. Residents were frustrated at the lack of concrete evidence of improvements in their living conditions. Some who had no children locked their shacks during the week and slept on city streets while begging or collecting scrap materials for recycling. Key members of the Canaansland committee, including some of the women who wanted to set up the creche, found menial jobs far from Canaansland. They left before dawn and returned after dark. On weekends they slept in. Because of this, the Canaansland Development Committee ceased to function. The children no longer had a forum to express their ideas and air their opinions.

Meanwhile, affordable housing was indeed built on the families' former squatter site in Johannesburg and the adjacent vacant lot on High Street: but only for the

Figure 5.11 On the rooftop of the Ubuhle Buyeza Centre

benefit of people with steady incomes higher than those in Canaansland. Belgian and Norwegian development funds have made it possible for the tenants in one section to pay low rents and for those in another to receive a monthly housing subsidy so that they can buy their homes. The former mortuary has been converted into a creche and recreational centre for their children. On 6 May 2000, a story in the Saturday Star announced that:

'A former squatter settlement in Newtown, Johannesburg, has been transformed into an appealing 126-unit housing complex for low-income earners…. If the vehicles in the parking lot are anything to go by, residents…appear to be mixed between low- and middle-income earners….'[30]

REFLECTIONS

Children are aware of the larger socio-political context. They develop a sense of social identity that is personally experienced as a hierarchy of social status, domination and power. These hierarchies are reflected in their neighbourhoods and are important in the development of personal identity.[31] The children at Canaansland found themselves at the bottom of the social hierarchy, subject to prejudice, and relatively powerless. This inferior status derived from three characteristics over which they had no control: poverty, race and childhood. The characteristics had visible identifiers.

First, the people at Canaansland were clearly needy. In common with children elsewhere, those at Canaansland were well aware of how their socio-economic background might affect others' views of them.[32] They tried to avoid being tagged with the pejorative label 'squatter' when away from home, by dressing neatly and keeping the location of their homes secret.

Being poor carries with it a socially assigned powerlessness that derives from the view that the poor are not entitled to share equally in facilities and services.[33] Because Canaansland residents had invaded others' land in the city, they could not expect to receive basic services such as sanitation and potable water there. This led outsiders who lived in suburban homes to associate the residents with filth and squalor, and to treat girls and boys at Canaansland with contempt. Such treatment may have long-lasting effects, for *'children's dignity is fragile, their self-awareness (whether based in individual or group identity) is in the process of development'.*[34]

At Thula Mntwana, the people of Canaansland were merely a small segment of a much larger, needy population and were threatened by their neighbours when they appeared to be given favours. The manner in which the Canaansland residents and their children were relocated was a striking example of their level of disenfranchisement. Many people had committed themselves to upgrading the original Canaansland site according to the children's insights and recommendations; but these positive indicators of the children's worth were badly eroded by their sudden relocation to an inhospitable environment that offered no provision for their health, recreational and educational needs. The construction of the promised play and study facilities at the new venue helped to assure the children that they were still worthy of consideration. The mayor's visits reinforced their sense of value.

> *The children at Canaansland found themselves at the bottom of the social hierarchy, subject to prejudice, and relatively powerless. This inferior status derived from three characteristics over which they had no control: poverty, race and childhood.*

Second, as regards race, the children at Canaansland were African in a neighbourhood of mainly Indian people, with mostly white people in low-cost housing to the North and Northwest. Racial discrimination had been legally entrenched and had focused on African people for so long before the African National Congress came to power in 1994 that it was still strongly evident in business centres, schools and other public places. The children experienced social exclusion on grounds of race when they wanted to enter public places and use public facilities, and they found that they were unable to attend schools of their choice. African passers-by abused them on site, but when they were out in the neighbourhood and not perceptibly 'squatters', people of other race groups felt free to abuse them verbally and physically because they were African.

Last, the state of childhood made the girls and boys at Canaansland relatively powerless in the presence of adults. They were expected to spend part of each day on

---

BOX 5.3

A Chronology of Project-Related Actions

FEBRUARY–APRIL 1997
Girls and boys from Canaansland take part in GUIC research.

MAY 1997
The mayor hosts a workshop for children and researchers to present their findings. Specific improvements are agreed upon and prioritised.

NOVEMBER 1997
Canaansland is relocated to Thula Mntwana, 44 kilometres from the city centre.

JANUARY–APRIL 1998
Children are fed through an emergency nutrition scheme financed by the Nelson Mandela Children's Fund.

1998
Team efforts reduce hostility between residents from Thula Mntwana and the former Canaansland.

1998–1999
Children's representatives are invited to meetings of the Canaansland Development Committee to discuss relevant issues.

1999
The mayor opens the Ubuhle Buyeza Centre for children and signs an agreement with Unicef to make Johannesburg 'child-friendly'.

1999
The Gauteng Department of Housing and Land Affairs approves finance to transform Thula Mntwana into a

township and the City Council lists Thula Mntwana in its fast-track development programme. Site studies and feasibility studies are completed.

2000
Residents of Thula Mntwana are told that the area is to be upgraded and that basic services will be provided, and residents register for stands. The Gauteng Department of Housing and Land Affairs decides on a participatory planning process.

MARCH 2000
A woman is appointed for the first time to chair the Thula Mntwana Steering Committee.

2000
The Canaansland Development Committee falls apart. Children no longer have a voice on any residents' committee.

2000
The Metro Council seeks children's views at four sites and appoints a project manager to run the Child-Friendly Cities programme.

OCTOBER 2000
The Southern Local Council announces that relocation of all the people in Thula Mntwana is again on its agenda. Residents' representatives strongly oppose this.

---

chores and errands for parents and other grown-ups, and African tradition required that they treat grown-ups with respect and never query their decisions and commands. In time, the adults of Canaansland realised that the girls and boys had evaluated their urban living conditions sensibly, and had made recommendations for improvements that would better all of their lives. This led to the unusual situation of children being able to voice their ideas at meetings of the Canaansland Development Committee. However, the committee had influence in only a small

area of Thula Mntwana and its disintegration meant that children could no longer put forward their ideas.

It is not required of South Africa, nor any other country that has ratified the Convention on the Rights of the Child, to guarantee the economic, social and cultural rights of children. Their duty is only *'framed in terms of doing what they can achieve, in the light of their available resources',* but the availability of resources to meet the rights of children is not always a clear issue.[35]

In South Africa, the right of children to shelter has

Figure 5.12 Playing in the Ubuhle Buyeza Centre playground

been used successfully since March 2000 to delay official efforts to evict squatters in two provinces. Defendants have argued that suitable alternative housing must be provided for children and their families before shacks are demolished, so as not to contravene Section 28 of the country's Constitution.[36]

Since 1997, the Gauteng Department of Housing and Land Affairs has introduced various initiatives in an effort to work with the poor in humane ways to ease housing problems. Since people tend to settle on land owned by local or provincial authorities, it was decided to earmark as much land as possible for release for settlement. If people erected shacks on privately owned land, the purchase of the land for settlement would be considered. People would be granted rights of tenure at these sites and could then apply for housing subsidies.[37]

In April 1999 the Department of Housing and Land Affairs approved funding for the development of Thula Mntwana.[38] Within a year all site studies and feasibility studies required prior to the establishment of a new township were complete and the Local Council was authorised by a special Power of Attorney to transform Thula Mntwana into a township: Kanana Park Extension. Development was located within the Greater Johannesburg Metropolitan Council's fast-track programme. Four thousand plots would be allocated. Security of tenure would be granted and by 2001 or 2002, it was expected that the General Plan of Approval (GPA) would be passed and basic services would be provided.

A commitment was made to undertake development at Thula Mntwana as a participatory process. This would take the form of mass meetings on site and local councillors would attend the monthly meetings of the Thula Mntwana Steering Committee. In March 2000, a Liaison Officer was appointed to interact with the Local Council, and the residents of Thula Mntwana elected a woman, for the first time, to chair their steering committee.

The children of Thula Mntwana were not barred from the steering committee meetings. Since residents presumed that the meetings were for adults, however, children were not expected to voice opinions there and they were effectively excluded from the participatory process. Despite this exclusion, continued contact with the children has shown that the increased self-esteem and self-efficacy that they gained from the GUIC process has not completely eroded. They have redirected their energies to achieving success at school in anticipation of finding good jobs that will lead to better living conditions for themselves and their families. A fifteen-year-old boy explained the children's view, in light of what had happened to the people of Canaansland: '...*If you do not have an education you are just like paper blowing in the wind.*'

Adults of Canaansland realised that the girls and boys had evaluated their urban living conditions sensibly, and had made recommendations for improvements that would better all of their lives.

Even though the story of the Canaansland children has ended in this way, the Mayor of Johannesburg has seriously tried to incorporate children's right to participation into his office's practice.[39] In 1999 he signed an agreement with Unicef, on behalf of the Greater Johannesburg Metropolitan Council, which committed the Council to making the city 'child-friendly.' In the year 2000 this process began in a practical way: four city segments were selected and a sample of children living in each were invited to evaluate their neighbourhoods and to recommend improvements, using a variety of Growing Up in Cities methods for data collection and public presentations. There are plans to include in the process a second squatter site, and possibly other sites as well, in 2001. At the same time, a project manager has been

appointed to ensure that the children's recommendations are implemented wherever possible, and to drive the child-friendly city initiative forward in Greater Johannesburg. In these ways, the experience gained with the children of Canaansland continues to spread its influence.

ENDNOTES

1. For a study by children of issues within two informal settlements in Zimbabwe, see Chinyenze-Daniel, McIvor and Honeyman (1999).
2. South African Department of Housing (1994, p. 21).
3. Stevens and Rule (1998, p. 1).
4. Statistics South Africa (1996, 1997).
5. cf. Reeves (1998).
6. May (1998).
7. Reeves (1998).
8. Mabetoa (1994, p. 87).
9. cf. Holden (1993).
10. Swift (1998).
11. Ennew (1998).
12. Boyden and Ennew (1997), Fine and Sandstrom (1998), Hengst (1997).
13. Rädda Barnen (1996, p. 7).
14. Swart-Kruger (2000, 2001).
15. Swart-Kruger (1994).
16. Van Bueren (1998, p. 43).
17. Magona (1990, p. 45).
18. Translated from isiZulu.
19. Rädda Barnen (1996).
20. Swart-Kruger (1997), Swart-Kruger (2000).
21. Swart-Kruger (2000).
22. Abrader (1997), Ndlela (1997).
23. Dizon (1997).
24. cf. McBride (1998).
25. Petition no. HL07038.97, reproduced verbatim in Swart-Kruger (2000).
26. Translated from IsiZulu.
27. Adult Basic Education and Training.
28. Meetings included representatives from Canaansland, Thula Mntwana, GUIC, the Nelson Mandela Children's Fund, the Southern Local Council and the Gauteng Department of Housing and Land Affairs.
29. A study financed by the Jacobs Foundation.
30. Dyanti (2000, p. 6).
31. Foster (1994), Hengst, (1997, p. 47), James, Jenks and Prout (1998, p. 201).
32. Hengst (1997), Sutton (1996).
33. cf. Colton et al (1997), Richter (1994).
34. Ennew (1998, p 30).
35. McBride (1998, p 110).
36. Tabane (2000), Mokwena (2000).
37. Gauteng Department of Housing and Land Affairs (1998, p 8).
38. Gauteng Department of Housing and Land Affairs (1999a, 1999b).
39. This initiative was undertaken by Isaac Mogase, Mayor of the Greater Johannesburg Metropolitan Council from 1995 to 2000.

REFERENCES

Abrader, G (1997) 'Fordsburg squatter camp goes up in smoke as residents are moved', *The Star,* Johannesburg, 17 November, p. 3.

Boyden, J and Ennew, J (eds) (1997) *Children in Focus — A Manual for Participatory Research with Children,* Rädda Barnen, Stockholm.

Chinyenze-Daniel, M, McIvor, C, and Honeyman, A (1999) *Do Not Look Down on Us,* Save the Children Fund, Harare.

Colton, M, Drakeford, M, Roberts, S, Scholte, E, Casas, F and Williams, M (1997) 'Child welfare and stigma: Principles into practice', *Childhood,* vol 4(3), pp. 265-284.

Dizon, AM (1997) 'Impact of eviction on children.' Unpublished report for the Urban Poor Associates (UPA) in cooperation with the Asian Coalition for Housing Rights (ACHR) and the United Nations Economic and Social Commission for Asia and the Pacific (UN-ESCAP).

Dyanti, A (2000) 'Inner-city slum becomes a jewel', *Saturday Star,* Johannesburg, 20 May, p. 6.

Ennew, J (1998) 'Shame and Physical Pain: Cultural relativity, children, torture and punishment' in Van Bueren, G (ed) *Childhood Abused: Protecting children against torture, cruel, inhuman and degrading treatment and punishment,* Ashgate, Aldershot.

Fine, GA and Sandstrom, KL (1988) *Knowing Children: Participant observation with minors,* Sage, Newbury Park.

Foster, D (1994) 'Racism and Children's Intergroup Orientations: Their development and the question of psychological effects on minority group children' in Dawes, A and Donald, D (eds) *Childhood and Adversity: Psychological perspectives from South African research,* David Philip, Cape Town.

Gauteng Department of Housing and Land Affairs (1998) *SINESU, We have a plan,* Gauteng Provincial Government, Johannesburg.

Gauteng Department of Housing and Land Affairs (1999a) 'Approved project list', Unpublished report, 20 April, Gauteng Provincial Government, Johannesburg.

Gauteng Department of Housing and Land Affairs (1999b) 'Multi-year strategic management plan: 1999/2000 – 2003/2004', Unpublished report, Gauteng Provincial Government, Johannesburg.

Hengst, H (1997) 'Negotiating "us" and "them": Children's constructions of collective identity', *Childhood,* vol 4(1), pp. 43-62.

Holden, R (1993) 'An argument for the validation of self-reliant technology and informal settlements in newly urbanised areas in South Africa', *Planning,* No 129, pp. 61-69.

James, A, Jenks, C and Prout, A (1998) *Theorizing Childhood,* Polity Press, Cambridge.

Mabetoa, M (1994) 'Cycles of Disadvantage of African Families in South Africa', in Sono, T (ed) *African Family and Marriage Under Stress,* Centre for Development Analysis, Pretoria.

Magona, S (1990) *To My Children's Children,* Africasouth New Writing, David Philip, Claremount.

May, J (1998) *Poverty and Inequality in South Africa,* Praxis, Durban.

McBride, (1998) 'The violation of economic, social and cultural rights as torture or cruel, inhuman or degrading treatment', in Van Bueren (ed) *Childhood Abused: Protecting children against torture, cruel, inhuman and degrading treatment and punishment,* Ashgate, Aldershot.

Mokwena, M (2000) 'Court ruling on rights of informal settlers challenged', *The Star,* Johannesburg, 12 May, p. 3.

Ndlela, S (1997) 'Squatters are to be forcibly removed to Weiler's Farm', *City Vision,* Johannesburg, 21 November, pp. 1, 6.

Rädda Barnen (1996) *Children on their Housing,* Rädda Barnen, Stockholm.

Reeves, J (1998) 'The move from slums to suburbs', *Saturday Star,* Johannesburg, 21 February, p. 9.

Richter, L (1994) 'Economic Stress and Its Influence on the Family and Caretaking Patterns', in Dawes, A and Donald, D (eds) *Childhood and Adversity: Psychological perspectives from South African research,* David Philip, Cape Town.

South African Department of Housing (1994) *A New Housing Policy and Strategy for South Africa,* White Paper, Department of Housing, Pretoria.

Statistics South Africa (1996) *Statistics in Brief RSA,* CSS, Pretoria.

Statistics South Africa (1997) *Statistics in Brief RSA,* CSS, Pretoria.

Stevens, L and Rule, S (1998) *Upgrading Gauteng's Informal Settlements,* vol 1, The Community Agency for Social Enquiry, Johannesburg.

Sutton, SE (1996) *Weaving a Tapestry of Resistance: The places, power, and poetry of a sustainable society,* Bergin & Garvey, London.

Swart-Kruger, J (1994) 'Black latchkey children in South Africa' , in Sono, T (ed) *African Family and Marriage Under Stress,* Centre for Development Analysis, Pretoria.

Swart-Kruger, J (2001) *Children of Thula Mntwana: Growing Up in Cities.* 26-minute video directed by S. Cameron and co-produced by Streetwise South Africa and UNESCO-MOST.

Swart-Kruger, J (1997) *Growing up in Cities: Children's participation in urban evaluation,* (Video) Unit Video & Sound/Photography, University of South Africa, Pretoria.

Swart-Kruger, J (ed) (2000) *Growing up in Canaansland: Children's recommendations on improving a squatter camp environment,* Human Sciences Research Council and UNESCO-MOST Programme, Pretoria.

Swift, M (1998) 'The Challenge of Keeping Participatory Processes on Track towards the Achievement of Practical Goals', in Johnson, V, Ivan-Smith, E, Pridmore, P and Scott, P (eds) *Stepping Forward: Children and Young People's Participation in the Development Process,* Intermediate Technology Publications, London, pp. 42-45.

Tabane, R (2000) 'Squatters ignore government pleas to leave; case rests on possible contravention of constitution if children have no shelter', *The Star,* Johannesburg, 12 May, p. 3.

Van Bueren, G (ed) (1998) *International Documents on Children,* 2nd rev. ed., Nijhoff, The Hague.

Victor, R (1998) 'Angry Diepsloot squatters block road after their shacks are demolished', *The Star,* Johannesburg, 4 May, p. 3.

West, B (1998) 'Inner-city squatter settlement set alight', *The Star,* Johannesburg, 26 June, pp. 1-2.

CHAPTER SIX

Tales from Truth Town
Children's Lives in a South Indian 'Slum'

Kanchan Bannerjee and David Driskell

Sathyanagar, a small self-built settlement on the edge of Bangalore (India), is presented through the eyes of its children. What emerges is a place of contradictions: a place where children have lives of real hardship and exposure to environmental hazards and political injustice; and simultaneously a place where children benefit from sustaining social networks, cohesive cultural beliefs, and diverse settings for play and engagement in their community. An effort to build on these strengths through a participatory process of community development is described, along with the barriers that this initiative faced. The lessons learned can be applied by development agencies and other organizations which seek to empower marginal communities and their children.

This is the story of a small self-built settlement in southern India. Like many similar settlements in India and throughout the developing world, it is a place that outsiders — including many middle-class Indians — would describe as dirty, squalid, poverty-stricken and depressed. It is, both in the classification scheme of the state bureaucracy and in the local nomenclature of its residents, a slum.

The name of the settlement is Sathyanagar, which roughly translates from the original Sanskrit as 'truth' *(sathya)* 'town' *(nagar)*. In retrospect, it is a fitting name for a place to explore the lives and perspectives of young people, recounted in their own words. The stories shared by Sathyanagar's young people — as documented by the Growing Up in Cities project in early 1997 — speak some basic truths about their lives and the place where they live. These are stories of severe economic hardship, environmental hazard, and social and political injustice. They

speak of young people thrust into adult roles at the age of six or seven; of hours spent each day in household chores such as fetching potable water; of children exposed to open sewer drains in their daily play; of people's lives cut short by disease and violence.

Yet these stories also describe young people with an astonishing degree of energy, self-reliance and optimism, cultural traditions and pride, human inventiveness and resilience. These are stories told by children who, in many cases, could quite safely be described as *confident, connected,* and *happy* — words seldom used to describe young people in many of the Growing Up in Cities sites who enjoy much higher levels of material well-being.

This juxtaposition — of children leading culturally and emotionally rich, happy lives within the context of a comparatively poor and environmentally degraded place — is the seeming paradox of the Indian Growing Up in Cities site, and a central theme of Sathyanagar's story.

But like all themes, it does not apply to all of the people in the story. Nor is it as simple as it may appear at first glance. This is not a naïve, romantic story about poor people content with their station in life, living happily in abject poverty. Such stories serve only the interests of those who wish to retain the inequities of the status quo.

The story of Sathyanagar, despite its uplifting optimism, is also a story of official neglect, broken promises, wasted resources and squandered opportunities. It is a story that casts an unflattering light not only on inefficient, ineffective and sometimes inept or corrupt bureaucracies and politicians, but also on misguided development agencies and mismanaged non-governmental groups. It is the story of young people making their way in the world, as best they can, in spite of the official adult world's failure to meet their most basic needs.[1]

THE SETTING: MODERN INDIA AND BOOMING BANGALORE

India is one of the truly remarkable stories of the modern age, defying any easy categorisation. It is both industrialised and agrarian, tradition-bound and cutting edge, fiercely democratic and beholden to ingrained systems of bureaucracy and patronage. It encompasses an immense diversity of languages, religions, ethnicities and caste groups. It is a place where every generalisation can be countered by a dozen readily apparent contradictions.

India also has one of the world's fastest growing populations. Having recently passed the one billion mark, it is expected to surpass China as the world's most populous country in the coming 20 to 30 years. While the country's well-known mega-cities are among the world's largest, the population remains predominantly rural. In 1991, according to the Census of India, only 26 percent of the country's population was urban. However, in absolute numbers, that translated into more than 215 million people living in Indian cities in 1991, an urban population far exceeding the total population of most other countries.[2]

India's burgeoning population has placed a tremendous strain on the country's resources and infrastructure. While the country has made great strides since independence a half-century ago, it continues to face seemingly insurmountable obstacles in its ongoing development programme. Although it has built up an industrial economy that places it among the world's top 15 producers, has reached virtual self-sufficiency in agricultural production, and has developed a substantial middle class, India continues to experience high levels of malnutrition and struggles with some of the world's highest poverty rates.[3] Across a wide range of development indicators (infant mortality, literacy, access to clean water, and so on), India has a long way to go in meeting the basic needs of its population.

Figure 6.1 Bangalore is a rapidly growing city of over 5 million people. It is rich in traditional culture as well as an important global centre for information technology.

© DAVID DRISKELL

Figure 6.2 Panoramic view of Sathyanagar, as seen from the embankment of the railway line

One of India's development 'success stories' in the past two decades has been the growth of its information technology sector, much of which is based in the southern city of Bangalore, capital of the State of Karnataka. Situated high on the Deccan plateau, about 1000 metres above sea level, Bangalore is located at the very centre of the southern tip of the Indian subcontinent.

Founded in 1537 by the chieftain Kempe Gowda and named Bangaluru in the local language of Kannada, the city has passed through the hands of several rulers, the last of them prior to Independence being the British, who further developed Bangalore as a cantonment city. Today Bangalore is a city of monumental public buildings, large parks, military establishments, scientific institutions and a fast-growing information technology sector that has attracted many multinational corporations and earned Bangalore a reputation as India's 'Silicon Valley.'

Partly because of its economic promise as a centre for information technology, Bangalore has been one of Asia's fastest growing cities over the past twenty years. With a current population of over 5 million, the city is projected to reach 7 million in the early years of the 21st century.[4] Such levels of growth have severely overbur-

dened the city's infrastructure and profoundly impacted the quality of life. Bangalore's claim as the 'Garden City' or 'Pensioner's Paradise' of India is being threatened by haphazard growth, high levels of pollution, increasing densities of development, escalating land prices and housing costs, and urban sprawl that is destroying traditional agricultural lands. Electrical power cuts are a regular occurrence, and access to water (or lack of it) is becoming one of the defining issues for the city's future.

In many ways, Bangalore is the essence of modern India — a fascinating mix of traditional culture, colonial influences, and new technology; a city being overwhelmed by its own success, and a society being transformed by the forces of the global marketplace.

SATHYANAGAR: A SETTLEMENT ON THE EDGE OF TRANSFORMATION

History

The self-built settlement of Sathyanagar was created more than 30 years ago when a group of displaced people staked their claim on a piece of land on the northeast

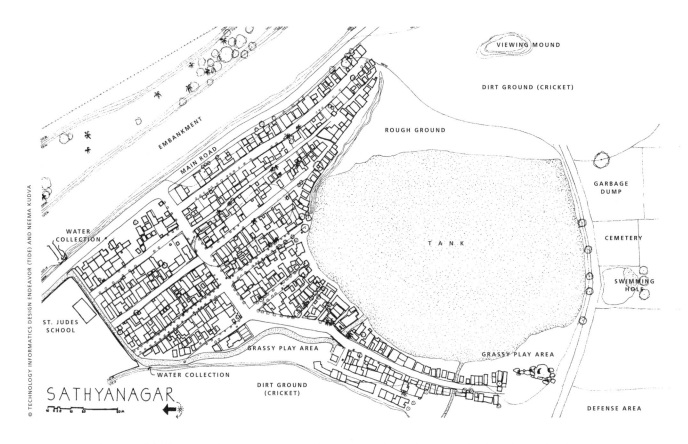

Figure 6.3 Sathyanagar is laid out on a clear street pattern, with approximately 550 houses. It is bordered by an abandoned, swampy tank (water reservoir), a railway line, and a military area.

periphery of Bangalore. Originally migrants from rural areas in the neighbouring states of Andhra Pradesh and Tamil Nadu, these settlers had first located in temporary housing in the centre of Bangalore, in areas around the railway yard, or in low-income areas adjacent to Sathyanagar.

As is common to self-built settlements, Sathyanagar sprang up on left-over land that was not considered particularly desirable for urban development: in this case, a dry lake bed located in between a military establishment, a railway line, an industrial storage area, and an abandoned and overgrown tank (water reservoir). Today, a middle class residential area is also located nearby, as are several other low-income, self-built settlements.

As is also common in self-built settlement patterns, the original group of 12 families multiplied quickly,

mainly on kinship lines, as relatives came and joined them in Sathyanagar. In the 1970s, they organised themselves into a registered cooperative society and, armed with proof of their intentions, convinced a sympathetic politician to grant them land tenure. As part of this process, a layout plan was developed for the community, organising a clear street pattern and distributing the land into 60- by 40-foot and 30- by 40-foot parcels. Thus, Sathyanagar began its development with two key advantages that are not always available to self-built areas: land tenure and an organised pattern of development.

At the time of registration in 1972, Sathyanagar had 152 houses. Today, the original parcels and structures have been subdivided, developed, and populated to the point that there are approximately 550 houses, with a population of over 3000. The process of densification is likely to continue given the recent extension of the Bangalore Municipality to include Sathyanagar and the surrounding area within the urban limits of Bangalore. It was partly due to this act of annexation that Sathyanagar was selected as the site for the Growing Up in Cities project. It provided an opportunity to explore a community about to undergo more intensive urbanisation and, for local decision makers, might offer policy and planning guidance based on the needs of young people living in such areas.

Built Environment

Although Sathyanagar is on the edge of a quickly urbanising area and surrounded by areas of intensive development, the settlement itself has the appearance and feel of a village. Approached from the nearby Banaswadi Main Road — a heavily trafficked, shop-lined thoroughfare — the primary route leading to the settlement is a dusty, potholed lane running parallel to the raised embankment of a railroad line. Progressing along the lane, the chaotic urban atmosphere of the main road recedes and a quieter, less intense atmosphere emerges.

The primary entrance to the settlement, and the only access point for vehicles, is from the road running parallel to the railroad tracks. At this point, the roadway becomes a narrow dirt lane that is the domain of pedestrians, bicycles and pushcarts, with only an occasional auto-rickshaw, car or small truck interrupting the flow of street activities.

The settlement originally consisted of mud-built homes with thatched roofs, as is typical in nearby rural communities. However, over time, many of these structures have been replaced by cinder block constructions with corrugated asbestos roofs. In some cases, better-off residents have added second stories to their dwellings in an ongoing, cumulative process of home improvement. Most structures are residential, although a number of small shops have been created in the front area of homes facing the main roadway of the settlement, and a number of small industries operate in homes and adjacent structures. Community facilities include a small Catholic church, several small Hindu temples and shrines, a government school building (which is nearly always padlocked shut), an informal school and technical centre run

TABLE 6.1	
Community Profile	

LAND AND POPULATION

Land Area	4.05 hectares (10 acres)
Dwelling Units	550
Population	3200

LANGUAGE SPOKEN AT HOME*	PERCENT OF HOUSEHOLDS
Tamil	85%
Telegu	10%
Urdu	3%
Kannada	2%

RELIGION	PERCENT OF HOUSEHOLDS
Hindu	90%
Christian	7%
Muslim	3%

* Kannada is the official language of Karnataka State, of which Bangalore is the capital. Tamil and Telegu are spoken in the neighbouring states of Tamil Nadu and Andhra Pradesh respectively. Urdu is a language originally from North India that is today the predominant language among Muslims throughout India.

by a local non-governmental organisation called the Development Education Society (DEEDS), and a toilet complex that has been recently completed by the local office of a national NGO called the Centre for Environment Education (CEE).

Environmental Quality

As is common in urban India, particularly in low-income settlements, the environment in Sathyanagar is significantly degraded. In Sathyanagar, as in the rest of Bangalore, two of the most problematic issues are water and sanitation.

'The gutters are dirty and there is no flow of sewage and so it stinks.' (Murali Kumar, age 11)

The lack of potable water was consistently ranked as the most significant issue facing the community, by young and old residents alike. It was a central theme in children's interviews (especially for girls), interviews with

© GANESH, AGE 12

Figure 6.4 Young people's drawings gave strong emphasis to the issue of water, typically displaying two or more water sources, often very prominently.

© DAVID DRISKELL

Figure 6.5 Residents collect drinking water from one of two holes punctured in a water pipe that runs through the community.

parents, and in the children's drawings, each of which included a water icon in some form. Some drawings even depicted the full range of water sources available at the site (see Figure 6.4).

Water has long been a critical issue for the entire Bangalore area, and the distribution of water from the Cauvery River (piped in from a distance of over 100 kilometres to serve as the main source of potable water for the city) is a source of continuing friction between the states of Karnataka and nearby Tamil Nadu. The city's only other major source of water is the Tippagondanahalli Lake which threatens to dry up every summer.

Most, if not all, surface water in Bangalore is contaminated with sewage (as is the tank, or reservoir, adjacent to Sathyanagar), and groundwater supplies are either too polluted for consumption (due to sewage as well as industrial and commercial pollutants) or, increasingly, no longer available due to over-extraction.[5] In Sathyanagar, two bore wells have been abandoned and only one (deeper) well provides water. However, due to pollution, the water can only be used for limited purposes. For drinking water, residents rely on a tenuous supply provided by two punctures in a water pipeline that traverses the area.

The process of carrying empty jugs to one of the two water pipe locations, waiting in line, filling the jugs, and then carrying them back to their homes occupies hours of the day for many residents, including children. A typical day may involve more than a dozen trips back and forth to the water pipe to fetch the day's water supply, with some children rising in the very early morning hours to collect water before the lines begin to form.

Water pollution issues are largely linked to the other major environmental issue in Sathyanagar: sanitation. While an open drainage system has been installed in the settlement and was being lined with new granite stones during the course of the Growing Up in Cities project, most of the system has not been designed with adequate slope to facilitate drainage, resulting in large stretches of standing sewage in the open drain system. Equally problematic was the destination of the untreated sewage that did drain: the adjacent tank area, where some residents do their wash and younger children sometimes play (although many of the children who were interviewed were aware of the problem and steered clear of the area).

'Because there is not enough, there are fights to catch water. They should have two water taps for every line of houses.' (Shankar, age 13)

Employment

The residents of Sathyanagar are engaged in a wide range of income-generating activities. Most of the men are daily wageworkers in the construction industry, in cement factories, or hired casual labour in the nearby railway yard. However, they are typically not employed all six days of the week. A small number are self-employed. Within the settlement area, there are four small commercial kitchens which make 'potato crisps' for sale to wholesale centres; three tiny general stores; two bakeries; and a couple of family-run tailoring shops. There are also several auto-rickshaw drivers, car drivers, and mechanics working in nearby repair workshops.

Most of the women take jobs as maidservants in the nearby middle-class areas of Cox Town and Banaswadi. A small number work at the multinational Kissan Products Factory, a large manufacturer of processed food products such as jams and ketchup. A fair number stay at home and earn income by rolling incense sticks (*agarbattis*) and stringing flowers into garlands. Another popular source of income is selling vegetables at the nearby market places. Children pitch in and help their mothers in all these activities. Many children are also involved in the local shops and other commercial operations within the settlement area, and a number of older boys work outside Sathyanagar.

THE GROWING UP IN CITIES PROJECT

The Growing Up in Cities project in Bangalore worked with 38 children (18 girls and 20 boys) from the ages of 10 through 14. These children represented a cross-section of the community's linguistic and religious groups, as well as the full range of available schooling options.

As in all of the Growing Up in Cities sites, interaction with the children involved formal and informal observations, one-on-one interviews, children's drawings of the local area and walking tours. Photographs taken by the children were also used as a method to gain insight into their lives and views of their environment.

In Sathyanagar, project work was largely carried out by a team of young researchers (all in their twenties),

trained and managed by the authors under the auspices of CEE, the NGO that had recently overseen development of the new toilet complex in Sathyanagar. Students in Environment Science at a local college were also invited to participate in the initial project training activities, and several became actively involved in the project's research activities. The project also involved staff from two other local NGOs: DEEDS, which operates the informal school and job training centre in Sathyanagar, and Technology Informatics Design Endeavor (TIDE), which carried out a community survey and preliminary mapping of the site as part of the project's activities. NORAD, the Norwegian aid agency, provided funding for the local project work, although the funding was subsequently cut short by unilateral action of the CEE programme coordinator (as discussed later in this chapter).

YOUNG PEOPLE'S LIVES

Through the various project activities, young people in Sathyanagar spoke about their lives and the place where they live: what they like about it, what they would like to change, and what they see for its future. A number of key themes emerged from the children's stories.

Busy Lives, Adult Responsibilities

Most children in Sathyanagar lead very busy lives, filled with responsibilities that are typically the domain of adults in middle-class Indian families and most Western countries. The two sample 'daily activity logs' in Table 6.3 illustrate the activities and daily schedules that are

TABLE 6.2

Participants Profile (N=38)

Male, 18   Female, 20

AGE	# OF PARTICIPANTS	AGE	# OF PARTICIPANTS
10	6	13	11
11	5	14	4
12	10	15	2

TABLE 6.3

Daily Activity Logs

Following are two examples of daily schedules for children living Sathyanagar:

A day in the life of Valli (GIRL, AGE 13)

6:00	woke up, brushed teeth, had a wash, helped with house chores
7:00	walked to Byapanahalli to deliver packed lunch to my father who works in Bangarpet
8:00	returned home; had breakfast
8:30	did the dishes; swept the floor and tidied the house
9:00	went to school at the Non-formal Centre
13:00	returned from school
13:30	washed and had lunch
14:30	went to the tailoring class at the Non-formal Centre
16:00	returned from the tailoring class; walked up to the bridge — fetched six pots of water
16:30	swept the doorstep clean
17:00	had a wash; braided my hair; played with Sanjeevani (friend)
17:30	fetched the cow from the grazing patch
18:00	carried packed dinner for my father who was working late
19:00	waited for my mother, who works at the Cantonment station (as a cleaning woman) to return from work
20:00	had dinner with my mother
21:30	went to bed

A day in the life of S. Anand (BOY, AGE 12)

4:00	woke up; went to collect water for storing
5:00	studied and finished school homework
6:30	changed my clothes; had a cup of tea; played near the church
7:30	came home, had breakfast
8:00	walked to school
9:00 – 12:30	school
12:30	lunch break — had a quick snack and played
13:00	more school
16:00	close of school; walked back home
17:30	reached home; washed and had lunch
17:00	went to play in the open ground behind the community toilet complex
18:00	returned from play; helped mother at vegetable shop
18:30	went to the neighbour's house to watch TV
20:00	returned home and had dinner
20:30	went to bed

typical for children in Sathyanagar.

Nearly all of the children are awake by 6 o'clock, with some rising as early as 4 o'clock to help with household chores before beginning their day in school or other work activities. Morning hours are typically filled with household chores such as cleaning the house, working in the kitchen, washing up, and looking after siblings. In addi-tion, many children (especially girls) help in the process of collecting water — a task that may take an hour a day or more.

After their morning chores, children attend school or, if they have dropped out of school, go to work. Of the 38 children involved in the Growing Up in Cities research, four had dropped out of school (two boys, two girls).

These children typically work at full-time jobs, either in a home-based industry (typical for girls) or in nearby shops or factories (typical for boys). One boy now works full-time as an assistant at a mechanic's workshop, while another delivers newspapers by bicycle to various areas in the city.

After-school hours provide an opportunity for some play, continued household chores, and/or part-time wage-earning work, either in the home or a local business. For two girls whose families keep cows, it is their duty to bring the cows home after school. In a tailor's family, the girls recycle remnant pieces of fabric into "scrunchies" (hair-bands) to be sold in the market. A 12 year old boy helps his mother at their greengrocer's shop, while some other children work in a factory in the local area making potato chips. An 11 year old boy works after school hours in a tailor's shop sewing buttons on shirts, earning 25 paise (about US$ 0.0058) for every button. Many children also accompany their parents to the work place during the school summer vacation and are employed for odd jobs on a short-term basis.

Interestingly, various forms of work have become so much a routine in children's lives that many did not mention it in their initial interviews when asked 'Do you work for anybody here in Sathyanagar or anywhere else?' It was only through the 'daily activity log' or subsequent informal conversations that their work-related activities came to light.

Limited Access to Education

'I would like to be a teacher when I am grown up, to teach all the young kids in this place, because no good teachers are there.' (Anand, age 12)

For most of the children interviewed, the morning and early afternoon hours are spent in some form of schooling, with school times and workloads varying based on the type of school attended. Most residents in Sathyanagar attend 'aided' schools, which are run by private institutions but are substantially subsidised by the State government. Many also attend the non-formal school located in Sathyanagar, operated by DEEDS. A few children attend private institutions, but most lack the re-

sources to pay exorbitant private school fees. One of the few children interviewed who did attend a private school was Anand (Table 6.3), who studies in the 6th grade at Maria Niketan School (a 15 minute walk away) run by a group of Christian missionaries. Valli, however, attends the non-formal school in Sathyanagar that is run by DEEDS. These two examples are reflective of the widely followed practice of investing in education for boys (particularly the eldest boy) while opting for free government or NGO-run schools for girls.

> *Most children in Sathyanagar lead very busy lives, filled with responsibilities that are typically the domain of adults in middle-class Indian families and most Western countries.*

State-run schools are available to children in Sathyanagar, with some children travelling a considerable distance to attend. However, many of the children are unable to take advantage of this instruction due to schedule conflicts and the need for them to contribute to the family income or household management. Children from Sathyanagar must also overcome language barriers, since government instruction is in the official state language of Kannada while most of them are fluent only in their mother tongues of Tamil or Telegu.

Although a small government school facility is located within the settlement, it is seldom used. In fact, for the duration of the Growing Up in Cities project, the building remained padlocked, with no sign of a visit from the government-sponsored teacher who is supposed to provide instruction there on a regular basis.

The DEEDS-operated school at Sathyanagar fills a void in the local schooling system and is highly valued by the children. It provides basic skills training, including basic life skills such as personal hygiene, with the objective of facilitating their admission to the mainstream schools. Because the school admits dropouts and non-starters of varying ages, it does not have any formalised grade demarcations. It also operates on a fairly flexible schedule, allowing children to meet their familial and work obligations without having to risk expulsion. Another important factor is that the school's instructors are fluent in the children's native languages of Tamil and Telegu as well as the local 'official' language of Kannada, which is the focus of instruction. DEEDS also offers vocational training programmes at another small facility in Sathyanagar that many of the older children attend to develop income-producing skills.

One issue raised by many of the young people during their interview was the lack of a quiet place to study. Given their cramped home environments and the noise and disruptions throughout the area, it was often necessary for them to find an out-of-the-way corner in which to study, or to either stay up late or get up early (so long as a light source could be found).

Never a Dull Moment

Although their lives are filled with chores and school responsibilities, children in Sathyanagar take advantage of every spare moment to have fun, and never seemed to be at a loss for things to do. In fact, during the several month process of conducting the research activities, not a single child in Sathyanagar was heard to utter what is perhaps the most common phrase among Western youth: 'I'm bored.'

> *Although their lives are filled with chores and school responsibilities, the children in Sathyanagar take advantage of every spare moment to have fun.*

Creative and energetic play. Despite their material lack of play equipment, children could be found engaged in all manner of play activities: playing tag, rolling an old tire with a stick, drawing in the dirt, exploring an adjacent open space, playing Gilli Dandu (a popular game played with two sticks), or even building a makeshift 'temple' complete with an idol and a ceremonial *pooja* (worship service).

For boys, the most visible and popular play activity was cricket. This typically took place on the two large,

Figure 6.6 Children incorporate the cultural ceremonies around them into their play activities. Here, the children enacted their own ceremonial procession and *pooja*.

flat open spaces on the periphery of the settlement area. The largest of these spaces was the site for Sunday afternoon cricket tournaments, pitting teams from Sathyanagar against teams from adjacent settlements.

For girls, play activities were usually located closer to home; they spend time with friends and play on the nearby streets (which are void of auto traffic) or in the small niche areas between homes. Protected spaces such as the non-formal school or the rooms located above the new toilet complex — when they were available — also served as play areas. However, in general, girls had fewer play opportunities than boys as they were typically expected to help more around the home and given less free rein to explore areas away from the home or the homes of relatives.

'At home they scold me if I play. They say I am too grown-up for that. So I run off to my aunt's place… There she does not mind.' (Ghousiya, age 14)

Television and the cinema. Although very few house-holds in Sathyanagar own television sets, most of the children had access to television in some form, and nearly all were in tune with Indian cinema and its stars. There are two homes with satellite dishes in the community, which provide cable connections to individual homes for a monthly fee. Watching television is a common social activity, with neighbours gathering to watch their favourite programmes. However, given their busy schedules and limited access to television, few children reported watching more than an hour or two of television per week, if that, and most focused specifically on Tamil and other Indian-language programmes. Some children also reported visiting a nearby cinema.

'The day we heard that movie star Ananth Nag was expected in our area, we danced and played, while we waited for him to arrive.' (Karthik, age 12)

Sundays. Sunday is considered a special day of the week by all of the children, as well as by the community as a whole. It typically means longer play hours, and the opportunity to engage in special activities. Older boys might go down the road to watch a movie in the 'tent' cinema housed in a temporary barn-like structure, or they might play in an organised cricket tournament with other settlements in the area. For several children, the high point on a Sunday was an 'oil bath,' with an oil massage for the head and the luxury of heated bath water. Sunday is special also because the meal may include a meat dish or a dessert.

'On Sundays we have a special lunch with a meat dish, and I have more work, more dishes to wash.' (Sumathi, age 12)

Safety and Freedom of Movement

Young people in Sathyanagar feel safe within the boundaries of the settlement area, and are very familiar with the places and people there. However, outside the boundaries of the immediate area, the range of movement is significantly different for boys and girls.

Freedom to move within the immediate area. Most of the children have been living in Sathyanagar all their life, and several of them have extended family members living

there as well. All of them move freely throughout the settlement. There is a strong feeling of safety within the area, but a high level of awareness about the people and places to be avoided (which of course vary according to each person).

Limited range for girls outside the immediate area. For girls, there is a marked difference in the range of movement they have at the community's periphery. They are familiar with most parts inside Sathyanagar, but they are not very familiar with what lies beyond its boundaries. Boys, on the other hand, move very confidently even to contiguous settlements, such as Naganapalya, Byapanahalli and Seva Nagar, a couple of kilometres away.

Parental restrictions on the free movement of adolescent girls stem from the anxiety caused by the absence of mothers from the home, as well as fears related to potential teasing or sexual abuse.

'Father says don't go too far from home. When I ask what is the reason, he says, "Just do as I tell you to".' (Valli, age 13)

'The menfolk are very bad in Byapanahalli [an adjacent settlement]. They use indecent language...and tease young girls.' (Mala, age 12)

'I only go to my sister's house or my uncle's house. If I go to my neighbour's house, my mother scolds me. She says I should stay at home and learn house-work.' (Lalitha, age 11)

Limited knowledge of the city. On occasion, children travel to the city centre in the company of adults, to places such as the City Market (a major wholesale distribution centre for vegetables, hardware items and cloth), far-flung suburbs to visit relatives, or even to picnic spots such as the Lalbag Botanical Gardens and Nandi Hills. But these trips are few and far between. Most children were only able to describe the larger city in relatively vague terms, with limited knowledge about the places to be found there.

Most children also reported taking trips to places outside the city, usually in a train or bus, to their village or town of origin once every three or four years to visit grandparents and attend family functions.

A Rich Variety of Places

'There are hiding places here, to play hide-and-seek.'
(Raju, age 10)

Early in the research process, the children were asked to make a drawing of the area around where they lived, showing the places where they go regularly and places that are important to them. These drawings expressed a number of interesting facts about the local area and the places where they spend their time — their own homes, their relatives' and friends' homes, their school, water collection points, and areas within the settlement used for play.

But the drawings made by the children depicted only the inner circle of movement, excluding significant features in the areas adjoining the community. In fact, few of the drawings depicted very prominent places immediately adjacent to the settlement area, such as the water tank or military area. While this may be because they misunderstood the drawing exercise instructions, it is more likely that it reflects Sathyanagar's very clear boundaries, both in physical terms and in the minds of its residents. Asked to draw 'the area in which they live,' the children understood this to mean Sathyanagar itself, and drew an image that reflected that definition, leaving out adjacent areas that are outside Sathyanagar even though they might visit those areas on a frequent (even daily) basis.

It was only later in the process, during walking tours of the site with some of the boys and after a certain level of trust had developed, that a variety of special places were revealed. These 'hideaways' provide a rich variety of natural spaces that support a wide range of play activities, from active group play to nature exploration and solitary, quiet play.

One of these spaces was a secluded strip of land between the abandoned railroad tracks and the adjacent industrial area. Here, in an area physically and visually blocked from the rest of the community by the railroad embankment (yet less than 100 metres from Sathyanagar's main road), lay a magical world quite removed from the noise and activity of the nearby developed area, as well as from the interfering eyes of adults. With a quiet

© S. R. PRAKASH

Figure 6.7 Boys were free to roam in adjacent areas, where a rich diversity of natural settings could be found. These special places were highly valued by the children who were able to access them.

glade of trees, a small meadow and meandering channel of water, it was a small paradise in which Sathyanagar's young people had uncommon access to nature.

A similar area lay on the opposite side of the tank, hidden among the reeds and grasses to be found along the tank's edge. Here there is a tiny seasonal pond that children use for 'fishing' and swimming, revelling in their community pool despite its shallow, muddy waters.

The richness of these natural environments was quite unexpected to the members of the Growing Up in Cities team, as the children had not mentioned them in their earlier interviews and discussions. It is hard to say whether this came out of a desire to keep these special places a secret, or if it was due to a lack of understanding as to what they were being asked. It was quite evident, however, that these places held a special attraction for the children and were frequently used. It was equally evident that there was a clear gender distinction of access and use, with only boys demonstrating their knowledge and use of these areas. None of these areas was well known to parents or visited by adults. While adults in the area were certainly aware of these places, there was no indication that they knew how much the boys valued them or how often they visited them.

Within the immediate Sathyanagar area, girls and younger children identified their favourite places as being the playground (a large open area suitable for running and group games), followed by home and then school. Most of these children could not identify a 'secret place' as distinctive from their favourite place, and several said they had no secret place. For example, Valli said that she had no secret place, but identified her favourite place as an area by the lake where she could enjoy the grass and wild flowers that 'looked colourful as a peacock.' One of the few secret places was identified by a 10-year old boy, who said that his secret place was a small storage shed where he would hide after a scolding from his mother.

Many of the children also had places they felt were 'dangerous,' where they were afraid to go. These included a small nearby cemetery ('there are ghosts in that place'), the military area ('the guards will capture me and pour tar on my head'), and a dilapidated house near the railway track ('it is lonely and scary'). Parents also identified unsafe places that they asked children to stay away from, including a large drainage ditch that has been the site of a few accidents, the streets of a nearby settlement that were reported to have rough-mannered youth, and the adjacent military area where trespassers were not welcome.

A Vibrant Social and Cultural Life

In addition to the rich variety of physical places in the local area, children spoke of a vibrant social and cultural life within the settlement, and their stories reflected their active role in it.

Religion and ritual. Religion and other aspects of traditional culture are an integral part of children's lives in Sathyanagar. This is expressed physically in the form of several small temples within the settlement area, as well as a small church building, and socially in a variety of community activities, festivals and holidays. Although children seemed aware of religious affiliations (Sathyanagar is predominantly Hindu but has Christian and Muslim families as well), their play activities and friendships make little to no distinction. Most of the children — including Hindu and Muslim children — included the

> *With few exceptions, children's attitudes about the future were largely positive, with visions of a future Sathyanagar in which current problems had been addressed through practical means.*

church building as a prominent feature in their drawings, attributed with important meaning even though the building itself is quite small and differentiated only by the small cross over its entrance. They also mentioned visiting the temples or church regularly to pray or participate in festivals and, regardless of their religion, engaged in play activities that reflected religious rituals.

Extended family networks. Most of the children have close relatives living within Sathyanagar or nearby areas, and some have extended family living within their home. Typically, children spent considerable time at relatives' houses, often with aunts or cousins who were involved in looking after younger children. Older children themselves sometimes played a role in looking after younger cousins. These extended family networks played an important role in children's daily lives. However, in some instances, children reported relatives' homes as off-limits due to a family quarrel.

Social issues. Children were aware of, and seemingly candid about, issues such as alcohol abuse within the family (usually an issue associated with men), as well as in the community as a whole. 'Drunk' and 'rowdy' men were cited by both boys and girls as one of the biggest

© DAVID DRISKELL

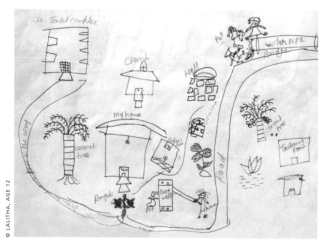

© LALITHA, AGE 12

Figure 6.8 Most of the children included the church as a prominent feature in their drawings even though the building itself is quite small, differentiated only by the cross over its entrance.

dangers in the local area. Several children also cited smoking as a problem in the community.

Environmental Care and Management

Children were well aware of the environmental conditions in their local area, and had numerous suggestions for how to improve them, as well as optimism about the future. However, while care of the home environment was evident in their stories and activities, care for the local environment as a whole, or any notion that they themselves could bring about positive changes, was not.

Signs of care and neglect. There were many signs of local residents' efforts to maintain and improve the quality of their home environment, from continual additions to their houses to daily cleaning activities, including sweeping the main entrance and daily decoration of the threshold with *rangoli* (intricate designs made with rice flour) — a tradition passed on to the young girls of the community. But such signs of concern rarely went beyond the doorstep. While some children reported efforts by their families or neighbours to sweep the street or clear the drain in front of their home, there was no maintenance system either at the community level or at the street level, and signs of neglect were evident. However, it was hoped that the recent incorporation of Sathyanagar as an official part of the municipal area would bring needed improvements from the municipal authorities.

Practical suggestions for change. One of the questions in the interview asked children about the changes they would like to see carried out in the area. Their responses reflected a range of adult-like concerns and practical suggestions: tar the road, install a water tap next to each home, clear the garbage, improve the drainage so that rainwater would not overflow into their homes. Not one child asked for a children's park or play equipment, nor did they have fanciful, unattainable visions for the future. Several of them also pointed to concerns about social issues, wondering why the sale of cigarettes should not be banned and why shops selling alcohol should not be closed down.

'Once a week I'll get the workers to clean the drains. Water all the plants. Everyone should say that Sathyanagar is a lovely place.' (Shankar, age 13)

Hope for the future. Children were keenly aware of the environmental problems and drawbacks of their local area, and expressed concern about the potential for further pollution and environmental damage. Nonetheless, with few exceptions, children's attitudes about the future were largely positive, with visions of a future Sathyanagar in which current problems had been addressed through practical means. Most children saw the community as having got better through their childhood years and on a path to further improvements in the future. This positive attitude about the future was further reflected in response to the question: Where would you like to live when you're grown up? Nearly all of the children who were interviewed did not hesitate in answering: 'Sathyanagar.'

'…Sathyanagar will be so good, they will write about us in the newspaper.' (Ghousiya, age 14)

PERSPECTIVES FROM MIDDLE-CLASS CHILDREN IN THE AREA

To provide a counterpoint to the views and perspectives of young people in Sathyanagar, an afternoon session was organised with middle-class children from the ages of 8 through 14 living in an adjacent residential area, located only 15 minutes away from Sathyanagar. The afternoon consisted of an abbreviated version of several Growing Up in Cities methods, including drawings, one-on-one interviews, and small group discussions.

While spontaneity and enthusiasm were our overwhelming first impressions in our interactions with young people in Sathyanagar, the first impressions we had from the assembled group of middle-class youngsters was that they were serious and somewhat tentative. This impression was largely created by the solemnity with which they approached the drawing exercise, and their concern about making 'a mistake.' Despite repeated assurances that this was not a test in any way, and that 'mistakes' were not a possibility, many of the children insisted on using a straight-edge to make their drawings, made extensive use of pencils and erasers, and asked for clean sheets of paper when they felt they had made an irreparable error.

Through the drawings, interviews and discussions, several notable differences between the two groups of children emerged.

Less creative play. In general, the children in the middle-class sample engaged mostly in structured and 'pre-set' play activities, such as playing cricket, going to movies, watching TV, playing hide-and-seek, playing scrabble, or playing computer games. While some of these play activities overlapped with activities popular with children in Sathyanagar, there were few signs of the more spontaneous, creative play that was evident in the settlement.

More concern regarding school and future career options. The ambitions of the middle-class children included professions such as computer engineer, doctor, model, architect, teacher and army officer. In most cases, it reflected the profession of their parents, and most of the children were fairly knowledgeable about the path they would need to follow to realise their ambition. On the other hand, a vast majority from the sample group in Sathyanagar expressed a desire to become teachers, with the next most popular occupation being a 'government job,' followed by wanting to run a small business. However, few of the children in Sathyanagar had an understanding of the training and resources that would be necessary.

Less familiarity with the surrounding community. The geographical range of movement for these children was much more restricted and supervised, even for boys, than for the children in Sathyanagar.

Equal concern regarding environmental issues. Both the middle-class children and the children of Sathyanagar were unanimous in their desire for more trees, less traffic and cleaner roads.

Attitudes Toward Sathyanagar

In addition to asking them about their own lives, children in the middle-class group were shown some photographs of everyday life in Sathyanagar — without any mention about where the place was located or what it was like — and asked to give their reactions.. They spontaneously drew comparisons to places they had seen before, although none of them connected the place as being so close to their own neighbourhood:

'It looks like a rural area.'

'I saw a similar place as we were driving along the highway.'

'It looks like a village street with cattle and dogs.'

Other observations reflected assumptions or judgements about the place and its people based on only a few images of the local streetscape:

'They are poor people…they haven't built proper houses.'

'They do not get enough food and do not have proper clothes.'

'Children have no restrictions; they play on the street.'

'There is no park here, and no television either.'

'They don't send girls to school.'

But other comments reflected a certain level of awareness of the situation:

'Children here have a very different life, they work when very young.'

'They don't have water, children help their mothers carry water.'

'The government is not taking proper care.'

And some comments even drew attention to potentially positive aspects of the place:

'There are no vehicles to be seen; it must be less polluted.'

'They have freedom to move around.'

> *Both the middle-class children and the children of Sathyanagar were unanimous in their desire for more trees, less traffic and cleaner roads.*

PARENTS' PERSPECTIVES

Parents of children in Sathyanagar were interviewed to provide insights on how they perceive their children's lives and their use of the local area. In juxtaposition to children's own views, many of the parents had a more critical view of Sathyanagar, with nearly all expressing concerns about crime and potential violence in the area due to quarrels between individuals, families and groups. Many of them identified places such as the tank, railway tracks, and military grounds as being off-limits to their children since they saw these places as dangerous or illegal.

Like the children, parents were very concerned about environmental problems in Sathyanagar, particularly the lack of reliable and safe drinking water and sanitation issues, including pollution in the adjacent tank. However, while children generally felt that these problems would be addressed and that conditions in the area were improving, their parents were generally less optimistic. Parents also cited issues related to the lack of health care facilities and the frequent illnesses suffered by children.

Parents were also more critical of the educational opportunities available to their children, with the provision of a good education cited as one of their highest concerns for both sons and daughters. Some of the parents cited the lack of teachers and facilities, while others placed blame on their children for not studying hard enough.

Strictness and discipline varied considerably between parents, with some expressing strict rules that limited the range of their children's movement and activities. Others expressed far fewer restrictions and indicated that their children were allowed to travel fairly significant distances on their own, although specific locations such as the tank or military ground might still be considered as off-limits. In general, girls had more restrictions than boys, as reflected in children's own accounts. However, in nearly every case, the restrictions identified by parents did not seem to be uniformly followed by the children, with their actual range of movement differing from the range established by their parents.

Last, it was interesting to note that many parents expressed disappointment with their children for not working enough or studying enough. They were critical of the 'bad influence' of other children and youth in the area, and claimed that their children spent too much time playing games or wasting time. These attitudes may, in part, be the result of different generational standards regarding work and play, since many parents grew up in rural agricultural settings where work hours tend to be longer.

THE POLITICS OF PATRONAGE AND NEGLECT

The stories and perspectives of Sathyanagar's young people were surprising and enlightening. Project team members were perplexed by how these children could be so positive, energetic and enthusiastic when faced with such difficult circumstances. It was a topic to which our conversations continually turned, with the assumption at first being that we were not asking the right questions, or

> *Project team members were perplexed by how these children could be so positive, energetic and enthusiastic when faced with such difficult circumstances.*

that the children were simply caught up in the excitement of a new and interesting activity, or that they were eager to show their community in a positive light to a group of outsiders even if that light was not entirely realistic or revealing. In the end, we came to accept their input and stories, and to speculate on the meanings and lessons that lay beneath. For many team members, it was an experience that challenged their previous perceptions of 'slums.' In the words of one staffer, '[The children in Sathyanagar] helped me get over the idea that a slum is a filthy smelly place and that the people there are dirty, violent or generally bad'.

Unfortunately, our initial assumptions were not transformed when we explored the perspectives and practices of local officials and government agencies charged with planning for the local area. On the contrary, these experiences reinforced our predisposition to view local development and decision-making processes as hostage to a system of political patronage, a fragmented bureaucracy, and corruption at nearly every level. The few politicians or bureaucrats who seemed to sincerely want to meet the needs of local young people were ill-equipped to do so in light of entrenched power relations and the complex bureaucracy. Even more disheartening was the nearly complete lack of connection between

what local officials viewed as the needs of local young people (opportunities for sports and recreation) and what young people expressed as their needs (adequate clean water and sanitation).

Politics and Development

During the time that the Growing Up in Cities project was underway, there were two dominant political parties in Sathyanagar as well as Karnataka as a whole: Janata Dal (which was in power at both the national and state levels) and Congress (India's traditionally dominant party since Independence). Both parties have long been active in the Bangalore area, and have established strong footholds in lower-income communities such as Sathyanagar, where they have become adept at influencing the outcomes of elections by bestowing various forms of largesse on the local community.

While politics is always intertwined with issues of economic power and control over resources, the 'rawness' of the relationship stands out when seen in the context of economic hardship in a place like Sathyanagar. For local party members, political activism can secure both economic and social status, and maintaining (or obtaining) political power has become as much of an economic issue as it is an ideological one.

Because of its international links and overall visibility, the Growing Up in Cities project was understandably a focus of much interest within the community. Although initial contact was made with recognised community leaders (representing both parties) to gain their support for the project, it was not long before various rumours were circulating within the community about the project, its intentions, and its potential outcomes (few of which had anything to do with the actual project goals). Similarly, it was not long before people began to assume that the project was associated with (and therefore credited to) one party over another, despite early efforts to position the project as a non-partisan, non-political activity.

As a result, midway through the project activities, members of the GUIC team were both verbally and physically threatened by local activists of one of the political parties. Though nobody was hurt, the decision was immediately taken to halt all project activities until the leaders of both parties could restate their support for the project and ensure the safety of team members.

As part of the effort to defuse this crisis, the authors had the opportunity to visit the home of the local Corporator of the municipal government (the elected representative for the area in which Sathyanagar is located). This meeting proved productive both in terms of re-establishing the project's local political support and its position as a non-political activity, and in providing insights into the perspectives and operations of a local politician.

In the relative opulence of her home, and surrounded by her party cadre and staff, the Corporator professed her support for the project and its participatory goals, but said that she saw little or no need for such forms of participation because she felt herself to be in tune with the needs of the local population (including its young people) and certain that she could and would provide the necessary resources. She spent the majority of the meeting expounding upon an extensive list of projects that she claimed to be underway or planned, ranging from drainage improvements (which were underway at the time) to a new hospital facility. When questioned about the needs of young people she quickly responded that she had plans for a new play area for them and left it at that.

For the Corporator, 'participation' consisted of residents being able to request favours and assistance. It did not extend to community dialogue about needs and priorities, or resident involvement in determining what would be in their own best interest. Rather, the role of the politician was to evaluate the merits of individual requests, decide on the most appropriate course of action, and call upon the resources available to her as a politician to carry out her plans. 'Participation' as we understood it was not an issue in her eyes. The only issue was accessing and coordinating the necessary resources, targeting them to the issues as defined by the Corporator, and ensuring that every project contributed to, and sustained, local support for the Corporator's party.

'The streets are cleaned only if the MLA (elected member of the State Legislature) is going to visit our area.'
(Mahesh, age 12)

Ad Hoc Planning and Bureaucratic Neglect

As part of the project, efforts were also made to try to understand the structures and processes by which planning and development decisions were carried out in Bangalore (the purpose being to identify the best time and place to influence the process in order to promote the interests of community residents).

In hindsight, it is not surprising that nobody was able to explain these processes in a clear, succinct, or comprehensive manner, even among those who were regularly involved. In part, this is because the bureaucracy is so complex and the roles of various ministries and departments so fragmented and overlapping that nobody really understands exactly how the process is supposed to work. Not only is there no coherent and consistent system of comprehensive planning, but it is also a system so susceptible to manipulation and coercion that it has ceased to function in any predictable manner. Planning is ad hoc, highly political, and largely controlled by major development interests, contractors and landowners.

> *Even more disheartening was the nearly complete lack of connection between what local officials viewed as the needs of local young people (opportunities for sports and recreation) and what young people expressed as their needs (adequate clean water and sanitation).*

Unfortunately, government efforts to reduce the influence of money and power on bureaucratic decision-making have not necessarily improved the situation. Senior civil service officials are regularly rotated in their posts, with most of them serving a maximum of two years in any one position or location. Although this turnover may decrease the likelihood of senior officials becoming beholden to local interest groups, it also means that officials have little time to develop a comprehensive understanding of the issues facing their constituencies so that they can target limited resources to the places where they are most needed. Rather, their understanding of community needs is based on broad generalisations, and they operate in a largely reactive mode in response to a seemingly endless series of individual requests — major and minor — from the community.

This mode of operation was perfectly illustrated when the authors attempted to interview the regional director of the government's 'Slum Board' — the government entity charged with planning and service delivery for Bangalore's slums (as officially defined and registered by the government). As we waited for our turn to speak with the director, we had the opportunity to see a typical series of interactions, in which individuals and families asked the director for assistance with their grievances, disputes, and special situations, ranging from requests for a loan to help cover marriage costs to arbitration of a family feud. He gave his opinion, advice or assistance, then directed his staff to follow up as necessary.

When it was our turn, we explained the Growing Up in Cities project to him and requested the opportunity to ask a few questions regarding his perceptions of young people's needs in places like Sathyanagar and his attitudes regarding young people's participation in the slum improvement process. However, we were not able to present our questions as the director immediately interpreted our brief presentation as a request for assistance, assured us that he supported young people's participation, and suggested we organise a citywide gathering of children from the slum areas to participate in a sports competition for which he would provide the buses to make it happen. He then thanked us for coming to him, asked us to keep in touch on the progress with our efforts, and turned his attention to the next petitioner.

MISINFORMATION, MISMANAGEMENT AND MISSED OPPORTUNITIES

Contemporary development practice often begins with the assumption that the involvement of NGOs is critical, especially at the local level.[6] Indeed, this was the assumption when the Indian Growing Up in Cities project was initiated, and therefore an alliance was formed with CEE (Centre for Environment Education) to carry out the project work. This national-level NGO, funded in part by the Indian government, has offices in Bangalore and had worked previously in Sathyanagar to design and build a new community toilet complex. Using a system design that would capture methane gas for cooking and compost for fertiliser, the toilet facility had a full-time manager to deal with maintenance and management issues, and included two open-air rooms on the first story for use in various community activities.

The activities envisioned for the project and the budget were considerably expanded, due in part to the strong desire to fund only activities with measurable outcomes.

Initial inquiries and discussions about the Growing Up in Cities project with CEE staff resulted in a strong expression of interest from local staff members, as well as from an influential programme coordinator who was then primarily based in New Delhi, but who continued to manage projects for CEE in Bangalore. It was felt that Growing Up in Cities would serve as a natural extension of CEE's previous community-based work, and provide an opportunity to branch out into a more comprehensive and participatory approach to community development and environmental improvement.

After reviewing several possible sites, it was decided to focus the project efforts on Sathyanagar because CEE had a working relationship with residents there and it was an area recently annexed by the Bangalore City Corporation, providing an opportunity to look at a peripheral urban area on the verge of much higher levels of urbanisation. It was also decided to undertake the Growing Up in Cities activities as part of a larger community planning effort that would focus on actions to improve the local area, and to place that effort within a larger regional planning programme, being pursued by CEE with support from NORAD (the Norwegian aid agency), to collect data and prepare plans for the recently annexed areas in this part of Bangalore. NORAD had supported the toilet complex development and sev-

© S.R. PRAKASH

Figure 6.9 The rich diversity of natural settings provided the young people (especially boys) with a much-needed refuge and supported highly valued play experiences.

eral other CEE initiatives under the direction of the same CEE programme coordinator who would oversee the Growing Up in Cities work.

At the encouragement of NORAD and the programme coordinator, the activities envisioned for the Growing Up in Cities project and the accompanying budget were considerably expanded. This was due in part to the strong desire to fund only activities with tangible, measurable outcomes rather than 'research' activities, and the desire to fund a small number of large projects rather than a large number of small projects.

The final proposal submitted to NORAD was titled 'Sathyanagar Pilot Study and Comprehensive Plan.' It outlined a year-long schedule of activities that would include participatory evaluation of the local area, a community-wide social survey, development of a Geographic Information System (GIS), preparation of a Community Action Plan, and a variety of public information and education materials. It also outlined the participation of other organisations, including local government agencies and DEEDS (the local NGO operating the non-formal school and job training in Sathyanagar) and described the project's objectives, staffing, schedule and funding. The Community Action Plan would serve as a blueprint for community improvements, identifying and coordinating actions that residents could implement themselves, as well as actions that could be taken by local authorities and/or be supported by development aid agencies.

Project activities were initiated in January 1997, focusing first on the background data collection (including the community survey and development of the GIS) and on the participatory evaluation activities with young people (including team training and carrying out the Growing Up in Cities methods). These initial activities were to provide the basis for a subsequent participatory planning workshop with both adults and young people, and for developing the Community Action Plan.

As project activities began to get underway, several 'warning signs' indicated (at least in hindsight) that things were perhaps not what they seemed. For example, on the very first day of interviews with children at the site, several of the children pointed out that the toilet complex (in which the interviews were being conducted) had been developed on what had previously been their favourite play space in Sathyanagar. This came as a surprise to several of the local CEE staff, as well as to one of the authors who had been told by the CEE programme coordinator that the toilet project had been undertaken with extensive community participation, including the participation of children. This and other incidents made it clear that the claims and reality of previous participation efforts were two different things.

'We used to play on this patch of ground… now they have built community toilets on it.' (Shankar, age 11)

Other warning signs could be found in the way in which the local project staff were being managed by the New Delhi-based programme coordinator, with unilateral decisions based on incomplete and often inaccurate information. Staff in the Bangalore office never seemed to be completely aware of who was supposed to be working on what, or even the basic status of the office's various projects. The initial project proposal submitted for Growing Up in Cities had even been significantly modified by the funding agency without the local staff being informed.

The distant and unpredictable nature of programme management was exacerbated by the problematic manner in which many of the local staff members were

treated. Staff efforts were typically deemed to be inadequate or unacceptable and several staff members were threatened with having their jobs terminated.

As the months of project work progressed, the situation between the programme coordinator and the local management team became increasingly strained. The lack of effective communication channels contributed to misunderstandings. These came to a head when preparations were underway to conclude the initial participatory research activities in Sathyanagar and prepare a summary presentation for the Urban Childhood Conference in Trondheim, Norway, that July — an event at which

> *It also raises the fundamental isues of NGO ethics and accountability. Who is responsible for ensuring that an NGO is working in a community's best interest?*

eight Growing Up in Cities sites would be represented. Feeling that she and CEE were not being properly acknowledged by the international project in the conference preparations, the programme coordinator decided to halt all work on the project and to withdraw CEE's support, reallocating the remaining project budget to other work efforts.

Although this decision was upsetting and frustrating, the responses from local staff members were rewarding in their own way. Several members relied on their income from CEE and understandably did not want to jeopardise their employment, but they had also developed a strong commitment to the project and to the young people in Sathyanagar. On their own initiative, they decided to continue their work on the project in the evenings and on weekends. This made it possible to complete the remaining participatory activities that represented the Growing Up in Cities portion of the work programme. In addition, because the project had worked closely with DEEDS, it was possible to implement at least one response to the issues raised by Sathyanagar's young people: the need for a quiet place to study. In 1998, a 'Centre for Children' was developed by DEEDS with the participation of

Sathyanagar's young people, and funding provided by Norwegian children through the Norwegian Broadcasting Company's 'Children's Hour' programme.

The fact that a single programme coordinator undermined the efforts of an entire project team — with no recourse to address the issue at the local, national or international level — illustrates the obstacles faced by young people and disenfranchised communities when it comes to exercising their rights, including their right to define their own development priorities. It also raises the fundamental issues of NGO ethics and accountability. Who is responsible for ensuring that an NGO is working in a community's best interest? The fact that even well-reputed and well-intentioned organisations such as CEE and NORAD failed to support this local participatory initiative illustrates the formidable barriers that stand in the way of translating rhetoric about participation into actual practice. Their failure, despite the quality of their organisations and the international connections of the Growing Up in Cities project, raises significant questions about the possibility of success for genuine community-based planning. Without an effective institutional framework and systems to promote ethics and accountability, there is a very real risk that NGOs can undermine legitimate community interests, leaving local residents without an established mechanism, such as an election, through which they can change the situation.

LEARNING FROM TRUTH TOWN

The stories shared by Sathyanagar's young people speak to some basic 'truths' about their lives and the place where they live. Our experience in working with them and with the various organisations and actors that affect their lives has also shed light on some basic 'truths' about the nature of the development process and the challenges of participation. Although these truths are based on interactions with a small group of young people in a single place and at a specific moment, they do provide valuable insights and lessons that are worthy of consideration and application in other situations and contexts.

Factors That Contributed to Children's Well-Being

The 'paradoxical poverty' of the Indian Growing Up in Cities site, like that of the Argentine site,[7] left us searching for clues as to how young people could be so apparently confident, self-aware and resilient in a social and physical environment that was so demanding, relentless, and (at times) threatening and oppressive. Following is a summary of what stood out as being some of the key factors affecting the lives of young people in Sathyanagar.

Cultural identity. The local culture — steeped in tradition, myth and ritual — provided children with a strong sense of identity. They knew who and what they were, and they had a strong sense of belonging as well as pride.

Social networks. Extended families and the close-knit (though sometimes fractious) community gave young people a sense of safety and the ability to move freely throughout the local area. Although this movement was more restricted for girls, all of the children appeared to be completely at ease within the immediate area and very familiar with it. It was also evident that parents were deeply concerned about their children's well being, and that by and large children felt that they were valued and important members of the community.

Responsibilities. Young people's sense of being valued was strongly reinforced by the expectations and responsibilities placed upon them both at home and in the community at-large. While there may be negative repercussions from working at a young age, for the children of Sathyanagar their work had the benefit of instilling a strong sense of belonging and of being needed.

Natural diversity. One of the surprises revealed by Sathyanagar's young people was the rich diversity of natural settings that were available in their local area. These trees, ponds and grassy areas provided a much-needed refuge and supported highly valued play experiences. However, planners and decision makers do not understand or appreciate these features and qualities, and it is unlikely that they will be preserved as the area undergoes further urbanisation.

Location and layout. Sathyanagar's location on the fringe of the Bangalore metropolitan area provided access to natural settings as well as urban amenities and excitement — features that young people valued. The settlement's physical layout also limited vehicle traffic and helped retain a self-contained village atmosphere, enhancing its function as a place where young people felt safe and free to move around on their own.

Basic services and facilities. Although Sathyanagar's residents face many hardships, including severe degradation of their local environment, there are several NGOs that are providing basic services and facilities to fill the void in government services, especially in education and job training. However, as the story of Growing Up in Cities demonstrates, the roles of these NGOs can sometimes be problematic, with no established mechanism for holding them accountable to the local community.

Land tenure. Though young people were not aware of the issue, the fact that residents had title to their land undoubtedly had a strong impact on the community's feelings of ownership, security and pride — feelings that had been passed on to young residents.[8]

A culture of democracy. India is proud of its status as the world's largest democracy and, imperfect though the system may be, people in communities such as Sathyanagar understand and exercise their right to vote. Though they may not receive attention and services they deserve from government agencies and officials, there is a commonly held expectation that such services *are* deserved. The question is not one of 'do we have a right to expect this?' but rather 'how can we best access that which is rightfully ours?'

Lessons for Planners and Development Organisations

Given the social, cultural and environmental resources that Sathyanagar contained, it is tempting to think about what might have been achieved through the comprehensive process of community-based planning that was originally proposed, which would have built upon existing strengths and addressed important needs. Reflections on what went wrong point to a number of lessons that may have value for others involved in planning and

development processes. These lessons are applicable whether one is working at the local, regional, national or international levels, and within a governmental, non-governmental or multilateral setting.

> *Factoring in qualitative measures leads to a much richer understanding of young people's lives and the issues they face, and reveals existing resources to be conserved as well as problems to be addressed. It also leads to far different conclusions about what should be done to enhance community quality for children and youth.*

Qualitative measures are essential for understanding young people's lives. A statistical analysis of quantitative measures of the well-being of Sathyanagar's young people would certainly not have yielded the same understanding of their lives as did the participatory exploration of their life quality. Based on quantitative measures alone, Sathyanagar would easily rank as one of the worst-off places for young people among the Growing Up in Cities sites. Factoring in qualitative measures leads to a much richer understanding of young people's lives and the issues they face, and reveals existing resources to be conserved as well as problems to be addressed. It also leads to far different conclusions about what should be done to enhance community quality for children and youth.

'This is the first time someone has asked me what I like and dislike.' (Sumithra, age 12)

Research cannot be divorced from action. Throughout the initial fund-raising phase of the project, potential funding agencies consistently indicated that they had no interest in funding 'research projects.' While safeguards need to be in place to ensure that research is linked to action, and that research results are put to good use, the almost complete lack of support for research-related activities was troubling and, perhaps, indicative of why

BOX 6.1

Putting Participation into Practice

The experience in Sathyanagar demonstrated a number of the obstacles that exist for participatory evaluation and planning, and pointed to several ways in which development aid agencies, governments and NGOs can support genuine processes of participation that build on people's strengths, in reality as well as in rhetoric.

Restructure the criteria and procedures used by funding agencies. Although many funding agencies espouse participatory ideals in their programme brochures and publicise participatory practices in their project descriptions, the reality is that few, if any, funding agencies operate in a manner that actually supports local participation efforts. Most funding agencies limit the range of issues or types of projects for which their funds can be used, want to know ahead of time what the project outcomes will be, prefer to fund a few big projects rather than numerous small ones, prioritise quantitative, project-oriented measures of success over qualitative and process-oriented measures, and establish strict timelines for the start and finish of each project. Funding agencies need to commit themselves to long-term investments and solutions, provide greater flexibility for local determination of funding priorities, support small projects, encourage project phasing, and value process outcomes as well as project outcomes. The message that 'the ends justify the means' — a message unintentionally yet strongly advocated by many funding agencies — needs to be removed from the funding equation.

Provide local management and monitoring. Participatory projects cannot be managed from a distance. When the process is valued as highly as other project outcomes, project management and communication must be daily and face-to-face. Similarly, project monitoring and evaluation cannot be achieved in a single visit or even several visits over the course of a project. While an outside perspective can certainly be useful, most evaluation visits tend to be staged events put on by local staff for the benefit of the visiting evaluator. Actual project work is often put on hold as staff members focus their attention on the preparation of a presentation and related materials. Reflection and evaluation must be a regular part of any participatory project, and should be conducted in a manner that actively involves project staff as well as local residents in identifying the project's strengths and weaknesses, identifying areas for improvement, and ensuring accountability.

Cultivate talented, reliable staff. International and national agencies need to cultivate talented, reliable staff at the local level, since it is here that the success or failure of participatory programmes will be determined. Local managers and staff should be considered as, and valued as, the most important and influential people in the organisation, and sufficient organisational resources must be made available to support them in their ongoing work efforts. Ineffective or unethical staff and inappropriate management should not be tolerated.

Operate using participatory principles. Organisations working to promote participatory forms of development must internalise participatory principles and methods in their own operations. Espousing participatory principles outside the organisation and then operating in an authoritarian manner within the organisation will undermine credibility, and will eventually undermine the ability to undertake participatory programmes.

Develop partnerships and a broad-based support network. A successful programme of participatory community development requires the active involvement of a range of groups and individuals, from local government agencies and elected officials to service organisations, community groups, technical professionals, and individual residents. The Sathyanagar project was able to move forward (though in a limited capacity) after its funds were cut off because of the support from local staff and DEEDS. The project's ability to move forward would have been considerably enhanced if the network of support had been broadened at an earlier date to include government departments, other NGOs, and a coalition of funding sources.

Encourage reflection and evaluation, and value success in all its forms. Critical reflection and evaluation are at the very core of a participatory approach to community development. It requires that participants consider both the strengths and weaknesses of the process and its outcomes, recognising and valuing success while always searching for better ways to do things the next time around.

so many development projects fail to achieve their objectives or, too often, result in more harm than good. Research and action are interdependent. Neither is viable without the other.

Natural settings must be integrated into the urban environment. The story of Sathyanagar reinforces what research on children's environments has consistently shown: access to natural settings has an irreplaceable value in children's lives.[9] Planners and decision makers need to understand the value that these settings have, and work to preserve them as part of the urban fabric.

> *Critical reflection and evaluation are at the very core of a participatory approach to community development.*

Resources for resilience must be recognised, valued and sustained. Research on resilience in children at risk has demonstrated that resilient children do not possess unique qualities that set them apart from other children. Rather, in the midst of adversity, they have been able to secure important resources that foster healthy and competent human development.[10] These resources include a close relationship with a parent figure who provides warmth and structure, a supportive extended family network, connections to pro-social organisations and adults beyond the family, effective schools, and opportunities to be sociable and to develop a sense of self-confidence, self-esteem, and faith. At their best, children's environments function with redundancy: if a resource is lacking in one place, it can be found at another. In many ways, despite its very real socio-economic disadvantages, Sathyanagar provided resources for resilience.

Participation must be real and meaningful. It is only by understanding and building upon the rich human and cultural capital that exists in communities such as Sathyanagar that the dynamics of successful development can be fostered. This type of understanding can only be gained through an inclusive and participatory process that involves residents of all ages in identifying 'resources for resilience' as well as issues for action. Local residents — especially women and children — need to be engaged in these processes because they are the ultimate experts on their daily lives and local conditions. They must have a voice in the planning and decision-making process, and a real stake in the long-term development and sustainability of their community. They should be treated as partners in the development process rather than as victims in need of help.

Facing the Challenges of Participation

The last 'lesson' for planners and development organisations — that participation must be real and meaningful — is recognised by many, but practised by few. If the experience in Sathyanagar illustrated anything, it is that people's conceptions of 'participation' vary widely, and that many definitions of participation are essentially self-serving. Successful participation requires more than a set of participatory methods. It requires an understanding of, and a commitment to, participatory principles from those involved at any level: organisations, including funding agencies, project staff and residents themselves.[11]

It would be easy to say that the Sathyanagar project was unsuccessful because the funding was stopped and the Community Action Plan was never developed or implemented. But this would fail to recognise what the project did achieve and the successes that it did have. These include the new Study Centre, as well as less tangible outcomes such as staff training and experience in participatory methods, the noticeable shift in staff attitudes towards 'slum' areas, and young people's pleasure and enthusiasm in thinking about the place where they live and articulating their ideas about it. The project also contributed to the establishment of a new NGO named JYOSHIKA (meaning 'cluster of buds') in Bangalore, which is working with the Government to promote educational opportunities for children from low-income families and basic literacy for youth. Most important, it has provided an opportunity for young people in Sathyanagar to communicate their stories to a global audience of people who, it is hoped, will find some truths in the stories they have heard and an opportunity to apply those truths in the places where they themselves live.

POSTSCRIPT

The Growing Up in Cities research in Sathyanagar was conducted in 1997. Four years down the line, there are signs that some positive changes have already occurred or are in progress at Sathyanagar.

On recent visits, the Government school within the settlement was indeed working, with a few children playing outside and a teacher visible in the doorway. Most noticeably, the streets inside Sathyanagar were freshly tarred, making them look wider and uncluttered, and the city transport service had made improvements, introducing two bus routes that connect the Sathyanagar area to the centre of Bangalore, though the frequency of service is very low. The 'Centre for Children' that was set up with funds from the Norwegian Children's Hour has also proven successful, housing a library and study centre for students, providing a meeting place for members of the Children's Club, and conducting skill development programmes.

On the negative side, children have lost access to one of their valued play spaces as the tank-bed area has been rendered 'out of bounds' — literally and figuratively — by the army authorities who own the area and have cordoned it off with stone slabs all along the boundary.

Also of note, the funding agency NORAD has changed its strategy of intervention in India by involving local government officials in coordinating and helping to monitor the programmes undertaken by NGOs. There is no verdict as yet on whether this strategy has been successful at countering the types of mismanagement that were evident in the Sathyanagar experience.

Perhaps of most interest to Sathyanagar's residents, the local 'leader' (i.e. the politician) informed us that a substantial amount of money had been paid collectively by local residents as charges for getting piped water to their homes. They hope the wait will soon be over.

ENDNOTES

1   For an abridged adaptation of this chapter that emphasizes implications for development policy, see Driskell, Bannerjee and Chawla (2001).
2   Bose (1992, pp. 2-7).
3   Chatterjee (1992, p. 5).
4   Badrinath (1995).
5   Ibid.
6   See UNDP (1999) and World Bank (1999).
7   See Chapter 2 of this book by Cosco and Moore, 'Our neighborhood is like that! Cultural richness and childhood identity in Boca-Barracas, Buenos Aires.' For further discussion of 'paradoxical poverty' in places that are poor in material resources yet rich in social, cultural or other critical resources see McKendrick (1998).
8   The South African Growing Up in Cities site demonstrated the contrasting effects of insecure land tenure on children's lives, as detailed in Chapter 5 of this book by Swart-Kruger, 'Children in a South African squatter camp gain and lose a voice.'
9   Chawla (in press).
10 Masten and Coatsworth (1998).
11 For an overview of participatory principles as well as methods and case studies, see Hart (1997) as well as Driskell (2001). For further analyses of conflicts between funding agency practices and processes which actually support beneficiaries' self-determination, see Nieuwenhuys (1997) and Satterthwaite et al. (1996, chapter 6).

REFERENCES

Badrinath, G D (1995), *Urban Environmental Profile of Bangalore,* IHS, Rotterdam.

Bose, A B (1992), *The Disadvantaged Urban Child in India,* Innocenti Occasional Papers (The Urban Child Series, Number 1), UNICEF, Florence.

Chatterjee, A. (1992), *India: The Forgotten Children of the Cities*, part of the Urban Child in Difficult Circumstances series, UNICEF, Florence, Italy.

Chawla, L (in press), "Spots of time: Different ways of being in nature in childhood" in Kahn, P.H. and S. Kellert (editors), *Children and Nature,* MIT Press, Cambridge, MA.

Driskell, D (2001), *Creating Better Cities with Children and Youth: A Manual for Participation,* UNESCO Publishing/Earthscan, Paris/London.

Driskell, D, Bannerjee, K and Chawla, L (2001), 'Rhetoric, reality and resilience: Overcoming obstacles to young people's participation in development', *Environment and Urbanization,* vol 13(1), pp. 77-89.

Hart, R (1997), *Children's Participation,* Earthscan Publications, London.

Masten, A S and Coatsworth, J D (1998), 'The development of competence in favorable and unfavorable environments,' *American Psychologist,* vol 53(2), pp. 205-220.

McKendrick, J (1998), 'Families and family environments in Manchester', *Transactions of the Manchester Statistical Society,* vol 1995-1997, pp. 1-27.

Niewenhuys, O (1997), 'Spaces for the children of the urban poor', *Environment and Urbanization,* vol 9(1), pp. 233-249.

Satterthwaite, D et al. (1996), *The Environment for Children,* Earthscan Publications, London, chapter 6.

UNDP (1999), 'Ten years of the human development report' in *Human Development Report 1999,* Oxford University Press and UNDP, New York, pp. 16-24.

World Bank (1999), 'Introduction: New directions in development thinking' in *World Development Report,* 1999/2000, Oxford University Press, New York, pp. 1-30.

CHAPTER SEVEN

Large but Not Unlimited
Freedom in a Nordic City

Hanne Wilhjelm

The Norwegian Growing Up in Cities project was carried out in two districts of Trondheim, and was thus able to compare young people's lives in an old working-class neighbourhood where inhabitants united to initiate a process of progressive local improvements, with an equally old residential area where the priorities of large institutions and highway construction have dominated the urban scene. In both settings, the perspectives and needs of local children have often been secondary to the interests of adults. Although Norway has some of the most advanced guidelines in the world for the promotion of the interests of children and youth in environmental planning, many difficulties exist in their implementation.

This chapter examines how urban transformations affect children's everyday lives, whether the urban changes be small and cumulative, or large and dramatic. The chapter will further consider how children living in two urban areas of the same city are influenced by their specific surroundings, by the differences and similarities these neighbourhoods may have. It will start with a brief introduction to the city of Trondheim, the two sites, and some important elements of childhood in Norway.

As an architect and urban planner, I was attracted to these districts because of my interest in how the continuous transformation of urban areas affects children's lives. In particular, I am interested in what happens to play spaces that children spontaneously claim or create, and also how the childhood domain has been increasingly lost through privatisation and urban development. Each area will be described from the perspectives of the children living there and from my own perspective; and in the course

of these stories the chapter will highlight planning issues with particular relevance to children.

From the children's perspective, the advantages of the Norwegian welfare state are evident. This chapter describes how a country, with a highly developed principle of equality instilled in its population, manages the social and physical environment in a way that makes it accessible to children and youth, and provides opportunities for free expression and development. It will examine the discrepancy between the rhetoric of the nation's planning policies and the more complex reality of how the city is constantly changing and how these policies are actually administered. In conclusion, it will discuss the obstacles that hinder implementing Norway's planning legislation, and suggest some ways to bridge the gap between the child-centred assumptions of planning policy and the realities of urban decision-making.[1]

A NORDIC CITY: TRONDHEIM

Located by a fjord, Trondheim is the third largest city in Norway, with a population of about 147,000. Located some 520 km south of the polar circle, the city enjoys a temperate coastal climate and yet experiences dramatic changes from season to season. In midsummer, daylight lasts for 24 hours while in midwinter it lasts only five hours.

In 1997 the city celebrated the 1000th anniversary of its founding. Up to the 14th century, Trondheim was the seat of both king and bishop. With its cathedral — the northernmost cathedral in Europe — it has been the centre of the nation's religious life and a regional centre for business and government for the past 1000 years. In 1910 the first Institute of Technology in Norway (later NTNU) was established, and Trondheim became important as a centre for the country's technological development and higher education.

Møllenberg and Elgeseter were the sites chosen as locations for the Growing up in Cities study. Both of these districts border on the ancient but still dynamic city centre, which is ringed on three sides by the River Nid and on the fourth by the Trondheim Fjord. Møllenberg lies across the river on the city's east side, while Elgeseter lies on the south side. I will use the concepts 'district' and 'area' to describe Møllenberg and Elgeseter although both are admini-stratively parts of one inner city area. The districts were chosen not for the purpose of making comparisons, but to provide more diverse sets of insights into the lives of young people growing up there.

These districts were established as residential areas around the turn of the 19th century. At that time, industrialisation was increasing rapidly, accompanied by a steady flow of labour migration to the city. At the turn of the 20th century, 50 percent of Trondheim's population lived on the east side of the river. This area continued to be very densely populated until the end of the Second World War, when a second period of urban expansion allowed families to migrate to the suburbs.

As early as the 1960s it was thought that building a highway around the centre would solve the city's traffic problems. Discussions took place as to whether these large roads should pass through the districts of Elgeseter,

Bakklandet, and Møllenberg. The result was uncertainty about the future status of the environment, with declining upkeep of the buildings as the outcome. After massive involvement by the residents and students living in these areas, public opinion and protest succeeded in stopping plans for the ring highway.

Urban development in Trondheim has followed the general European tendency of valuing architectural heritage and promoting conservation. Despite the similarities in historic legacy of these districts, urban development has varied considerably from one district to the other. Whereas Møllenberg has become more residential, Elgeseter has lost much of its residential status and has been confined on two sides by the Regional Hospital in Trondheim (RIT) and the main campus of NTNU.

CHILDREN AND LAND USE PLANNING

Norwegian law shows a long history of concern for children's well-being and rights[2]. In 1981 the Norwegian government appointed the world's first Commissioner for Children, often referred to as the Children's Ombudsman. The same year as Norway ratified the United Nations Convention on the Rights of the Child (CRC), a number of actions were taken to strengthen the position of children in relation to land use planning. One measure was to require by law that the municipalities appoint a children's representative to defend children's interests during the preparation of cases connected with land use.[3] Another measure was the National Policy Guidelines (NPG) passed by the Government to promote the interests of children and adolescents in matters subject to planning legislation. Section 4d in the NPG reads:

'The municipality shall organize the planning process to make sure that the points of view concerning children as the affected party are brought to light and that different groups of children and young people are given an opportunity to participate themselves.'[4]

The reform was 10 years old in 1999, but its effects have not yet been thoroughly evaluated,[5] and we do not know whether these policy intentions have been effective in prac-

© FJELLANGER WIDERØE AS

Figure 7.1 Aerial photo of the city of Trondheim, including Møllenberg (in the background) and Elgeseter (on the right)

tise. There is, however, an urgent need to investigate this since Norwegian urban centres are growing. From 1960 to 1980 population growth in small urban settlements was the dominant trend in Norway.[6] Now Norwegian cities and towns are growing in population, not because of immigration, but because of an increase in births.[7] Nevertheless, Elgeseter and Møllenberg belong to the category of city districts that have experienced a strong decrease in population, particularly in the number of children. In the case of Elgeseter, the number of dwellings has decreased, while in Møllenberg population changes have come about through changes in demographic composition — elderly people and families with children have moved out and students have moved in.[8]

In districts like Elgeseter and Møllenberg, urban planning has determined to a large extent the physical condi-

tion of the neighbourhoods. Since the first Norwegian planning legislation for urban areas was passed in the 1920s, land use planning has been widely used to structure and direct the evolution of urban landscapes. A later revision aimed to integrate physical and socio-economic planning: it named municipalities as the local planning authority, and placed emphasis on citizen participation in the planning process.[9]

Norwegian municipal planning authorities have three important instruments for reinforcing their work with children as participants. These are the Convention on the Rights of the Child, the general provision in Norwegian legislation for public participation in planning (for all age groups), and the National Policy Guidelines to promote the interests of children and adolescents in matters subject to planning policy. In order to understand the relation between plan and reality, and how this is connected to children's lives, I will try to put into context childhood in this part of the world.

GROWING UP IN NORWAY

For children growing up in Trondheim, as in other Scandinavian cities, the structural components include the family, the home, the public school and the neighbourhood.

It is taken for granted that Norwegian children 'belong' to their parents and that a stable family life is the best social environment for a child. It is also taken for granted that residential stability is a condition for a good childhood, and that having to move several times during childhood is damaging to a child's attachment to people and place.[10] Many Norwegian children have access to a second 'home', such as a cottage in the country, and many of them occasionally go to relatives living in the countryside, to where their parents had grown up, or to foreign countries for vacation.

Over the last few decades, changes in the structure of work have also changed children's lives. The majority of mothers have joined the workforce and the number of children enrolled in kindergarten and after-school programmes is increasing. Women and younger children leave the home for many hours during the day, while older children have the possibility of choosing on their own whether or not to stay indoors or outdoors when they return home after school. During afternoon and evening hours, they are allowed into friends' and other people's homes with less ceremony than grown-ups. Although most Norwegian children now have a room of their own, childhood is typically associated with a life outdoors, with the street as well as with nature, rather than with the indoors.[11]

The vast majority of Norwegian children living in the city attend the public school in their neighbourhood. Many children also take part in afternoon activities, for example at the public music school or sports clubs for girls or boys, since the school generally does not organise sports activities. However, activities connected with school orchestras (brass bands) are highly valued by many Norwegian schools, parents and local communities. Thus, afternoon

© HANNE WILHJELM

Figure 7.2 Playtime at Småbergan

activities for children in the city have a great diversity and consequently many children attend two to three afternoon activities per week, while other children attend none at all. The extent of involvement in afternoon activities and leisure programmes depends on social class, on the parents' involvement in what their children do, and on the time available.

Many popular ideas about what a good and 'natural' childhood should be link children and nature. It is generally held in Norway that the weather should not stop you from having an outdoor life. Therefore babies are taken outside to get fresh air even on cold winter days, and children from an early age are expected to play outdoors on their own in all kinds of weather. Norwegian ideas about childhood focus on self-governed free play among peers in an outdoor environment. Norwegian notions of childhood are thus not primarily associated with protected gardens or play areas, but with freedom, friendship, certain kinds of innocent rough play (self-management) among children and explorations of patches of wilderness in their local communities.[12]

Both boys and girls have a large degree of freedom to move around in their local environment. It is unusual for children in the city to be driven to and from school on a regular basis by their parents or others. Parents rarely keep their children inside or accompany them outdoors because of fear of crime or other dangers. Like other Scandinavian children, children in Trondheim are regarded as being able, according to their age, to manage freedom of movement in their own small neighbourhood, in the district, and in the city centre.

SAMPLE AND METHOD

This study has been carried out by a team consisting of myself (at the time, a researcher at the Norwegian Centre for Child Research), and two graduate students from the Department of Geography at the Norwegian University of Science and Technology (NTNU). Seven students (four men and three women) from NTNU assisted the team.

The 35 children with whom we worked ranged in age from nine through 13 years. The oldest would hardly like to be called children, preferring instead to be called young people or adolescents. Following the United Nations definition of a 'child' as anyone under 18, I have chosen to refer to all of them as children.

Principals and school boards at the three primary schools that enrol children from Møllenberg and Elgeseter gave us permission to introduce the project to the pupils. I did not choose the sample: it was the children who chose to join the project after receiving information and an invitation to participate. A 'snowball' effect was created when friends or groups of friends decided to take part. In terms of gender distribution, another effect was observed: when, in a certain class, the first ones to join were 11 year old girls, it was difficult to recruit boys from the same class. Thus the Møllenberg study shows an over-representation of girls, while the gender distribution is the opposite for Elgeseter. Although the children should not be considered

TABLE 7.1

Participants Profile (N=35)

Male, 19   Female, 16

AGE	# OF PARTICIPANTS	AGE	# OF PARTICIPANTS
9	2	12	5
10	12	13	4
11	12		

TABLE 7.2

Community Profiles

MØLLENBERG

Land Area[17]	34 hectares (84 acres)
Population	3523
Population Age 7–15	231

ELGESETER

Land Area (see endnote 16)	65.6 hectares (162 acres)
Population	2632
Population Age 7–15	165

as being particularly competent to describe how they perceive their environment, it is important to be aware that some of them might have considered their own competence when they volunteered to take part in the project.

When granting permission for the project, the Data Inspectorate emphasised that the children had to participate voluntarily, and with their parents' consent.[13] Consequently, the sample could be biased with regard to representation of the social and economic composition of the residents in the two areas. However, since we knew exactly where the children lived, we also knew that the sample covered all sub-areas of the two districts with regard to housing and, to some extent, their social structure. The type and size of the dwellings, and whether they were owned or rented, gave us an indication of the economic situation of the families.

Møllenberg has never been characterised by a homogeneous social class.[14] A few generations back, there was a large number of children from working class families, but today this is no longer the case. The children in our sample lived in newly renovated wooden houses owned by the family as well as in deteriorating municipal blocks of rented flats. The children from Elgeseter also came from mixed social backgrounds. They lived in municipal apartment buildings, well-kept wooden houses with courtyards or gardens, and blocks of flats owned by housing cooperatives.

Our group of children was also representative of the general Norwegian family pattern, which means that nearly all children live together with both parents or with their mother.[15] Approximately half of Norwegian children have one sibling and a quarter have two or more siblings. However, the great majority get siblings, half-siblings or stepsiblings in the course of their childhood. A quarter of our children (9) lived with one of their parents, and most of these had to relate to two local environments since they stayed with both the mother and the father.[16]

> *When 16 Møllenberg children gave priorities for improving their area, the traditional need for more green areas and better playgrounds came at the bottom.*

Reflecting the general geographic stability of the Norwegian population, the majority of the sample had lived in the same area all of their life, and many of them in the same street or the same house.[18] A fifth of the sample (7) came to Trondheim with their parents as refugees, and have maintained an active affiliation with their homeland. The largest share of children (5) from refugee families lived in the Elgeseter district.[19]

To supplement the interviews, observations, informal talks and guided tours adopted from the original 1970s GUIC study, we had children take photographs. Altogether, the children took 401 photographs of their areas, and for 80 percent of the Elgeseter pictures and 50 percent of the Møllenberg pictures they wrote commentaries that described the image and why they had taken it (a selection of their photos and captions illustrates this chapter).

Almost all of the children drew maps of where they spent their time and indicated their range of movement on city maps or aerial photographs.[20]

In addition, my graduate assistants and I interviewed a number of employees of the Trondheim municipality, of government institutions such as the Norwegian State Housing Bank[21], and representatives of some developers in the two districts. Although information from the municipal authorities and developers in the two areas was important, the material presented by the children living in Møllenberg and Elgeseter constituted the foundation for the project.

MØLLENBERG

Møllenberg was developed at the end of the 19th century with a mixed population. The owners of the apartment houses lived on the first floor facing the street, and their tenants lived in the basement, in the loft, or at the back facing the yard. Today, the distribution of social classes is identical in Trondheim and in Møllenberg, although the dwellings in Møllenberg that have not been renovated house students in increasing numbers.[22] Several studies of Møllenberg have been conducted using the adult part of the population as informants. Before urban renewal started in the late 1970s, residents' complaints about the physical environment referred mainly to lack of insulation and sanitary facilities in the apartments, the amount of motor traffic, and the danger from traffic.[23]

At that time it was clear that the environment was problematic for younger children, whereas conditions were beneficial for older children. So, with good reason, families with young children moved out as housing production gained pace in the suburbs. The Møllenberg population has grown in recent years, but a lack of attractive outdoor areas is still a main reason why families with school-age children want to move out of the area. Although the number of 7–12 year olds has increased, they account for a smaller share of the population. Thus the GUIC children belong to families who have chosen to stay, and only two of the 18 children in our Møllenberg sample said that their family would like to move.

Like other areas close to the centres of towns or

Figure 7.3 Map of Møllenberg by Lene (11 years old)

urban areas elsewhere in Norway, Møllenberg has lost much of the earlier prolific commercial activity that thrived in the small shops on the ground floors of its buildings. There are many synergetic reasons for this change, for example a centralisation of the commodity trade, higher rents, and solid financial gain in building or rehabilitating housing. Although a great number of small enterprises remain, many buildings have vacated their ground floor commercial spaces and their attractive shop windows have been lost to residents.

Children from Møllenberg: Neighbourhood Narratives

The children from Møllenberg describe a district that has attractive wooden houses, small green backyards, and a local park that is appreciated and used. It has a school that is one of the most important buildings in the district, both as an architectural monument and as a meeting place for the community during and after school hours. The children know that they live in an attractive area and are proud of their district. They mention, for example, that Møllenberg has 'the longest street' of small wooden houses

to be found in Norway. Renovating, painting and improving the houses, or building new ones, are all part of a continuous process which the children notice and regard as a natural part of the environment. In these initial descriptions a large majority said that they liked their neighbourhood and very few negative aspects came to light:

'Møllenberg is fine. There are lots of dogs, lots of fences which it's fun to climb over, and lots of back yards.' (10 year old girl) …*'Quite pleasant, easy to make friends here. I'm sure you will like it here.'* (13 year old girl)… *'I live in a nice home, in a very fine old house.'* (10 year old boy)… *'I like it here: poor climate and lovely nature. I live below the fort near to the bicycle lift in a small brick house and below us are some blocks of flats.'* (10 year old boy)… *'I like being everywhere.'* (10 year old girl).

The advantages and disadvantages of the area can be glimpsed through the accounts of a 10 year old girl, Marianne, and a boy of almost 11, Michael.[24] Marianne lives on the top floor of an apartment building built before the turn of the 19th century, where the site has been utilised to a maximum degree and the buildings have very small courtyards. Michael lives in a similar house in the centre of the district. The children focus on the blocks nearest to their homes, although Michael's range spills over into the city centre and Småbergan, a small wooded area. Both children describe a freely explored, intimately known area.

During a guided tour of their neighbourhood, Marianne and her friend lead me over several broken fences to the interior of her own block. They show me some of the small treasures to be found there, such as traces of cat's paws in a concrete floor and 'secrets' under the tiles. They demonstrate an equally detailed knowledge of nearby blocks and of private areas to which they officially do not have access: for example, the backyard behind a bakery where we take in the fragrant smells from the ventilation outlet, or a new extension being built on a restaurant. They also guide me to a playground for small children where they sometimes meet but seldom spend much time. Marianne narrates:

'There's fine nature and asphalt and also a small garden here, and lots of broken fences. There is just a small fence between us and the apartment house next door. There are

lots of bicycles. Our neighbour's ugly backyard is on the other side of the wall. The roof of our neighbour's house is good to have when we sit outside on our veranda because it shields us, so that everyone who passes along the street cannot see us when we are sitting there....'

What about the traffic?

'Hm! – Little traffic where I live, just where I live cars pass by very seldom, but in Kirkegaten there is a lot of traffic, the street next to where I live.'

And the parked cars?

'Silly, they let out oil and that is silly, where they are parked, it drips from the cars when they drive away. I and her, my best friend, have started a kind of oil-thing club...yes, we had it before, when we collected the oil in buckets and mixed it with water and then poured it down the sink. That wasn't very smart.'

And if there were less traffic?

'Much better if we could toboggan in the street, run around in the street, then we would have to have something else... cars that run on a battery or bicycles.'

What do you think it will be like in the future?

'Much more traffic, there'll be much larger buildings and a lot of pollution — nothing else.'

Do you have too little time?

'Ah...Hm...Both yes and no...I go to gymnastics and music school here at Bispehaugen. I would like to go to swimming training, but I don't have time for that. And I would like to learn to dive...and then I would like to go climbing. I have the time for that, but don't have the money for it. It's expensive. I don't have any climbing gear or anything, and anyway, there aren't any climbing courses for children. No, I don't get bored.'

Many of Michael's school friends live outside the Møllenberg area. In spite of this, his photographs show his own little neighbourhood consisting of the nearest city blocks. The text gives the clear impression that he values his environment. On the photograph showing the view from his room he wrote, *'I took this picture because I enjoy it here.'* He is one of the very few project participants who is an active user of a home computer. He calls himself a computer freak. During his interview, Michael showed a lot of interest in his environment, as shown by his answers.

Figure 7.4 'Upper Møllenberg street with parked cars'

What would you tell a visitor about Møllenberg?

'I would say that it is very old, because it has been here from before the war. This house of ours is about a hundred years old. There are some strange things, and the neighbourhood doesn't have a lot of traffic, and not so much pollution, even though we live on the corner of the street that has the most traffic, and Småbergan at any rate is nice. I'm mostly at home or else at school. I go there every day. Work most of the time, am there sometimes after school hours, then with... all my friends.... I go to tae kwon-do every Tuesday and Thursday, out at Innherredsveien. Here I go out of the city, but I go into the city too, to Ram and Rom [computer software shop] ... See most of the computer games...see if I find anything interesting...I don't like violent games... Well, I do like violent games when they're funny. I'm usually by myself at Ram and Rom.'

And in other places?

'Brun and Libris [bookshops], they have lots of games there too. Oh yes—and in the Trondheim market square, I went there once, bought clothes together with my mother. I'm there mostly with my mother.'

Which places do you enjoy the most?

'First at home, and then the Trondheim market square, I don't mean just the houses, but around there, and then Småbergan. When I have gone there I have tobogganed or ridden on jet skis with my friends.'

What do you think the place will look like in the future? *'There will be more shops then. New houses, because the buildings are so very old already. We live on the street in Møllenberg with the most traffic. E6 is 500 metres away, that is hell. And the parking places ought to become pavements, then there would be some place to cycle. Many of the cars have their wheels on the pavement.'*

The Architect's Møllenberg

During the first year of the project I moved to Møllenberg to become a neighbour to the children and be able to observe their everyday lives. Møllenberg has the appearance of a rigidly planned urban grid. The streets running east-

west follow the contours of the landscape, and the streets running north-south start at the top of the sloping terrain and run downwards towards the former industrial areas on the flatter land along the fjord. In their narratives the children primarily characterised the area as having two-storey wooden houses containing several families. However, from my point of view the area is not quite so homogeneous. The district also has four-storey apartment buildings and other more modern blocks of apartments from the 1930s and from more recent years. Only a few plots in some specific city blocks have a shabby appearance, but these are disappearing month by month. Møllenberg, a neighbourhood close to the city centre with a nostalgic flavour, is attracting investment by residents and investors who like to speculate in the housing market.

It was winter when I moved in, and there was no vegetation until the spring. Several of the streets are planted with trees, and most of the courtyards have been rehabilitated. Many of the city blocks have outdoor areas for common use and places where younger children can play. Not all the city blocks have been developed for maximum utilisation. One city block remained undeveloped and became the 'park' for the area. In the afternoons the outdoor environment at the kindergarten and the schoolyard are widely used by children in the area. In addition, the proximity to large green areas, including Småbergan around Kristiansten Fort, a 17th century military installation, is a great advantage for Møllenberg as well as for other surrounding districts.

My observations did not give me the impression that there were many children. Which children we would be able to meet often depended on the time of year, if not the time of day. Many cancelled appointments with the research team, for example, if a warm and sunny spring day enticed them to do other activities. In late autumn, when the sun goes down at six o'clock, most people are inside in the evenings, but in the evening hours in January, when the sun goes down at three in the afternoon, children often play in the snow under the light from the street lamps and the moon. The changing seasons and the unpredictability of the weather provide possibilities for a diversity of activities.

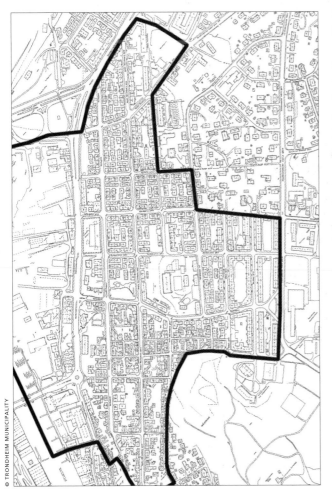

© TRONDHEIM MUNICIPALITY

Figure 7.5 The study area marked on the map of Møllenberg

RENEWAL FOR WHOM?

For both the public authorities and the people living in Møllenberg, the principal objectives of urban renewal have been to conserve the stock of buildings, improve court-yards and green areas in the district, and regulate traffic. These are aims that everybody can agree upon, but do children and adults have the same priorities?

When 16 Møllenberg children gave priorities for improving their area, the traditional need for more green areas and better playgrounds came at the bottom. Their own priorities (with the number of children who proposed each one indicated in parentheses) were:

• maintenance of and changes to buildings (6)
• less traffic and safer streets (6)
• welfare measures of various kinds (5)
• improvement of green areas and playgrounds (4)

As mentioned above, Norwegian planners and architects usually think in terms of better green areas for children to play in when they consider improvements. Just like other adults here, they hold the deeply ingrained Norwegian belief that outdoor living in natural areas is vital. But since Norwegian children living in cities do not have immediate access to natural environments any more than children in other urban areas around the world, their needs for good environments have to be addressed without reference to this strongly rooted cultural belief. Faced with this reality, discussions on the wishes of children living in an urban area like Møllenberg are difficult to promote.

For us it was not surprising that few of the children at Møllenberg directly expressed a wish for new green areas, because it is difficult for adults and children alike to see where such areas could be found. However, this is not the same as saying that the children did not value 'green.' Besides the local parks, they described and photographed their own backyards, indicating small flowerbeds, grass and bushes, and the woods. Urban renewal led to well-kept small courtyards that meet the needs of young children under supervision. The children described these areas as boring, as places to meet briefly, but not as places to stay. The children's preferences were divided into public territories, group territories, and private spaces that were not

necessarily in accordance with the official divisions of categories.[25] The older children living in the most densely populated part of Møllenberg favoured the schoolyard since the yard was the only open territory where they could meet in the afternoons without being overly supervised by adults.

Figure 7.6 Møllenberg in winter

Møllenberg is representative of the majority of 'well-functioning' city districts in Scandinavian countries where few plots are not actively used. Small green areas that could have served to extend the facilities available to our group of children are usually in private hands. In addition, adults, who are often retired people living at home, define the outdoor environment to suit their calm lives.[26] Their tidy and well-kept surroundings contrast sharply with the rougher and flexible outdoor areas that provide the best opportunities for play.[27]

The dilemma illustrated in the following case shows the conflict between the meaning of green space in the minds of planners and developers and the meaning that it often holds for children. The example here shows how a planning process can take place without drawing in children from the area concerned.

Near the school in Møllenberg there was a site with a small two-storey house from the 1950s, a badly maintained garage, and a private garden. Some of the children referred to the unkempt garden as a green area. Marianne's text to her photograph of it reads: 'A wood I like very much in Møllenberg.' Johanne had also taken a photo of this 'wood', with her friends in the foreground, pointing to the trees. Lene had taken a photo of wood anemones on the site, and her text reads: 'I think the picture looks as if it is in a wood, but it is in the middle of Trondheim. I think it's *beautiful*.' During my inspections of the site in 1999 I found no traces of children's play. But this does not alter the fact that this private property was a valued space for the children. It was perhaps one of the few remaining green areas that could have been turned into a public play area, consistent with requirements in the NPG.

The developer of the location made various propositions for buildings on the site, against which residents protested for various reasons — some because the proposed new buildings would not conform to the traditional architecture, others because the new density of residents would exceed the limits they considered suitable. Still others thought that the formal play area for a block of neighbouring apartments would be impaired. The developer's plans were discussed back and forth without anyone suggesting preserving the 'wood', as it was privately owned and earmarked for house construction in the local development plan. In the eyes of the municipality and the developer, the agenda for the building issue did not concern children. A few of the residents did refer to the NPG and argued that the site should be considered as a green area for a district with few green resources.

> In the eyes of the municipality and the developer, the agenda for the building issue did not concern children.

The plan for the site was completed by the end of the year 2000 and ideas for a play area will never be realised. Children's interests came far behind other interests, since the question about architectural styles dominated the planning agenda and probably will continue to do so in similar cases. Here, as in other building or planning cases, considerations for one particular interest overshadowed the others.

© MARIANNE (10 YEAR OLD GIRL)

Figure 7.7 'A wood I like very much in Møllenberg'

Traffic-safe, but not Traffic-free

The visions associated with children's wishes for change, for example broader sidewalks, can lead to a paradox; what do adults do when children's proposals for improvements are far removed from the possibilities that adults tend to choose? The problems of traffic and parking that the children's narratives illustrated are issues that Norwegian society today is far from willing to acknowledge or act upon.

The dominant position of motorised traffic became more evident in the children's pictures and written descriptions, whereas in their initial verbal description of the area it was the buildings, rather than the streets, that were emphasised.

In the 1970s only two percent of the surveyed adult residents evaluated the district as traffic-safe for children, and almost half considered traffic to be a serious danger.[28] The city's effort to improve the area in the 1970s was summed up as follows: 'The traffic regulation measures must be regarded as a successful part of the total efforts to make Møllenberg a better district to live in...the residents (adults) are less anxious.'[29] For the adult population, traffic-related problems such as accidents and pollution have to a large extent now been solved. Finding a space for parking in the evenings might still be difficult, but this is not considered a reason for people to move out of the district.

When the Møllenberg children talked about traffic they were conscious of its dominance and extremely enthusiastic about reducing it. Although traffic occupied a major place in their narratives, this does not imply that it limited their radius of action. They were aware of the two streets with heavy traffic that encircle the blocks to the north and south. During the interview we asked the children what they thought about the traffic, and the changes that might occur if there were less. Their comments revealed the impact that traffic has had on many of the children:

'It would be better because then we could move about freely without our parents getting worried.' (11 year old girl)… *'Perhaps there would be more children playing outside.'* (13 year old girl)… *'It would be very nice to live here. More people would spend time outdoors.'* (11 year old boy)…. *'There would be cleaner air and less noise, and it would be safer to cross the street.'* (10 year old boy)…. *And the parked cars? 'I would remove the cars… They're in the way for those who play football.'* (13 year old girl)

In brief, their wishes were for fewer parked cars and less traffic and many of the children proposed solutions to the problems. Kenneth (10 year old boy) suggested a parking garage when we asked about parked cars: 'I don't like them, I think there should be parking places nearer to school. A basement [garage], like the one under the low-price supermarket in the city centre.' Johanne, an 11 year old girl, produced a photograph of part of a street where pedestrians have priority and cars drive at minimum speed. The photo showed the sign *'Drive carefully, children at play.'* Her text to the photo read: 'This is a street where the cars drive very slowly. I think the people who have put up the sign should put up more of these signs in other places.' To reduce pollution and traffic, other children suggested battery-run cars, bicycles, and even horses. Regardless of their suggestions, it was clear from their answers that fewer cars would give them more space for play, especially in winter when they wanted to use the steep roads for tobogganing. Even though the area has some good off-road slopes, the temptation to use their sledges or the sole on their boots to slide in the streets was so great that they did this secretly at times, although it was not allowed.

From my point of view, the traffic is not generally heavy since there is only one street with heavy traffic in the area.

Figure 7.8 Kirkegata dominates Møllenberg by its width.

Unfortunately it is a street that many of the children have to cross over on their way to school. There are, however, many parked cars, and the city blocks appear to be lined with them despite one-sided parking in several streets. There is an evident disparity between the large asphalt areas and the narrow pavements where the children can play. But it would be difficult for the authorities to change the conditions the children have referred to: broader sidewalks would obviously lead to fewer parking spaces.

The Møllenberg children do not talk specifically about traffic as being dangerous, but are fully aware of the possibilities that fewer cars would offer. They describe traffic first and foremost as an urgent problem of space. Yet public concern over urban renewal has not resulted in easy answers to the problems raised by the children. A district that was planned a hundred years ago cannot possibly have enough space for the number of cars that today's lifestyle brings with it. Nor can Møllenberg reverse the trend and become a museum community.[30] Even if the municipality were to restrict parking space for new development projects, there would still be far too many cars. Thus the demand for fewer cars becomes both a radical and almost revolutionary suggestion.

ELGESETER

Although urban centres are growing as a result of increased economic activity and population growth, some districts will nonetheless undergo a change in character and lose their population base. Well-functioning residential areas may suddenly and reluctantly find themselves being transformed. Major changes in infrastructure, like new highways and a concentration of commercial activity, can 'roll over' small residential areas. The result can be unacceptable noise, dust and danger from traffic, or a decrease in the number of local shops. Homes are turned into offices, and the area becomes desolate from a residential perspective when institutions have expanded beyond their originally planned limits. These changes will produce new social codes for how the environment is used and understood.

As in Møllenberg, traffic is a major concern of residents in Elgeseter. In addition, two large and powerful institutions — the hospital and the university — dominate Elgeseter. It is therefore marked by a struggle between competing land use interests, and the situation illustrates the difficulty of maintaining citizen participation in urban transformation processes. From 1970 to 1999, the population in Elgeseter declined from 5241 to 2632, with a corresponding decline of 7-15 year olds from 400 to 165.[31]

Elgeseter According to its Children

Children in Elgeseter, unlike children in Møllenberg, did not say that they belonged to a special district. When asked where they lived, they named a certain street, or a neighbourhood within the district, or said that they lived in an area close to the city centre.[32] Elgesetergate, the southbound main road from the city centre, splits the area into two parts. The east side turns towards the university and the west side turns towards the hospital. Elgeseter is not a cohesive city district, even though — when using the typological elements developed by Kevin Lynch in *The Image of the City* — one can easily find its boundaries and landmarks.[33]

The children here also described their area in generally positive terms. Their initial descriptions tell of quiet residential neighbourhoods, which they do not regard as part of the district's total and dynamic whole. In contrast

to the descriptions from the Møllenberg children, they go into much more detail about how the area might develop in the future.

Magnus, an 11 year old boy, described the district in terms of what he could do there:

'A lot of people live in this area both old and young. It's easy to get to know people here. And there's a lot of snow — it's fun to play in the snow, on the slopes near the university. It's fun in the winter. I like where I live.'

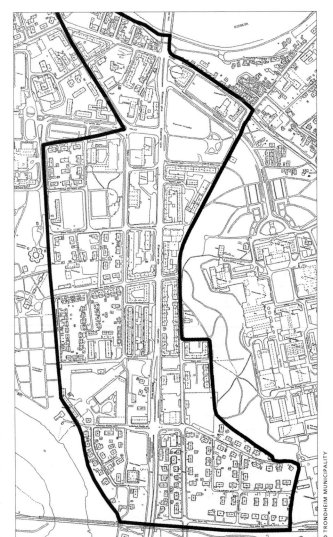

Figure 7.9 The study area marked on the map of Elgeseter

© MORTEN (11 YEAR OLD BOY)

Figure 7.10 Map of Elgeseter by Morten (11 years old)

Louise, a 10 year old who belongs to one of the refugee families in the area, says that she likes Elgeseter because she feels more free here than in any of the five other places where she has lived. In Elgeseter, she can go with her mother, brother Mehram or friend Melissa to her favourite places, such as Finalen, a park in the middle of the district, or across the bridge to the grassy riverbank beside the cathedral, or to the library. Like most other refugee children, she does not have access to recreation facilities, such as a family cabin for holidays in the forest or along the shore, or relatives to visit nearby. The resources in the vicinity of her home are therefore especially important for her.

'When there is no snow on the ground Mummy takes out my little sister in her pushchair. I usually go with her, either on my bike or walking beside her. Mehram and I share a bicycle. We also ride my father's bicycle when he is not using it. My mother and I may decide to go for a walk after we have had dinner. We go either to Finalen or to the kindergarten past the football stadium. In summer we go down to the river. We take a picnic lunch, which we eat on the grass near there. Melissa and I do the same, but by ourselves. Melissa and I often agree beforehand to meet at Finalen. We cycle round the block there and on the football ground if there's nobody kicking a ball around. Sometimes we use the swings and other things. Afterwards either Melissa comes home with me or I go home with her. Then we do our homework, look

at TV and talk. Both Melissa and I like to read. We go together to the library to borrow books, but I also borrow the books Melissa has at home. Sometimes I'm allowed to stay overnight with her.'

Louise and the rest of the children from the east side of Elgeseter pass through the university campus on their way to school, while the children from the west side attend a school in the city centre. Louise thinks she has a long way to walk to school because it takes her up to half an hour to get there, and it can be long and tiring. She goes first to Melissa's house, and from there they walk to school together. Since her little brother started school, she walks home with him a couple of days a week. When her parents, brother or Melissa aren't free to travel with her, however, her world becomes much smaller:

'If Mehram comes with my mother and me to Finalen, I play football with him. Otherwise, I spend most of the time after school close to where I live. I cycle around the block with Melissa, play "jumping the elastic" in the streets behind my house and kick a ball around with the small children in the neighbourhood. Mummy says that I must not stray far from home…I'm very bored at times.'

Harry, an 11 year old who lives with his mother, within walking distance of his father, is an example of a child who takes advantage of the rich cultural resources that the city offers. Musically talented, he attends the public afternoon-school for music, plays the accordion and the piano, and sings in the boy's choir of the cathedral. Elgeseter gives him a base from which he can move out into the city. Whenever possible, he plans activities with his friend Gisle who, like himself, divides his time between two separated parents. Harry narrates:

'We live on the second floor of the block. I don't know many who live in this block. There are hardly any children living in the block except Gisle. Gisle is in the same class as me and his father lives one staircase over from us. My bedroom window looks out on the backyard, towards Elgesetergaten, where the cars are parked. I sometimes find it difficult to sleep at night because of the traffic. There's traffic all the time, especially on weekends and in the summer. There is a block building between us and Elgesetergaten, which dead-

ens the noise a bit. But it's comforting to hear a few cars otherwise it might feel a bit creepy — too quiet...I like to listen to music, all kinds of music. Sometimes I go to Trondheim market square to buy CDs at the music shops there. My mother doesn't like that very much. She doesn't like me to be there, because of drunks and others who hang around there...I like to go to Finalen, because there we can do what we want: for example, play football, or let off fire-crackers, which the father of one of my friends buys in Sweden. I go to Finalen a lot in the summer. We meet there in fact. It is a sort of meeting place for us, but for others too. In the park itself there are usually only boys. The girls keep to the playground...I have sometimes cycled to the city centre, down to the fish market, for example, but only when I have asked if I can beforehand. Usually I cycle together with friends — Morten and Gisle. When Gisle is living with his mother, Morten and I sometimes cycle over Stavnebrua [a bridge over the river for pedestrians and cyclists] and up to where his grandmother lives.'

Between the district and the city centre, Harry's world gives him scope for development.

The Architect's Elgeseter

In the 1970s I was one of a group of university employees who drove into the area every day from the north over the Elgeseter bridge, swung into a parking space between two residential areas and parked my car in the assigned spot. Like other university employees, I had an essentially functional relationship with Elgeseter, mainly through the use of this typical urban space, at the time paved with gravel, now covered with asphalt.

> When I returned to the area in 1995, the dominance of Elgesetergaten, with its 33,000 cars on a typical day, was overwhelming.

In many ways the district can serve as a reference to architectural and planning ideas. Elgeseter was not, and is not now, homogeneous. We can find farmhouses from the 18th and 19th centuries, Jugendstil apartment houses in

Elgesetergaten and, representing the modern tradition, the high-rise blocks of the hospital and the municipal administration building. Neighbourhoods with wooden houses for one, two or four families in the 'garden town' are based on English town planning traditions. The residential areas show many good qualities when considered separately as neighbourhoods, but for visitors neither these nor the large green areas around the district compensate for the district's disorderly impression.

When I returned to the area in 1995, the dominance of Elgesetergaten, with its 33 000 cars on a typical day, was overwhelming.[34] This central artery carries a heavy flow of traffic, dust and exhaust gases (especially in winter), and those willing to risk crossing it need to do it at a run.

While the children describe their own small and quiet residential areas, I see the area as a whole marked by large contrasts and by the proximity of the two large institutions, the hospital and the university, towering high over this part of Trondheim.

WHEN HOUSING IS THE LOSER IN THE URBAN DYNAMIC

In the course of our work on this project, the situation in the district was dominated by several important planning issues, such as building extensions to the RIT and the future fate of the common open area, Finalen. Both of these issues have great relevance for the Elgeseter children's outdoor environment.

Urban Renewal Did not Reach Elgeseter

In Elgeseter, urban renewal never translated into an overall effort to upgrade the district. As mentioned above, the district contains a mixture of municipal apartment houses that are rented out to families, well-kept privately owned wooden houses with gardens, and blocks of flats owned by housing cooperatives.

Essentially four elements determine the dynamics of the urban fabric at Elgeseter: Elgesetergaten, the hospital with its extensions, the university with its extensions, and Finalen. As stated above another important element has been the dramatic reduction of the district's population.[35]

There are more elderly (over 60 years of age) now than in the 1960s, whereas the number of children has fallen. These demographic changes, caused by a uniformity of housing in parts of the area and by migration to the suburbs, are ordinary urban phenomena. With regard to the children's environment, it will be particularly interesting to see how the smaller number of children will affect their possibilities of finding friends and playmates close to their homes.

Keeping the Hospital at a Distance

The vulnerability of residential areas in the face of large land interests can be illustrated by a reference to the expansion plan for the hospital, named 'RIT 2000'. When we began the Growing Up in Cities project in Trondheim in 1995, the city government had started work on the municipal area plan for the district and had already given the hospital permission to expand, despite residents' demands for an environmental impact assessment in accordance with the Planning and Building Act. When the local development plan was adopted, I suspected that the hospital's expansion might completely dominate the area. My suspicions were confirmed as RIT nearly doubled its area to 225 000 square metres, and the cost for the expansion increased from 2.4 billion to 3.5 billion Norwegian crowns. The role of the hospital in Elgeseter had become that of a 'cuckoo in the nest.'

The proposal that won the competition for the expansion claimed that: 'RIT shall be integrated both physically and socially with the city. The hospital shall not be felt to be an institution, but an open part of the city with a diversified environment and innumerable activities...'[36] According to the municipality: 'The city planning vision for RIT 2000...can be summarised as a wish for an "urban society"; integration with the city, versatility, human dimensions, an expression of "greenness", i.e. conditions that prevent alienation.'[37]

What, then, did the GUIC children have to say about the hospital's development? Neither the public authorities nor the developer had asked them — despite the fact that Norwegian guidelines demand that in planning issues affecting children the municipality shall consider their points of view. Nor did our children show an awareness of the hospital and its plans. Despite the hospital's and the municipality's claims that the hospital seeks integration with the city and that it was nearby and visible, the children hardly mentioned this large and powerful institution when describing their environment. Only a few of them drew the hospital in their maps, and hardly any of them were concerned about having one of the country's largest building sites as their neighbour for many years to come. Anders (12 year old boy) and Harry were the only two among the 17 children who documented the hospital in their photographs.

Figure 7.11 'The hospital before the enlargement to RIT 2000'

It is difficult to conceive how children's rights can best be respected in such a huge case of land use planning and development as the RIT. And it is hardly surprising that the children were not especially interested, since it is difficult for anyone who is not directly involved to grasp the dimensions of such a big development project. People living north of the hospital have protested against impairment of their residential area, but the residents of Elgeseter began to make their opinions known only very late in the planning process. Both the primary school and the County Governor expressed concern about the problems that may arise in connection with the children's way to school. There are probably only few who really believe that the hospital's goals for urban integration will be fulfilled.

Traffic is a Burden

Despite the positive features that Elgeseter's parks and convenient geographic location offer, a number of the children expressed dismay over the level of traffic along Elgesetergaten, and the noise, dust and pollution that it generates.

'It would have been better if there had been fewer cars and traffic in the area. I have asthma. Lots of exhaust gases. Sometimes I wish I had a facemask... If I could change anything I would like the motor traffic to go through a tunnel, with a pedestrian area on top. This would give more space for us to run around in the streets. I would like to see cars without exhaust, with an air-cleaning thing on the exhaust pipes.' (11 year old boy) *'Here, over Elgeseter bridge I pass every day on my way to school. In the background you see the Cathedral. And cars — they pollute terribly, there is only one thing to say: Cough-Cough.'* (12 year old boy, photo text) *'I don't use Elgesetergaten on my way home from school because there is so much exhaust there, not because I'm not allowed to.'* (11 year old boy) *'No, I don't spend any time along Elgesetergaten...lots of disturbance, noise and dust in the spring. It is really awful. If it could be different where I live I would certainly suggest moving Elgesetergaten.'* (11 year old girl)

Other children seemed to accept the traffic as an inevitable part of the environment. When a 9 year old girl was asked about the types of changes that she anticipated, she replied, 'Perhaps new colours on the houses, perhaps more cars.'

> *Traffic safety appeared to be achieved by children avoiding the heavily travelled roads by their own preference, or by parents making these roads 'out of bounds'.*

Here, as in other urban environments, traffic safety appeared to be achieved by children avoiding the heavily travelled roads by their own preference, or by parents making these roads 'out of bounds.' This situation parallels that found in the United Kingdom by Mayer Hillman

Figure 7.12 Elgesetergaten, the southbound main road from the city center

and his colleagues. Safety from traffic was achieved at the expense of reducing children's free range and independent mobility.[38] A small study initiated by the Highway Authority showed that few children were out on Elgesetergaten. The report concluded that:

'There is a certain relationship between the recorded level of accidents and whether or not people feel safe. Most people feel safe, and the danger from traffic does not seem to limit the use of the road. There are very few children in the streets, however, and the parents' fear of traffic accidents may explain why they do not allow their children to go there.'[39]

Nevertheless, children in Elgeseter have many good reasons to cross Elgesetergaten. For example, in winter they find on the west side the ice skating rink, and on the east the slopes of the university campus for skiing and tobogganing. The risks are illustrated by this conversation with Melanie (10 year old), when I asked her whether she was afraid of the traffic:

'No, I'm not afraid of the traffic. When we are together with my mother she says, You must only cross over when it's green. [Melanie distorts her voice to sound like her mother warning her to cross only when the pedestrian signal turns green.] She doesn't understand anything.'
And when you are alone?
'You know: there where Ronja lives. Me and Ronja, we're not allowed like to run across the road.... He [an uncle]

*saw us and waved to us. He told Ronja's mother, who was
damned cross with us.'*
So you take risks?
'Yes, we run across the road on red.'

In addition, our work in Elgeseter has made us aware of a
paradox in an area where the usual conflict between the
world of adults and the world of children is not so obvious. Open-air parking spaces filled with cars during working days can be attractive areas for play and exercises on
bicycles in the evenings and on weekends in the summer.
In the future, when new office buildings and parking-
garages occupy these open areas, possibilities for the
children to enjoy these spaces will be lost.

Finalen Is Important

Finalen is the most important place for social contact, play,
and ballgames for the GUIC children. The gravelled area
has been used for ball games for 50 years and is maintained
by the municipality's Department for Parks and Recreation.
Its use from 1980 until now has been safeguarded by a confirmed local development plan. But plans are not worth
much more than the paper they are written on if politicians find it right to change the land use of the area. Like
the 'cuckoo in the nest', the hospital proposed to expand
its territory for buildings to Finalen in the summer of 2000.
However, when an alliance of forces, including the GUIC
team, engaged in advocacy for children's interests to save
the area, the hospital's proposal was turned down. The
majority of members in the City Council voted in favour of
Finalen. We might therefore expect that the hospital will
become less of a threat to common outdoor life in the
district for a time. On the other hand, the 'cuckoo' is un-
fledged and may return with new demands.

Louise describes her visit to Finalen and the park occupies a dominant place in Harry's descriptions as well.
Although it is difficult to divide our sample of children from
Elgeseter into several categories for analysis, I find some
recurring common features concerning their use of time
in the afternoons. It is the boys from the west side of
Elgeseter who use Finalen as a place to meet and play
football, and it is the girls from the east side, who do not
have a private garden to play in, who meet there. The boys

Figure 7.12 Finalen in summer

from the east side tend to go back over the hill to their
school playground at Singsaker to play basketball or some
other ballgames on the asphalt. The children's use of outdoor recreation areas varies with the seasons and their
different needs; but for the children of today and generations to come, Finalen can be expected to remain an
important place, and symbol, of public life.

TAKE THE CHILDREN'S SUGGESTIONS SERIOUSLY

The GUIC material gathered in Trondheim showed many
common characteristics among the children's use and
evaluations of their city. Freedom in how children use time
and space is a deeply rooted concept in Nordic cultures.
Accordingly, the children, like the majority of children
growing up in urban areas in Scandinavia, shared a large
degree of independence from which both boys and girls
benefited. The parents of 9 year olds in the sample set clear
limits to their children's range of movement. But already
at the age of 10 or 11, children were allowed to go to the
city centre without being accompanied by parents or older
siblings, as long as they told where they were going and
came home at the agreed time. They moved around freely
in their local environments without important parental

restrictions and they had great freedom to form their own social relations. They had friends whom they visited at home and many of them were able to spend the night with a best friend.

Due to the geographical location of Møllenberg and Elgeseter, the city centre was an accessible resource for children older than 10 or 11, and most of them went there on their own, with others being accompanied by friends. Not all travelled widely through the city, but the majority made frequent use of public cultural facilities such as cinemas, the indoor swimming pool, and the library. They visited shops and public areas and became familiar with the 'city' in a comfortable way, even though many of them knew where they might meet people addicted to alcohol or narcotics.

> *Planners who have experienced children's participation in the planning process have found that children possess useful and important knowledge that no one else in the community can provide.*

Despite the resources and freedoms that they enjoyed, these children had little or no voice in the urban transformations that affected their lives. The Trondheim municipality could have initiated a system of participation for the planning and building issues that have been described here, but it never did. Up to this time the municipality has not taken advantage of the GUIC project to draw children into their planning process, although the children's comments have been communicated through seminars, meetings, and letters. Thus Trondheim is neither different from the majority of cities around the world, which tend to ignore the requirements of the Convention on the Rights of the Child, nor is it different from many municipalities in Norway, which ignore the explicit language calling for participation in the National Policy Guidelines and the Planning and Building Act.

In conclusion, we who are interested in giving children a voice should ask ourselves how it might be pos-sible to make planning more transparent and take children's viewpoints and their use of the local environment into account. The Trondheim study suggests two areas where participation could be increased not only for children, but also for those who belong to less influential segments of the adult population.

Rights and Obligations

First we must examine the status of rights that are already established. Laws and guidelines are of little use if people are not aware of their right to be consulted when they are affected by physical changes in their environment. Requests for greater public participation and greater transparency in planning, as found in documents like the United Nations Habitat Agenda and the Norwegian legislation on the management of land and resources, should be made more public so that both children and adults are aware of them. The population, the politicians and the public administration must realise that some have obligations so that others can have rights. If children are going to exercise their rights to participate in planning processes where the results will affect their lives, developers and the public, represented by administrators and politicians, have to provide a common ground for discussions, and in this way fulfil their obligations.

Work related to Agenda 21, including Local Agenda 21 planning, might provide useful experience with public debate on important environmental issues. In this context, a dialogue between developers and planners on one side, and the population — including children and adolescents — on the other, would help bring to light different standpoints regarding how the urban environment should evolve in the future. The participation of children and adolescents, the managers of tomorrow's environment, should be of utmost interest.

In the case of Møllenberg, planners and politicians might be more likely to take action in the right direction — for example reduce the street surface for private cars — if they knew the views of the area's children about parking. Planners who have experienced children's participation in the planning process have found that children possess useful and important knowledge that no one else in the community can provide. The town planners in

Trondheim are currently working on a municipal area plan for the western district close to the centre of Trondheim. On my frequent visits to the municipal offices, I received some signals indicating that the planners were more open to children's perspectives than they had been up to this point. Perhaps this is a small legacy of the GUIC project.

The Children's Perspective

More than before, we must be aware that discussions and reports concerning our physical environment need to link conditions to context. A small issue for an adult may be a big issue for a child. For example, when I returned to Elgeseter in 1995, my references were earlier experiences of the area and I was particularly concerned with Elgesetergaten as a dominating physical element in the environment. In my first notes from the study, I tended to focus on the destructive nature of the 'boulevard', rather than on the qualities that the children brought home to me in their descriptions of the residential areas. Their positive attitudes neither made Elgesetergaten less of an environmentally destructive traffic artery, nor did they remove the dangers to which the children were actually exposed, but they did show me how they coped with this special environment. Here is another example: Louise lives near large green areas at the university, but it is the caretaker's carelessness, when he strews gravel over flowerbeds and shrubs, that she talks about when describing her environment.

One problem we face when we try to understand children's perspectives is that most adults have forgotten what it was like to be a child.

One problem we face when we try to understand children's perspectives is that most adults have forgotten what it was like to be a child. We need children's collaboration in order to get essential information about their everyday lives. Another problem is avoiding the pitfall of sentimentality in forming our construction of children's worlds.[40] We have to go beyond our own adult perspectives in order to take children's perspectives seriously.

ENDNOTES

1. Wilhjelm (1995, p. 434).
2. Flekkøy (1995).
3. Wilhjelm (1995, p. 436).
4. Ministry of Environment (1994, p. 5).
5. Wilhjelm (1997).
6. Myklebost (1984).
7. Sørlie (1995); Østby (1998, p. 34). Østby, Lars and Halvard Skiri (1998) Befolkningen, Sosial utsyn (The population, Social survey). In Lyngstad, Jan et al (ed) Sosialt utsyn 1998 (Social servey 1988). Oslo – Kongsvinger: statistisk sentralbyrå (Statistics Norway).
8. Students make up 1/3 of the population in Møllenberg and 1/4 in Elgeseter. Siiri (1997, p. 4 and p. 12).
9. Naustdalslid and Tombre (1997, pp. 2-3).
10. Gullestad (1997, p. 27).
11. Gullestad (1997, p. 28).
12. Gullestad (1997, p. 27).
13. In Norway, permission is needed for research involving children. The Data Inspectorate shall ensure that the rights of the individual are not violated.
14. Trondheim Kommune (1985, p. 6).
15. Statistics Norway (1999b).
16. Studies have shown that one in five children living in a household with only one of the parents lives within walking distance from the other parent. Jensen (1992, p. IX).
17. The land areas used here consist of the central parts of the two districts where the children live. Trondheim Kommune (1999a); Statistic Norway (1970, 1980 and 1990).
18. In 1996, change of residence from one municipality to another numbered 41.8 per 1000 of the population. Statistics Norway (1998, pp. 188-189).
19. In 1998, 8.5 percent of the population in Trondheim were immigrants. 4.3 percent of the population came from Third World countries. Statistics Norway (1999a).
20. We used aerial photographs from Fjellanger Widerøe AS. The municipality supplied paper copies of maps in the scale 1:5000 and 1:2500.
21. The over-riding goal for the government's housing policy after 1945 was to provide enough housing. The State Housing Bank was up to the 1980s the major source of financing for new production of housing, including the renewal of areas like Møllenberg. Martens (1993, p. 33); Naustdalslid and Tombre (1997, pp. 77-79).
22. Frøyen (1992, p. 45).
23. Hovden (1975, p. 109).
24. The narratives from Marianne, Michael, Louise and Harry are partly similar to narratives in the master thesis of Skare and Rogers. Skare (1998); Rogers (1999).
25. Skare (1998, pp. 150-154).
26. Guttu and Martens (1998).
27. Moore (1990).
28. Hovden (1975, p. 68).
29. Haakenaasen (1981, p. iii).
30. MacEwen (1974, p. 9).
31. Trondheim Kommune (1999a); Statistic Norway (1970, 1980 and 1990).
32. The municipality has used the designation Elgeseter. Rogers, however, on

the basis of her studies is in doubt as to whether this use of place name agrees with the earlier and current residents' conception of their district. Rogers (1999, p. 206).

33 Lynch (1960).

34 Trondheim Kommune (1999b).

35 Rogers (1999, p. 103).

36 Prosjektsekretariatet RIT 2000 (1997, p. 18).

37 Byplankontoret (1997, p. 2).

38 Hillman (1993, p. 18).

39 Selberg (1995, p. 7).

40 Tiller (1973, p. 13).

REFERENCES

Byplankontoret, Avdeling Byutvikling, Trondheim Kommune (1997) *Elgeseter Bydelsplan: Delrapport arealbruk* (Municipal Plan for Elgeseter: Report on spatial use), Trondheim Kommune, Trondheim.

Flekkøy, M G (1995) 'The Scandinavian experience of children's rights' in B Franklin (ed), *The Handbook of Children's Rights,* Routledge, London, pp. 176-187.

Frøyen, Y K (1992) *Virkninger av Byfornyels: Møllenberg* 1973-1990 (Impact on urban renewal: Møllenberg 1973-1990), Trondheim Kommune, Bolig og Byfornyelsesseksjonen, Trondheim.

Gullestad, M (1997) 'A passion for boundaries: Reflections on connections between the everyday lives of children and discourses on the nation in contemporary Norway', *Childhood,* vol 4(1), pp. 19-42.

Guttu, J and Martens, J-D (1998) *Sentrumsnære Byboliger: Survey til beboere i sju norske byer* (Inner city housing: Survey among dwellers in seven Norwegian cities), (NIBR-prosjektrapport; 1998:10), Norsk Institutt for By-og Regionforskning, Oslo.

Hillman, M (1993) 'One false move... A study of children's independent mobility: An overview of the findings and the issues they raise', in Hillman, M (Ed) *Children, Transport and Quality of Life,* Policy Studies Institute, London.

Hovden, J (1975) *Møllenberg, Bevaring og Rehabilitering eller Totalsanering?: En intervjuundersøkelse av beboerne i en utsatt gammel bydel i Trondheim* (Møllenberg, preservation and rehabilitation or the clearance of a slum? A survey among dwellers in an old city district in Trondheim), Norges Tekniske Høgskole, Trondheim.

Haakenaasen, B (1981) *Virkninger av Trafikkløsninger: trafikksaneringen i Rosenborg/Møllenberg-området i Trondheim* (Consequences of traffic regulations: Restructuring the traffic in Rosenborg/Møllenberg district in Trondheim), Transportøkonomisk Institutt, Oslo.

Jensen, A-M (1992) *Det Vaklende Faderskapet? Barns familier etter samlivsbrudd* (Vacillating fatherhood? Children's families after the family breaks up), Norsk Institutt for By-og Regionforskning, Oslo.

Lynch, K (1960) *The Image of the City,* MIT Press, Cambridge, Mass.

MacEwen, A (1974) 'Traffic in historic towns', *European Heritage,* No 2, pp. 5-9.

Martens, J-D (1993) *Norwegian Housing,* Norsk Arkitekturforlag, Oslo.

Ministry of Environment (1994) *Children and Planning: National Policy Guidelines to Promote the Interests of Children and Adolescents in Planning,* Ministry of Environment, Oslo.

Moore, R C (1990) *Childhood's Domain,* MIG Communications, Berkeley, California.

Myklebost, H (1984) 'The evidence for urban turnaround in Norway', *Geoforum,* vol 15, no 2, pp. 167-176.

Naustdalslid, J and Tombre, E (1997) *Compendium of Spatial Planning Systems and Policies,* Norsk Institutt for By-og Regionforskning, Oslo.

Prosjektsekretariatet RIT 2000 (1995) *Utbygging av Regionsykehuset i Trondheim: Melding etter plan-og bygningslovens bestemmelser om konsekvensutredninger* (Extension of the regional hospital in Trondheim: Notification according to the provisions for environmental impact assessment in the planning and building act), Sør-Trøndelag fylkeskommune og RIT 2000, Trondheim.

Rogers, B (1999) *Elgeseter — Et Ikkested?: En studie av barns nærmiljø i et livshistorie-og barneperspektiv* (Elgeseter – a non-existing place? The study of a children's local community from the life history and perspective of a child), Hovedfagsoppgave, Norges Teknisk-naturvitenskapelige Universitet, Trondheim.

Selberg, K (1995) *Idédugnad Elgeseter Gate* (Workshop – Elgeseter Street), Statens Vegvesen Sør-Trøndelag, Trondheim.

Siiri, R (1997) *Studentenes Bosted i Trondheim* (Student housing in Trondheim), Trondheim Kommune, Trondheim.

Skare, C D (1998) *Planen og Virkelighetene: En studie av barns arealbruk på Møllenberg og Kolstad* (The plan and the reality: a study of children's land use in Møllenberg and Kolstad), Hovedfagsoppgave, Norges Teknisk-naturvitenskapelige Universitet, Trondheim.

Statistics Norway (1970, 1980 and 1990) *Folke-og Boligtelling* (Population and Housing Census), Statistics Norway, Oslo.

Statistics Norway (1999a) *Andel Personer med Innvandrerbakgrunn: Ikke vestlig. Pst. og Andel personer med innvandrerbakgrunn: Vestlig. Pst.* (Part of population with immigrant background. Not western. Percent. Part of population with immigrant background. Western. Percent) [www.ssb.no], Statistics Norway. [Accessed 10.9.99], Oslo.

Statistics Norway (1999b) *Barnestatistikken, SSB: Barn 0-17 år, etter familietype og hjemmeboende søsken uansett alder. 1. Januar 1997* (tabell) (Statistics about children, SSB: Children 0-17 years of age, by relationship. Siblings regardless of age. 1 January 1997 [www.ssb.no/emner/02/barn_og_unge/del1/tabell/162_03_0.shtml], Statistics Norway. [Accessed 21.9.99], Oslo.

Sørlie, Kjetil (1995) *Norsk Bosettingsutvikling ved et Generasjonsskille* (Norwegian pattern of settlements at the advent of a new generation) Samfunnsspeilet Norwegian Statistics 4/95, pp. 33-37.

Tiller, P O (1973) 'Noen synspunkter på forskning om barns vilkår' ('Some aspects of the conditions for research on children') in Tiller, P O (ed) *Barns Vilkår i Norge. Et seminar om forskning, praksis og administrasjon* (Children's conditions in Norway. A seminar about research, practice, and administration), Institutt for anvendt sosialvitenskapelig forskning, Oslo.

Trondheim Kommune (1999a) *Befolkningsstatistikk* (Population statistics), Trondheim Kommune, Trondheim.

Trondheim Kommune (1999b) *Tall om trafikk i Trondheim: Nøkkeltal fra trafikk— statistikker 1990-98* (Figures about traffic in Trondheim: Key figures–statistics 1990-98), Trondheim Kommune, Trondheim.

Trondheim Kommune and Møllenberg beboerforening Rosenborg (1985) *Formningsrettleder for Møllenberg—Kirkesletten—Rosenborg i Trondheim* (Design guide for Møllenberg–Kirkesletten–Rosenborg in Trondheim), Trondheim Kommune og Rosenborg og Møllenberg beboerforening, Trondheim.

Wilhjelm, H (1995) 'Children and planning – a recent Norwegian reform to improve the physical environment of children and adolescents', *Children's Environment* (12) 4, pp. 434-443.

Wilhjelm, H (1997) *Rikspolitiske Retningslinjer for å Styrke Barn og Unges Interesser i Planleggingen–En gjennomgang av evalueringer og forskning* (National policy guidelines to promote the interests of children and adolescents in planning — an examination of evaluations and research), Norsk Senter for Barneforskning, Trondheim.

Østby, L and Halvard, S (1998) Befolkningen, Sosial Utsyn (The population, social survey), in Lyngstad, J et al (eds), *Sosialt Utsyn 1998* (Social 1998), Statistisk sentralbyrå, Oslo.

CHAPTER EIGHT

Between Fences
Living and Playing in a California City

Ilaria Salvadori

In Oakland, California, Growing Up in Cities was carried out with children of Cambodian and Mexican immigrants who shared an apartment housing complex in the city's disadvantaged Fruitvale neighbourhood. The project participants revealed fear and ignorance about the city around them, combined with an intense creative use of their immediate housing environment. Building on this creativity, the project initiated a participatory design process which engaged the children in envisioning improvements to their housing site. In the process, the children began to tear down the fences around them both literally and figuratively.

HOW EVERYTHING STARTED: THE PROCESS

MAY 1997

I am driving along the freeway. It is hot, almost a summer day. The skyscrapers of downtown Oakland appear and disappear in the rearview mirror. I will pick up eight children to take them to Berkeley to draw the final site plan of our project.

In Oak Park, I see Eva and Mia ready to go, two Mexican girls all dressed up as if it were a special day. They have long, beautiful hair all curled and shiny. The Cambodian girls are screaming and yelling my name: 'Ilaria', 'Hey, Ilariaaaaa!.' They want to pick friends to bring with them, to share the new adventure. Unrealistic expectation, because there is no extra room in the two cars our team is driving.

'Eight', I said, 'eight.' I feel bad for the others who won't be able to come. Keo, 15 years old, is still in her apartment on the upstairs level and I have to go to pick her up. She doesn't look ready at all, sitting on a chair in a sunny spot on the balcony. She doesn't feel like coming. Looking down into the courtyard, she says: 'They are all small kids…. I changed my mind.' I want her to come, Keo with her quiet presence and her firm will: 'Please, you know it is important.' I feel like a little child asking her mother for something special. She looks at me, then she moves indolently toward the stairs, a sign that she is coming with us.

Now everybody in the courtyard wants to come. I start feeling annoyed: 'Come on, it's not a field trip… The field trip is in June, as I said, all right?.' All the small Mexican children are surrounding me: 'Can I come?… Can I come?.' It goes on like that for a while, until I manage to get to the car with the eight 'lucky ones' who only a week ago seemed generous to have signed up as volunteers.

Half of them have never been to Berkeley before, though it is only a few miles away from their homes.

NOVEMBER 1996

I heard about Oak Park for the first time on a day in November, while eating Vietnamese food in a restaurant in downtown Oakland. An energetic man in his early thirties is at the table with me, and the woman who introduced me to him a couple of hours earlier is facing us. This man seems to understand immediately what I am looking for and what my goal is. 'I have in mind a range of possibilities', he announces. 'You just have to call and try.' I scribble the phone numbers he gives me on the back of my research proposal. 'I think this group of people could be very interesting for you. …They are not a nonprofit organisation or anything like that. They are a group of volunteers who work with the children, tutoring them. I have a contact here', he says, opening his thick address book.

The food is getting cold, and I am lost in this labyrinth of names and youth programmes mentioned during his high-speed presentation. Dan is the director of one of the most successful nonprofit organisations conducting youth participatory research and action in Oakland, and a main promoter of Proposition K (named also 'Kids First') that secured the allocation of more funds for youth programmes at the city level. 'A very kind, visionary man', I think, while riding the eastbound train that will take me home. By the time I am back in Berkeley, only a name is left. It lays there, in the back of my mind: 'Oak Park, Oak Park.'

'Oak' like 'Oakland' or like 'oak tree.'

DECEMBER 1996

'Dinner is served at 6 p.m. on Monday. You will then present your ideas to the group.' Alyson is a student of city planning at the University of California at Berkeley. After our previous meeting during which I presented my proposal to her, she decided to open the door of Oak Park. Alyson has her home in Oak Park. She is a volunteer, working with the children, dedicating most of her free time to the children living with her. The church-based project she works with is named 'Oak Park Ministry.'

The first thing you see when you approach Oak Park Apartments is a very tall palm tree, looking as if it were growing out of the building itself, its large thick leaves perforating the roofs of the apartments. Right after that, when your eyes travel down the tree trunk, you see the wide parking lot where many people of different ages are hanging out. At the opposite end is the courtyard's entrance with four-foot high fences surrounding the trees and many, many children all over the place. A lively, warm atmosphere surrounds you, like the four walls that surround this courtyard. You feel safe here, watched and protected by many families, many open doors along the walls of the two-storied building, many eyes looking at you.

My first impression is of a motel with only children as clients.

Everybody is outside and loud music is coming from some of the apartments.

We eat dinner at apartment number 11, the home of David, another volunteer from the Oak Park Ministry. After dinner and after my presentation, Alyson takes me along the first floor balcony. There are about 28 one-bedroom apartments on the second floor, and another 28 below, all looking onto the courtyard. Many doors are open. A Cambodian family is living here: a father with his five children. Three of them are now playing on the bed; two are writing words in a notebook. 'He is teaching them Cambodian', Alyson explains. I smile at him, without understanding really where I am.

FEBRUARY 1997

Alyson and I decided to give the project the form of a regular class, meeting weekly like an after-school programme. A small presentation in Alyson's apartment — number 43 — will start the process. The presentation will be about the research I intend to conduct and the role of the children in it. Alyson already invited several children to sign up on a list, and about 14 have done so: 13 Cambodians and one Mexican (Eva), all 9–14 years old. Eva explains to me that there are many Mexican kids 'who have not been invited to the class', even though they make up almost 50 percent of the child residents in Oak Park. Later eight more Cambodian children will volunteer.

A week later, I will go back on a beautiful warm Tuesday night with Martha, one of the three graduate students who are going to help me with the research. We will go door to door, speaking to the Mexican families, with Eva with us, translating from English into Spanish. We inform them what the class is about, and ask for permission for their children to participate. After one evening, our outreach adds four new children to the group, and two others will join the group as the project takes shape.

> *You feel safe here, watched and protected by many families, many open doors, many eyes looking at you.*

GROWING UP IN CITIES IN OAKLAND, CALIFORNIA

The project I conducted in Oakland using Growing Up in Cities methodology took place at the smallest site of all the GUIC projects. The participants were children of immigrant workers in a housing complex in the middle of the Fruitvale neighbourhood of Oakland. I conducted the research together with three other students at the College of Environmental Design at the University of California at Berkeley, under the supervision of Professor Randy Hester from the university, and Michael Schwab from the California Wellness Foundation. At the time, Professor Hester was teaching a class on 'Sacred Landscapes', about the relationship of individuals and communities to landscapes across the world. GUIC's methodology and goals became our field of study, an attempt to depict a vivid landscape that could represent the living conditions of a specific community in the United States. In spite of the small area covered by the research — one housing project — the results revealed significant issues concerning children in the industrialised western world and their societies' responsibilities to create appropriate environments for child development. Our results came from a rich range of observation and other means of data collection, generated by both social and spatial analysis.

This chapter is divided into four parts. The first part gives a general overview of the physical and socioeco-

© ILARIA SALVADORI

Figure 8.1 The courtyard is the social and physical center of Oak Park.

nomic characteristics of the city of Oakland and the neighbourhood of Fruitvale where our research took place. The second part takes the reader into the Oak Park community to get a sense of its children's daily lives and their perceptions of the city where they live. The GUIC methodology is described and its results are used to illustrate the geographies of this specific community of children. The third part discusses the children's isolation and alienation from their environment; and a fourth and final part describes a participatory design process as an attempt to restore this disrupted relationship.

The chapter addresses the crucial role of participation in studies of how children relate to their environment. The richness of the results that GUIC methods offer is connected to children's active participation in addressing issues of change, stewardship and the improvement of the physical world of which they are a part.

VOICES FROM THE CITY

Oakland and its Young People

Oakland is a major urban area on the east side of the San Francisco Bay in California. Its population of 400,000 people is extremely diverse: approximately 45 percent of the population is African-American, 20 percent Anglo-American, 10 percent Mexican-American, 7 percent Chinese-American, and one percent Cambodian-American, with a smaller population of Latino, Vietnamese, Korean, American Indian, Eskimo and other ethnic groups.[1]

About 97,000 children live in Oakland: in other words, about one quarter of the population is under 18 years of age. Of these, less than half speak only English at home. According to 1990 census data, 24 percent of all Asian-American children in Oakland speak English 'not well or not at all', compared with 41 percent of Asian-American adults. Among Latino families, 16 percent of the children fall in this category, compared with 35 percent of the adults.[2] The Oakland schools are enriched with students from over 30 different language groups, but the challenge of providing second language instruction is enormous. Nevertheless, children of immigrant families understand the language and culture of their adopted home more quickly and effectively than their parents. Thus they carry the additional burden of mediating between the adults in their household and the outside world.

In a nation where non-Caucasians are often denied equal opportunity in education and employment, it is not surprising that incomes in Oakland, which has such a large non-white population, are low: 36 percent of its African-American households earn less than $15,000 per year, as do 32 percent of its Asian-Americans, 25 percent of its Latino-Americans and 20 percent of its Anglo-Americans. One in three non-white children of colour in Oakland is growing up in poverty, and many are subject to periodic food shortages.[3]

There is a great deal of public fear in Oakland, much of it directed towards older children and youth. Indeed, youth are often stigmatised in the inner cities of the United States, and Oakland is no exception. The issue of public safety is often cast as a problem of youth violence

and crime, although only five percent of all juveniles are arrested, and of these arrests less than one in ten is for a violent crime.[4] However, the homicide rate of young black men has increased dramatically, and this has been used as a main rationale for a variety of 'get tough' policies affecting all young people: for example, increased policing, youth curfews, trying children in court as adults, and campaigns to address gang violence. Most public discourse about youth crime fails to acknowledge the economic, physical and political causes of youth violence. Recent research conducted by youth in Oakland as part of a project promoted by the Children and the Environment Group found that youth violence is partly due to a lack of safe spaces for young people and a lack of opportunities for them to get the help and support they need. By joining together with other youth organisations, and with help from public advocates, young people drafted a petition calling on the City Council to set aside 2.5 percent of the city budget for youth centres and services. They collected the 50,000 signatures needed to get the measure on the ballot for the November 1996 elections, and the measure was passed, with an allocation of $5 million per year over the next 12 years. This is a success story, and hopefully it will lead to positive changes for Oakland's children; but for the present Oakland, like many other children's environments, is still poisoned by fear of young people, especially African-Americans.

> *About 97,000 children live in Oakland: in other words, about one quarter of the population is under 18 years of age. Of these, less than half speak only English at home.*

The Neighbourhood

The site of my research is in the Spanish speaking Fruitvale neighbourhood located on the east side of the San Antonio district, which is bordered on the north and the south sides by two main freeways. The area has been defined since 1994 as a Federal 'EEC' area or 'Enhanced Enterprise Community.' To be defined as an EEC area, a

© ILARIA SALVADORI

Figure 8.2 Oak Park Apartments housing complex

district must have more than 35 percent of its population living below the poverty rate.[5]

In contrast to the present, in the late 19th century the San Antonio district was considered an affluent and respectable area to live in.

'Originally carved from the estate of Luis Maria Peralta, the area now known as Fruitvale began to attract German and Portuguese immigrants in the 1850's. Drawn to California for the same promise of a better future that continues to draw people here today, they planted orchards that turned the once stark landscape into a veritable garden. The peaches, pears, apples and lemons that grew so abundantly in the California sun provided a good reason to call the area Fruitvale. The combination of rural charms and relatively easy access to Oakland's and San Francisco's growing business districts soon brought prestigious residential subdivisions, and in 1884 when Watson Bray built a home for his daughter Emma and her new husband Alfred Cohen at 1440 29th Ave., Fruitvale was an up-and-coming suburb. The homes built here were among the most stylish in the Bay Area....'[6]

Other distinguished residents besides Alfred Cohen, chief attorney for the Central Pacific Railroad, were Julia Morgan, one of the most important architects in California, and the writers Jack London and Louis Stevenson. In 1906, after the San Francisco earthquake, many working class Caucasians came to the area from across the Bay,

> *Most public discourse about youth crime fails to acknowledge the economic, physical and political causes of youth violence.*

increasing the housing demand and starting to create the landscape of today: large apartment buildings next to Victorian houses. During the Second World War, African-Americans from the South moved to Oakland, further increasing housing demand. A large Latino population was already living in the area at this point, working in canneries. In 1949, the #880 freeway opened, providing an alternative route around the neighbourhood and its businesses and bypassing East 14th Street, which had been one of the main boulevards and commercial centres of the district. As one of the consequences, middle class white residents left the area and moved to the suburbs, and economic disinvestment followed the migration. In the 1970s, the Vietnam War brought more ethnic diversity, as a federal resettlement policy introduced Vietnamese, Cambodians and Mien refugee families to the area. A second wave of immigration followed in the 1980s and, in the meanwhile, repeated waves of immigration came to the area from Mexico.

The physical infrastructure of the San Antonio district is in poor condition today: roads and public buildings need repair, shops are scarce, and there is a high level of pollution. The challenge to live a healthy, productive life here is extreme, and children growing up here struggle with a sense of hopelessness. There is also a great deal of public fear concerning the neighbourhood, often attributed to youth violence and crime. By the same token, though the streets can be dangerous because of drugs and violence, there are also many community-based projects and programmes designed to encourage self-help and mutual support for young people and residents. Among them, it is worth mentioning the Spanish Speaking Unity Council, which is promoting numerous physical improvements at a neighbourhood level, and the Community Health Academy, which funds youth-led programmes and projects in the neighbourhood.

The Site in the Neighbourhood

'Children should not be allowed to play in the building corridors. This can disturb others in the building. Also children can be injured in the hallways, since they are not appropriate for playing. No children can play or climb the trees because they can get hurt. This is strictly prohibited. The parents of any children found playing in the trees will receive a termination of tenancy letter. No children can ride their bikes in or around the corridors of the parking lot. Furthermore, no children at all are allowed to play in the parking lot. Also, no children can play with any hard balls anywhere in the apartment. No one is allowed to socialize in the parking lot.'

From the amendment to the rental agreement, Oak Park Apartments

Where East 16th Street crosses 29th Avenue, in the heart of the Fruitvale district, is located Oak Park, a small apartment complex of some 50 units. Built in the 1950s as a motel, it is now private rental housing. Its two-storied structure has a square plan with one-bedroom apartments facing an enclosed courtyard. The building is connected to the street by two parking lots divided by a small private lot with a two-family duplex.

About 100 children live in Oak Park. Residents are almost 50 percent Cambodian political refugees who emigrated to the United States around 10 years ago, and 50 percent Mexican immigrants on temporary jobs who came two to five years ago (see Table 8.1). The third group of residents is a Christian community (about 15 people) of urban missionaries and community organisers who converted most of the Cambodian children of Buddhist background to Christianity. This group plays an important role in the Oak Park community and in the children's lives, organising (on a volunteer basis) on-site educational and recreational activities, residency classes for parents, and Bible readings. At the beginning of this

TABLE 8.1	
Community Profile	
Site	1.2 hectares (3 acres)
Housing typology	one-bedroom apartments
Households	48
Population	about 200
RELIGION	**PERCENT OF HOUSEHOLDS**
Christian	60%
Buddhist	40%
ETHNICITY	**PERCENT OF HOUSEHOLDS**
Cambodian	55%
Mexican	40%
Caucasian	5%

research, the Mexican kids seemed to neither participate in these activities nor interact with the community organisers. Most of the children involved in the GUIC group were in fact Cambodian under the tutoring of the Oak Park Ministry.

In spite of the management's attempt to control the space, as expressed by the above text of the Oak Park Apartments Rental Agreement, visitors like myself who come here for the first time are struck by the many children playing around the courtyard. A reporter of the local newspaper *Street Spirit,* who visited Oak Park two years after my arrival, describes this experience:

'A visit to Oak Park Apartments on a warm evening shows the tight community in full flower. The apartments surround a courtyard with a couple of dozen children playing. On one side of the courtyard, an impromptu soccer game with the older kids is in full motion. On the other side younger children are playing softball or hopscotch. In between are the fenced-off planters of the community garden with their struggling bok choy and strawberries. A tamale vendor and ice cream man sell their wares to residents before moving to other spots in the San Antonio neighbourhood. An old car seat serving as a bench outside an apartment is overloaded with younger children playing. Adults visit family and friends and the laughter drowns out the poverty.

'You don't have to look far to see the other side of the coin. Broken glass litters the parking lot. Every apartment has serious deferred maintenance—from rodent infestation to broken plumbing.'[7]

HOW THE CHILDREN OF OAK PARK SEE THE CITY

Methods

I carried out the research with student assistants from February through May 1997. During these months I worked with a group of 28 Mexican and Cambodian children from 10 through 14 years of age. As an addition to our small research team from the University of California at Berkeley, I found it extremely important to hire a young person inside the community as a research assistant. An 18-year-old Cambodian resident, Rath Pal, offered precious help in the organisational aspects of the process. Moreover, she eased our communication with the community, offering insights and advice. Even if we structured the meetings with the children in weekly after-school classes, the children often found it difficult to respect this schedule. When I was ready to start at the

Children of immigrant families understand the language and culture of their adopted home more quickly and effectively than their parents. Thus they carry the additional burden of mediating between the adults in their household and the outside world.

set time, Rath would have the children gathered in the courtyard and ready to begin. Not having an institution or organisation office to work in, we gathered all the children into Alyson's one-bedroom apartment on the second floor of the complex. Even though these cramped conditions generated a rather chaotic workspace, these restrictions often enhanced collaboration and cooperation among the children. Sometimes the group was

divided into two and the activities were repeated in two sessions to allow children more space and concentration. The 'after-school class' was a good structure for our research, and for the children it became a chance for socialisation among the two different ethnic groups, as children found numerous chances to play or interact with each other between activities. As part of the afternoon schedule, we shared snacks, which became a good opportunity to give the children more responsibility in terms of setting up before eating and cleaning up afterwards. Chores were listed on charts and volunteer work was ranked by points. Children accepted the structure of our activities well and welcomed this system, especially because it brought a new and different variety to their daily routine of activities and play.

TABLE 8.2

Participants Profile (N=28)

Male, 13   Female, 15

ETHNICITY AND SEX	NUMBER OF PARTICIPANTS
Cambodian – Male	12
Cambodian – Female	9
Mexican – Male	3
Mexican – Female	4

The protocol for GUIC calls for a minimum of the following methods: formal and informal observations, and a structured interview with each child, including a drawing of the area where the child lives and a schedule of daily activities. Our team decided to introduce some additional methods of analysis to better understand the children's lives and perceptions. Therefore Oak Park children took photographs to illustrate the geographies of their daily lives, and identified photos of city landmarks to demonstrate their familiarity with Oakland. The former activity served as a particularly successful tool to maintain the children's attention and enthusiasm. At the same time, the researchers conducted both spatial and behavioural on-site observations, often just before or after meetings with the children. Numerous informal conversations with the children's parents, social workers, and the Christian missionaries turned out to be a precious source of knowledge and understanding about the community.

After we began with a group of 14 children, the project was accepted enthusiastically by the children as a new game, a new recreational opportunity. The final number of children who participated in the main activities of the GUIC protocol increased to 28.

The Unknown City

Children in Oak Park have a scarce knowledge of the outside world. Coming as they do from low-income families, some of whom receive welfare benefits, their chances of travelling on vacations are remote. Limited economic resources keep them mostly at home. When they were asked where they spend their vacations, most children answered 'at home' or 'nowhere.' Even at the local level, they have limited spatial mobility. Our research showed that the children failed to perceive the geographical borders of Oakland as a meaningful boundary. In the photo identification exercise, when they were asked to recognise images of city landmarks, few of them could identify local sites within a one mile radius from Oak Park. Not being aware of its borders, the children didn't perceive Oakland as a whole.

The children's failure to comprehend Oakland as a geographical entity is illustrated by Table 8.3, which gives the children's responses to the question, 'What is the furthest place that you have been in Oakland?' Apart from a few Oakland landmarks reached by car with their parents or on school trips, the places that the children mention are mostly located outside the county or even outside California. This vague perception of the city contrasts with the children's perception of Oak Park as the densely inhabited place of their daily experience.

A Precious Pearl in a Hard Shell

If the outside is considered a 'foreign' territory, the space inside the boundaries of Oak Park, on the contrary, is perceived as a very positive, active space. Children described Oak Park as 'a big, crowded place' that they liked, 'full of trees, with a lot of space to play.' 'Pretty', 'noisy', 'big', and 'kind of dusty' were some of the words they used. They reported that it has a 'big parking lot', 'a lot of trees', 'a big courtyard', 'a lot of apartments', 'a laundry place', and 'a lot of dirt to play in', and that it is 'a beautiful place', a 'fun place' with 'nice people', 'a lot of kids' and 'a lot of Cambodian people' where 'you can make a lot of friends.'

TABLE 8.3	
What is the furthest place that you have been in Oakland? (N=28)	
RESPONSES*	
3	Don't know
2	Lake Tahoe (Nevada); San Leandro (California); Oakland Zoo; Church; Jack London Square
1	Pittsburg (California); Nevada State; Lucky Store; San Francisco; Boston; Canada; Washington; Reno; 98th Avenue; Bay Bridge; Toys R Us; Cambodian store; Alameda; a store we drive to; Harbor House – Dan drives us there

* *Number of children giving each answer listed*

The children felt so strongly connected to this space that they identified Oak Park with the term 'neighbourhood.' When they were asked to make a drawing of their neighbourhood, 20 children out of 24 drew the space contained in the boundaries of the apartment building complex itself. The squared courtyard, the apartments and — with more ambiguity — the parking lot were what the children considered their own territory. No place in the immediate surroundings of Oak Park or in the more distant city appeared in these drawings. Among the other four children, nine-year-old Efrain drew some streets surrounding Oak Park, but added that his parents 'don't let me go by bike in the streets because black people can hit me or take the bike away from me.' He also included a dead-end street located on the north side of the building where he sometimes played with his brother. With few exceptions, the children's enclosure within Oak Park was confirmed by their inability to identify city landmarks, as mentioned above, and by their focus on the housing complex when they used words and images to describe their favourite places in their daily geographies.

The courtyard, the place most of the apartment windows look into, is the social and physical centre of Oak Park. When the children were asked about their 'favourite places inside and outside Oak Park', almost 100 percent mentioned 'my home' (meaning the interior space of the apartments), and 95 percent mentioned the courtyard. Not only is the courtyard a prominent central place in the children's lives, but it flexibly contains numerous different activities, which define its complex identity. It is the 'living room' for social interactions for which the one-bedroom apartments lack space, the 'playground' where different games take place, the 'public square' for social events, and the 'garden' where the trees grow. The courtyard embraces social meanings for the children: one Cambodian boy, for example, called his own living room 'my little courtyard.' In this practice of identifying this place with its activities, the children of Oak Park are similar to the younger children described by the geographer Yi-Fu Tuan:

'The first grade pupil when he looks at the picture of the village is more likely to ignore its broader spatial setting; he may not even recognize it as a village, his attention being focused on its parts — the church, the school, the shop and the road. . . . Indeed [the child's] primary interest seems not to be the physical environment but the people in it, what the man or the little girl is doing.'[8]

When asked to draw their neighbourhood and all the important places in it, the children described specific details of the apartment complex and the activities happening there.

What are those activities?

An analysis of the research material shows several repetitively identified 'place typologies' that are defined by their actual physical characteristics and by the activities that take place there. The courtyard, as stated above, is the eclectic space containing most of these elements.

The most important element is the four-foot high metal fences that surround the areas where the trees are planted. The fences fragment the courtyard space, creating smaller areas of activity. Moreover, they are them-

Figure 8.3 Cambodian children's use of space — organised play in the parking lot

selves objects of play, used mostly as monkey bars, with the adjacent space becoming 'the playground', or as apparatus to climb up into the trees. The fences also surround dirt areas, creating enclosures that are defined by the children as 'gardens.' This manipulation of the meaning of the fences from obstacles to opportunities for play, from negative elements to functional means to define subspaces in the courtyard, is a typical act of 'spatial semantics' here in Oak Park. The fences create gardens, form barriers for games of hide and seek, separate the marble field from the digging dirt area, and function as supports to climb into the trees they enclose.

Trees represent another important locus of activity and are the only natural element of the neighbourhood that the children mentioned. Given the highly urbanised character of the area and these families' limited mobility, the children are not exposed to other natural features. The only other one they mentioned — the creek running by the school — was a forbidden place that the children defined as 'the river where many people died.' 'The creek close to school — the principal said that many people died there. It is dangerous because it is slippery and you can fall', explained 11 year old Sunlarry.

In their drawings, the children depicted different kinds of trees, some real and some fantastic: fruit trees, a palm tree and other unspecified kinds. The palm tree is a landmark of Oak Park, with its tall silhouette and large crown, although some children considered it dangerous because of its large leaves 'that could fall down on people's heads.' All of the children used the rest of the trees for climbing or to play with their roots and surrounding dirt.

The corridors, especially on the second floor, are a very important social place connecting the interior of the apartment with the outside. Small children can play there while they are watched by their siblings from inside the apartment and from the courtyard below, an activity that many Cambodian girls included in their drawings. Mexican girls, from the first floor where their apartments are, use the perimeter of the courtyard in the same way. Girls from both ethnic groups watch their siblings even if their mothers are at home. This common practice is a chore that often blends into play activities in the courtyard.

Figure 8.4 Informal use of space — climbing fences and trees

The plain courtyard contains no walls or furniture for sitting and hanging out. Nevertheless, the children's great creativity in manipulating traditional functions of courtyard features and putting them to new uses is one of the most striking results evident in this research. This pervasive 'redistribution of meaning' in an environment that lacks so many basic resources for its children is a

mode of action that we observe here in Oak Park both in the practice of play and more generally in other daily activities. 'I took a picture of a little bench', wrote Mia, when she framed the curb of the corridor by her apartment with her camera. Stairs and curbs become 'benches' for sitting and interacting. Mia mentioned the stairs as 'an important place where to meet friends.' And when she took a picture of 'her five-year-old cousin on a swing', the swing was actually an old rug hung between two ropes.

Ethnic and Gender Differences in the Use of Space

Although all of the children used Oak Park spaces intensively in their daily activities and play, the interviews, observations and photographs taken by children showed both similarities and differences, and a lack of social interaction, in the Cambodian and Mexican children's use of space. This social distance was reflected in their physical separation during play, which was reinforced by separation according to gender.

Mexican boys use the space through movement, especially crossing the courtyard and the parking lot with their bikes. Mexican girls move along the perimeter of the courtyard, relating to the interior of the apartments to watch siblings or to take orders from parents. They concentrate on more spatially limited areas, such as outside the apartment doors and the stairs and steps where they sit to chat or meet their best friends. They also take great account of the space inside the house, that they are proud of keeping tidy and clean. Most of the Mexican girls took pictures of their beds, with dolls neatly displayed as a sign of order and cleanness.

Cambodian girls get together to chat in the same way along the corridor on the balcony of the second floor, outside their apartment doors. They also take care of siblings, both from the balcony and sometimes from the courtyard when they are playing there. Cambodian boys, on the other hand, use not only the space of the courtyard but also the parking lot and the backyard of the Wongs' house (a single family house beside the parking lot, which is inhabited by a group of Cambodian refugees who previously lived in Oak Park). Although the boys generally used space in an extensive way, several differences were found between the two ethnic groups. The parking lot, a contested area in the geography of Oak Park, was mostly used by Cambodian boys to play structured team games such as football. Other groups managed to appropriate this space occasionally. Cambodian girls played the 'Lucky cart' game, pushing shopping carts from the Lucky drugstore chain around the area. The Mexican boys sometimes used the space to play soccer when nobody else was claiming it. The 'basketball court' located in the Wongs' backyard was exclusively reserved for some of the older Cambodian boys.

> *The children's scarce knowledge of the outside and their limited mobility in the urban environment generate a fear of the unknown.*

This separation in the use of space, which has resulted in rare interactions between the two groups, can be related to the physical arrangement of the apartments. The more desirable apartments on the second floor are inhabited by the Cambodian families, who were the first to move into the Oak Park complex.[9] The Mexican families all live on the first floor. In their living quarters, too, the two groups are spatially segregated.

Competitive and Cooperative Play

During our observations and through other data, we discovered a strong relationship between different types of play and the degree of cooperation they fostered. We observed two fundamentally different types of play in the courtyard and the parking lot.[10]

The first kind, 'organised play', includes team games or other well structured games, and it emphasises rules and hierarchy. Rules are like a language that has to be decoded, that reflects the characteristics of a specific culture. They are taught and learned, and in the culture of the United States, they encourage competition, separation between groups, and a division of roles within a group. Football is an example, which appeared to be played only by Cambodian boys. Most of the Cambodian boys, in fact, showed a football game in their drawings of

Oak Park, with cars relegated to the sides of the parking lot and imaginary football field lines drawn across the space. In separate groups, the children also played marbles in the dirt areas, and alligators on the lawns. There were even two different versions of hopscotch, one of them being 'Cambodian hopscotch.'

The second type of play, 'adventure play', emphasises the interpretation and manipulation of reality. Rules are created while the games are taking place and they are imitated, exchanged and transformed. Creativity, absence of hierarchy, openness and irony are encouraged. Cooperative games of this kind were played all over Oak Park and by the same number of children in each ethnic group and, in some cases, by children of the two groups together. As a curb can become a 'little bench' and fences can become 'monkey bars', in the same way a shopping cart can become a car running around the courtyard, dirt areas can become gardens, and swings can be built with ropes and pieces of cardboard. Along with this shift from original functions to new ones, these games involve a shift from competition to cooperation.

Looking Inward

'Parents are scared I might get kidnapped, or get lost, or somebody with a gun could kill me.' (Jennifer, 9 years old)

Both the physical structure of the housing complex — its walls facing an interior courtyard and its entry recessed from the public space of the sidewalk — and the psychological perception of the surrounding environment orient the children's lives inward. The children's scarce knowledge of the outside and their limited mobility in the urban environment, as discussed above, generate a fear of the unknown: in this case, a fear of neighbourhood public places. Forbidden to go almost anywhere around the neighbourhood, the children spend all day inside the perimeter of the housing complex, fantasising about the danger outside.

In these children's views, the streets are dangerous because of traffic and assaults. Owned by nobody, they are battlegrounds for adult men and the police. 'Sometimes I can get distracted and get beat up by people, by bad people', says Sunlarry, an 11 year old. The 'outside'

TABLE 8.4

What is the most dangerous place in the neighbourhood? (N=28)

RESPONSES*	
4	Parking lot; AC Mall; None
3	Streets
2	Corner store; parks; creek at Hawthorne School
1	School yard; fishing place near the bridge; around the corner; shortcuts; close to apartment 1 (where Mexican people live); everywhere outside Oak Park; inside Oak Park at night

* Number of children giving each answer listed

then becomes a tricky environment where danger can be just around the corner. Around the corner is where 'gangs of bad boys do drug dealing', where children may be 'murdered or shot', where 'mom is scared I might be kidnapped.' Outside places are distant places that are not safe.

In his discussion about practices of exclusion in urban settlements, David Sibley wrote:

'The construction of community and the bounding of social groups are a part of the same problem as the separation of self and other. Collective expressions of fear of others, for example, call on images which constitute bad objects for the self and thus contribute to the definition of the self. The symbolic construction of boundaries in small groups which have been studied by social anthropologists has its counterpart in the marking off of communities in developed western societies.'[11]

Identity built upon difference generates often opposing dynamics in the community, and sometimes episodes of racial tensions within the community and between the community and the outside world.

Racial stereotypes germinate in these children's minds as they repeat racist remarks they have heard from their parents. The 'Other' is dangerous, like an unknown place. They are afraid of images of places they cannot experience and people they cannot meet. There-

fore, 'empty houses from where people moved away' are dangerous but, if asked, they cannot name one they have been to. Streets are places where people 'might take me away or take things from me' and where 'someone stole some money from an old man.' The area outside AC Mall is dangerous because somebody stole a necklace once from a friend, and 'bad people, drug dealers walk there.' Drug dealing is also associated with the local park. Even the parking lot is sometimes dangerous, like the outside. A Cambodian girl is afraid that some Mexican men might take her if she goes to the parking lot.

Whatever it is — street, park, parking lot — the fear is not personally experienced but imagined. 'They [African-American men] just look at us. My mom told me that if somebody looks at you he wants to kidnap you', says 9 year old Sunlalina.

FICTIONAL HOPES: BLURRED FUTURES

During the interviews, a striking discrepancy emerged between the children's ideas about the future and the real environment that surrounded them. The back of the coin of the dangerous streets described above are icons of wealth presented by the media: Los Angeles, palm trees, motels, the hills. When the children were asked 'In 10 years, where would you like to live?' they let their minds travel across the flatland of Oakland up to the hills where the topography of this part of the world marks social status. Here they could have a view of the Bay and a better, wealthier life; or across the Bay, where they might go to San Francisco, to mansions and large houses with many rooms.

Braver minds dared to think of far away dream lands: Florida, where friends are living; 'Tennessee', where cheaper food and larger houses would guarantee an improved life; 'somewhere pretty and where I would be able to afford it' someone else echoed. One child chose Detroit because, 'I think it's a better place to live.... On TV I saw a lot of nice people and they are not in gangs.' Motels, cheap food and even Great America — the promised land — were the landscapes of their future.

This naive enchantment with imagined places, mixed

with mature concerns about affordable housing and healthy communities, resemble the great contradictions these children live in their daily life. Material life is hard for many of these children, who live in overcrowded rooms in often substandard conditions. They perceive their homes in Oak Park as safe, but the reality is that their apartments are also small and less than modest. Their daily struggles are challenging. Their futures are blurred. Instead of being built with the resources and strengths of the community where they live, they imagine their future taking place 'somewhere else' where land is cheaper and the American Dream is still alive and kicking.

TABLE 8.5	

In 10 years time, where would you like to live?
(N=28)

RESPONSES*	
8	In a house in L.A.
7	Somewhere else (somewhere safe, somewhere pretty that I could afford)
4	Texas (in Dallas, Texas: I want to make a new life)
2	In Tennessee (the house is not little...it is big); up in the hills
1	In a motel; Great America (an entertainment park in Silicon Valley, California); Florida because my mother has friends there; San Francisco in a five-room apartment; Detroit: I think it is a better place to live...; On TV I saw a lot of nice people...they are not in gangs

* Number of children giving each answer listed

REASONABLE EXPECTATIONS: THE PARTICIPATORY PROCESS

Following this initial research phase, I embarked with the children on a participatory process to design renovations of the community's common spaces. This double focus on the existing condition of the place, while thinking and envisioning future possibilities, gave a rich and stimulat-ing quality to my work in the community. This was a choice made together with representatives from the Oak Park Ministry at the beginning of the process, as we both shared the same philosophy about the importance of promoting change after conducting an environmental analysis in a community.[12]

The creative energy that the children used in turning their poor environment into complex fictional geographies prepared them for the imaginative redesign of their site. By channelling this energy into participatory design, the children were able to think about new possibilities to improve the physical conditions of their daily surroundings. The shift from competition to cooperation during adventure play was another inspiring practice that I tried to incorporate into every activity that I developed with the children.

We began the process with focus group discussions to assess needs and wishes for the community. The children then translated their first ideas into collages. On black and white photocopies of the existing Oak Park setting, they overlapped new images, which composed views of the place's possible future. Animals, trees, together with many consumer items and a pool at the centre of the courtyard, appeared on the children's collages. During this phase, nobody changed the main existing elements of the place nor removed the fences.

We then moved on to exploring forms and materials and their combination in space. I showed the children slides of playgrounds and public places around the world, and they discovered that the ground is not necessarily paved with concrete, trees are not always fenced in, and that gardens can have flowers, benches and edges. We connected new images to old words.

We constructed a three-dimensional model with moveable elements and tried different designs for the space. The elements were divided into existing elements (to be removed or shifted) and new ones (to be added). The children particularly loved this activity, as they liked to feel the tactile character of the objects, to play and try different possibilities. Several plans emerged that I documented through photographs. We then discussed and agreed on one final plan for the courtyard, which the children presented to their parents.

© ILARIA SALVADORI

Figure 8.5 Making the collages: Eva, Mia and Nayelli

What did the children envision for the space? The main projects that emerged for the improvement of Oak Park were intended for three main areas: the courtyard, the parking lot, and a narrow piece of vacant land located at the back of the apartment complex. For the improvement of the courtyard, the children divided the large space into smaller subspaces and created several niches diversified by different materials for play: sand areas for younger siblings, smooth paved areas for roller blading and other games, benches and tables under the trees for everybody to use, circulation paths, and more green on the balconies overlooking the courtyard.

In the parking lot, the children drew lines for both football and soccer fields, hung a basketball hoop to create a new basketball court, and created a mural on the parking lot wall depicting the residents of Oak Park. They got this latter idea after a field trip to visit the Precita Eyes Mural Art Center in San Francisco, a nonprofit organisation formed by a group of artists with the goal of beautifying and preserving the character of the Spanish-speaking Mission neighbourhood. The children enjoyed the trip and were enchanted by the stories and images of the murals, which they had seen first on slides and afterwards on site.

As a third project, the children proposed developing a vegetable garden at the back of the building. For a long time the site had been closed and blocked by wooden boards, and therefore the children called it the 'secret garden'. They proposed growing a garden here, to be managed by the children as a pilot project for the first phase, with a second phase involving both children and adults in a larger scale production of crops for the whole community of Oak Park.

Effect of the Process on the Oak Park Environment

'Fences define, protect, confine and liberate. They tell us where we belong.... Fences join the public and private. Remove a fence, invite chaos. Erect a fence: you are home. Fences give order.... They frame space and encourage people to perceive land as a patchwork of properties.... Fences make space into place.'[13]

All through the development of the research, the fences and their psychological role in Oak Park were the subjects of an ongoing debate. Objects of order from many adults' point of view, they were objects of play for most of the children. Either way, they were objects that everybody had always taken for granted, to which nobody objected. When I first entered the space of the courtyard, I was puzzled by the odd effect of the fences on the overall space, and felt outrage at this explicit control of the residents as tenants of the apartments. Speaking with the children, I realised that they considered the fences simply part of the landscape, just another element like the trees, the palm at the centre, or people occupied in different activities. They never questioned their presence. When they talked about changes, they suggested plans to 'replace the fences with different ones' or to 'change the fences with prettier ones' or with 'newer ones' — never considering the space without them.

Then, one March afternoon and three months into the project, Dan, a member of the Oak Park Ministry and the manager of the housing complex at that time, told the children to clean up the courtyard. One Mexican boy started to cut and tear the metal wire apart with the help of the other children, until only the naked poles of the fences were left standing in half of the courtyard. Up to that point, we had only discussed the fences' removal in an informal, intermittent way.

The courtyard remained in this condition for several weeks because parents, the manager and members of the ministry did not know what position to take. They were torn between the authority they had to maintain and their astonishment at the children's bravery. ('Put the chain link back up!' was their first order, followed by 'Complete what you started!') After several weeks, they

decided to remove the poles and the remaining wire. So the fences disappeared from Oak Park for good.

The children's creation of the three-dimensional model and their new vision for Oak Park has not reduced their fear of the outside world nor enhanced their knowledge of the city. It has, however, given them a language that they will be able to remember and articulate in their dialogues with adults in their community, and a foundation for the construction of a new tolerance and a new ecology. In the middle of the suddenly fenceless courtyard in Oak Park, a small community garden has been started, thanks to a community grant for youth-led projects. Before other ideas the children had could be

> *The shift from competition to cooperation during adventure play was another practice that I tried to incorporate into every activity that I developed with the children.*

implemented, larger changes needed to take place. The Oak Park Ministry began to push for renovations in the apartments, too long kept in substandard condition, by filing a lawsuit against the slumlord of the housing complex and beginning a dialogue with media and City of Oakland representatives about the poor environmental conditions in which many silent communities are living in urban areas of our western 'civilised' countries. How much the first visions developed by the children through Growing Up in Cities research have influenced this initiative for change is difficult to measure. The children's visions and initiative, however, have been the first step toward change.

CONCLUSION

The research with Oak Park children presented some themes that can be linked to the current larger body of critical theories of children's social relations and experience in public space. These themes relate to the increasingly shrinking range of possibilities for children in pub-

Figure 8.6 Three dimensional model: paving the courtyard

Figure 8.7 Three dimensional model: parking lot and apartments in the background

lic space, children's perception of safety and their relationship to parents' ideas and sanctions, and children's ability to create 'ecological niches' of meaning to resist their exclusion from public areas.

Children in Oak Park valued their own home as the primary and safest nucleus of their daily lives. In her study of 115 children's urban experience in Los Angeles, Shirl Buss also discussed the home as the centre of children's lives. She defined it as 'an oasis or cocoon,

which is sometimes surrounded by a more violent, unpredictable universe.'[14] This emphasis on the home can be linked to the increasing privatisation of public space in US cities.[15] In the new language of contemporary urban environments, complexity means disorder, unpredictability means danger. The urban environment, in other words, is no longer perceived as a learning playground, but as a threatening unknown terrain. As a result of this withdrawal from the public realm, children are often kept at home by their parents, and playing in the street is often considered the most forbidden activity of all.

Several authors have discussed the relationship between children's ability to map the activities that they perform in a territory and their range of mobility.[16] Connected to mobility is the potential for informal learning, which Chawla and Salvadori define as 'what children learn by direct contact with the cities beyond their school walls, as they move through urban spaces in play, travel and everyday routines.'[17] Children's scarce mobility in their own environment, as shown by the maps drawn by the children in Oak Park and the responses of children interviewed in other cities,[18] represents a threat to the potential for informal learning about urban ecosystems and civic values.[19]

Both in Oak Park and in Buss's study of Los Angeles, children's negative perceptions of the public realm stood in contrast to the positive attributes that they conferred on private spaces of consumption. Order and control, the two main characteristics of these private spaces, were seen by the children (and their parents) as signifiers of safety. When the children of Oak Park were interviewed about their idea of the future, they clearly showed their appreciation of spaces such as malls, entertainment parks and video arcades. The artificial character of these private spaces and the activities they afford often merge with the images of youth in the media and advertisement industries. The children also showed many items of wealth and consumption in their collage images. 'I want to live in a house in the hills', explained a child in Oak Park (the hills are where the rich live). 'The malls have things you need: fresh air, families together, clean restaurants and stores', echoed a child from Watts in Buss's study.[20]

This filter created by the media and parents' beliefs may radically affect children's perceptions of the environment and its dangers. When Blakely interviewed 42 parents in multi-ethnic neighbourhoods in Queens, New York, she found that most parents reported fear and worry about social threats to their children, and many associated their own fear with fear in their children and their reluctance to leave the home or go far from their parents' side.[21] She noted that these anxieties were based mostly on second-hand information, such as local legends or stories from the media.

In another study by Kelley, Mayall and Hood, we find a discrepancy between parents' and children's accounts of risk.[22] Children internalised parents' accounts based on the nature of the parent-child relationship and the assumption that parents have a responsibility to protect their children and therefore they know what is right for them. These findings can be related to the fears of the Oak Park children, who often recited their parents' or other relatives' stories about dangers. In Oak Park, the children's lack of direct experience of danger, despite a

> *Children in Oak Park valued their own home as the primary and safest nucleus of their daily lives.*

high level of fear, corresponds to the results of Kelley, Mayall and Hood's study. Moreover, all the studies cited here indicate that both parents and children tend to externalise risk. The outside, in contrast to the home, is dangerous and populated by threatening anonymous characters.

The nature of perceived risks varies with age and gender. In her fieldwork in New York, Blakely noted that parents had different attitudes toward danger depending upon whether their child was a boy or girl.[23] They kept girls inside more than boys, and allowed the boys a larger range of movement. This difference held true across ethnic groups. In London, O'Brien and her colleagues found that ethnic girls were especially confined.[24] Similar differences were found in Oak Park. The girls primarily used the space inside the house or its immediate premises. In interviews, the girls were more likely than boys to mention the fear of being kidnapped or hurt by a stranger.

These geographies of fear and danger attenuate the once rich texture of the public environment and cause children to withdraw into the private, restricted sphere of the family and the home. This discussion should not end, however, with this diminishment of the public realm. The Oak Park research and the other case studies in this book teach us that children are resourceful in creating alternative geographies in spite of the restrictions created by the adult world. These meaningful spaces can be the starting point of a new ecology, where children can become more confident actors in their community as well as agents of change in the outside world.

ENDNOTES

1 U.S. Bureau of Census (1990), 'Census of population and housing', 'Table P9: Race.'
2 Ibid., 'Table P28: Age by language spoken at home and ability to speak English.'
3 Ibid., 'Table P87A: Race of householder by household income in 1989.'
4 Meucci and Redmon (1997).
5 An EEC designation makes a community eligible for special funding for a number of antipoverty programmes.
6 Spanish Speaking Unity Council (1997, p. 8).
7 'Oak Park Apartments yanked from slumlord', (1999), p. 1.
8 Tuan (1977, p. 31).
9 Second floor apartments are generally better maintained, less exposed to rats, better ventilated, and more exposed to sunlight.
10 Moore (1986).
11 Sibley (1995, p. 45).
12 Hart (1997).
13 Dreicer (1996, p. 8).
14 Buss (1995, p. 345).
15 Loukaitou-Sideris and Bannerjee (1992).
16 Hart (1979), Matthews (1992), Chawla and Salvadori (2001).
17 Chawla and Salvadori (2001).
18 Blakely (1994), Buss (1995), O'Brien et al (2000).
19 Chawla and Salvadori (2001).
20 Buss (1995, p. 349-350).
21 Blakely (1994).
22 Kelley, Mayall and Hood (1997).
23 Blakely (1994).
24 O'Brien et al (2000).

REFERENCES

Blakely, K (1994) 'Parents' conceptions of social dangers to children in the urban environment', *Children's Environments,* vol11(1), pp. 16-25.

Buss, S (1995) 'Urban Los Angeles from young people's angle of vision', *Children's Environments,* vol 12(3), pp. 340-351.

Chawla, L and Salvadori, I (2001) 'Children for cities and cities for children: Learning how to know and care about urban ecosystems' in Berkowitz, A, Hollweg, K and Nilon, C (eds) *Understanding Urban Ecosystems,* Springer-Verlag, New York.

Dreicer, G (ed) (1996) *Between Fences,* Princeton Architectural Press, New York.

Hart, R (1979) *Children's Experience of Place,* Irvington Press, New York.

Hart, R (1997) *Children's Participation: The theory and practice of involving young citizens in community development and environmental care,* Earthscan Publications, London.

Kelley, P, Mayall, B and Hood, S (1997) 'Children's accounts of risk', *Childhood,* vol 4, pp. 304-324.

Loukaitou-Sideris, A and Banerjee, T (1992) *Private Production of Downtown Public Open Space: Experiences of Los Angeles and San Francisco,* School of Urban and Regional Planning, University of Southern California, Los Angeles, CA.

Matthews, M H (1992) *Making Sense of Place: Children's understandings of large-scale environments,* Harvester Wheatsheaf, Hemel Hempstead.

Meucci, S and Redmon, J (1997) 'Safe spaces: California children enter a policy debate', *Social Justice,* vol 24(3), pp. 139-151.

Moore, R (1986) *Childhood's Domain: Play and place in child development,* Croom Helm, London.

'Oak Park Apartments yanked from slumlord', *Street Spirit,* vol 5 (7), p. 1.

O'Brien, M, Jones, D, Sloan, D and Rustin, M (2000) 'Children's independent spatial mobility in the urban public realm', *Childhood,* vol 7(3), pp. 257-277.

Sibley, D (1995) *Geographies of Exclusion: Society and difference in the West,* Routledge, London.

Spanish Speaking Unity Council (1997) 'History comes alive at Cohen-Bray House', *Fruitvale Foreword,* vol 1, p. 8.

Tuan, YF (1977) *Space and Place: The perspective of experience,* University of Minnesota Press, Minneapolis.

© HANNA WOLOWSKA

CHAPTER NINE

Adapting During a Time of Great Change

A Return to Warsaw

Piotr-Olaf Zylicz

Twenty-five years after the first Growing Up in Cities research in Powisle, the project returned to this old working-class district of Warsaw to listen to young people present their lives, after the radical change from Communism to a free market system. Thus Powisle becomes a window to glimpse how dramatic social, political and economic changes are influencing the lives of young people in eastern Europe. The 10–15 year old residents of Powisle compared the district with the rest of Warsaw and described their daily lives, hopes and fears, as well as their views of contemporary politics. They also shared their sense of powerlessness in their city, along with their desire to take positive actions for the environment.

What is so unique about the lives of young people living in Powisle, a central and relatively poor district of Warsaw, to attract the attention of scholars for a second time? Since a Polish research team under the direction of Professor Tadeusz Tomaszewski first participated in the Growing Up in Cities project in the 1970s, major political and social changes have occurred, affecting the lives of Polish teenagers. As a psychologist at the Institute of Psychology trying to understand how young people in Powisle are faring under these completely different political circumstances, I have eagerly taken up this work begun by my older colleagues.

I invite readers to accompany me on a visit to look again, some 25 years later, through the window of Powisle into Eastern Europe. To begin, I will describe some specifics about our site of investigation. Then I will discuss how dramatic social, political and economic changes are influencing the daily lives of young people in this district. In many ways, this context is similar for young people in other parts of Eastern Europe, in countries like Bulgaria, Romania, Latvia, the Ukraine and the Czech Republic, which formerly belonged to the Soviet political and military bloc and are currently undergoing comparable transformations.[1]

The main body of this chapter consists of children's voices gathered by my student collaborators and myself while meeting and interviewing 80 boys and girls, from the ages of 10 through 15, who live in Powisle. Our participants' voices are authentic expressions of their lives marked by ordinary and extraordinary expectations, hopes and fears. Unfortunately, adults in Poland, as elsewhere, usually show little interest in listening to these

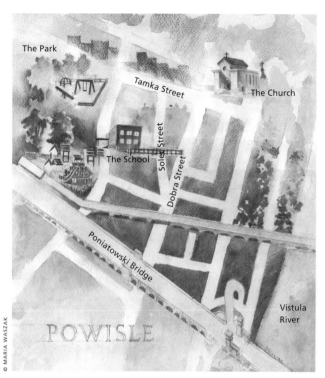

© MARIA WASZAK

Figure 9.1 Site of the Growing Up in Cities project in Powisle

voices of young people to learn from them about their lives. Let it be a time for change in this domain as well.

POWISLE YESTERDAY AND TODAY

To understand Powisle today, it is necessary to present it in the larger context of Warsaw, the capital of Poland. The history of Warsaw goes back to the 13th century, which from a Polish perspective is not unusually old. Not far from Powisle, there is the Old Town with many historic churches, old tenement houses and picturesque narrow streets. All of the contemporary Old Town, however, is a reconstruction because 85% of all the pre-war buildings in Warsaw were destroyed by bombings and the systematic destruction of the city by Hitler's armies during the Second World War. The war also broke the continuity of the city's history in terms of its population and the chain of successive generations. Out of a pre-war population of 1,300,000, more than 650,000 people died,

including almost all of the large Jewish community who, before the war, had constituted a colourful multinational fabric of Warsaw inhabitants. This is why we can say that present-day Warsaw, with a population of almost 2 million, is to a large degree a city of new people and new buildings.

This post-war architecture reflects general trends in construction during the last five decades. The Palace of Culture and Science, erected by the Soviet Union, is considered by many symbolic of the 1950s. It is the tallest building in Poland, towering more than 200 metres high, with an eclectic facade that resembles those of similar buildings all over the former East bloc. From the 1950s to the 1970s, numerous huge apartment buildings were built to meet the housing demands of a rapidly growing population. The buildings of this era are architecturally undistinguished. The current period of transformation to a capitalist society shows a new permissiveness in terms of colour and form. Those who design new apartment buildings, for example, attempt to make them look original and aesthetically pleasing. Recently, financial and business centres have begun to dominate.

Although the site of our research — Powisle — lies in the centre of the city, it has remained to some extent outside the mainstream of city life and these changes. One reason is that it is separated from Warsaw proper by a steep hill. Another is that it has a strong local tradition. For some people Powisle is unique and charming, and they wouldn't think of moving away. My good friend, Elzbieta, who has resided in Powisle most of her life, told me once:

'When I was abroad I used to long solely for Powisle. You know it is in the heart of the city but our daily life is like that of a little provincial town. People know one another pretty well and you always have to say hello while walking here. At 8 pm the district social life is over and everyone is at home.'

For many centuries, Powisle was a district of poor people, people figuratively and literally 'at rock bottom', as the district is situated along the Vistula River, below the escarpment where the more affluent boroughs are located. Although at present Powisle is inhabited by people of varied social status, we still find here relatively more social pathologies and people living in difficult housing conditions than in 'upper' Warsaw. Unlike the other districts of the city, there are a substantial number of families in Powisle whose ancestors had ties to this place.

The local architecture includes old, pre-war buildings, closely attached to one another and built along narrow streets that are constantly crowded with cars. More recent buildings from the 1960s and 1970s stand

TABLE 9.1	
Community Profile	
Land Area	65 hectares (160.2 acres)
Population	no official or unofficial records on a community scale
Elementary schoool	1
Public playground	1
Playing fields outside of school	0
Swimming pool	0
Youth clubs	0
Church	1
Hospital	1
Bookshop	1

out, as they are considerably taller than the former — giving the area little architectural unity. Not much has been built here during the transformation period, due mainly to the lack of open space. In recent years colourful store window displays and billboards have appeared, and many houses have been repainted, at least in the front. In some respects, not much has changed in Powisle since the first Growing Up in Cities study in the 1970s. The statements recorded then remain valid today: 'The district is sufficiently provided with shops, repair shops, and other services, but it lacks cultural and recreational centres. There is no space for playgrounds or sportfields.'[2]

For the present study, the research team returned to observe the life of children and young people in the original study area: the part of Powisle that lies between a central bridge and Tamka Street, which is one of the two main thoroughfares that connect the district to the 'upper' city. The escarpment and the Vistula River, bordered by a broad and very busy avenue, form the two other boundaries of the area. The area of investigation can be considered in terms of a 'developmental niche' as proposed by Super and Harkness.[3] It is relatively small (about 65 hectares), with a dense network of apartment buildings, an elementary school, a church, a hospital, a famous theatre, a large and fairly new playground, and a terrain owned by nuns which is inaccessible to the public. The only soccer fields and basketball courts are located on the school premises. It might appear to be an area where young people would rather not live, as it has insufficient places for playing games or socialising with others, such as youth clubs. The finding of Weist and colleagues[4] that it is generally less stressful and psychologically problematic for young people to live in suburban or rural areas than in the centre of a city may seem particularly true for Powisle's youth. However, the feelings of the young people living here are much more complex.

THE YEAR 1989 AND AFTER

By understanding the everyday lives of young people in Powisle at the end of the 20th century, we can to some extent see into the lives of their peers living in other big cities in this region of Europe. It should be noted, however, that the pace of transformation differs considerably from country to country in Eastern Europe, especially in terms of the quality of changes taking place, standards of living, and the degree of maturity of their democratic institutions.

The great majority of young people living here can observe rapid economic and social changes taking place around them: emerging wealth, unemployment (a previously unknown condition), widespread crime, many tempting, newly available (yet often inaccessible) products, and the restoration of democracy. Young Poles,

Czechs or Romanians, especially those living in cities, hear it being said around them that their countries must 'join Europe' — as if they had not yet been part of the 'real' Europe. They take for granted that they can now read a free press and travel across Europe without needing special visas (if they can save enough money). They drink authentic cans of the once forbidden Coca-Cola, watch American films, and generally know foreign musicians better than the musicians of their own country. It is often easier for them to quote the score of last Saturday's Chicago Bulls game or Mike Tyson's current problems, than to assign major Polish politicians to their political parties. The streets are now full of billboards, and youth magazines are much more colourful than 10 years ago. In shops they can now get French or German rollerblades and American baseball bats (if they come from an affluent family). Elementary school children no longer need to wear ugly monochromatic uniforms, and paragraphs about the superiority of the Communist party and the Soviet system have been deleted from their textbooks. Many young people know that their future depends on a good education, which today is easier to obtain, but this education now frequently requires at least as much money as skill. In 1989, only about 7 percent of the young Poles of university age were in higher education, whereas the proportion now is about 20 percent. However, almost all of the new universities are private.

A 1997 Unicef report on children in Eastern Europe sums up their situation with accuracy, highlighting a condition which unfortunately remains virtually unchanged:

'Overlooked by the planners of economic reforms…the social crises for hundreds, thousands and millions of vulnerable children across the region remain unchecked. Amidst economic stabilisation and regeneration, the social reform is piecemeal and uncertain in its aims, strategies and funding.'[5]

There are two truths about the economic situation for countries in Eastern Europe. The 'average' economic truth is this: for the majority of these countries, macro-economic indicators are good. Since 1989, the Polish currency has become much stronger in relation to Western European currencies. The national level of unemploy-

ment in Poland, which had fallen in the past few years, has increased recently and now oscillates around 14 percent — which is notably lower than in other countries, such as Russia and the Ukraine. On the other hand, offsetting these gains, there is a growing gap between rich and poor. There is an increasingly better life for the elite, while middle and lower classes are struggling.[6]

Figure 9.2 Typical block-like buidings of post-war Warsaw

Nowadays, it is more difficult to be less affluent. The poor are ashamed of their poverty; and it is important to note that in many countries in Eastern Europe, the level of child poverty has been increasing on average one and one-half times faster than the general level of poverty.[7] Under the Communist regime, with the exception of a few high-ranking party supporters, the majority of the people lived on a comparable socio-economic level. Today, both on television and in the neighbourhood of Powisle, it is possible to see some people who are rich or very rich.

It is particularly difficult to be a child in a family where someone is unemployed — which is a new phenomenon in all the countries of the region. Children suffer from unemployment for financial reasons, as well as from the frustrations experienced by their parents. At the same time, a great many employed parents are forced to work longer hours than before. As a consequence, parents have less time for their children, as demonstrated by the fact that in the mid-1990s, one in ten Polish children aged seven to nine was left without adult supervision for over two hours a day.[8]

Ever higher rates of divorce are also influencing the situation of children. The worst situation in this respect is in Estonia, where there are now more divorces than marriages. As the Unicef report observed: 'One might have expected families to pull together in times of economic crisis. But the huge pressures of the transition appear to be splitting families apart and eroding parental responsibilities.'[9]

In recent years, the number of families with only one child has increased rapidly.[10] If this trend continues, Eastern European societies — particularly in urban environments — will soon be dominated by children who have no siblings. In Bulgaria, in 1995, the average woman in her childbearing years gave birth to 1.2 children, and in Poland the situation is not much better. There are many underlying causes. First, the cost of raising a child is increasingly high. In the majority of the countries in the region, state health services, as well as education, have become to a large extent insufficient, and parents are compelled to use more expensive private services. Second, it is more difficult than before to balance a professional and family life: for instance, it is not easy today to take a leave of absence from work to care for a sick child. Third, in recent years, the number of people who choose not to have children has increased. For example, in Poland, 24 percent of the women between the ages of 18 and 44 have declared this to be their choice.[11] In some parts of Eastern Europe, the tragic state of the natural environment is used as an important argument for not having children.

The poor condition of the environment is not the only threat young people face. In recent years the health condition of children and young people has deteriorated, mainly due to malnutrition. In many countries of Eastern Europe, especially in the countries of the former Soviet Union, there is a considerable increase in the occurrence of the so-called poverty diseases, such as diphtheria and tuberculosis, among children and youth.[12]

Police reports show another disturbing trend.[13] In the past ten years in Poland, the number of juvenile offences has increased by two-thirds. Most of these are committed by boys aged 13 through 16 who have failed classes and are frequently absent from school. Often they are runaways from home or juvenile welfare institutions. We can observe a similar pattern of more crimes being committed against young people.

In addition to these external signs, there are some aspects of the transformation which are more difficult to depict. Young people now have to sort their way through bewildering sets of alternatives: national traditions or cosmopolitan thinking; leftist theories and the collectivism of socialism or the ethos of individualism and personal responsibility of capitalism; religious idealism or the cult of unrestricted consumerism embodied in the slogan, 'I consume, therefore I am — and please don't disturb me.' It is primarily young people who are prone to react to contemporary problems by joining nationalistic, paramilitary or racist groups, and blaming Jews, gypsies or immigrants from a poorer country for their economic problems. At the same time, it is young people who are least burdened by the past, the old conflicts and stereotypes, and who seem best equipped to participate in the changes taking place.[14]

In 1989, only about 7 percent of the young Poles of university age were in higher education; the proportion now is about 20 percent.

Since 1989 much has changed in Poland: political and economic independence from Russia has been reached, democratic institutions have been installed, and personal and minority rights are fairly well protected. Poland has become a full member of the North Atlantic Treaty Organization and it is expected to join the European Union in a few years. For most adults in Poland, 1989 was a breakthrough and turning point in national history. But children seem to live through these changes, absorb them and adjust to them often without thinking about them. For participants in our research, this date often meant nothing, or it was simply one of the dates which they must memorise for examinations. When 12 year old Ula was asked 'What has changed in Poland over the past years?', she thought a moment and then replied, 'Well, it is difficult to say, but I know for sure that separate containers were supplied for collecting glass and paper'. Given that children apprehend the world around them first through their own immediate environments, it is important to understand what everyday life is like for children in Poland today.

TABLE 9.2				
Participants Profile (N=80)				
Male, 39 Female, 41				
AGE	# OF PARTICIPANTS		AGE	# OF PARTICIPANTS
10	3		13	17
11	3		14	41
12	5		15	11

© HANNA WOLOWSKA

Figure 9.3 Parks and playgrounds are favourite places to 'hang out'.

RESEARCH IN POWISLE

We met the participants in our research through the help of the authorities of the local elementary school. With their teachers' consent, we contacted young people who lived in the area we had designated, and explained to them that we would like to find out what they thought of life in Powisle and which changes they would like adults to implement there. Since our meetings took place during classes, many of the children were happy that they were excused from attending two consecutive classes for the period of about one and one-half hours that was required for each interview. Most Polish urban schools set high educational standards, which are often enforced through authoritarian teaching methods. Therefore most children eagerly and enthusiastically accepted our invitation to take part in the meetings outside of class. Some older

boys, however, thought that drawing and talking about their lives may be an activity suitable for girls, but not for boys.

A considerable majority of children participating in the research attended the seventh and eighth grades, the two highest grades in Polish elementary schools. The lower grades, fourth through sixth, were represented by a smaller number of children. Thus this study reflects the district primarily from the viewpoint of young adolescents. Because of the relatively large sample of 13–15 year old participants, I estimate that the research team probably met over half of the young people of this age living in the study area.

Because there has been little recent migration into Poland, all of the participating children were probably of Polish origin, although some of them had different ethnic roots as indicated by their non-Slavic names. Their religious backgrounds were probably also homogeneous, as most people in Polish society are Roman Catholic, and Warsaw is no exception in this respect (compared with some Greek Orthodox regions in the east of the country). In terms of actual religious practice, however, differences among the children's families were probably substantial. Given Powisle's history, most of the participants came from families of low economic status.

During the research meeting, each child drew the neighbourhood where he or she lived and answered the standard GUIC questions. They also compared their perceptions of Powisle with those of the rest of Warsaw, and played a game called 'Dongs' that simulated financial investments in the district. The results of these meetings are summarised in the following sections.

HOW DOES MY NEIGHBOURHOOD COMPARE?

The first thing I wanted to understand was how these young residents evaluated Powisle. For this purpose, older participants aged 13 through 15 were asked to describe the two categories of 'my neighbourhood' (whatever part of Powisle he or she identified with) and 'Warsaw' by filling out a semantic differential: a scale composed of pairs of contrasting adjectives.[15] A statistical analysis of means enabled us to observe similarities and differences in participants' perceptions of Powisle and the rest of Warsaw. (See Table 9.3.)

The mean evaluations of 'my neighbourhood' demonstrate an overall positive image. All of the means, except one, are closer to the positive adjective of a given pair. The only exception is the category 'noisy-quiet': Powisle appears to be a little noisier than quiet. This perception is understandable, since the area we investigated is surrounded by busy streets which reflect Warsaw's dramatic increase in traffic since 1989. In the original 1970s study, noise was also mentioned as a salient negative quality of the area.[16]

At the same time, Powisle appears to be less interesting and less important than the city of Warsaw as a whole. This lesser importance attributed to Powisle can be explained by its lack of places of interest, and the fact that cafes, expensive shops, sports fields and important events are located primarily in other parts of the city. Although participants did not find their area particularly quiet, they perceived the city of Warsaw as much more noisy, rowdy and crowded, which reflects objective differences.

Let us now look at the views that the participants expressed during the interviews. When asked if they felt more like inhabitants of Powisle or Warsaw, about twice as many participants identified themselves with the city as a whole rather than with their neighbourhood. (In the 1970s, Lynch also noted 'a lack of identification with the area' among young Powisle dwellers.[17]) Several children stated that they think of themselves as inhabitants of both Powisle and Warsaw. Those who said they feel more attached to Powisle had interesting explanations for their affiliation. Most frequently, they emphasised the fact that this is where they live ('because I've been living here since I was born'), or that they rarely go outside their

TABLE 9.3	Mean evaluations for 10 attributes

Perceptions of 'My neighbourhood' and 'Warsaw' (N=55)

	1	2	3	4	5	6	7	
Pretty			● □					Ugly
Good			● □					Bad
Interesting			□ ●					Boring
Pleasant				● □				Unpleasant
Cheerful			●	□				Sad
Friendly				□ ●				Hostile
Important			□ ●					Unimportant
Quiet				●		□		Noisy
Peaceful			●		□			Rowdy
Uncrowded			●			□		Crowded

□ WARSAW   ● POWISLE

neighbourhood ('because I'm in Powisle all the time, I never go outside'). When posing such questions one has to make sure that the question does not force an arbitrary answer. When asked which segment of the city she most identified with, 15 year old Monika said, 'I have never really thought about it.'

> *When asked if they felt more like inhabitants of Powisle or Warsaw, about twice as many participants identified themselves with the city rather than with their neighbourhood.*

In an attempt to find out how the participants represent 'my neighbourhood', we asked them to draw their neighbourhood and all the places important to them.[18] First, we paid attention to the size of the area drawn. Our participants' images of 'my neighbourhood' frequently coincided with the part of Powisle that constituted our major area of research. They identified four boundaries of their neighbourhood: the hill, the river, the road and railway viaducts, and Tamka Street. Tamka Street might not seem like a boundary to adults, but the area north of this street appeared to be a 'different land' to many children. A boy affiliated with the local gangs suggested that this other area is controlled by a different teenage group, attending a different school, but for the majority of children an unwritten tradition seemed to forbid them to go there.

The analysis of the drawings revealed that 'my neighbourhood' was most often delineated by important, frequently visited places, typically within a radius of 200 metres from home. These important places — the child's house and its immediate environment, school, a friend's house, the park, church or local stores — were usually shown disproportionately big in relation to other objects and drawn with a degree of detail. Often, the child's home was drawn in the middle of the drawing. The closer the objects were to the periphery, in general, the smaller they appeared. The youngest participants, especially girls, created the most beautiful drawings in terms of colour and detail. Older teenagers (aged 14–15) usually drew carelessly, depicted a relatively small number of details, and avoided using colours, as if in fear of revealing themselves.

What the participants drew in their maps was reflected in their interviews. Not surprisingly, the majority of participants mentioned their home and school as the places where they spent most of their time during a typical weekday. They gave parks the third most frequent mention. A playground had been built recently in one of the parks, and the older participants revealed that they go there primarily to 'hang out' since Powisle lacks places where young people can meet. Streets and playgrounds were mentioned almost equally as often, and were reported twice as often as sports clubs, friends' homes or stores.

I did not classify our participants' most favourite places, since they were frequently connected with highly personal and idiosyncratic experiences. Let some of the participants' statements serve as examples. Fourteen year old Michael admitted with some embarrassment that a meat store was most important to him 'because I'm sent there everyday to do shopping.' For Monika (aged

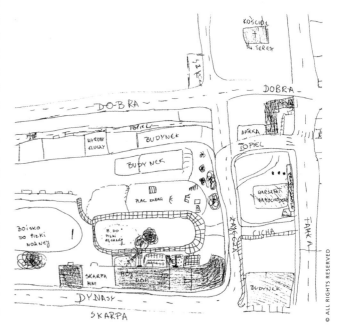

Figure 9.4 Child's drawing showing the centre of Powisle

15) one of the playgrounds in the neighbourhood was particularly important: 'I'm here at least three times a day, because I walk my dog here.' Ania (aged 15) said something nobody else said about the local park: 'There's a tree there that I used to climb...the only tree I ever climbed in my life.' For 14 year old Iza, a significant place was her friend's room: 'It's clean and nice at her place; she's got lots of closets.' (Adults often fail to appreciate how important and fascinating the closets at a friend's home can be.) When participants said previously that they often spend their time at home or school, we were not certain whether this was good or bad, because many children dislike school; but there are also children like Agnieszka (aged 15) for whom school 'is like a club where you come to meet your friends.'

Because there have been frequent reports in the media about 'toxic parents', I thought that young people might rarely speak positively of their homes. Surprisingly, many children described their house, or a part of it, as their favourite place. 'This is a place', Danusia (aged 15) told us, 'that is always peaceful, where there are lots of things to do, where one can relax and be with one's family.' Fourteen year old Malgosia associated home with a nice atmosphere and the smell of cake. To Witek (14 years old) home was primarily an oasis: 'It's cool in my house; I can lie down and listen to my music and nobody disturbs me.'

If we managed to gain the trust of our young participant during the interview, he or she would frequently tell us about favourite places that needed to remain hidden from other people, apart from 'the authorised gang members.' We hope the reader will understand that, even though we are not bound by an oath, we cannot reveal the precise location of these meeting places, nor can we tell in which tower of the bridge there is a secret hiding place. Let us merely quote 14 year old Ola here (for which she will hopefully forgive us), who confessed 'that there's a hole under the stairs in school where we would sit for hours after classes.' It is a trivial statement only for those adults who have forgotten how finding one's own secret place in the world was once important.

Not all homes, however, are so wonderful. It is not coincidental that the area we studied has daycare centres

---

BOX 9.1

A Typical Weekday

One day in the life of 13 year old Ania is fairly representative of the days lived by other children in the neighbourhood.

6:30	get up
6:40	walk the dog
7:00	have a wash
7:15	breakfast
7:25	leave for school ('I always go to my friend's house first, so I have to leave earlier')
8:00–15:00	school
15:15	walk the dog
16:00	French language extracurricular class
17:00	do homework
20:00	supper; watch 'Rambo' on TV
22:00	walk the dog
22:30	go to bed after having had a wash

The average time (per day) among respondents (N = 80)

Watching TV	1.5 hours
Playing (indoors and outdoors)	1.75 hours
Homework and tutorial classes	1.78 hours

---

run by the Powisle Foundation for children from dysfunctional families. For one of the boys — let's call him Piotr (14 years old) — this centre is a very important place in his life. As he describes it: 'It is very interesting there. I know many people. It is kind of my environment. Teachers are very good; you can really talk to them. You can learn to be responsible.'

When asked about problems in their area, 27 percent of the participants told us that there wasn't anything that particularly troubled them. The largest number of children (17 percent) complained of litter or excessively heavy traffic in narrow streets. Family and school chores and homework ranked next in terms of trouble.

BOX 9.2

The Powisle Foundation

The Powisle Foundation was created in 1991 in a 'bottom-up' process much like other NGOs. It took considerable time to convince local authorities that its low budget activities would be profitable for local residents, including young people facing diverse personal problems. There are still people who believe that it is the responsibility of the State and its agencies to provide citizens with all necessary support and services, but since the collapse of the former regime which had promised 'welfare for everybody', NGOs have begun to supplement the State, often with greater efficiency, and are winning increasing social acceptance.

Currently the Powisle Foundation runs several centres for socially and/or psychologically maladjusted children from all over Powisle. In 1997, long-term help was provided for about 100 children aged 5–15 (and some of their families) mostly suffering from severe problems in school and at home related to alcoholism and domestic violence. Most of the children attend the foundation centres for several hours daily. Each centre serves as a shelter and a place of emotional support. Individual tutoring and help in solving family or peer conflicts are offered. Children are taught to live responsibly in a group and in society, to resolve group conflicts, to satisfy their needs in congruence with the needs of others, and to learn what tolerance is all about. The centres are therapeutic communities where children participate in establishing standards and rules, controlling how they are obeyed, organising games, preparing food and doing other day-to-day activities that are part of running the centres. A nation-wide programme of similar centres has been described by Bronowski and Gabrysiak, and similar programmes in other countries have been described by Meyer and Farell. [19]

Does Powisle seem safe and quiet to our participants? In the 1970s study, Powisle was perceived as markedly less safe than a more modern district of apartment blocks on the periphery of Warsaw.[20] Today, children usually find the area safe. Powisle seems more quiet and peaceful to them than the rest of Warsaw, which has become more and more dangerous as shootings and bomb explosions have ceased to be unusual. Several children expressed the view that 'locals' are safe in Powisle, unless somebody from the outside shows up. One boy,

> *In the 1970s study, Powisle was perceived as markedly less safe than a more modern district of apartment blocks on the periphery of Warsaw. Today, children usually find the area safe.*

asked if he is sometimes afraid to walk in the neighbourhood, declared in a proud and confident voice that he is never afraid because 'I have a brother who is feared all over Powisle.' A few children admitted to being afraid of alcoholics, who can mug them and steal their money.

This is why the liquor store is among the children's least favourite places. Muggings can occur anywhere, and many children did not recommend walking in Powisle after dark, especially in the parks, near the bridges and by the river. Some of these answers reveal that there may be a risk of habituation to social pathologies. As one boy said, 'Cars are stolen, but otherwise it is peaceful here.'

HOW FAMILIAR IS THE REST OF WARSAW?

When we asked participants what places, apart from their neighbourhood, they knew in Warsaw, they rarely listed more than ten. Some participants were unable to mention any other place. One boy explained: 'I rarely go outside my neighbourhood.' Most frequently, they enumerated names of other Warsaw districts. Quite often I had the impression that the children quoted them as mechanically as they did the names of provinces or regions in their country. However, they clearly knew Warsaw stores, which they mentioned almost as often as they did the districts. Like adults, they appeared to treat going shopping as a kind of entertainment, usually enjoyed on weekends. Clothing and music stores were most important to them.

The third most frequently mentioned places were streets and squares, especially those located near Powisle, where our participants often walked on their own. Almost equally often they named the Palace of

© PIOTR-OLAF ZYLICZ

Figure 9.5 The dominant feeling was that the state of the natural environment in Powisle was deteriorating.

Culture and Science, a socialist-realist structure towering above the city. This building is as unsightly as it is useful. Many children visit it to go to a movie, a puppet theatre or a youth centre, or just to take an elevator to the top floor. In order of importance the other places outside of Powisle that children cited were cinemas, theatres, sports centres and fast food restaurants.

The fast food restaurants deserve special attention. McDonald's, Burger King and Pizza Hut are not only the names of places where one eats, but also places where many young people spend free time with their parents and with peers. There are no Polish chains of snack bars, and so a cheeseburger with a large order of fries is fast becoming a 'traditional national dish' of Polish youth.

NEIGHBOURHOOD CHANGES

So far we have been mostly concerned with the image of the district where participants live. I am going to focus now on whether children have perceived changes in their neighbourhood and how they evaluate them. As mentioned earlier, political and economic changes in the country have significantly altered the natural and built environment.

It is worth mentioning that when asked about the changes taking place in Powisle, as many as 42 percent of the participants declared that they observed none at all. Some young people simply said: 'Nothing's changed.' Others added interesting comments to explain why they thought so: 'I cannot see many changes…I might have got used to them.' Or, 'You know, living here I don't really see these changes…If I were an outsider, then maybe.' What appears as relatively recent to an adult, may seem ancient history to a teenager. Kasia (13 years old) admitted, 'I don't really remember how it used to be.'

TABLE 9.4

Perceived Changes in Powisle
Frequency of response among those who observed change (N=32; AGES=13–15)

CHANGES NOTICED BY CHILDREN	% OF CHILDREN
Changed street appearance	70
Changes in the natural environment	63
Renovated buildings	52
New buildings	41
New stores	41
New technical infrastructure (e.g.traffic lights)	38
General improvement in the look of the district	26
Demographic changes (more crowded streets, more strangers and poor people)	25
New recreational facilities for children and youth	25

The changes that participants noticed most easily were those that were most visible. Seventy percent of those who perceived changes talked about the streets: new street names, street lighting, new store fronts, newly repaired road surfaces and the like. A somewhat smaller number (63 percent) noticed the improvement or degradation of the ecology of the area. A few mentioned the increased amount of green space. However, the dominant feeling was that the state of the natural environment in Powisle was deteriorating. Children mostly objected to tree cutting and air pollution caused by the rapidly increasing number of cars. Table 9.4 shows the changes observed by children, ranked according to the frequency with which they were cited.

> *The dominant feeling was that the state of the natural environment in Powisle was deteriorating. Children mostly objected to tree cutting and air pollution.*

It is important to note that our participants paid attention to changes that affected all inhabitants and not only young people. We can also note that these young people were quite acute observers of reality. The fact that many referred to the natural environment demonstrates that Polish youth are sensitive to ecological issues. Some children, however, mentioned relatively small idiosyncratic changes, such as the installation of phone booths for the disabled or a new intercom in the child's building. Monitoring young people's reactions to transformations in Hungary, Van Hoorn and Komlosi observed that children tended to find changes more salient when they affected their own lives. The researchers' conclusion is worth repeating: 'The lack of deeper analysis reflected in their responses appears to reflect the lack of opportunity they have to discuss these issues in depth.'[21] I did not observe significant differences between the sexes in terms of the kinds of changes observed, although girls more often noticed the new look of stores, whereas boys paid more attention to playgrounds, bicycle paths and sports centres.

As a following step, I sought to learn how the participants evaluated these changes. I wanted to find out which changes they considered to be good or bad and whom they believed benefited most from them. Not to my surprise, new bicycle paths, playgrounds, more attractive streets and positive ecological changes (such as planting new trees) met with the participants' approval. In contrast, increased air pollution, the loss of trees, and increasing traffic in the streets and street markets were identified as bad changes. There was also a fairly universal sense of deteriorating public safety in the streets, because: 'There are more crooks, hooligans and thieves.' Some evaluations were surprising. Many children were irritated by the poles installed just before the beginning of our research to prevent parking on sidewalks, or the fences that had been put up to prevent walking on the grass, because they saw these as restrictions of freedom.

Figure 9.6 Powisle children usually find their area safe.

About 80 percent of those who noticed changes were of the opinion that these changes were for the better. At the same time, quite spontaneously, they often added a statement along the following lines: 'At present, some people are doing well and others are doing badly.' Our participants emphasised that the impacts of the changes vary significantly for different inhabitants of Powisle. 'Those who have money, are rich and can afford whatever they feel like are much better off. Less affluent people do much worse due to lack of money.' Not only money was judged important. As one of the participants observed, 'Older people find it more and more difficult to live because they have less strength and money.' A few other participants were of the opinion that the ability to live more comfortably was basically determined by the level of education: 'Those who are uneducated are not successful, as opposed to those who have a wide knowledge and are educated.'

DO WE HAVE ANY INFLUENCE IN THE NEIGHBOURHOOD?

Another series of questions aimed to discover if our participants felt that they could influence life in Powisle and if they would like to have a say in what happened in their neighbourhood. This issue of having influence over the environment is significant beyond the local level. The democratic changes of 1989 brought great hopes that a democratic society would develop in which (unlike in the past) many citizens would actively participate in creating social reality, and young people would learn what social participation is all about by actively taking part for the sake of their personal development and for the greater good. A growing number of advocates for children's rights are convinced that social participation is not to be reserved for adults and should be fostered and experienced at different stages of personal development, as 'democratic responsibility is something which does not suddenly arise in adulthood.'[22] I was interested to see if the powerful changes that have shaken Poland were reflected in the minds and actions of the young people in Powisle.

Almost all who were interviewed said that they had no such influence. Only about 10 percent of the participants believed that they had any impact on local affairs. Asked to explain what kind of influence they thought they had, several indicated that this was played out more in a social context: 'I have some influence over my peers'… 'If we hang out with our friends we have influence.' Other participants considered the meaning in terms of local initiatives undertaken by parents: 'My parents belong

to the residents' organisation.' One of the girls was convinced that she had some influence because she had been invited to a meeting of the residents of the apartment building where she lives, but her conclusion was quite significant: '…but because I'm underage, they don't yet listen to me.'

Young people in Powisle not only felt ignored… many deeply distrusted any political involvement in local or national affairs.

When we asked our young participants about adults seeking the opinions of young people, many times we heard: 'I have never come across such a case before.' Or it may have happened once: 'Some guy two or three years ago asked us about safety.' Many replied with regret that they were not treated by adults as partners: 'Adults sometimes ask questions, but they end up doing whatever they feel like doing'…'They think that we have no opinion'…'They probably don't care about us, or about our opinions'…'They are rather not interested in what young people would like.'

Young people in Powisle not only felt ignored, but questions about their attitudes toward politicians and politics showed that many deeply distrusted any political involvement in local or national affairs. When they were asked about their interest in politics, 43 percent declared that they did not care about political affairs, and 31 percent expressed an intense disapproval of politicians. Their pronouncements in this regard typically were that: 'Politicians only quarrel and are keen for money and power'…'They are directed solely by self-interest without trying to improve anything'…'They do not listen to people.' Fourteen percent of these adolescents wanted nothing to do with politics because they considered it a difficult and thankless profession. Only 12 percent spoke of politicians in approving terms.

At the same time, the resilience and optimism of youth were obvious, as most of the participants indicated that they would like to influence neighbourhood changes. Some said emphatically, 'I'd love to very much.' Usually our participants added immediately what they would like to do and what they would like to change. Most of their reflections were complex and thoughtful:

'I would like to build a youth club in Powisle. Right now, the only place where we can meet is the park. And then when we meet in the park, teachers and some parents accuse us (they must be bored) of doing some dirty stuff there. They imagine that everybody is drinking there or getting into fights. And such things never happen... If somebody goes to the park, then people think he is a hooligan. And where else can we meet? At our friend's place, where there is not enough space?... This is why I would like to build a club.'
Agnieszka, 15 years old

TABLE 9.5	
Investment Priorities in the Game of 'Dongs'	
HIERARCHY OF THE FREQUENCY OF CHOICES	AREA OF INVESTMENT
1	Renovating buildings and squares
2	Sports facilities and playgrounds
3	Parks and green areas
4	School
5	The poor (the homeless, the unemployed, sick people)
6	A meeting place for young people
7	Renovating streets and sidewalks
8	Eliminating pollution, cleaning up the area, adding recycling containers
9	Improving the management of street traffic

To further explore the changes that participants would like to make, I introduced as part of the research activities a game that I called 'Dongs.' The participants' task was to invest fake 'Monopoly' money in projects for the area. Participants were told: 'You have 100,000 Dongs. This is really big money. On what important projects for your neighbourhood would you spend it?' A large majority of the young people approached the task with great enthusiasm, and through their choices they revealed their priorities.

Their choice to invest in particular areas seemed to result from both their personal interests and their recognition of existing shortages or deficiencies. To my surprise, many participants declared their willingness to allocate part of the money for people in need, even though this was not an obvious way of 'investing' in the neighbourhood. It demonstrated their sensitivity to the needs of people who face difficulties and contradicted the image of young people as too 'cool' to be concerned with any social issues.

DO WE WANT TO DO ANYTHING FOR OUR AREA?

To verify whether these results corresponded to participants' actual involvement in their community, I asked them whether they ever took care of any part of Powisle or did anything of value for the area. Two-thirds answered, 'Yes, I did.' However, further questions revealed a fairly dispiriting picture. Most often their only relevant action was to participate in a programme called 'Clean Up the World' when they were pressured to take part in this effort to clean up their school environment once a year. All of the participants had probably taken part in this programme, but it must have been of so little personal importance to others that they failed to mention it. As one young Polish activist from another research study commented, 'On Earth Day, everybody talks and goes to clean up the forest, but the next day they act as always.'[23] Older generations of Poles, Hungarians and Russians were forced to take part in obligatory and mostly senseless 'social works' which fostered social passivity and a disregard for volunteering, and many of our young participants still seemed burdened by the bad experiences of their parents' generation. A few participants mentioned that their major contribution to the welfare of the locality was not doing certain things, such as not littering or not writing graffiti on the walls. Fortunately, we found other young people (around one third of those who

Figure 9.7 You don't need much to play happily.

declared personal involvement) who appeared to be actively participating in improving life in the neighbourhood. They freely undertook activities like shopping for an ill neighbour, helping the janitor with her work, or helping to build the local playground.[24]

Do these results mean that young people, in general, are not willing to get involved and help for the sake of their environment? Not at all. As many as 87 percent of our participants declared that they would act for their area if someone encouraged them. The problem is that there is usually no such 'someone' — an adult or anyone else who would motivate them to get involved. Grzegorz (14 years old) said: 'I would willingly paint, say, a fence...but provided that I would be asked personally by someone. If I just went out by myself to paint there might be people who will not like my work.' As Carleton

has noted, it normally takes time to awaken young people to their ability to initiate new ideas and accomplish them.[25] In a study of adolescents living in a much more affluent area, I found a similar lack of young people's involvement for the sake of their area and a lack of adults' motivating support.[26]

CONCLUSIONS

Powisle is an important reference point for the young people living there, despite the fact that most of them prefer to be considered inhabitants of Warsaw rather than Powisle. They do their best to adapt to what is an unfriendly environment for them in some ways, due to physical constraints and lack of support from adults.[27]

These young people want to act for the sake of their neighbourhood, but they feel that they are not invited to actively participate in improving life in Powisle. Adults want neither to share responsibilities nor to discuss issues relevant to young people in the area. Currently, Powisle's youth participate very little in local affairs. Even projects where adults mobilise young people for one-day events (such as Earth Day or 'Clean Up the World') are rare. Can we tolerate such a situation in Poland? This is, after all, the country of Janusz Korczak,[28] one of the earliest promoters of practical and effective local democracy exercised by children, who became a martyr in the Second World War for his love and support of children. And this is also a country proud of being instrumental in initiating the United Nations Convention on the Rights of the Child.

> *Without spending a great deal of money, parents, teachers and local authorities can do much to foster young people's sense of efficacy and well-being.*

Without spending a great deal of money, parents, teachers and local authorities can do much to foster young people's sense of efficacy and well-being in Powisle and elsewhere. The advantages will be shared by everyone involved. These benefits include less frustrated and more active, happy, involved and caring young people, more safety on the streets, less need for constraints like curfews for youth, and more people willing to take responsibility for the area in the future. Research clearly shows that youth participation fosters volunteerism in adults and incites them to take responsibility for the community in which they live.[29]

Adults can begin by trying to listen to their own children and to the children of their neighbours. Sometimes it takes time to find a suitable 'key', a way of asking and just 'being with' that enables insight into the complexity and specifics of children's personal experiences. Adults can learn about young people's challenges and resources not only through discussions, but also through methods

like those used in the Growing Up in Cities project and questionnaires like the "My Life Questionnaire", which can measure factors that protect youth against stressors of inner-city life, such as poverty, crime and violence.[30] However, adults often do not have time, or take time, to attune themselves to young people's voices. By careful listening and discussing, adults can learn much and young people can develop ways of self-reflection that will help them avoid obstacles and seize opportunities on their way to adulthood. They can better understand that their sense of powerlessness[31] is primarily due to the discouraging legacy of Communism and the social inequalities of capitalism, and to their age, rather than to their personal inadequacy. Both adults and young people can then put forth compatible proposals for improving life in the locality and try to put them into practice, at least wherever youth affairs are involved.[32]

The present study shows that we still have a long way to go to truly support the involvement of young people in our society. The young people of Powisle, of Warsaw and probably of hundreds of cities all across Eastern Europe are willing and waiting. It is time now for adults to change their deeply rooted habits and ways of thinking: time to really promote and support the participation of young citizens.

ENDNOTES

1 An imaginary line from the Baltic to the Black Sea divides Western and Eastern Europe. Although Poland lies in the dead centre of Europe, it has been associated historically with the eastern half (Davis, 1985).

2 Lynch (1977, p. 149).

3 The developmental niche theory attempts to describe the micro-environment of the child from the child's point of view in order to understand processes of development and the acquisition of culture (Super and Harkness, 1986; Harkness and Super, 1996).

4 Weist, Myers et al (2000).

5 UNICEF (1997, pvii).

6 UNICEF (1997), Toth (1997), Golovanova (1997), Pelnomocnik rzadu do spraw rodziny (1998b).

7 UNICEF (1997, p. 21), Golinowska et al. (1996).

8 UNICEF (1997).

9 UNICEF (1997, pix).

10 UNICEF (1997), Pelnomocnik rzadu do spraw rodziny (1998a, 1998b).

11 UNICEF (1997, p36), Pelnomocnik rzadu do spraw rodziny (1998b).

12 UNICEF (1997), Golinowska et al. (1996), Pelnomocnik rzadu do spraw rodziny (1998b).

13 Pelnomocnik rzadu do spraw rodziny (1998b).

14 Skarzynska and Poppe (1997) showed clearly that Polish youth in the 1990s-are both less patriotic and less nationalistic than their parents.

15 Osgood, Suci and Tannenbaum (1957).

16 Lynch (1977).

17 Lynch (1977, p. 152).

18 Exploring children's drawings enables us to have some insight into their 'cognitive maps' or images of the physical environment (Eliasz, 1993, pp. 100, 112).

19 Bronowski and Gabrysiak (1999), Meyer and Farell (1998).

20 Lynch (1977, p. 152).

21 Van Hoorn and Komlosi (1995, p. 20).

22 Matthews, Limb and Taylor (1999, p. 136). See also Chawla in this volume, Hart (1997), Miller and Goodnow (1995), Mírch (1998).

23 Carleton (1999, p. 6).

24 Young Poles tend to value as major life goals a 'happy family' and 'close friends' — that is, values pertaining to interpersonal relationships and cooperation. 'Conformity' and 'community' are ranked higher, in general, by young people 13–14 years of age than 17–19 year olds who value self-guidance and achievement more highly. (Skarzynska, 1993, 1995).

25 Annelise Carleton, personal communication.

26 Zylicz (1997).

27 This marginalisation of youth is not limited to Polish cities. See the chapters by Malone and Hasluck and Percy-Smith in this volume.

28 Korczak (1991).

29 Janowski, Musick and Wilson (1998), Youniss, McLellan and Yates (1987).

30 Weist, Albus et al (2000).

31 Joffe and Albee (1988).

32 Miller and Goodnow (1995).

REFERENCES

Bronowski, P and Gabrysiak, J (1999) 'Community-based drug prevention in Poland', *Drugs: Education, Prevention and Policy,* vol 6, pp. 337-342.

Carleton, A (1999) *Voices of Polish Youth: What motivates young people to action for the environment,* unpublished manuscript.

Davis, N (1985) *Heart of Europe: Short history of Poland,* Clarendon Press, Oxford.

Eliasz, A (1993) *Psychologia ekologiczna[Ecological psychology],* Institute of Psychology PAN, Warsaw.

Golinowska, S, Balcerzak-Paradowska, B, Kolaczek, B and Glogosz, D (1996) 'Dzieci w trudnych sytuacjach [Children in difficult circumstances]', *Raport IPISS,* vol 10, pp. 1-87.

Golovanova, N (1997) *The tendencies in the urban childhood's crisis: Researching and overcoming,* paper presented at the Urban Childhood Conference, Trondheim, Norway.

Harkness, S and Super, C (1996) *Cultural Belief Systems: Their origins, expressions, and consequences,* Guilford Press, New York.

Hart, R (1997) *Children's Participation,* UNICEF/Earthscan Publications, London.

Janowski, T, Musick, M, and Wilson, J (1998) 'Being volunteered? The impact of social participation and pro-social attitudes on volunteering', *Sociological Forum,* vol 13, pp. 495-519.

Joffe, J and Albee, G (1988) 'Powerlessness and psychopathology', in Albee,

G , Joffe, J and Dusenbury, L (eds), *Prevention, Powerlessness, and Politics,* Sage Publications, Newbury Park.

Korczak, J (1991) *When I am Little Again and the Child's Right to Respect,* University Press of America, Lanham.

Lynch, K (1977) *Growing Up in Cities,* MIT Press, Cambridge.

Matthews, H, Limb, M and Taylor, M (1999) 'Young people's participation and representation in society', *Geoforum,* vol 30, pp. 135-144.

Meyer, A and Farell, A (1998) 'Social skills training to promote resilience in urban students', *Education and Treatment of Children,* vol 21, pp. 461-479.

Miller, P and Goodnow, J (1995) 'Toward an integration of development and culture', *Items,* vol 49, pp. 2-6.

Mírch, S (1998) 'Social co-operation and practice in youth research', *Polish Psychological Bulletin,* vol 30, pp. 46-67.

Osgood, C, Suci, G and Tannenbaum, P (1957) *The Measurement of Meaning,* University of Illinois Press, Urbana.

Pelnomocnik do Spraw Rodziny (1998a) *Zalozenia polityki prorodzinnej [Principles of family politics],* Warsaw.

Pelnomocnik do Spraw Rodziny (1998b) *Raport o sytuacji polskich rodzin [Report on Polish families circumstances],* Warsaw.

Skarzynska, K (1993) 'Determinants of values accepted by youth', *Polish Psychological Bulletin,* vol 24, pp. 195-207.

Skarzynska, K (1995) 'Mlodziez '90: wartosci i mozliwosci mlodego pokolenia [Youth '90: values and opportunities of the young generation]', *Kolokwia Psychologiczne,* vol 5, pp. 143-153.

Skarzynska, K and Poppe, E (1997) 'Patriotyzm i nacjonalizm a spostrzeganie cech Polakow i innych narodowosci [Patriotism and nationalism in relation to the perception of Poles and other nations]', *Przeglad Psychologiczny,* vol 40, pp. 179-197.

Super, C and Harkness, S (1986) 'The developmental niche: A conceptualization at the interface of child and culture', *International Journal of Behavioral Development,* vol 9, pp. 545-569.

Toth, O (1997) 'Anxiety and lack of perspectives: Hungarian urban chidren', paper presented at the Urban Childhood Conference, Trondheim, Norway.

UNICEF (1997) *Children at Risk in Central and East Europe: Perils and promises,* UNICEF Child Development Centre, Florence.

Van Hoorn, J and Komlosi, A (1995) *Adolescents' constructions of rapid societal change: Hungarian perspective,* poster presented at the VIIth European Conference on Developmental Psychology, Cracow.

Weist, M, Albus, K, Bickham, N, Tashman, N and Perez-Febles, A (2000) 'A questionnaire to measure factors that protect youth against stressors of inner-city life', *Psychiatric Services,* vol 51, pp. 1042-1044.

Weist, M, Myers, C, Danforth, J, McNeil, D, Ollendick, T and Hawkins, R (2000) 'Expanded school mental health services: Assessing needs related to school level and geography', *Community Mental Health Journal,* vol 36 (3), pp. 259-273.

Youniss, J, McLellan, J, and Yates, M (1987) 'What we know about engendering civic identity', *American Behavioral Scientist,* vol 40, pp. 620-631.

Zylicz, P (1997) *The attitudes of Polish youth toward volunteering as a function of gender and social status,* poster presented at the Conference on the Practice of Social Influence in Established and Emerging Democracies', Cracow.

CHAPTER TEN

Toward Better Cities for Children and Youth

Louise Chawla

The results of the eight-nation revival of Growing Up in Cities that have been presented in this book are synthesised and compared with the four-nation study carried out by the project in the 1970s. These results are used as the basis for a set of indicators of the qualities that make communities either good places in which to grow up or frustrating and alienating, according to young people's own perspectives. The experience gained from the project, past and present, is applied to a series of recommendations for urban decision-makers who seek to establish effective programmes for engaging children and youth in improving their own life conditions and in creating more liveable cities for people of all ages.

CITIES AND OTHER HUMAN SETTLEMENTS

The preceding chapters have explored questions related to young people's relationship with their environment. What conditions make some children engaged and happy with the places where they live? Why do others feel marginalised and alienated from their communities? What strategies can unite city governments, non-governmental and community-based organisations, development agencies and educational institutions to create means for young people to invest their energy and hope in their local environment? How can participatory research and planning inform government and organisation policy? Through eight case studies, the preceding chapters have advanced some answers to these questions, and demonstrated opportunities and complexities inherent in taking action with young people to respond to their priorities. This concluding chapter will synthesise

these findings, compare the results of this 1990s version of Growing Up in Cities with Kevin Lynch's original work in the 1970s, and apply this body of experience to some general policy recommendations for creating better communities with children and youth.

The conclusions that follow come out of the specific context of this project: the experience of 10–15 year olds in low or mixed-income urban districts. In a world characterised by high rates of urban poverty, their experience is representative of many. They and others like them are the children who are most dependent on the resources of their immediate environment. With few exceptions, the usual round of their lives includes no trips away on weekends or holidays. Their local environment — what it offers or denies them — is their world. For children like these, the processes of community evaluation and improvement that the preceding chapters have described are particularly important.

At the same time, many of the results and recommendations that follow will be relevant to more privileged or less urban places as well. The second half of this chapter distils recommendations for effective participatory processes with children and youth: the articles of the Convention on the Rights of the Child regarding participation, echoed by similar sections of Agenda 21 and the Habitat Agenda, apply to all children everywhere.

> *Adults may know how to create community environments that promote health and safety, but children and youth are the experts on what fosters or fractures their personal sense of well-being.*

It is likely that many of the GUIC children's indicators of good or bad places in which to grow up extend beyond the project boundaries. The agreement among these young people as to what constitutes engaging or alienating places, across different nations and cultures and across 25 years in time, suggests that the project has uncovered enduring and widely shared needs and values: in the words of Lynch, who was already struck by the consistency with which young people judged their environments in the 1970s, the results suggest 'some human constants in the way children use their world.'[1] Indeed, what participants in Growing Up in Cities have said about significant community resources parallels the broad results of a generation of child-environment research in Western Europe, Canada, the United States and Australia that has included middle-income suburbs and small rural towns.[2] In the 1990s, as in the 1970s, Growing Up in Cities has been unusual in extending this tradition of child-based community evaluation to Eastern Europe and low- and middle-income nations of the South; but it has not been unusual in terms of what its children say.

Although this book's recommendations may apply to a range of human settlements, there are good reasons to give cities special attention. Not only are urban areas the home of more and more of the world's children, but for a number of social, economic and environmental reasons,

they form a particularly viable type of settlement that must be a key part of nations' planning for sustainable development. The high population densities in cities reduce per capita land use and provide economies of scale in improving living conditions and responding to environmental hazards, including lower costs per household for clean piped water, drainage, sewerage, waste collection and disposal, and the provision of electricity, natural gas and communication systems.

Urban densities make for easier access to education, health care, and natural and cultural treasures such as museums, theatres and parks. Although heavy traffic is an unsolved problem in many cities, cities nevertheless offer the best potential for reducing the use of cars and trucks through walking, bicycling and mass transport. They also allow for more efficient recycling and reuse of materials, and for more effective enforcement of environmental regulations. In the economic sphere, they provide families with varied opportunities for employment in both the formal and informal sectors, without excluding possibilities for subsistence urban agriculture.

In the social sector, cities have the best developed 'social economies' in the sense of locally controlled non-profit initiatives, such as community organisations, sports associations and after-school and youth clubs.[3] Several of the Growing Up in Cities sites have demonstrated the importance of these organisations in children's lives. Whereas the diversity of people who come together in cities can be a source of tension, on the whole it fosters cultural vitality and innovation. Not least in children's eyes, urban densities mean that friends and playmates are likely to live nearby. For all of these reasons, if cities are well planned, they can provide many advantages for children and for the attainment of a sustainable future.

In contrast to the reality that more and more of the world's children live in urban areas, and that investment in improving urban conditions is a means to a sustainable future for all children, development policies often continue to follow the pastoral ideal that associates children with nature, combined with the ideal of separate spheres for women and children, far from the dangers and dirt of the central city.[4] Rather than investing in urban life quality, development planning continues to reproduce low-density suburbs around the world, wasteful as they are in their consumption of land, capital and natural resources, and failing to meet many of women's and children's self-perceived needs. This is true of most suburban settlements — from the high-priced villas on the edge of Northampton in the United Kingdom, that Barry Percy-Smith described, to South African promises for the construction of low-cost 'Levittowns in the veld', which form the prototype for Thula Mntwana that Jill Swart-Kruger discussed.[5] In the children's perspectives that follow, readers will discover an alternative vision of how cities can provide homes where young people can meet their immediate needs and, at the same time, where the long-term need for a sustainable society can be served.

YOUNG PEOPLE'S PRIORITIES

Adults may know how to create community environments that promote health and safety, but children and youth are the experts on what fosters or fractures their personal sense of well-being. This level of life quality is ineluctably qualitative. The Human Development Index of the United Nations Development Programme,[6] which factors together life expectancy, level of education and adjusted per capita income, provides a quantitative indicator of physical, cultural and economic preconditions for the full realisation of human capacities; yet people can be physically healthy, well educated, economically privileged, but unhappy and unfulfilled. Growing Up in Cities explores the conditions by which young people themselves judge whether community resources adequately provide for their needs for self-development.

The criteria by which young people evaluate their local environments form important indicators for several reasons. Children's happiness is a good in itself, to be prized in the moment. A further benefit is that through satisfying experiences in the public realm, children have opportunities to grow into new roles and competencies. In the long term, the experiences of childhood form a foundation for the 'habits of the heart' of adulthood, in the sense of people's accustomed relationships to their community, public life and public space.[7]

What were young people's criteria? The answers that follow are based on participants' responses to a cluster of interview questions: How would you describe the area where you live? Where do you most like to be in your area? Are there places where you don't like to go? Are there dangerous places? Are there any places that feel like your own? Are there places where you feel like an outsider? Has the area where you live changed in your memory? Has it gotten better or worse? If you could travel into the future, what do you think this place would be like in 10 years time? If you could make changes in your place, what would they be? Ten years from now, where would you like to live? If most participants at a site described their area in positive terms, identified many nearby places where they liked to go, believed that conditions were changing for the better, or wanted to continue to live where they were, then the local environment was considered to satisfy children's own place priorities. Conversely, if participants described the area in negative terms, identified many disliked or dangerous places, felt that conditions were stagnant or getting worse, and wanted to move away, the local environment was judged to fail children.

Sources of Satisfaction

Among the eight project countries, children showed the greatest satisfaction with their neighbourhood at five sites: Sathyanagar, the self-built settlement on the periphery of Bangalore; Boca-Barracas, the old port district of Buenos Aires; Powisle, the working-class district of Warsaw; and the two locations on the edge of central Trondheim. (Young people were divided about the advantages and disadvantages of Hunsbury, the suburb outside North-ampton, but as this chapter deals essentially with urban quality, it will focus on the urban sites.) Distant as these places are from each other in geography and culture, the children valued them for similar reasons, and these can be summarised. Not all five communities illustrated all of these qualities, but they all gave their young residents reasons to feel generally comfortable and positive about where they lived.

© DAVID DRISKELL

Figure 10.1 Children highly valued places where they felt part of community life–where they could meet friends, feel accepted by adults, and observe or join in interesting activities.

Safety and freedom of movement. In all five locations, children felt generally safe and free to move about. For some children in Sathyanagar, Boca-Barracas and Powisle, this sense of safety and freedom was limited to their own 'turf' in their community, but for others in these places, and for nearly all in Trondheim, freedom to explore extended to neighbouring districts or the nearby downtown. This sense of security does not mean that these areas were free of all risks. In all places there were drunks, occasional fights or crime; and young Poles perceived a trend of increasing crime. Children could learn to avoid troublesome areas, however, so that in most parts of their communities they felt safe and therefore able to move about to find friends and interesting things to do.

Social integration. In all five locations, children described their communities as generally friendly, and felt free to use public and semi-public places. In Sathyanagar and Boca-Barracas, children reported this sense of friendliness in the most positive terms. In Sathyanagar, the unpaved streets, free of cars, served as immediately accessible gathering places. In Boca-Barracas, children reported feeling welcome in local shops and plazas, and a variety of community organisations provided them with special programmes. Observations at both locations showed that these children were treated as valued resources. Although the children of Sathyanagar were expected to be strictly obedient to adults, they were invested with real responsibilities that made them full-fledged actors in their community's social and economic life. In Boca-Barracas, the children's energy, creativity and playfulness appeared to be appreciated and accommodated.

A variety of interesting activity settings. Each location either provided numerous different types of activities, or in the case of Powisle and the Trondheim districts, easy access to downtown offerings. Although life might be routine for these children, they rarely complained about boredom. There were places to meet friends to talk, or play informal games or athletics, places for snacks and doing errands, and there was action to observe in the street or in other public places. It was usually possible to find activities of interest to observe or join.

> *In five locations, children described their communities as generally friendly, and felt free to use public and semi-public places.*

Peer gathering places. Each community allowed children to claim corners and niches of their own where they could play and socialise with friends. In Argentina, by tradition, each segment of society stakes out its own territory in the plazas, and thus there are areas for the old and young, sedate and flirtatious, for men, women, boys, girls and family groups. Within these spaces, some children had their own special meeting place for their own group of friends: 'our corner.' There were other meeting places in stores, coffee shops, sports arenas and community centres. In Sathyanagar, Elgeseter and Mollenberg, children could meet their friends on playing fields or in the streets, in spaces between houses, overgrown lots or undeveloped margins. Although there was a shortage of meeting places in Powisle, children managed to find some hang-out places, such as a playground or 'secret spaces.'

Cohesive community identity. Sathyanagar, La Boca, Powisle and the Mollenberg district of Trondheim had clear physical boundaries that made them distinctive geographical entities. Riven as it was by a major highway, Elgeseter was divided in its identity; but in Elgeseter, as in Møllenberg, children could claim the historic downtown as part of their territory. History and culture also figured importantly in children's sense of Sathyanagar and Boca-Barracas. The children of Sathyanagar knew that their settlement had been built by their parents, and therefore they understood its history as an upward progression. Ninety percent of the residents were Hindu and 85 percent Tamil, so that most of the children shared the same stories, songs and celebrations. They took part in decorating festival shrines, and the girls helped create traditional designs on the ground with coloured powders, called *rangoli*. In Boca-Barracas, the children knew that famous authors, painters and musicians had lived in the brightly painted area called 'La Caminita' and that tourists sought out this neighbourhood. They also knew that the tango had spilled out into the world from the dance halls of La Boca. This artistic heritage lives on in tango dancing by all ages in local plazas and coffee shops, street music and colourful murals. At carnival time, children marched and danced in elaborate displays of the *murga*. Nearly all of the population was Catholic, so that the Church also provided a unifying identity.

Green areas. A feature that was not present at all sites, but that was valued where it was available, was green space for play and discovery. In addition to flat green fields for pick-up games and organised sports, children valued tree-shaded parks or safe overgrown 'wild' areas such as the vegetated lake bed, grove of trees or ditch where boys went swimming at the edge of Sathyanagar. In Trondheim, this type of area was represented by overgrown lots and park edges, and in Powisle and Johannesburg by parks with trees. In Northampton, children sought out the banks of the Nene River and its

flood plain. In the restricted territory of Oak Park, they clustered around the few courtyard trees. As limited as accessible green places were in these city settings, children often used them intensively for play and exploration. At most locations, when children were asked what they would like to change for the better, their recommendations included more trees, parks or gardens. Dangerous areas, however, like the polluted Marybyrnong River in Braybrook, Braybrook's barren flat 'reserves', or the veld surrounding the new Canaansland location, were little used.

The extreme deprivation of the squatter camp children in Canaansland, Johannesburg, threw into relief the three other advantages listed below that children at the other sites appeared to take for granted. In Canaansland, the absence of these resources was painfully felt.

> *Sometimes places were set aside for young people's use, but they were so sterile, featureless or littered that young people avoided them.*

Provision of basic needs. In all of the sites except Canaansland, all or most children enjoyed the basic security of food, water, shelter and access to sanitation. The provision may have been rudimentary, as in the case of the outside water pipes and communal toilets in Sathyanagar, but it was accessible.

Secure tenure. Growing Up in Cities participants came from a variety of housing types: from rented apartments in most cases; from small parent-owned homes in some cases in Australia and Norway; and also from housing cooperatives where squatters had negotiated legal standing in Argentina. In contrast, the children in Canaansland lived in anxiety over whether or not they could keep their homes. Their experience of eviction contrasts with that of the children of Sathyanagar, whose parents also came to the city as homeless migrants who squatted on marginal land, but who succeeded in negotiating secure land tenure and therefore were able to invest in a continuous upgrading of their homes without fear of losing them.

A tradition of community organising and self-help.
Three of the five locations where children expressed
satisfaction with the area in which they lived had a
history of successful community organising. In Boca-
Barracas, a long history of voluntary associations had
culminated in the creation of a network of 45 community
organisations that cooperated to offer social services
and programmes to influence city hall. In Sathyanagar,
the entire community was a testimony to its residents'
initiative and resourcefulness. The Møllenberg district of
Trondheim was distinguished by its residents' successful
resistance to a highway plan in the 1970s — which had
initiated a spiral of cumulative renovations. The absence
of such a tradition in Elgeseter and Powisle gave a negative side to these communities' stories. Residents in
Elgeseter had little voice, squeezed as they were between
the highway and the large powerful institutions of the
hospital and university. In Powisle, the children's disbelief and cynicism about the possibility of participation
or the value of political action reflected the repressive
legacy of Communism.

Sources of Alienation

At half of the Growing Up in Cities sites, participants did
not feel integrated into a community that provided
friendly meeting places and engaging activities. In Northampton, Melbourne, Oakland and Johannesburg, young
people expressed a sense of alienation because they were
feared or distrusted by the adults; because they themselves feared crime, traffic or harassment; or because
their environment offered little to do. Young people in
these locations lived and moved in limited enclaves of
relative security within larger territories that they perceived as hostile, dangerous or boring.

Stigma and social exclusion. In Melbourne and Northampton, media reports about the 'youth problem' tended
to stigmatise all adolescents, but especially those from
low-income families. Criminal convictions of a few youth
put many under suspicion, and especially youth who
gathered to hang out in groups. Whereas this seemingly
aimless gathering to be seen, to talk and socialise had its
accepted place within Buenos Aires plazas, there was no

public place for it in England or Australia. At these sites,
when young people tried to colonise corners for themselves, they reported being repeatedly told to move on
by police or local adults. At the bottom of the hierarchies
of age and class, the children in the Johannesburg squatter camp reported being kicked and spat on for playing
on the sidewalks. As Karen Malone and Barry Percy-
Smith have argued in their chapters on Melbourne and
Northampton, under these conditions young people's
rights to be part of the social, cultural and leisure life of
their community were not only denied to them, but they
were considered troublesome for trying to accommodate
to places that were available, no matter how limited. In
this way the lack of appropriate gathering places for
youth became concealed under the perception of youth
as a problem.

Boredom. Sometimes places were set aside for young
people's use, but they were so sterile, featureless or littered that young people avoided them. The Braybrook
'reserves' are one example, although in terms of the land
area they cover, they more than adequately provide for
recreational open space by quantitative measures of land
use. The small playgrounds that Melbourne and North-

Figure 10.2 Where there were no safe places for socialising and
participating in community life, young people expressed high levels
of alienation.

ampton offered might be stimulating for young children, but they were no substitute for a range of lively, accessible places for older children.

> *Criminal convictions of a few youth put many under suspicion, especially youth who gathered to hang out in groups.*

Fear of harassment and crime. Sometimes young people drew their own lines to keep their local environment at a distance. The most extreme examples were the immigrant children of Oak Park, Oakland, who perceived themselves to be surrounded by an alien and threatening culture where anything might be done to them at any time. As a consequence, their out-of-school environment ended at the boundaries of their housing site. In Melbourne, Northampton and Johannesburg, the children navigated around 'zones of avoidance': for girls, often places where men might harass them; and for all, places associated with drug use or bullying.

Racial tensions. In areas of recent immigration, fear of violent crime, harassment, or bullying was racially defined. In Oakland, the Mexican and Cambodian children feared their African-American neighbours. In Melbourne, African boys sometimes reported being challenged by police or peers on the basis of their racial difference. The native African children of the Johannesburg squatter camp reported being frequently accused of crime by Asian shopkeepers. In these areas, lines drawn by fear or stigmatisation were also lines of race.

Heavy traffic. To some degree, traffic was a problem in all locations except for Sathyanagar with its dirt roads and the new Canaansland camp after eviction. Children faced not only the risk of moving cars, but for street play they had to adapt to the 'space left over after parking.'

Uncollected trash and litter. In Northampton, Melbourne, Johannesburg and Buenos Aires, the children read littered parks and streets and piles of uncollected refuse as ugly and as signs of neglect for their area.

Lack of basic services. When basic services like water, sewerage, waste collection, and park maintenance were missing, young people complained about more than just physical deprivations. In Canaansland, the lack of sewerage, waste collection and adequate clean water put the children of the camp at increased risk of disease, but they did not talk about the problems in these terms. What was of direct consequence to them was the inconvenience and increased burden of work that these deprivations caused, and the indignities of dirt and shame that they suffered as a result.

Sense of political powerlessness. When the children at the eight Growing Up in Cities sites initially learned of the project goals, all doubted that they would ever have a chance to make their ideas for environmental improvements a reality. All were sceptical that adults would ever take their ideas seriously. At some sites, this general sense of being discounted as a young person was intensified by other doubts. The children of Canaansland doubted their abilities to speak well or draw, marked as they were with the stigma of being squatter children. As they saw some of their ideas taken seriously and implemented in visible form, they were gradually able to see themselves as part of the same political system that incorporated others. In Powisle, the children expressed a deep distrust of politics and politicians, echoing sentiments ingrained in their parents' generation during the era of Communist control. In both countries, a history of political repression had left a legacy of self-doubt or doubt about the political system that will have to be overcome before new generations can feel themselves full members of civil society.

GROWING UP IN CITIES NOW AND THEN

One of the special features of Growing Up in Cities in the 1990s is that it can draw historical comparisons with project results in the 1970s. With 25 years separating them, how do these child-based measures of environmental quality compare? Lynch summarised the results of the four 1970s sites under general topics such as *'the image of the locality'* or *'range of action'*, which are not the same as the indicators listed above; however, when his discussion of each topic and excerpts from the national reports are read closely, it is evident that the environmental qualities that were important to children in the 1970s remained significant in the 1990s.

Under the topic of *'unprogrammed space'*, Lynch noted the importance of peer gathering places. As he described these spaces, they were the local streets, courtyards, staircases, sports facilities, city centre attractions, and other hangouts where young adolescents could 'talk and meet and walk about together', 'play informal pick-up games' and 'mess around.'[8] They were the places that children talked about, according to Lynch, 'when asked about what they choose to do, the places they are interested in, how they spend their time, or how they would like to.'[9] In the 1990s, meeting places that young people could claim as their own had lost nothing of their importance. In the past and present studies, some potential meeting places were ruled out because of fear due to 'bad men', robbers and drunks.

> *The environmental qualities that were important to children in the 1970s remained significant in the 1990s.*

Some of the unprogrammed spaces that Lynch described fall under the category of *'green areas':* tree-shaded parks, natural areas and wastelands. Lynch noted that children were sometimes ambivalent about the natural areas within their reach, such as nearby hills and riverbanks, because they considered them dangerous, even as they were drawn to them as territories where they could act independently.

Lynch's topic of *'boredom and engagement'* combines the negative quality of nothing to do with the positive quality of diverse interesting activity settings. Boredom was a salient feature in the 1970s as well as the 1990s. As Karen Malone's chapter on Braybrook has shown, in the 1970s, as in the 1990s, young people described this Melbourne suburb as overwhelmingly boring. Then, as

now, some young Australians had a wide range of movement, but Lynch noted that their environment was so featureless that they were 'exposed to a more restricted variety of people, activity, and place.'[10] At the opposite end, in terms of access to interesting activity settings, the children of Cracow and Powisle, in Poland, were just a short walk away from many things to see and do in their old city centres.

In the 1970s, as in the 1990s, young people in Braybrook associated their location with social stigma. In Lynch's words, 'In Melbourne (Braybrook) people think of themselves as being at the bottom of society', even though in material terms they had more than families at the other three sites. 'If these Australians have hopes for themselves or their children', he noted, 'it is to be somebody else and to get away.'[11] For these young people, their environment embodied social exclusion.

In the past as in the present, heavy traffic restricted children's lives. In the 1970s, children in Powisle already competed with moving traffic and parked cars in order to find outdoor space for play. Children in Toluca, the provincial capital of the state of Mexico, could only meet in parks and playgrounds because traffic had already taken over their streets.

An important determinant of alienation in the 1970s was geographic isolation. Children suffered from feeling far from the centre of things in two high-rise Polish housing projects on the peripheries of Cracow and Warsaw, and in Ecatepec, which was then on the frontier of the metropolitan expansion of Mexico City. In the 1990s, the children of Canaansland found themselves in this predicament after their community was resettled far out in the veld. After resettlement, they feared the surrounding veld, as the children of Ecatepec feared the dried up lake bed that surrounded their *colonia,* which they associated with ditches, dangerous men and piles of trash. More fortunate than the children of Canaansland, the children of Ecatepec could consistently name their school as a favourite place.

In the 1970s, the locations with the most positive community identity were Las Rosas, a well-defined community on the outskirts of the provincial city of Salta in northern Argentina, and Bystra Podhalanska, a Polish village that was included for the purpose of a rural comparison. In both places, children played an important part in local life, believed that their locality was changing for the better and, in most cases, wanted to remain there when they grew up. They drew maps that showed consistent geographical boundaries, illustrated with vividly drawn details. Like the children of Sathyanagar, the children of Bystra contributed many hours of work to the local economy. Similar to Sathyanagar, Boca-Barracas and Møllenberg, children in Las Rosas had witnessed a tradition of self-help: residents progressively added on to their small houses, and at the time of the 1970s study, a neighbourhood association was building a public swimming pool. Just as the children of Sathyanagar participated in religious festivals and rituals, and as the children of Boca-Barracas danced the tango and joined in the annual carnival parade, the children of Las Rosas were an integral part of a ten-day Christmas pageant which drew spectators from all over Salta. Lynch noted that Las Rosas was described by its children as friendly, protected, and fun, and that it had 'the appearance of a hopeful and active community, however meagre its means.'[12] The same words could be applied to the contemporary sites with a robust community life.

As noted before, Lynch was surprised by how similar the criteria were that children used to assess their areas, despite great differences in culture, geography and city form. 'Policy makers are well advised to suspect findings imported from other nations' he cautioned. 'Yet the similarities we find in these disparate cases indicate the possibility of some human constants in the way children use their world.'[13] Twenty-five years later and in even more disparate environments, most of these constants in terms of what children like and dislike about their communities remain substantially unchanged.

A few new concerns appeared in the 1990s, however, and some concerns that were briefly mentioned in the 1970s showed increased importance in the 1990s. Heavy traffic—already a problem in Toluca, Mexico and inner-city Warsaw and Cracow in the 1970s — increasingly dominated Powisle, Warsaw in the 1990s, and was mentioned as a threat by children in Melbourne, Northampton, Trondheim and Johannesburg. Environmental

complaints, that were mentioned occasionally in the 1970s, became more insistent in the 1990s: air pollution from heavy traffic; river pollution; tree cutting; uncollected trash and litter; and lack of sanitation and piped water. In the 1970s, some participants in Braybrook, Melbourne named new ethnic groups as part of the deteriorating conditions that they envisioned for the future. By the 1990s, racial tensions among residents from African, Asian and European backgrounds had become part of the community's reality; and migration and refugeeism were important to the stories of Canaansland, Sathyanagar, Elgeseter, and Oak Park in Oakland. In the 1970s, a few children mentioned a fear of 'bad men'; and then, as now, girls were more likely to be kept close to home or only allowed to travel in groups. In the 1990s, fear of crime and drug use kept the immigrant children of Oak Park restricted to their housing site, and many children in Canaansland, Braybrook and Semilong confined to small areas. In Powisle, several children noted an increase in crime as an unwelcome post-Communist change.

All of these concerns that the children voiced correspond to statistics that show high rates of traffic congestion, pollution, migration, crime and drug use in many cities of the world.[14] Global demographic statistics also show that an increasing proportion of children grow up in single-parent, female-headed households.[15] As a consequence, there is a need for formal and informal community resources to help 'parent' children, as shown in Robin Moore and Nilda Cosco's chapter on Argentina. Finally, political powerlessness was not explored in the 1970s, an era that predated the Convention on the Rights of the Child.

A note is due about television — already an important component of children's use of time in Poland, Australia and Argentina in the 1970s. By the 1990s, television was a feature of children's lives in every Growing Up in Cities setting — including battery-operated sets in some of the shacks in Canaansland, and highly-prized sets in a few Sathyanagar homes that neighbouring children visited for communal viewing. Despite television's temptations, GUIC reports now and then suggest that in the limited discretionary time that children had left after school, homework, chores and television viewing, freedom to get out into their local community remained an important dimension of their lives.

CHILD-BASED INDICATORS OF ENVIRONMENTAL QUALITY

The results of Growing Up in Cities in the 1970s and 1990s, summarised above, form a list of child-generated indicators of a good place in which to grow up: social integration, peer gathering places, a variety of activity settings, safety and freedom of movement, a cohesive cultural identity, and green areas. Background factors that emerged through site comparisons were secure land tenure, a tradition of community self-help and provision for basic needs. Children described the following indicators of an alienating place: stigma and social exclusion, boredom, fear of harassment and crime, racial tensions, a lack of basic services, uncollected trash and litter, too much traffic, geographic isolation, and a sense of political powerlessness.

TABLE 10.1

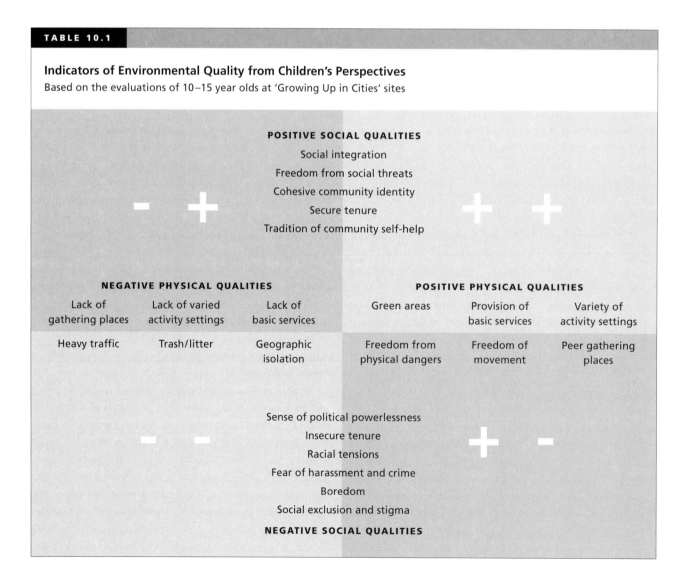

Indicators of Environmental Quality from Children's Perspectives
Based on the evaluations of 10–15 year olds at 'Growing Up in Cities' sites

POSITIVE SOCIAL QUALITIES
Social integration
Freedom from social threats
Cohesive community identity
Secure tenure
Tradition of community self-help

NEGATIVE PHYSICAL QUALITIES			**POSITIVE PHYSICAL QUALITIES**		
Lack of gathering places	Lack of varied activity settings	Lack of basic services	Green areas	Provision of basic services	Variety of activity settings
Heavy traffic	Trash/litter	Geographic isolation	Freedom from physical dangers	Freedom of movement	Peer gathering places

Sense of political powerlessness
Insecure tenure
Racial tensions
Fear of harassment and crime
Boredom
Social exclusion and stigma
NEGATIVE SOCIAL QUALITIES

These indicators describe a *sociophysical* environment. They refer to social perceptions and behaviours that are enacted in physical arenas. In their positive form, they imply places where people of all ages can interact congenially, where groups of friends can gather, where young people feel safe and free to move about, where a community can perform the activities and rituals that define its identity, and where local resources motivate a community to join together for common goals. Carol Werner and Irwin Altman term spaces of this kind 'secondary territories', and argue that they are critical for healthy child development.[16] On the other hand, indicators of alienation assume the absence of such places. In the words of the architect Christian Norberg-Schulz, 'Life takes place.'[17]

If the physical and social qualities of a place are represented as two axes, then the child-based indicators that emerged from Growing Up in Cities in the 1970s and 1990s can be distributed as shown in Table 10.1. As they are lived, places fall in the quadrants between the axes, where social meanings and activities are embodied in the physical resources that places afford or lack. For

---

TABLE 10.1 (continued)

POSITIVE INDICATORS

Social integration: Children feel welcome and valued in their community.

Cohesive community identity: The community has clear geographic boundaries and a positive identity that is expressed through activities like art and festivals.

Tradition of self-help: Residents are building their community through mutual aid organisations and progressive local improvements.

Safety and free movement: Children feel that they can count on adult protection and range safely within their local area.

Peer gathering places: There are safe and accessible places where friends can meet.

Varied activity settings: Children can shop, explore, play sports and follow up other personal interests in the environment.

Safe green spaces: Safe, clean green spaces with trees, whether formal or wild, extensive or small, are highly valued when available.

Provision for basic needs: Basic services are provided such as food, water, electricity, medical care and sanitation.

Security of tenure: Family members have legal rights over the properties they inhabit either through ownership or secure rental agreements.

NEGATIVE INDICATORS

Social exclusion: Children feel unwelcome and harassed in their community.

Stigma: Residents feel stigmatised for living in a place associated with poverty and discrimination.

Violence and crime: Due to community violence and crime, children are afraid to move about outdoors.

Heavy traffic: The streets are taken over by dangerous traffic.

Lack of gathering places: Children lack places where they can safely meet and play with friends.

Lack of varied activity settings: The environment is barren and isolating, with a lack of interesting places to visit and things to do.

Boredom: Children express high levels of boredom and alienation.

Trash and litter: Children read trash and litter in their environment as signs of adult neglect for where they live.

Lack of provision for basic needs: When basic services like clean water and sanitation are lacking, children feel these deprivations keenly.

Insecure tenure: Children, like their parents, suffer anxiety from fear of eviction, which discourages investment in better living conditions.

Political powerlessness: Children and their families feel powerless to improve conditions.

Note: These columns are adapted from Swart-Kruger, 2001

the 10–15 year olds in the Growing Up in Cities project, place identity appears intimately connected with their need to develop a positive self-identity through social integration with their peers and adult society. Considering that these young people are in transition from childhood to adult roles, this is not surprising.

Another way of viewing these child-based indicators is to note that they fall along four dimensions of place identity, whose negative or positive poles define the experiences of place alienation or place attachment: from *exclusion* to *integration, stigma* to *positive status, fear* to *security,* and *boredom* to *engagement.* Each dimension combines social and physical components, as children's personal experiences of integration, status, security and engagement—or their contraries—are acted out through the opportunities and constraints that places afford.

Earlier in this chapter, it was noted that standard quantitative measures of life quality — such as per capita income, level of education, and life expectancy — need to be supplemented by people's own qualitative perceptions of conditions for human development. The challenge is to relate these two levels of measurement. Some of the preceding chapters in this book have placed young people's experience in the larger context of economic and political decision-making in their countries: disinvestment in inner cities in England; business subsidies and national debt repayments at the expense of housing for the lowest income groups in South Africa and Argentina; entry into the free market system in Poland; the priority given to highway construction and institutional expansion over neighbourhood protection in Norway.

The unemployment, piece work, part-time employment or informal employment of many of these children's parents represent the most probable future for the children as well; this economic insecurity can be attributed to a global economic system that favours the free flow of capital, speculative investment, depressed commodity prices, cheap labour and the maximisation of profit for a few over social protection and the creation of adequately payed jobs for the majority.[18] Corruption and patronage are also common elements of this economic system, as are inadequate or unenforced environmental regulations. Almost all children in this study have been affected by

© NILDA COSCO AND ROBIN MOORE

Figure 10.3 The communities that children favoured were rich in social capital from a child's perspective.

one or more of these economic problems in one form or another, and some acutely so. In these cases, economic decisions at the national and international level have translated into risk and hardship on the ground.

Despite these connections, the problem remains that we do not yet have a 'child-centred understanding of poverty', as this book's chapter on Argentina has argued.[19] The results of Growing Up in Cities suggest that, if we did, we would have to give attention to many community characteristics that are altogether absent from standard economic measures. The urban communities where many children spoke positively about where they lived covered a wide economic range: from Møllenberg and Elgeseter in the social welfare state of Norway (which guarantees general material well-being to all its citizens), to Powisle, whose citizens historically had their basic needs met under Communism and which is now part of a currently strong Warsaw economy, to the economically marginal communities of Boca-Barracas, Sathyanagar and, in the 1970s, Las Rosas. The qualities common to all of these places were children's perception of the place as on the whole friendly and secure, where as a consequence they could move about and do things with friends. This unifying characteristic may be described as a fund of social capital from a children's perspective. A number of these communities revealed additional assets in terms of social capital: the children's sense that they had valued roles; an interesting street life; rituals, art and festivals that celebrated community identity; and histories of community organising and self-help. These social advantages, enacted in the streets, shops and public places of the community, appeared to outweigh standard economic indicators. On measures of per capita income, housing quality, material possessions, sanitation and provision of public utilities, health services and education, for example, Sathyanagar and Boca-Barracas ranked below the project sites in Australia, England and the United States: yet the latter sites were places where young people expressed high levels of alienation.

These observations are *not* a justification for disinvestment in housing, infrastructure or other basic needs. As the children of Canaansland have eloquently shown, when children lack provision for basic needs, they suffer doubly: from the lack of shelter or sanitation itself, and from feeling themselves outside their society's circle of care. Children are also not able to see invisible threats to their well-being, such as pollutants in the air or microorganisms in the water that may need to be treated.[20] When deciding on environment and development issues, these observations make a strong case for giving more weight to social capital as it is defined by children and experienced in the places of their daily lives.

In opposition to these results, the dominant economic model since the Second World War defines development as an increasing integration into the industrialised free market, measured by rising levels of disposable income and rising consumption of material goods. The appropriateness of this model for all nations and societies has been challenged on a number of grounds.[21] The results of Growing Up in Cities suggest that it is also inappropriate for children. What children highly valued were a safe, engaging community life in public spaces and organisations, acceptance by adults, and ability to play and socialise with friends in public spaces or in areas of their own. Identifying and preserving these sources of community satisfaction, and learning how to foster them where they are missing, would represent a radically new direction for development policy.[22]

Two final comments are in order related to indicators of development and children's environments. When we consider the worldwide increase in single-parent, female-headed households, as well as households where both parents work outside the home, combined with many parents' low wages and long work hours, community quality for children becomes especially significant. Although family relationships are undeniably important, children in the age group studied by Growing Up in Cities need to interact with a wider network of social support.[23] As this chapter on Boca-Barracas has shown, community organisations and adults can act as surrogate family, providing children with welcoming people and places outside the home. As the chapter on Braybrook has shown, when these friendly surroundings are missing, the result can be long hours spent alone, or limited to hanging out with one or two friends in the confinement of apartments: an impoverishment of social and environmental experience at a time when young adolescents should be moving out into a wider world.

> *Identifying and preserving sources of community satisfaction, and learning how to foster them where they are missing, would represent a radically new direction for development policy.*

Finally, congruence can be observed between the values expressed by the children in Growing Up in Cities and the models of sustainable development that stress a fair provision of basic needs for everyone; beyond this level of general health and welfare for all, there must be a focus on improving the social, cultural and environmental quality of life rather than increasing material consumption. The importance of projects such as Growing Up in Cities is that they suggest children's own perspectives of social, cultural and environmental quality, and therefore the importance of involving children in development of this kind.

EFFECTIVE PARTICIPATION

The results of Growing Up in Cities, past and present, indicate that young people need to be involved in determining how their communities work for them because young people's views on community problems and resources often differ significantly from adults' views. At many of the project sites, government authorities believed that they knew best what young people needed, and therefore they had no reason to consult them. The results of Growing Up in Cities show, however, that authorities often do *not* know best; in the 1990s, as in the 1970s, the project succeeded in exposing 'the misperceptions of planners.'[24]

But how does participation work most effectively? In the 1990s, one of the project's main purposes was to create model participatory processes that could suggest some answers to this question. As the previous chapters show, this was an important phase of the work in Argentina, Australia and South Africa, and to a lesser degree in India and the United States. At the first three sites, the project managed to institutionalise young people's participation in different ways: in Australia, through a middle-school curriculum and the city council's consultation with youth on recreation issues; in Argentina, through a mobile environmental education unit and community-based organisations; in South Africa, through a community development organisation and the eventual inclusion of participatory research in a Child-Friendly Cities initiative. These successes were partial in the sense that no site managed to achieve more than limited government allegiance to the principle of young people's participation. Nonetheless, within the spheres in which project members worked, they have left marks that continue to produce good effects. Each of these models was unique, responding to the particular political, social, economic and environmental constellation of each location, and yet they share some common agreements about what constitutes effective participation and what makes its realisation possible.

In June 1996, the leaders of each Growing Up in Cities site met in Trondheim, Norway, to prepare for project fieldwork. Because one of the goals was to replicate the methods of Lynch's original Growing Up in Cities project, the research agenda was predetermined. On the 'ladder of children's participation' proposed by Roger Hart, Growing Up in Cities would be characterised as 'adult initiated, shared decisions with children' rather than 'child initiated.'[25] There was consensus, however, that after children evaluated their communities, they would determine their own priorities for environmental improvements and, wherever possible, participate in their design and implementation. Although the GUIC project did not originate with child-initiated concerns and methods, it is authentically participatory in that it is based on a respect for children and their views, at whatever level children feel able to contribute, and therefore avoids the 'tokenism', 'decoration' and 'manipulation' that Hart classified as non-participation.

> *The cornerstone of all authentic participatory processes is listening. For the children involved in the GUIC project, being listened to appeared to have a powerful effect.*

Much that passes for participation in government, non-governmental organisations and planning practice, however, falls under tokenism, decoration and manipulation. As project leaders conducted their work, not only had they to contend with city officials who were convinced that they already knew what children needed, they also had to contend with well-intended but misguided officials who believed that they had achieved participation if children sang a song at a ceremony. Other politicians were quick to coopt the GUIC process by having publicity pictures taken with the project children, although they never followed up on anything that the children proposed.

One of the preconditions for effective participation, therefore, is *training* in what true participation involves and different means to achieve it (see Box 10.1). Site directors for Growing Up in Cities undertook this training together at the initial project workshop in 1996. In 1997 and 1998, directors from several project sites led a two-

Major Components of Effective Programmes for Child and Youth Participants

Training in authentic participation and different methods to achieve it

Listening to young people and their families

Systematic research — qualitative as well as quantitative — when the information gathered is intended to inform policy making

Networking to create alliances of people at local, municipal and national levels who will use their influence to see that children's needs are responded to and some of their ideas are implemented

Lobbying to keep children's right to participate a salient political issue.

part workshop in collaboration with the MOST Programme of UNESCO and the Averroes European Training Centre, a Dutch institute for multicultural awareness and education. This workshop series attracted international representatives from UNICEF, city governments, planning offices, universities and non-governmental organisations, and it has become a prototype for similar workshops in other parts of the world. In Buenos Aires, project leaders took the approach of training trainers when they enlisted the staff of the Green Van to spread the Growing Up in Cities model around the city. In South Africa, work is underway to create short certificate courses and postgraduate studies in participatory research and planning with children. Just as there are many models for authentic participation, there are many approaches to training, depending on resources and needs. What all have in common is an effort to communicate principles of effective programmes, including respect for young people's inherent dignity, firm but flexible structures for involving young people's ideas and energies and defining their areas of responsibility, and a commitment to moving forward to realise at least some of these ideas.[26]

The cornerstone of all authentic participatory processes is *listening*. In the case of Growing Up in Cities, this took the form of systematic qualitative *research*. For small projects that involve small groups of people, *listening* — that is, being truly open to what people have to say — can be informally structured. For any project which seeks to influence government policy, this *listening* needs to be carefully and systematically structured: in other words, it requires research. It needs to select representative or strategic sites, involve children who represent a cross-section of the population of interest, and make note of children who are not willing or permitted to participate. It needs to ask questions and follow methods consistently, and it needs to ensure that all children involved have a chance to speak and to have their responses count equally. It needs to involve a number of people in the analysis — ideally including some children — in order to ensure that the analysis will be reproducible. These basic research guidelines have been summarised in *Children in Focus: A Manual for Participatory Research with Children* and *Creating Better Cities with Children and Youth*.[27]

In seeking funding for the Growing Up in Cities sites, project leaders faced a common reaction among aid agencies, foundations and government offices that they do not 'waste money' on research. In many cases, research has earned this reputation when it has consisted of surveys and close-ended questions that press respondents into predetermined categories in order to generate reports that are an end in themselves. Research of this kind, however, is fundamentally different from the open-ended participatory action-research that Growing Up in Cities involves. To reject research categorically leaves unsettling questions. Do aid agencies, foundations and government offices prefer to disburse funds without information about where these funds are most needed or how effectively they are used? If organisations collect information, do they prefer to do so unsystematically? Although the reaction that 'we don't do research' invites these questions, it remains a common position.

For the children involved in the GUIC project, being listened to appeared to have a powerful effect. The South African chapter described how the children of Canaansland moved from initial shame over what they assumed to be the inadequacy of their words, drawings and ideas

— having internalised a sense of inferiority as squatter children — to increased self-assurance after they learned that they and their ideas would be treated with respect. Similarly the children in Braybrook moved from an apathetic conviction that they and their views were unimportant, to enthusiastic creativity when they had a chance to contribute to transforming their environment for the better. Although participation may serve extrinsic purposes in terms of concrete community improvements and more child-sensitive policies, it also appears to foster an intrinsic sense of self-esteem and self-efficacy that is a basic preparation for citizenship. A new project-related direction for work is to document the transformations in children who are involved in environmental projects such as Growing Up in Cities.[28]

If there is one cardinal rule that characterised the work of project leaders who sought to move Growing Up in Cities from its research to action phase, it is *'Network, network, network.'* If any ideas of young people are

> *Participation may serve extrinsic purposes in terms of concrete community improvements and more child-sensitive policies, but it also appears to foster an intrinsic sense of self-esteem and self-efficacy that is a basic preparation for citizenship.*

realised, it is because adults with authority, influence and resources see the importance of their contributions. These people need to be identified, and whenever practical, put in touch with each other through more or less formal networks committed to children's rights and participation. In Jill Swart-Kruger's words, they are people in power who 'talk straight' about children's rights to participation, rather than just voicing rhetoric without action. The observation of Lyn Campbell, the children's representative in the city government of Christchurch, New Zealand, and advisor to Growing Up in Cities–South Africa, suggests how time consuming and difficult the task of finding these people may be. In her words, 'You

bang your head on all the doors until you find the ones that open.'[29] These people can be at the local, city, or national level — or at all three — depending on the scope of the project goals and the politics of the area. Often overlooked because of its 'humble' level, but often invaluable to individual children, this networking includes encouraging strong members of the community to look out for the most vulnerable, alerting them to children's needs and getting them to talk with each other and provide support for the weakest families.

As the South African chapter showed, the priorities that emerge from a final community action plan involving young people and their families can typically be divided into three categories: changes that the community can do for itself; changes that the government can and should do; and changes that require external funding. To get government action and external funds, a further ingredient of effective participation is *lobbying*. Even the best disposed politicians, city government officials and foundation managers have many constituencies and interests competing for their attention. Therefore project leaders need to combine the ability to establish a rapport with children and low-income families, research and training skills, political and fund-raising acumen, and a knowledge of how to use the media — or they need to be able to put together a project team that combines these skills. Many politicians will find it tempting to appear in newspaper or television reports that show them on the side of appealing children who want to improve their neighbourhood. Once promises have been made, it often takes dogged work to get government officials to live up to their promises. At this point, a network of supporters who can challenge officials is crucial.

These observations should make two things clear. One is that it takes special people to make successful community development with children possible: people who are not only sensitive and committed to children, but who also know how to implement the right strategy and assemble, fund and motivate this political process.[30] A second observation is that if children are to participate in significant environmental change, the process requires strong adult commitment and facilitation. Children's participation is really about a partnership between children

© MELINDA SWIFT

Figure 10.4 Truly listening to children and valuing their ideas is a fundamental principle of authentic participation. Here children in Johannesburg prepare to share their evaluation of their squatter camp at a workshop in the mayor's office.

and adults. Horelli, analysing three case studies of children's involvement in urban planning in Finland, Switzerland and France, also emphasises this point.[31]

The movement for children's rights is often compared to the movement for women's rights, but there is a critical difference. Women have a maturity and actual or latent political power that children lack. As they become empowered, they can run for office and other positions of influence and elect politicians who will be responsive to their needs. Children cannot. Children lack physical, economic and political power. Although they may learn, through adult-initiated examples of participation, how to move to child-initiated projects, when the time comes to implement their ideas they will still need adults who will stand beside them and ensure that they are treated with respect. For large achievements, they need support

from governmental and non-governmental organisations. The movement for children's rights, including children's participation, requires a partnership of influential adults working with children, their families and their communities, with ongoing support and facilitation.

A final point that cannot be overemphasised is that the process described here benefits not only children but also their communities. As the opening chapter of this book noted, community participation has been an accepted principle of development theory since the 1970s, and its implementation is increasing once again. In the United Nations *Human Development Report 1997* on the eradication of poverty, the first priority for action is that, 'Everywhere the starting point is to empower women and men and to ensure their participation in decisions that affect their lives and enable them to build their strengths and assets.'[32] A review of seven successful programmes for urban poverty reduction found that each programme included increased participation and options for decision making by community members.[33] What projects like Growing Up in Cities seek to do is to keep alive the principle of the Convention on the Rights of the Child that children, too, have the right to a voice in decisions that affect their lives.

POLICIES AND PRACTICES TO FACILITATE PARTICIPATION

Barriers and Opportunities

During the 1997 and 1998 UNESCO/Averroes workshops mentioned above, participants were asked what kind of statements they anticipated from people who would object to young people's involvement in community development. They were quick to list them: 'It is too difficult and time consuming.' 'Children are unreliable and unstable in their ideas.' 'Children make mistakes.' 'They can't foresee long-term consequences.' 'They have no technical background.' 'Adults will build up false expectations because children can't understand practical constraints.' 'Adults were children once, so they know what children need.'[34]

To these challenges could be added many common barriers on the side of city governments, development agencies and universities: a lack of understanding about what effective participation means; distant, misguided and sometimes corrupt bureaucracies; pressure to disburse funds on expensive capital construction rather than on facilitating many small grassroots efforts; pressure to keep development agency staff numbers low although successful grassroots efforts require skilled monitors and mentors; prejudice against research, and especially action research; academic traditions that hinder interdisciplinary and community-based research; and systems that evaluate success in terms of products rather than process, and through solely quantitative indicators rather than a combination of qualitative and quantitative measures. On the side of communities, there is often a distrust of politicians and agency representatives

---

BOX 10.2

Recommendations to Increase Children's Participation

Invest in people who can facilitate children's participation through training, lobbying, networking and supportive work with children and their families.

Institutionalise children's inclusion through a variety of measures that make children's involvement in decisions that affect their lives part of practice as usual.

Use qualitative as well as quantitative indicators of children's well-being.

Recognise action research as a significant contribution to agency planning and academic prestige.

Build on community strengths by making loans, grants and other forms of support available for grassroots initiatives that capitalise on people's energies, resources and goals.

Strengthen city and local authority and budgets to respond to community initiatives and needs.

Create community-based curricula for school and out-of-school programmes that involve young people in studying and improving their local environment and life conditions.

---

and a learned passivity.[35] Not least, participation is about real power sharing: between adults and children; between the sexes; between majority and minority groups; between the privileged and the underprivileged; between politicians and their constituencies; and between central office staff and field workers. People who have power usually don't want to share it.

Nevertheless, there are contemporary forces that favour children's participation, that have enabled Growing Up in Cities to go further with its goals in the 1990s than it could in the 1970s. Most important, there is the Convention on the Rights of the Child, which has made the principle of children's right to a voice in decisions that affect their lives an element of international law, and which has dictated the inclusion of this principle, often with specific reference to environmental decision-making, in numerous other agreements: from the international level of Agenda 21 and the Habitat Agenda, to the regional level of the African Charter on the Rights and Welfare of the Child, to the level of Local Agenda 21s and inclusive models of municipal budgeting.[36] Concurrently, there is the spreading democratisation of societies and, with it, a recognition that children need to learn active roles in civil society. There is concern over growing disparities between rich and poor, and the impoverishment and exclusion of a growing number of people; at the same time, there is growing evidence that broad-based participation is an essential ingredient of effective models to achieve social equity. Slowly, there is an acknowledgement on the part of development agencies and social welfare organisations that these models require a decentralisation of control so that decision-making and funding allocations can respond to grassroots initiatives. All of these trends are partial and imperfect, but together they lend weight to the inclusion of children in community-based efforts to evaluate and improve local environments.

Recommendations to Increase Children's Participation

Where Growing Up in Cities has succeeded in moving from an evaluation of young people's experience of problems and resources in their local environment to the implementation of participants' suggestions for improving local conditions, it has represented a broad alliance of people and organisations that included, in different locations: municipal officials, city agency staff, officials on the regional or national level with responsibility for urban planning or child welfare, development agencies, non-governmental organisations with an interest in children, community-based organisations, schools, universities and, not least, parents and other community members. These broad-based networks are essential for two reasons: to make action on the local level possible, and to use local experience to inform more child-sensitive policy on the city-wide, regional or national level. Drawing on the project's experience, it is possible to make recommendations to strengthen the dialogue between policy and practice that is vital to improving children's life quality (see Box 10.2).

Invest in people who can facilitate children's participation. As this chapter has noted, children's participation depends on committed adult support. If cities and development agencies want children's participation to happen, they need to support people who can provide the facilitation, networking, lobbying and training that successful participation requires. This recommendation runs counter to conventional policies of development planning, which have historically concentrated on large capital constructions such as highways and airports, and which have historically been measured by their efficiency in terms of low staff ratios for the number of dollars spent. A serious intention to reduce poverty and include children and youth in development planning requires the alternative strategy of training and supporting people who can catalyse and facilitate community planning processes, which then tend to involve modest material costs for construction, or which may lead to projects where communities achieve full cost recovery.[37] People-centred and child-centred development requires a shift from a primary investment in capital construction and *products* to a primary investment in *people* and *process*. Development offices will not only require new funding formulas, but new ways of monitoring the quality of work of this kind.

> *Broad-based networks are essential for two reasons: to make action on the local level possible, and to use local experience to inform more child-sensitive policy on the city-wide, regional or national level.*

It should be noted that people who can lead participatory processes come from many backgrounds. In the examples in this book, they have come from universities, non-governmental organisations, private offices of planning and design, city government offices and community organisations. They have been distinguished by their commitment, their ability to establish strong rapports with low income children and their families, and their ability to motivate others through strategic training, networking and lobbying. To encourage children's inclusion in community development, it is necessary to support people of this kind who can mediate between communities and policy makers.

Institutionalise children's inclusion. Growing Up in Cities has consisted of site by site efforts to create model projects that can dramatise the benefits of including children in community evaluation and development. The ultimate goal, however, is for processes of this kind to become 'practice as usual' in order to integrate children's perspectives into planning and policy. To this end, several mechanisms have been recommended to ensure that children are taken into account: a representative for children at the metropolitan level and in smaller municipal divisions, with input into decisions that affect children indirectly as well as directly, including budget decisions; the creation of children's councils and other organisations with advisory powers and real powers of review over decisions that impact children's lives; the creation of curricula that involve children in the study and improvement of their local environment, in both formal and non-formal programmes of education; and the creation of certificate courses in children's rights and participation.

> *Growing Up in Cities demonstrates that a study of their own local environment and lives can motivate young people to enthusiastically practice skills of writing, speaking, reading, drawing, measuring, design and calculation through an approach that makes learning more relevant and applied.*

Use qualitative as well as quantitative standards and indicators. Since the United Nations Conference on Environment and Development in 1992, there have been various initiatives by governments to determine environmental standards for development and regulation through processes that include citizen participation.[38]

There is also a growing recognition that the definition of development goals needs to include the voices of the poor who are most dependent on the resources of their immediate environment.[39] Yet the problem that Kevin Lynch noted many years before remains, namely that standards and goals usually focus on quantifiable things, and 'the very precision and concreteness of these successful standards tend to devalue other aspects of the environment.'[40] Therefore it is important to combine quantitative and qualitative measures.[41] Growing Up in Cities presents methods for deriving measures of urban quality from children, always one of society's most vulnerable groups.

Recognise action research as a significant contribution to agency planning and academic prestige. One difficulty that Growing Up in Cities had to negotiate is that many development agencies and non-governmental agencies dismiss community-based research as irrelevant, while many universities dismiss applied participatory research as insignificant. The result is that development decisions are usually made without the systematic inclusion of community members' perspectives and ideas, and researchers who could do work of this kind often go unfunded, or work without incentives from their universities in the form of recognition and promotions. Where this circle of disinvestment and disincentive is broken, as this book's chapters on Argentina, Australia, and South Africa demonstrate, universities can make an important contribution to community revitalisation. This contribution can be institutionalised with formal alliances among universities, government offices and community organisations through which universities assist communities in gathering information that can be used to formulate better government policies.

Build on community strengths. The processes that Growing Up in Cities promotes can be seen as a strategy to improve community quality and stability by giving children and their families reasons to believe that they can better their lives. This strategy involves meeting communities halfway by capitalising on existing energies, resources and goals, and by making funds available as they are needed for grassroots initiatives, thus strengthening community members' sense of control over their lives. Processes like this can be used proactively in order to prevent children and their families from falling into homelessness and other extreme circumstances.

Strengthen city and community-level authority and budgets. As noted at the beginning of this chapter, cities offer many potential advantages in terms of economies of scale, density of settlement, access to services, resources and social capital in the form of human creativity and cultural diversity. Therefore the creation of well-managed cities that promote health and social development without excessive levels of natural resource consumption must be a central strategy of sustainable development that seeks to balance social and environmental needs. Many city governments, however, lack the necessary authority and funds to carry out these responsibilities. Yet metropolitan governments are much more accessible to community groups, including groups of children, than are distant officials in national capitals. Therefore support for participatory community development must include support for government at the levels closest to citizens.[42]

Create community-based school and after-school curricula. Growing Up in Cities demonstrates that a study of their own local environment and lives can motivate young people to enthusiastically practice skills of writing, speaking, reading, drawing, measuring, design and calculation through an approach that makes learning more relevant and applied. Rather than seeing projects like Growing Up in Cities as an expensive activity for children in addition to their outside of school and after-school programmes, the examples of Growing Up in Cities in Australia and Argentina demonstrate how these projects can strengthen institutions by introducing new methods and ideas and by creating alliances among teachers, youth workers and resource people within government, universities, non-governmental organisations and private planning and design agencies.

FRUIT OF AN OLD MAN'S REASON AND A CHILD'S SEASON

Since its revival in 1994, Growing Up in Cities has expanded into new areas of the world and new forms of practice. No matter how it may be extended or adapted to new circumstances, it remains a legacy of Kevin Lynch. As such, it is the legacy of a passionate urbanist and humanist. Lynch's writings reveal his never tiring fascination in observing how cities function for all the people who live there. He understood that the history of cities — as well as the history of the word 'city' itself — lies close to the heart of the meaning of civilisation. Behind the words 'city' and 'civilisation' lies the Latin *civis,* or citizen. Other derivations from this root are 'civil' and 'civic.' For Lynch, one of the great measures of a civilisation is the quality of the experiences that its cities afford its citizens. In opposition to attempts to evaluate cities primarily in terms of generation and circulation of capital, or efficiency in service delivery, or aesthetic form, Lynch maintained that cities are first and foremost places where people live and work, and that they are to be evaluated primarily on the quality of their citizens' lives.

The introductory chapter of this book noted that while he was composing *Growing Up in Cities,* Lynch wrote a foreword to the book *Environmental Knowing* that opens with a question that motivated much of his work. He sought to understand not only how cities function, but how they can best function for people. 'What interchange between people and their environment', he wrote, 'encourages them to grow into fully realized persons?'[43] Throughout the course of his career, he refined his explanation of what this person-environment relationship at its best involves. Growing Up in Cities can be understood to be Lynch's exploration of the meaning of this relationship in childhood and early adolescence.

Near the end of his life, Lynch condensed this career-long labour into five 'performance dimensions' of good city form.[44] A city at its best, he stated, promotes *vitality* in terms of physical health for individuals and society (a criterion which implies that cities must be managed in ways that protect the regional and global ecosystems on which human health depends). It embodies *sense,* in terms of a clear physical identity in harmony with people's sensory and mental capabilities and cultural beliefs. It offers *fit,* in terms of adequate and adaptable behaviour settings where people can play many roles. It gives *access,* in terms of convenience in reaching activities, resources, services, information and other people and places. It allows *control,* in terms of giving those who live and work in urban places power to create, repair, modify and manage them. A good city provides all of these dimensions with efficiency and justice. A fully-realised human life, it follows, would reflect these dimensions of place experience.

These five dimensions of good city form can be taken as general categories for indicators of how well cities function for their citizens. All of the qualitative child-based indicators that have been summarised in this chapter can be divided among them. Some standard quantitative indicators, such as infant mortality rates or average years of education, fit under categories such as vitality or access. What cannot fit are quantitative indicators of economic growth, such as average per capita income or gross domestic product, that fail to include justice in distribution or to take into account that economic gains for some may involve losses in local control or human and ecosystem health for others.

Growing Up in Cities presumes a conceptualisation of development that is based on interdependent well-being for individuals, communities and environments, rather than short-term measures of economic growth. Not only are the project children's priorities for their communities consonant with Lynch's five dimensions of good city form, but they are in harmony with a model of sustainable development that combines social justice with environmental protection. Beyond the provision of basic needs, the children have emphasised social and environmental goods rather than increasing material consumption. They have sought social integration in friendly communities, a sense of belonging to a cohesive community with a proud tradition of cultural expression and co-operative improvement, secure residences, places to meet friends, engaging things to do in safe streets and public places, freedom from crime, and freedom of movement. When green areas that could be put to playful uses were available, these were valued too. When the children were given chances to help design and shape their environment, they responded with enthusiasm. From qualities such as these, sustainable human settlements can be made.

As a record of processes for including children and youth in evaluating the places where they live, this book does not seek to present the last word on young people's experiences and ideas. Although Growing Up in Cities may have uncovered a general consistency in young people's likes and dislikes at the eight-nation sites described in this book and at the four-nation sites in the 1970s, as important as any indicator that emerged is the young people's participation in their articulation. The indicators summarised in this chapter may provide general guidelines for creating child-friendly environments, but in each community these guidelines need to be defined in terms of local resources, barriers and opportunities. Furthermore, local networks that involve both children and adults must be formed to create places to which inhabitants can commit themselves in a spirit of identification, care and love. This book seeks to be an invitation to this ongoing dialogue that constitutes one form of interchange among people (and between people and their environment) through which cities and citizens can move toward the realisation of their best potentials.

ENDNOTES

1. Lynch (1977, p. 12).
2. Medrich et al (1982), Chawla (1992, 1994a,1994b), Eubanks Owens (1988), Gosset (1996), Hart (1979), Homel and Burns (1985), Horelli (1998), Moore (1980, 1986), O'Brien et al (2000), Schiavo (1988), Van Vliet (1981), Wooley et al. (1999).
3. Roseland (1997), UNCHS (1996, Chapt. 13).
4. Chawla (1994c), Hayden (1984), Noschis (1992, 1995).
5. For strategies of the alternative 'smart growth' movement that favors the densification of city and town cores as an alternative to suburban and exurban sprawl, see Stoel, Jr. (1999).
6. UNDP (1998).
7. Bellah et al (1985).
8. Lynch (1977, p. 13).
9. Ibid, p. 15.
10. Ibid, p. 23.
11. Ibid, p. 11.
12. Ibid, p. 30.
13. Ibid, p. 12.

14 UNCHS (1996).

15 Bruce, Lloyd and Leonard (1995).

16 Werner and Altman (1998).

17 Norberg-Schulz (1980, p. 6).

18 Brecher and Costello (1998), Korten (1995).

19 McKendrick (1998).

20 Satterthwaite et al (1996).

21 Ackerman et al (1977), Daly and Cobb, Jr (1994), UNDP (1999).

22 See also Bartlett (1999, 2001), Morrow (1999, 2001).

23 Swart-Kruger (1994).

24 Lynch (1977, p. 1).

25 Hart (1997).

26 For a description of strategies for creating programmes that correspond with these principles, see the project's manual, *Creating Better Cities with Children and Youth* (Driskell 2001).

27 Boyden and Ennew (1997), Driskell (2001).

28 First steps in this direction have been an assessment of project sites in South Africa (Griesel, Swart-Kruger and Chawla, in press), an article by Chawla and Heft (2002) and a symposium on 'Children's Participation in Community Settings' in Oslo in June 2000, which formed the basis for *PLA Notes* (Number 42, October 2001).

29 Lyn Campbell, in a comment during a workshop on 'Participatory practices for involving children in urban planning', Urban Childhood Conference, Trondheim, Norway, 12 June 1997.

30 Malone (1999), Stoecker (1999).

31 Horelli (1998).

32 UNDP (1997, p. 6).

33 Anzorena et al (1998).

34 Driskell, unpublished report on a workshop on 'Creating better cities with children and youth', Soesterberg, The Netherlands, July 1998.

35 Bartlett et al (1999).

36 Abers (1998), Lafferty and Eckerberg (1998).

37 Anzorena et al (1998).

38 Abbott (1996), Renn, Webler and Weidemann (1995).

39 Chambers (1997), World Bank (2000).

40 Lynch, undated proposal for 'A study of environmental quality in areas of new growth', M.I.T. Archives, Kevin Lynch Collection, Box 14, Folder 51.

41 Marsella, Levi and Ekblad (1997).

42 Bartlett et al (1999).

43 Lynch in Golledge and Moore (1976, pv).

44 Lynch (1981).

REFERENCES

Abers, R (1998) 'Learning democratic practices" in Douglass, M and Friedmann, J (eds) *Cities for Citizens,* John Wiley, Chichester, pp. 39-65.

Abbott, John (1996) *Sharing the City,* Earthscan Publications, London.

Ackerman, F, Kiron, D, Goodwin, N. Harris, J and Gallagher, K (eds) (1997) *Human Well-being and Economic Goals,* Island Press, Covelo, CA.

Anzorena, J, Bolnick, J, Boonyabancha, S, Cabannes, Y, Hardoy, A, Hasan, A, Levy, C, Mitlin, D, Murphy, D, Patel, S, Saborido, M, Satterthwaite, D and Stein, A (1998) 'Reducing urban poverty', *Environment and Urbanization,* vol 10 (1), pp. 167-186.

Bartlett, S (1999) 'Children's experience of the physical environment in poor urban settlements and the implications for policy, planning and practice', *Environment and Urbanization,* vol 11 (2), pp. 63-73.

Bartlett, S (2001) 'Children and development assistance', *Development in Practice,* vol 11 (1), pp. 62-72.

Bartlett, S, de la Barra, X, Hart, R, Missair, A and Satterthwaite, D (1999) *Cities for Children,* Earthscan, London.

Bellah, R, Madsen, R, Sullivan, W, Swidler, A and Tipton, S. (1985) *Habits of the Heart,* University of California Press, Berkeley.

Boyden, J and Ennew, J (1997) *Children in Focus: A Manual for Participatory Research with Children,* Radda Barnen, Stockholm.

Brecher, J and Costello, T (1998) *Global Village or Global Pillage,* 2nd ed, South End Press, Cambridge, MA.

Bruce, J, Lloyd, C and Leonard, A (1995) *Families in Focus,* The Population Council, New York.

Chambers, R (1997) *Whose Reality Counts?,* Intermediate Technology Publications, London.

Chawla, L (1992) 'Childhood place attachments' in Altman, I and Low, S (eds) *Place Attachment,* Plenum Press, New York, pp. 63-86.

Chawla, L (1994a) 'Childhood's changing terrain', *Childhood,* vol 4, pp. 221-233.

Chawla, L (1994b) 'All over town', *Small Town,* vol 25 (2), pp. 4-15.

Chawla, L (1994c) *In the First Country of Places: Nature, Poetry, and Childhood Memory,* State University of New York Press, Albany.

Chawla, L and Heft, H (forthcoming in 2002) 'Children's competence and the ecology of communities', *Journal of Environmental Psychology,* January.

Daly, H and Cobb Jr, J (1994) *For the Common Good,* 2nd ed, Beacon Press, Boston.

Driskell, D (2001) *Creating Better Cities with Children and Youth,* UNESCO Publishing/Earthscan, Paris/London.

Eubanks Owens, P (1988) 'Natural landscapes, gathering places, and prospect refuges', *Children's Environments Quarterly,* vol 5 (2), pp. 17-24.

Gosset, C (1996) 'Perceptions of environmental health by children in cities' in Price, C and Tsouros, A (eds) *Our Cities, Our Future,* WHO Healthy Cities Project Office, Copenhagen, pp. 178-185.

Griesel, D, Swart-Kruger, J and Chawla, L (in press) 'Children in South Africa can make a difference: An assessment of Growing Up in Cities in Johannesburg', *Childhood,* vol 9.

Hart, R (1979) *Children's Experience of Place,* Irvington Publishers, New York.

Hart, R (1997) *Children's Participation,* Earthscan, London.

Hayden, D (1984) *Redesigning the American Dream,* W W Norton, New York.

Homel, R and Burns, A (1985) 'Through a child's eyes' in Burnley, I and Forrest, J (eds) *Living in Cities,* Allen and Unwin, London, pp. 103-115.

Horelli, L (1998) 'Creating child-friendly environments', *Childhood,* vol 5 (2), pp. 225-239.

Korten, D (1995) *When Corporations Rule the World,* Kumarian Press, West Hartford.

Lafferty, W M and Eckerberg, K (eds) (1998) *From the Earth Summit to Local Agenda 21,* Earthscan Publications, London.

Lynch, K (1976) 'Foreword' in Moore, G. and Golledge, R (eds) *Environmental Knowing,* Dowden, Hutchinson and Ross, Stroudsburg, PA, pp. v-viii.

Lynch, K (1977) *Growing Up in Cities,* MIT Press, Cambridge, MA.

Lynch, K (1981) *A Theory of Good City Form,* MIT Press, Cambridge, MA.

Marsella, A, Levi, L and Ekblad, S (1997) 'The importance of quality-of-life indices in international social and economic development activities', *Applied and Preventive Psychology,* vol 6, pp. 55-67.

McKendrick, J (1998) 'Families and family environments in Manchester', *Transactions of the Manchester Statistical Society,* vol 1995-1997, pp. 1-25.

Medrich, E, Roizen, J, Rubin, V and Buckley, S (1982) *The Serious Business of Growing Up,* University of California Press, Berkeley.

Moore, R (1980) 'Collaborating with young people to assess their landscape values', *Ekistics,* vol 281, pp. 128-135.

Moore, R (1986) *Childhood's Domain,* Croom Helm, London.

Morrow, V (1999) 'Conceptualising social capital in relation to the well-being of children and young people', *The Sociological Review,* vol 47 (4), pp. 744-765.

Morrow, V (2001) *Networks and Neighbourhoods,* Health Development Agency, London.

Norberg-Schulz, C (1980) *Genius Loci,* Academy Editions, London.

Noschis, K (1992) 'The inner child and the city', *Architecture and Behaviour,* vol 8 (1), pp. 49-58.

Noschis, K (1995) 'The urban child' in Noschis, K (ed) *Children and the City,* Comportements, Lausanne, pp. 9-16.

O'Brien, M, Jones, D, Rustin, M and Sloan, D (2000) 'Children's independent spatial mobility I the urban public realm', *Childhood,* vol 7(3), pp. 257-277.

Renn, O, Webler, T and Weidemann, P (1995) *Fairness and Competence in Citizen Participation,* Kluwer Academic, Dordrecht.

Roseland, M (1997) *Eco-city Dimensions,* New Society Publishers, Gabriola Island, BC.

Satterthwaite, D, Hart, R, Levy, C, Mitlin, D, Ross, D, Smit, J and Stephens, C (1996) *The Environment for Children,* Earthscan Publications, London.

Schiavo, R (1988) 'Age differences in assessment and use of a suburban neighborhood among children and adolescents', *Children's Environments Quarterly,* vol 5 (2), pp. 4-9.

Stoecker, R (1999) 'Are academics irrelevant?—Roles for scholars in participatory research', *American Behavioral Scientist,* vol 42 (5), pp. 840-854.

Stoel, Jr, T (1999) 'Reining in urban sprawl', *Environment,* vol 41 (4), pp. 6-11, 29-33.

Swart-Kruger, J (1994) 'Black latchkey children in South African households' in Sono, T (ed) *African Family and Marriage Under Stress,* Centre for Development Analysis, Pretoria, pp. 135-157.

Swart-Kruger, J (2001) *'We Know Something Someone Doesn't Know...': Children speak out on local conditions,* unpublished report for the City Council of Johannesburg.

UNCHS (United Nations Centre for Human Settlements) (1996) *An Urbanizing World,* Oxford University Press, Oxford.

UNDP (United Nations Development Programme) (1997) *Human Development Report 1997,* Oxford University Press, Oxford.

UNDP (1998) *Human Development Report 1998,* Oxford University Press, Oxford.

UNDP (1999) *Human Development Report 1999,* Oxford University Press, Oxford.

van Vliet, W (1981) 'Neighborhood evaluations by city and suburban children', *American Planning Association Journal,* vol 47 (4), pp. 458-466.

Werner, C and Altman, I (1998) 'A dialectical/transactional framework of social relations' in Gorlitz, D, Harloff, H, Mey, G and Valsiner, J (eds) *Children, Cities, and Psychological Theories,* de Gruyter, Berlin, pp. 123-154.

Woolley, H, Spencer, C, Dunn, J and Rowley, G (1999) 'The child as citizen', *Journal of Urban Design,* vol 4 (3), pp. 255-282.

World Bank (2000) *Poverty Reduction Strategy Sourcebook,* World Bank, Washington, DC.

Research Guidelines

This appendix is an inventory of the main research methods followed at the eight country sites presented in this book. Some of the methods — in particular, the interviews and photographic documentation — were done at all sites; others at a few. For a detailed description of the Growing Up in Cities methods on which the book is based, see the project manual *Creating Better Cities with Children and Youth* by David Driskell (UNESCO Publishing/Earthscan, 2001). Another good reference is still the chapter on 'Original and Revised Guidelines' in *Growing Up in Cities,* edited by Kevin Lynch (MIT Press, 1977).

Observation

Informal observations: One of the most effective research methods is 'hanging out' in the community, noting where children are present, what they are doing, what the quality of housing is and how community life is organized in different places. Talk with community members in the process, and use this opportunity to introduce yourself and the project. This general familiarity with how the community works becomes a basis for determining where more formal observations and mapping will be useful, as well as identifying community leaders who may be helpful in moving the project forward.

Formal observations: After identifying key community places that are important in children's lives, observe them more carefully. Behavioural mapping, described below, is a useful way to do this systematically.

Mapping and Other Documentation

Maps of the study area: Collect existing maps, such as outline base maps and aerial photographs. They can be used as points of reference on which to relate children's range of movement, problem sites and resources, as well as points of discussion with children and community groups. If no maps exist, have 'space specialists' — such as members of a nearby geography, architecture or urban planning department — prepare a base map.

Behavioural maps: After you have identified key community places used by children and youth, prepare a base map of each selected place, and record on it the number of people present at different locations (by age group, sex and any other important categories at your site) and the activities that they are engaged in. Do this for different times of day or days of the week that show significant variation. If people are willing, talk with them about what they are doing and what the place means to them.

Vision maps: After the children have evaluated their area and defined their priorities for improving it, they can draw desired changes on a base map.

Gulliver's footprints: A useful method to record different age groups' memories and feelings about the study area is to unroll a large base map during a public festival or in a busy public place and encourage people of all ages to draw on it and annotate it. The finished map can serve as a point of departure to discuss how the area functions for its children.

Photographs: Make a systematic visual record of the study area through a 'photogrid' made at regular intervals around the community. Also take photographs during behavioural mapping and informal observations.

Child-taken photographs: One of the most revealing methods is to give the study children disposable or low-cost cameras and to send them out to take pictures of the places in the community that are most important to them, including those they like and dislike. Have them discuss or write commentaries on their pictures. The children can later organize their pictures into an exhibition to encourage public discussion about urban issues related to children.

Background data: Collect existing sociological, historical and economic data about the community, such as census records, local histories, old photographs, government reports and surveys.

Interviews and Other Activities

Child-led walks: After rapport with the study children has been established through interviews and other activities, invite small groups of children to lead you along their paths of movement through the area, showing you the places that they use, their favorite places, and places that they find problematic.

Role-plays: In addition to asking the children to share a schedule of their typical weekday and weekend in the course of the interviews, have groups of children role-play a typical day, showing where they go and the things they do. This activity is a good occasion to discuss differences between girls' and boys' places and activities.

Focus groups and small group discussions: As children's issues become evident, it is very useful to discuss them with small groups of children. This will allow you to better understand their perspectives according to age, sex and other characteristics, and to clarify the information that is emerging. It may be useful to discuss emerging issues with groups of parents and community leaders.

Interviews with parents: As children reveal their use of the study area, talk with some representative parents about their own perception of how the area works for its children, their rules regarding their children's use of the area, and changes that they have observed in the community and in children's lives.

Interviews with community leaders and urban officials: Discuss the study area and children's use of the city with community leaders and urban officials whose decisions affect children's lives. Get their views on how the area works for children, changes in the way the city has functioned for children over time, children's needs, and their plans to address these needs. In addition to gathering information, these interviews are good occasions to identify people with influence who may later help to realize some of the children's ideas for improving their area.

Community workshops: Because the goal of Growing Up in Cities is to put some of the children's ideas for improving their community into action, as well as to educate the public and urban officials about urban issues for children, it is important to have workshops and other public events to plan how to move from ideas to action. One type of workshop brings children and parents together with community leaders and city officials to discuss issues and draft action plans. Another is to have children work with urban designers and other community leaders to create visions and models for change that can be presented publicly and adopted for implementation.

Interviews with children: One-on-one interviews with a representative sample of children from the study area are an important source of insight into children's lives and feelings. They can be conducted in a number of ways: through one long interview; by breaking the questions into two or more short interviews; or by organizing a series of workshops with the children on different themes, using some one-on-one questions from the interview schedule along with a variety of group activities at each workshop. In one format or the other, the following questions were asked in all the Growing Up in Cities study sites. They are presented here in a two-interview format.

INTERVIEW #1

INTERVIEWER _____

CHILD'S REFERENCE # _____

DATE _____

Preparation

- Arrange for a place to work where there will be minimal interruptions and distractions.
- Begin by introducing yourself, and explain that you are trying to find out how young people use the place where they live and what they think about it. Obtain the child's permission to proceed with the interviews.

Identification

1. Record the following information:

NAME _____ AGE _____

ADDRESS _____

PHONE # *(if applicable)* _____

Residential History

2. How long have you lived in this area?
3. Have you always lived in the same house? *(if not, locate previous residences.)*
4. What were the locations where you lived before? *(if the child hasn't lived in the area all of his or her life)*
5. What type of house do you live in now? *(if there are different housing types that affect children's environmental experience)*
6. Do you go to school? Which school? Which grade? Half a day or a whole day?
7. Do you work for anybody, here in the area or anywhere else? For whom? Where? What do you do?
8. Do you visit places outside this area for recreation or vacations?
9. How would you describe the area where you live?

Drawing

The time required for this part of the interview will vary, but allow for approximately 45 minutes. Sometimes it is possible to arrange for the children to do the drawings in advance and bring them to the interview. Use large, durable paper, and have extra paper available if a child wants to enlarge the drawing space. A black marking pen of medium width is the basic drawing implement, supplemented with crayons for colour.

10. Would you please make a drawing or map of the area around where you live, and show me whatever you know in it?

Before discussing the drawing, ask the child's permission to make light pencil notes on the drawing as he or she explains it. To encourage discussion or additions:

- Show me on your drawing the places where you do things or spend your time, and the routes you travel.
- Do you go to these places by yourself or with somebody else?

At the end of the exercise, remember to ask the child to write his or her name, age, date, address and telephone number (if there is one) on the back of the paper. Also record the child's sex. If you think that you may want to exhibit or reproduce the drawing in any way, be sure to get the child's written permission, and determine whether the child would like you to use his or her real name or a fictional nickname. Whenever possible, involve the children in planning exhibitions or publications where their drawings will be used.

Place Knowledge and Use

11. Please tell me all the places that you know or use in your area, indoors and outdoors. *(Record this answer as a list with two columns for the place names and the child's comments about each place. Discuss each place through the following questions, and probe for specific activities, rather than generalities like 'play'.)*

- What do you do there?
- Do you go there alone or with others?
- What do you like or not like there?
- What would you change in this place if you could?
- Which of these places do you use most often?
- In which of these places do you spend the most amount of time?

12. What is the furthest place where you have ever been in the city?

Special Places

13. Of all these places, which are the most special to you or your favorite?
14. How would you describe this place to someone who had never been there, who wanted to know what it was like?

Problem Places

15. Are there places in your area where you don't like to go? Why don't you like it?
16. Are there places where you aren't allowed to go? Who forbids you? What are their reasons?
17. Are there places that you would like to enter but you cannot? What would you like to do there?
18. Are there dangerous places in your area? What makes them dangerous?

Place Ownership

19. Do you help take care of any places in your area? What do you do there?
20. Are there any places where you feel as if you own them? Which places? Why do you feel as if they are yours?
21. Are there places where you feel uncomfortable, like an outsider? Which places? Why do you feel like an outsider there?
22. Are there any places that nobody owns, that are abandoned?

At the end, close by thanking the child and asking:

• How do you feel about the interview?
• Is there anything you would like to add or talk about next time?

Explain that the next time you see them you want to talk with them about how they use their time and who they spend their time with, and any changes that they would want to make in their environment.

INTERVIEW #2

CHILD'S REFERENCE #

Introduction

When we met before, we talked about the places where you go, the things that you do, and what you think about them. Is there anything more that you want to say about it?

Today I want to talk with you about how you spend your time.

Daily Activity Schedule

23. Please tell me about what you did all day yesterday, in detail: where you went, what happened there, what you did, and the time when you did it.

Together with the child, record each event on a form that divides the day into 15-minute intervals. Be sure to record the day of the week. A variation is to draw a big clock face and record the child's activities in a circle around the clock hours.

24. Was there anything unusual about your activities yesterday? Was yesterday a typical day?
25. How does your schedule on the weekend compare? What would be different on a Saturday? Do you have a special schedule on Sunday?

Family Network

26. I also wanted to know about the people in your family and where they live. Who lives with you in your home?
27. Do any other members of your family live in your area?

Genealogy/Family Tree (optional)

28. *In some cultures, family networks are extremely important in shaping children's experience of place. If that is true at your site, you may wish to expand on the questions regarding family networks by explaining how to*

create a family tree and then drawing one with the child, noting where relatives live. For each family group on the tree, ask the child:

- How often do you see them?
- Do they come to your place or do you visit them?
- How do you get there?

Place Changes

29. Has this area where you live changed in your memory?
30. Has it gotten better or worse? Why?
31. If you could travel into the future, what do you think this place would be like in 10 years?
32. If you could make changes in your place, what would they be?
33. Ten years from now, where would you like to live?

Conclusion

34. Everything you have told me has been very interesting for me. I hope these questions have been interesting for you too. Is there anything else I should have asked?

Explain how you plan to use the information, and close with the following question:

35. Do you have any suggestions about how this information should be used?

Authors

KANCHAN BANNERJEE is a sociologist from Bombay University with a special interest in participatory activities with children and youth. She is currently Managing Trustee of 'Jyoshika', a Bangalore-based non-governmental organization whose work focuses on providing learning opportunities for children from low-income families. She designs training programmes for teaching staff, especially teachers in government schools, as well as instructional material for adult literacy programmes in low-literacy urban pockets. She served as co-director of the Growing Up in Cities project in Bangalore.

LOUISE CHAWLA has a masters degree in child development from Bryn Mawr College and a doctorate in environmental psychology from the City University of New York. She has carried out research and published widely in many areas related to children's environmental experience. She is currently Associate Professor in Whitney Young College, an interdisciplinary honors program at Kentucky State University, and Adjunct Professor in the Doctoral Program in Environmental Studies at Antioch New England Graduate School in the United States. From 1994-96, she was a Fulbright Scholar at the Norwegian Centre for Child Research. She serves as International Coordinator for Growing Up in Cities.

NILDA COSCO holds a diploma in psychopedagogy (psychology applied to the learning process) from Salvador University, Buenos Aires. She served for many years as Director of the National Lekotek Centre of Argentina, an institution that manages toy libraries, playrooms and programs for at-risk children in low-income communities. She is currently Educational Specialist for the Natural Learning Initiative, North Carolina State University, where she consults on the design and programming of spaces for play, leisure and non-formal education, and designs and delivers training courses on play and learning for children with and without disabilities. She served as co-director of Growing Up in Cities, Buenos Aires.

DAVID DRISKELL is an urban planner with a strong interest in community-based participatory planning. He was trained at Stanford University and MIT, and has helped design and implement participatory planning projects in the United States, Middle East and South Asia. He lives and works periodically in India, where he served as co-director of Growing Up in Cities, Bangalore. He is co-principal of Baird + Driskell Community Planning, and in 2002 will be a Visiting Scholar at the Einaudi Center for International Studies at Cornell University. He is also author of *Creating Better Cities with Children and Youth: A Manual for Participation,* which is based on Growing Up in Cities methods and experiences.

LINDSAY HASLUCK studied anthropology and history at Curtin University and archaeology at the University of Western Australia. Following work for state museums and extensive world travel to study indigenous groups, he has researched and published for Growing Up in Cities at three Australian sites and in Port Moresby, Papua New Guinea. He is currently employed as Unit Chair and Lecturer for the Postgraduate Diploma of Natural Resource Management at the Institute of Koorie (Aboriginal) Education, Deakin University in Victoria, Australia. In 2001, he was doing research on urban design in Peru.

KAREN MALONE is Asia-Pacific Director for Growing Up in Cities and Lecturer in Science and Environmental Education, Faculty of Education, Monash University. Her research interests are exclusionary and regulatory practices in the construction of landscape, safe and livable cities, and children as environmental designers. She uses participatory and narrative research methods, and has a keen interest in children's use of multi-media as a research tool. She was a finalist in the Australian National Museum Eureka Science 2000 awards and in 1998 was the first non-planner to give the Royal Australian Planning Institute memorial lecture.

ROBIN MOORE holds degrees in architecture (London University) and urban planning (MIT), and for most of his career he has worked in the field of landscape architecture as educator, researcher, author, and consultant. He is a principal in the firm of Moore Iacofano Goltsman, Professor of Landscape Architecture at North Carolina State University, and past president of the International Association for the Child's Right to Play (IPA). Through the Natural Learning Initiative, he is currently involved in the design or renovations of outdoor spaces for preschools, special education facilities and school grounds. He co-directed the Growing Up in Cities project in Buenos Aires.

BARRY PERCY-SMITH is Senior Research Fellow and Youth Research Coordinator at SOLAR (Social and Organisational Learning and Re-animation), an interdisciplinary action research and development centre at University College Northampton, United Kingdom. His doctoral thesis ('Multiple Childhood Geographies: Giving Voice to Young People's Experience of Place') involved an in-depth study of English childhoods. He is currently working on a range of research and change projects that develop policy and practice with and for socially excluded and vulnerable young people around issues of education, training, guidance, homelessness, youth offending and neighbourhood renewal.

ILARIA SALVADORI has a joint masters degree in City and Regional Planning and Landscape Architecture from the College of Environmental Design at the University of California-Berkeley. Her focus is on urban design and social aspects of the design of public space. She is also very much interested in environmental justice issues, people's behaviour in space, and their construction of place. She has experience in public participation with children in Northern Italy and California, and has worked on community development projects in the Tenderloin neighbourhood of San Francisco. She currently works at the Project for Public Spaces in New York.

JILL SWART-KRUGER is a Research Fellow in the Department of Anthropology and Archaeology at the University of South Africa. Her special research interest is children, youth and childhood. She is the South African director of the Growing Up in Cities project and founder of Street-Wise, a national programme for street children. She is a member of the Codesria Scientific Committee for Child Research in Africa, a founding member of the Commission on the Anthropology of Children and Childhood for IUAES (International Union of Anthropological and Ethnological Sciences), and serves on various reference groups in matters concerning children and youth.

HANNE WILHJELM received her degree in architecture from the Royal Academy of Fine Arts in Copenhagen. Her practice of architecture took her to Norway, where she has served in the Department for Regional Planning and Land Use in the Ministry of the Environment. During this period, she was head of the programme 'Children and Planning' which was established to implement the provisions of the Building and Planning Act and National Policy Guidelines related to the interests of children and adolescents in planning. At the Norwegian Centre for Child Research, she served as director for Growing Up in Cities, Trondheim. She is currently a Research Fellow at the Institute of Architectural Design, Oslo School of Architecture.

PIOTR-OLAF ZYLICZ has a masters degree in philosophy and a doctorate in psychology, and currently works at the Warsaw School of Advanced Social Psychology and the Institute of Psychology, Polish Academy of Sciences. His research interests focus on moral development and on the social and psychological determinants of youth volunteering. He directed the Growing Up in Cities project in Warsaw.

Index